The Cambridge Companion to Nabokov

Vladimir Nabokov held the unique distinction of being one of the most important writers of the twentieth century in two separate languages, Russian and
English. Known for his verbal mastery and bold plots, Nabokov fashioned a
literary legacy that continues to grow in significance. This volume offers a con-
cise and informative introduction to the author's fascinating creative world.
Specially commissioned essays by distinguished scholars illuminate numerous
facets of the writer's legacy, from his early contributions as a poet and short-
story writer to his dazzling achievements as one of the most original novelists
of the twentieth century. Topics receiving fresh coverage include Nabokov's
narrative strategies, the evolution of his worldview, and his relationship to the
literary and cultural currents of his day. The volume also contains valuable
supplementary material such as a chronology of the writer's life and a guide to
further critical reading.

THE CAMBRIDGE
COMPANION TO
NABOKOV

EDITED BY
JULIAN W. CONNOLLY
University of Virginia

CAMBRIDGE
UNIVERSITY PRESS

CAMBRIDGE UNIVERSITY PRESS
Cambridge, New York, Melbourne, Madrid, Cape Town, Singapore, São Paulo

Cambridge University Press
The Edinburgh Building, Cambridge CB2 8RU, UK

Published in the United States of America by Cambridge University Press, New York

www.cambridge.org
Information on this title: www.cambridge.org/9780521536431

© Cambridge University Press 2005

First published 2005
Reprinted 2007

Printed in the United Kingdom at the University Press, Cambridge

A catalogue record for this publication is available from the British Library

ISBN-13 978 0 521 82957 1 hardback
ISBN-13 978 0 521 53643 1 paperback

CONTENTS

NOTES ON CONTRIBUTORS

BRIAN BOYD is University Distinguished Professor in the Department of English, University of Auckland. He is the author of *Vladimir Nabokov: The Russian Years* (1990), *Vladimir Nabokov: The American Years* (1991), *Nabokov's* Pale Fire: *The Magic of Artistic Discovery* (1999), *Nabokov's* Ada: *The Place of Consciousness* (1985, second edn 2001), and "Annotations to *Ada*" (*The Nabokovian*, 1993–; as *ADAonline*, at http://www.libraries.psu.edu/nabokov/ada/index.htm). He is the editor of the Library of America's publication of Nabokov's English novels and autobiography (3 vols., 1996), and with Robert Michael Pyle, of *Nabokov's Butterflies* (2000). He is also editing, with Stanislav Shvabrin, *Verses and Versions* (Nabokov's verse translations), and with Olga Voronina, *To Véra* (Nabokov's letters to his wife). Among other work he also publishes on Shakespeare and on evolution and fiction, and is currently writing *Heads and Tales: The Origin of Stories*.

JULIAN W. CONNOLLY is Professor of Slavic Languages and Literatures at the University of Virginia. He is the author of *Ivan Bunin* (1982), *Nabokov's Early Fiction: Patterns of Self and Other* (1992), and *The Intimate Stranger: Meetings with the Devil in Nineteenth-Century Russian Literature* (2001). He also edited the volumes *Nabokov's* Invitation to a Beheading: *A Course Companion* (1997) and *Nabokov and His Fiction: New Perspectives* (1999). He has written extensively on nineteenth- and twentieth-century Russian literature.

NEIL CORNWELL is Professor of Russian and Comparative Literature at the University of Bristol. Among his authored books are *Vladimir Nabokov* (in the series "Writers and Their Works," 1999), *James Joyce and the Russians* (1992), and *The Literary Fantastic* (1990). He is also the editor of the *Reference Guide to Russian Literature* (1998) and *The Routledge Companion to Russian Literature* (2001). He has translated collections of the stories of Vladimir Odoevsky (*The Salamander and Other Gothic Tales*, 1992) and Daniil Kharms (*Incidences*, 1993), and his edition of Maiakovsky's *My Discovery of America* is forthcoming. He is currently completing a general study of the absurd in literature.

ALEXANDER A. DOLININ is Professor of Russian Literature in the Department of Slavic Languages and Literatures at the University of Wisconsin-Madison. He is the author of *Istoriia, odetaia v roman. Val'ter Skott i ego chitateli* (1988) and *Istinnaia zhizn' pisatelia Sirina. Raboty o Nabokove* (2004). He helped to edit and annotate Nabokov's collected works in Russian (5 vols., 1999–2000) and in French (Pleiade edition). He has written over 100 articles, with scholarly interest in Nabokov, Pushkin, Russian literature of the nineteenth and twentieth centuries, and Russian–English literary connections.

JOHN BURT FOSTER, JR. is Professor of English and Cultural Studies at George Mason University. He is the author of *Nabokov's Art of Memory and European Modernism* (1993), of numerous articles on the contexts of Nabokov's fiction, and of many other publications on nineteenth- and twentieth-century literature and thought. He recently completed a six-year term as editor of *The Comparatist* and has co-edited *Thresholds of Western Culture: Identity, Postcoloniality, Transnationalism* for the International Association for Philosophy and Literature.

GALYA DIMENT is Professor and Chair of the Department of Slavic Languages and Literatures at the University of Washington, Seattle. She is the author and editor of four books, including *Pniniad: Vladimir Nabokov and Marc Szeftel* (1997). She is currently co-editing a Modern Language Association volume on approaches to teaching *Lolita* and writing a cultural biography of Samuel Koteliansky, a Russian translator for Bloomsbury's Hogarth Press.

ZORAN KUZMANOVICH teaches literature and film at Davidson College. He writes on the relations among arts, ethics, and politics. Since 1996 he has served as the editor of *Nabokov Studies*.

PRISCILLA MEYER is Professor of Russian Language and Literature at Wesleyan University, Middletown, Connecticut. She published the first monograph on Vladimir Nabokov's *Pale Fire, Find What the Sailor Has Hidden* (1988), and edited Andrei Bitov's collected stories, *Life in Windy Weather* (1986). She is co-editor of collections on Gogol, Dostoevsky, and Nabokov, and has written articles on Pushkin, Lermontov, Gogol, Dostoevsky, Tolstoy, Nabokov, and Soviet prose writers of the 1960s–1970s.

Her most recent book is *How the Russians Read the French: Lermontov, Dostoevsky, Tolstoy* (forthcoming).

ELLEN PIFER is Professor of English and Comparative Literature at the University of Delaware. She has written five books and dozens of essays on modern and contemporary literature. Her numerous studies of Nabokov include *Vladimir Nabokov's* Lolita: *A Casebook* (2003), chapter four of her *Demon or Doll: Images of the Child in Contemporary Writing and Culture* (2000), and *Nabokov and the Novel* (1980). She has been Visiting Professor at the University of California, Berkeley, and the University of Lyon, France. Fellowships and grants include Fulbright and National Endowment for the Humanities awards.

BARRY SCHERR is the Mandel Family Professor of Russian at Dartmouth. His teaching interests center on both nineteenth- and twentieth-century Russian literature, comparative literature, and film. He has published articles on a wide range of topics in Russian poetry and prose, with special interests in the work and career of Maksim Gorky, literary figures of the early twentieth century, Russian verse theory, and the poetry of Joseph Brodsky. His books include *Russian Poetry: Meter, Rhythm, and Rhyme* (1986); *Maksim Gorky: Selected Letters*, which he co-edited and co-translated with Andrew Barratt (1997); and, with Al LaValley, he co-edited *Eisenstein at 100: A Reconsideration* (2001).

SUSAN ELIZABETH SWEENEY is Associate Professor of English at Holy Cross College. She has published many essays on Nabokov's work, including other accounts of his American literary career. Recent publications include "Looking at Harlequins: Nabokov, the World of Art, and the Ballets Russes," in *Nabokov's World: Reading Nabokov* (2002); "*The Enchanter* and the Beauties of Sleeping," in *Nabokov at Cornell* (2003); and "Executing Sentences in *Lolita* and the Law," in *Punishment, Politics, and Culture* (2004). A specialist in postmodernist fiction, she also studies revisions of such popular genres as mysteries, romances, ghost stories, and folktales, and co-edited the volume *Detecting Texts: The Metaphysical Detective Story from Poe to Postmodernism* (1999). She is now working on allusions to fairy tales in Nabokov's fictions about pedophilia.

LEONA TOKER is Professor in the English Department of the Hebrew University of Jerusalem. She is the author of *Nabokov: The Mystery of Literary Structures* (1989), *Eloquent Reticence: Withholding Information in Fictional Narrative* (1993), *Return from the Archipelago: Narratives of Gulag Survivors* (2000), and articles on English, American, and Russian writers. She is editor of *Partial Answers: A Journal of Literature and the*

History of Ideas. Current research interests include English fiction of the eighteenth and nineteenth centuries, James Joyce, Nabokov, and literature as historical testimony.

MICHAEL WOOD is Professor of English and Comparative Literature at Princeton University. He is the author of *The Magician's Doubts: Nabokov and the Risks of Fiction* (1994), *Children of Silence: on Contemporary Fiction* (1998), and most recently, *The Road to Delphi: the Life and Afterlife of Oracles* (2003). He writes frequently on film and literature for the *London Review of Books*, the *New York Review of Books*, and other journals.

BARBARA WYLLIE has contributed articles on Nabokov to the *Reference Guide to Russian Literature*, ed. Neil Cornwell (1998); *Nabokov at the Limits: Redrawing Critical Boundaries*, ed. Lisa Zunshine (1999); *Torpid Smoke: The Stories of Vladimir Nabokov*, ed. Steven G. Kellman and Irving Malin (2000); the special edition of the *Revue des études slaves*: "Vladimir Nabokov dans le miroir du XXe siècle" (2000); and the first of two festschrift volumes of the *New Zealand Slavonic Journal* in honor of Arnold McMillin (2002). Her book, *Nabokov at the Movies: Film Perspectives in Fiction*, was published in 2003. She is assistant editor of the *Slavonic and East European Review* at the School of Slavonic and East European Studies, University College London.

ACKNOWLEDGMENTS

I would like to express my deep gratitude to Linda Bree, Jacqueline French, and Alison Powell of Cambridge University Press for their invaluable assistance in the preparation of this volume.

NOTE ON TRANSLITERATION

The Library of Congress system of transliteration (without diacritics) has been used throughout the bibliographic references and the main text of the essays, with the following exceptions:

a.   For personal names in the main text, the letters ю and я are rendered as "yu" and "ya" at the beginning of the name, and the sequence ый and ий is rendered as "y" at the end of the name (e.g., "Yakov," "Yury," "Bely").

b.   The spelling used by Nabokov for names of figures in his works has been retained (e.g., "Chernyshevski" and "Koncheyev").

c.   We have retained the familiar English spelling of well-known Russian figures (e.g., "Tolstoy," "Gogol"). Soft signs occurring within well-known proper names (e.g., "Olga") are generally not denoted to facilitate reading for the non-specialist.

ABBREVIATIONS

Ada	*Ada, or Ardor: A Family Chronicle.* 1969. New York: Vintage International, 1990.
AnL	*The Annotated Lolita.* Ed. with preface, introduction, and notes by Alfred Appel, Jr. 1970. Revised edition: New York: Vintage International, 1991.
BS	*Bend Sinister.* 1947. New York: Vintage International, 1990.
CE	*Conclusive Evidence: A Memoir.* New York: Harper, 1951.
Def	*The Defense.* Trans. Michael Scammell in collaboration with the author. 1964. New York: Vintage International, 1990.
Des	*Despair.* 1966. New York: Vintage International, 1989.
En	*The Enchanter.* Trans. Dmitri Nabokov. 1986. New York: Vintage International, 1991.
EO	*Eugene Onegin. A Novel in Verse by Aleksandr Pushkin.* Trans. with commentary by Vladimir Nabokov. Bollingen Series 72. 4 vols. 1964. Revised edition: Princeton: Princeton University Press, 1975.
Eye	*The Eye.* Trans. Dmitri Nabokov in collaboration with the author. 1965. New York: Vintage International, 1990.
Gift	*The Gift.* Trans. Michael Scammell with the collaboration of the author. 1963. New York: Vintage International, 1991.
Glory	*Glory.* Trans. Dmitri Nabokov in collaboration with the author. 1971. New York: Vintage International, 1991.
IB	*Invitation to a Beheading.* Trans. Dmitri Nabokov in collaboration with the author. 1959. New York: Vintage International, 1989.
KQK	*King, Queen, Knave.* Trans. Dmitri Nabokov in collaboration with the author. 1968. New York: Vintage International, 1989.
LATH	*Look at the Harlequins!* 1974. New York: Vintage International, 1990.
Laugh	*Laughter in the Dark.* 1938. New York: Vintage International, 1989.

LDQ	*Lectures on* Don Quixote. Ed. Fredson Bowers. New York: Harcourt Brace Jovanovich / Bruccoli Clark, 1983.
LL	*Lectures on Literature*. Ed. Fredson Bowers. New York: Harcourt Brace Jovanovich / Bruccoli Clark, 1980.
LRL	*Lectures on Russian Literature*. Ed. Fredson Bowers. New York: Harcourt Brace Jovanovich / Bruccoli Clark, 1981.
Lo	*Lolita*. 1955. New York: Vintage International, 1989.
Lo Screen	*Lolita: A Screenplay*. 1974. New York: Vintage International, 1997.
Mary	*Mary*. Trans. Michael Glenny in collaboration with the author. 1970. New York: Vintage International, 1989.
NWL	*Dear Bunny, Dear Volodya. The Nabokov–Wilson Letters, 1940–1971*. Revised and expanded edition. Ed., annotated, and with an introductory essay by Simon Karlinsky. Berkeley: University of California Press, 2001.
NG	*Nikolai Gogol*. 1944. New York: New Directions, 1961.
PF	*Pale Fire*. 1962. New York: Vintage International, 1989.
Pnin	*Pnin*. 1957. New York: Vintage International, 1989.
PP	*Poems and Problems*. New York: McGraw-Hill, 1970.
RLSK	*The Real Life of Sebastian Knight*. 1941. NewYork: Vintage International, 1992.
SL	*Selected Letters, 1940–1977*. Ed. Dmitri Nabokov and Matthew J. Bruccoli. New York: Harcourt Brace Jovanovich / Bruccoli Clark Layman, 1989.
SM	*Speak, Memory: An Autobiography Revisited*. 1967. New York: Vintage International, 1989.
SO	*Strong Opinions*. 1973. New York: Vintage International, 1990.
Song	*The Song of Igor's Campaign*. Trans. Vladimir Nabokov. 1960. New York: McGraw-Hill, 1975.
Stikhi	*Stikhi*. Ann Arbor, MI: Ardis, 1979.
Stories	*The Stories of Vladimir Nabokov*. 1995. New York: Vintage International, 1997.
Ssoch	*Sobranie sochinenii russkogo perioda v piati tomakh*. 5 vols. St. Petersburg: Simpozium, 1999–2000.
TT	*Transparent Things*. 1972. New York: Vintage International, 1989.
USSR	*The Man fom the U.S.S.R. and Other Plays*. Introductions and translations by Dmitri Nabokov. New York: Harcourt Brace Jovanovich / Bruccoli Clark, 1984.

CHRONOLOGY

Dates before the departure of the Nabokov family from Russia in April 1919 are given in Old Style (Julian Calendar); the New Style date (Gregorian Calendar) is given in parentheses. In the nineteenth century, the Julian Calendar lagged the Gregorian Calendar by twelve days; in the twentieth century, the discrepancy grew to thirteen days. Thus, while April 10, 1899 – the date of Vladimir Nabokov's birth in Russia – was April 22 in the West, it became April 23 in 1900. The sources for the information contained in this chronology are Brian Boyd's two-volume biography of Nabokov (*Vladimir Nabokov: The Russian Years* and *Vladimir Nabokov: The American Years*), the chronologies Boyd prepared for the Library of America editions of Nabokov's English-language novels and *The Garland Companion to Vladimir Nabokov*, Michael Juliar's *Vladimir Nabokov: A Descriptive Bibliography*, the volume entitled *Nabokov's Butterflies* that was edited and annotated by Brian Boyd and Robert Michael Pyle, and Stacy Schiff's *Véra*.

1899   Vladimir Vladimirovich Nabokov (VN) born on April 10 (April 23) at 47 Bolshaia Morskaia Street, St. Petersburg. Parents are Vladimir Dmitrievich Nabokov (VDN [1870–1922]), a teacher of criminal law at the Imperial School of Jurisprudence, and Elena Ivanovna Nabokov (née Rukavishnikov [1876–1939]).

1900   Brother Sergei born February 28 (March 13).

1901   VN's Rukavishnikov grandparents die. Mother inherits country estate Vyra, and VN's uncle Vasily inherits country estate Rozhdestveno. Mother travels with Vladimir and Sergei to Biarritz, France.

1902   VN and Sergei learn English from British governess, Rachel Home. Sister Olga born December 24 (January 5, 1903).

1903   VDN responds to pogrom in Kishinev in April by writing article in journal *Pravo* that criticizes governmental attitudes fostering climate of anti-Semitism. Family travels to Paris and Nice in the fall.

1904   Russo-Japanese War begins in February. Nabokov family travels to Rome, Naples, and Beaulieu. National congress of zemstvos (local assemblies) meets in St. Petersburg, calls for major political changes (constitution, civil rights); final session meets in Nabokov home.

1905   January 9 (January 22) – "Bloody Sunday" – tsarist troops fire on demonstrators in St. Petersburg. VDN deprived of court title after denunciation of the incident in the St. Petersburg Duma (City Council). Family travels to Abbazia (now Opatija, Croatia) in February. VDN returns to St. Petersburg and renews involvement in political activity; becomes one of founders of Constitutional Democratic (CD) Party.

1906   Family returns to Russia. Swiss governess Cécile Miauton joins family. Sister Elena born March 18 (March 31). VDN continues pushing for major political reform in State Duma until its dissolution in July. VN tutored in Russian by village school teacher Vasily Zhernosekov. VDN becomes editor of *Rech'* newspaper.

1907   VN seriously ill with pneumonia; studies books on butterflies while recovering.

1908   VDN serves three-month sentence in Kresty prison for signing Vyborg Manifesto in 1906 calling for civil disobedience.

1909   Family travels to Biarritz, where VN falls in love with nine-year-old girl, Claude Deprès ("Collette" in VN's memoir *Speak, Memory*).

1910   VN pursues his interests in lepidoptery. Family travels to Germany in fall.

1911   VN enters Tenishev School in St. Petersburg. Brother Kirill born June 17 (June 30).

1912   VN studies drawing with Mstislav Dobuzhinsky.

1914   Composes first poem. Germany declares war on Russia. VDN called up for military service as reservist. St. Petersburg is renamed Petrograd.

1915   VN bedridden with typhus. After recovering, begins serious romantic affair with Valentina ("Liusia") Evgenievna Shulgina. In November he co-edits school literary journal, *Iunaia mysl'* (*Young Thought*), in which his first published poem, "Osen'" ("Fall") appears.

1916   Publishes translation of Alfred de Musset's "La Nuit de décembre" in *Iunaia mysl'*. Publishes collection of poetry entitled *Stikhi* (*Poems*) at his own expense. Poem "Lunnaia greza" ("Lunar Reverie") appears in journal *Vestnik Evropy*. Uncle Vasily Rukavishnikov dies, leaving VN his Rozhdestveno estate, worth several million dollars.

1917   February 27 (March 12) – February Revolution. Tsar Nicholas II abdicates; VDN accepts post in new Provisional Government. VN has appendix removed in May. Writes "Dozhd' Proletel" ("The Rain Has Flown"), the earliest poem he would include in his later collection *Poems and Problems* (1970). Makes selection of poems to appear in collection *Dva puti* (*Two Paths*) with Tenishev School companion Andrei Balashov (published 1920). VDN resigns from the Provisional Government with other members of the CD party. October 25 (November 7) – Bolshevik Revolution. VDN sends sons Vladimir and Sergei to Crimea to avoid their conscription into the Red Army; they are soon joined by their mother and siblings. Arrested and imprisoned for several days by the Bolsheviks, VDN leaves Petrograd and rejoins his family in December. VN composes first chess problems.

1918   German army takes Crimea in April. VN hunts butterflies, composes poems. After departure of German troops, VDN becomes Minister of Justice in Crimean Provisional Government.

1919   Facing approach of Bolshevik troops, Nabokov family departs Sebastopol for Athens on Greek ship on April 2 (April 15). From Athens, Nabokov family moves on to London. VN enters Trinity College, Cambridge, in October; begins studying zoology and then modern languages (French and Russian). Writes poetry in Russian and in English; also writes first entomological paper (published 1920).

1920   Nabokov family moves to Berlin; VDN helps establish Russian-language newspaper *Rul'* (*The Rudder*). VN's poem "Home" appears in *Trinity Magazine*; his poem "Remembrance" appears in *The English Review*. He also publishes Russian poems in *Rul'* using the pen name "Cantab."

1921   Publishes poems and the short story "Nezhit'" ("The Wood-Sprite") in *Rul'* in January, using for the first time the pen name "Vladimir Sirin." Finishes translation of Romain Rolland's *Colas Breugnon* (published as *Nikolka Persik* in 1922). During summertime visit to Berlin, falls in love with Svetlana Romanovna Siewert.

1922   On March 28, VDN is shot and killed while trying to defend Pavel Miliukov from assassination by two monarchist gunmen. In June, VN receives BA degree and moves to Berlin, where he becomes engaged to Svetlana Siewert. Receives commission to translate Lewis Carroll's *Alice in Wonderland*. Collection of poems entitled *Grozd'* (*The Cluster*) published in December.

1923 Poetry collection *Gornii put'* (*The Empyrean Path*) appears in January. Engagement with Svetlana Siewert ends because of her parents' concern with Nabokov's financial situation. *Ania v strane chudes*, Nabokov's version of *Alice in Wonderland*, is published in March. Two-act play entitled *Smert'* (*Death*) published in May. Nabokov meets Véra Evseevna Slonim (1902–1991) at a charity ball in May. Works as agricultural laborer in South of France during summer. Writes five-act verse play, *Tragediia gospodina Morna* (*The Tragedy of Mr. Morn*).

1924 Publishes several short stories, including "Kartofel'nyi el'f" ("The Potato Elf"), "Katastrofa" (translated as "Details of a Sunset"), and "Bakhman" ("Bachmann") in Russian periodicals. Drama *Polius* (*The Pole*) published in August. Nabokov supports himself by giving private lessons in tennis, boxing, Russian, and English.

1925 Marries Véra Evseevna Slonim in May. Writes first novel, *Mashen'ka* (*Mary*). Publishes stories, including "Vozvrashchenie Chorba" ("The Return of Chorb") and "Putevoditel' po Berlinu" ("A Guide to Berlin").

1926 *Mashen'ka* published in March.

1927 Short story "Uzhas" ("Terror") published in *Sovremennye zapiski*, the premier literary journal of the Russian emigration. Long narrative poem "Universitetskaia poema" ("A University Poem") also appears in *Sovremennye zapiski*.

1928 Novel *Korol', dama, valet* (*King, Queen, Knave*) published in September.

1929 Completes work on novel *Zashchita Luzhina* (*The Defense*). Novel appears serially in *Sovremennye zapiski* in 1929–1930. Collection of stories and poems entitled *Vozvrashchenie Chorba* (*The Return of Chorb*) appears in December.

1930 Short novel *Sogliadatai* (*The Eye*) published in *Sovremennye zapiski* in November. *Zashchita Luzhina* appears in book form.

1931 Novel *Podvig* (*Glory*) published serially in *Sovremennye zapiski*.

1932 *Podvig* published in book form. Nabokov travels to Paris to give public readings of his work. Novel *Kamera obskura* (*Laughter in the Dark*) appears serially in *Sovremennye zapiski* in 1932–1933.

1933 Adolf Hitler appointed Chancellor of Germany in January. *Kamera obskura* appears in book form.

1934 Novel *Otchaianie* (*Despair*) appears serially in *Sovremennye zapiski*. Son Dmitri born in May.

1935 Novel *Priglashenie na kazn'* (*Invitation to a Beheading*) published serially in *Sovremennye zapiski* (1935–1936). Nabokov translates *Otchaianie* into English.

1936 *Otchaianie* published in book form in February. English translation of *Kamera obskura* by Winifred Roy published with title *Camera Obscura*; Nabokov dissatisfied with translation. "Mademoiselle O," story in French, published in April. Véra loses job at engineering company because she is Jewish.

1937 Nabokov leaves Germany for a reading tour in January; he would never return. Essay on Pushkin, "Pouchkine ou le vrai et le vraisemblable" ("Pushkin, or the Real and the Plausible") published in March. Nabokov becomes involved in romantic liaison with Irina Guadinini in Paris. Travels with family to Cannes; ends affair with Guadanini. *Despair*, Nabokov's translation of *Otchaianie*, appears in England. Last Russian novel, *Dar* (*The Gift*), begins serial publication in *Sovremennye zapiski*; novel is published 1937–1938, with the exception of chapter four, which editors of journal refuse to publish because they disapprove of the treatment of its subject, the life of the nineteenth-century writer N. G. Chernyshevski.

1938 Two dramas, *Sobytie* (*The Event*) and *Izobretenie Val'sa* (*The Waltz Invention*), published. *Priglashenie na kazn'* appears in book form. *Laughter in the Dark*, Nabokov's translation of *Kamera obskura*, comes out in the United States. *Sogliadatai* (*The Eye*), a collection of short fiction, appears in October.

1939 Writes *The Real Life of Sebastian Knight*, his first English-language novel. Travels to England looking for employment. Mother dies in Prague. Germany invades Poland on September 1. France attacks Germany on September 7. Nabokov receives and accepts offer to teach summer course in Russian literature at Stanford University. Writes *Volshebnik* (*The Enchanter*).

1940 Germany begins invasion of France on May 12. Nabokov departs France soon afterwards with Véra and Dmitri aboard ocean liner *Champlain*. Arrives New York May 27. Vacations at summer home of Mikhail Karpovich in Vermont. Rents apartment in New York City. Meets Edmund Wilson. Writes reviews for the *New Republic* and the *New York Sun*. Works on Lepidoptera at the American Museum of Natural History.

1941 Gives lectures on Russian literature at Wellesley College. *The Event* is produced in New York City. Nabokov is driven to Stanford by former student Dorothy Leuthold; on route west, Nabokov discovers new species of butterfly he names *Neonympha dorothea dorothea* in Leuthold's honor (the butterfly has since been reclassified as a subspecies, *Cyllopsis pertepida dorothea*). Begins one-year appointment as Resident Lecturer in Comparative Literature at Wellesley College in the fall. Begins helping put Lepidoptera collection at Harvard's Museum of Comparative Zoology in order. Publishes articles on Lepidoptera in the *Journal of the New York Entomological Society*. *The Real Life of Sebastian Knight* is published by New Directions in December.

1942   Appointed Research Fellow at the Museum of Comparative Zoology. Short poem "The Refrigerator Awakes" becomes Nabokov's first poem published in the *New Yorker*. Long Russian poem "Slava" ("Fame"), which Véra later points to as showing Nabokov's central interest in the "otherworldly," appears in *Novyi zhurnal*.

1943   Begins teaching non-credit Russian language course at Wellesley College. Receives Guggenheim Fellowship to work on new novel, *Bend Sinister*. During summer, collects butterflies and works on novel in Utah.

1944   Short monograph entitled *Nikolai Gogol* published by New Directions. Nabokov appointed lecturer at Wellesley College.

1945   Collection of translations entitled *Three Russian Poets* published by New Directions. Poem "An Evening of Russian Poetry" published in *New Yorker* in March. First short story published in the *New Yorker* – "Double Talk" (later retitled "Conversation Piece, 1945") – appears in June.

1946   Works on lectures for course on Russian literature at Wellesley. Finishes *Bend Sinister*.

1947   *Bend Sinister* published in June. Nabokov offered teaching appointment at Cornell. Collection *Nine Stories*, containing stories translated from Russian as well as English-language stories, appears in December.

1948   Short story "Signs and Symbols" published in the *New Yorker* in May. Excerpts from *Conclusive Evidence*, first version of autobiography, published in the *New Yorker*. Nabokov moves to Ithaca and begins teaching Russian literature at Cornell.

1949   Continues to publish excerpts from autobiography and to teach at Cornell. Participates in writers' conference in Utah in July.

1950   Begins working on novel entitled *The Kingdom by the Sea*, which later evolves into *Lolita*. Discouraged, he is prevented from burning his early drafts by Véra. Begins teaching major course on European fiction at Cornell.

1951 *Conclusive Evidence* published in February. Nabokov continues work on *Lolita*. Near Telluride, Colorado in July, Nabokov catches first female of *Lycaeides argyrognomon sublivens*, male specimens of which he had studied at the Museum of Comparative Zoology. Nabokov later uses this setting for a key passage in *Lolita*.

1952 Teaches Russian literature and a course on the novel as a Visiting Lecturer at Harvard during the spring. Receives second Guggenheim Fellowship. *Dar* published in (complete) book form. Returns to Cornell to teach in the fall. Collection of Russian poems, *Stikhotvoreniia 1929–1951* (*Poems 1929–1951*), published in Paris.

1953 Takes leave from Cornell to work on translation of Pushkin's *Eugene Onegin*. Publishes first chapter of *Pnin* in the *New Yorker*. Finishes writing *Lolita* in December.

1954 *Drugie berega*, a revised Russian version of Nabokov's autobiographical memoir, published. Nabokov unsuccessful in finding an American publisher for *Lolita*.

1955 *Lolita* accepted for publication by Maurice Girodias, owner of Olympia Press in France. Named one of the best books of 1955 by Graham Greene in the London *Sunday Times*.

1956 John Gordon denounces *Lolita* in the London *Sunday Express*, sparking controversy over the novel. Nabokov's collection of Russian short stories, *Vesna v Fial'te i drugie rasskazy* (*Spring in Fialta and Other Stories*), published in New York. French government bans *Lolita* along with several other Olympia Press titles (ban is overturned in January 1958).

1957 *Pnin* published; receives nomination for National Book Award. The *Anchor Review* publishes passages from *Lolita* together with Nabokov's essay, "On a Book Entitled *Lolita*," and a critical essay by Fred Dupee.

1958 Nabokov's translation of Mikhail Lermontov's *A Hero of Our Time* is published. *Lolita* published by G. P. Putnam's Sons; achieves instant success. Collection of short stories, *Nabokov's Dozen*, appears. Nabokov takes a year's leave of absence from Cornell.

1959 Resigns from Cornell. Travels to Europe. Small collection of poetry entitled *Poems* appears. *Invitation to a Beheading*, Dmitri Nabokov's translation of *Priglashenie na kazn'*, published. *Lolita* published in England.

1960   Works on screenplay for *Lolita*. *The Song of Igor's Campaign*, Nabokov's translation of medieval Russian epic, published.

1961   Works on *Pale Fire*, finishes novel in December. Takes rooms in Montreux Palace Hotel, Switzerland.

1962   *Pale Fire* published. Stanley Kubrick's film version of *Lolita* released.

1963   *The Gift*, translation of *Dar* largely completed by Michael Scammell with Nabokov's corrections, appears in May. *Notes on Prosody* published.

1964   Nabokov's last public reading takes place in April, at Harvard University. His translation of *Eugene Onegin* with extensive notes and commentary published in June. *The Defense*, Michael Scammell's translation of *Zashchita Luzhina*, appears in September.

1965   Edmund Wilson's critical review of *Eugene Onegin* triggers heated debate in periodical press. *The Eye*, Dmitri Nabokov's translation of *Sogliadatai*, appears in the fall.

1966   *The Waltz Invention*, translation of *Izobretenie Val'sa*, published. *Despair*, Nabokov's revision of his early translation of *Otchaianie*, appears.

1967   Short-story collection *Nabokov's Quartet* appears. Revised version of Nabokov's memoir, *Speak, Memory: An Autobiography Revisited*, published. Nabokov's Russian translation of *Lolita* published.

1968   *King, Queen, Knave*, Dmitri Nabokov's translation of *Korol', dama, valet*, extensively revised by Nabokov, appears in April. Anthology entitled *Nabokov's Congeries* (later entitled *The Portable Nabokov*) published in September.

1969   *Ada* published in late spring. Joseph Papp stages Russell McGrath's adaptation of *Invitation to a Beheading* at the New York Shakespeare Festival in March.

1970   *Mary*, the translation of *Mashen'ka* by Michael Glenny and Nabokov, published in September.

1971   Musical based on *Lolita* – *Lolita, My Love* – has unsuccessful run in Philadelphia and Boston. Collection of poetry and chess problems entitled *Poems and Problems* published in March. *Glory*, Nabokov's translation of *Podvig*, published in December.

1972   *Transparent Things* published in October.

1973   *A Russian Beauty and Other Stories*, a collection of stories originally written in Russian, appears in April. *Strong Opinions*, a collection of interviews and notes, appears in November. Nabokov awarded the National Medal for Literature in the United States.

1974 *Lolita: A Screenplay* published. His last complete novel, *Look at the Harlequins!*, appears in August.

1975 A second collection of early stories, *Tyrants Destroyed and Other Stories*, appears in January.

1976 Third collection of early stories, *Details of a Sunset and Other Stories*, published in March. Nabokov sustains concussion from a fall, hospitalized for ten days. Later infection sends him back to hospital from June to September. Selects poems for extensive collection of Russian poetry entitled *Stikhi* (*Poems*) that will not be published until 1979.

1977 Hospitalized in Lausanne with fever and influenza from March to May. Returns to hospital in Lausanne in June. Dies on July 2. After cremation, body is interred in Clarens cemetery.

1991 Véra Nabokov dies on April 6.

JULIAN W. CONNOLLY

Introduction: the many faces of Vladimir Nabokov

Vladimir Nabokov was acutely aware of the image that readers and critics held of him. Deriding the notion that he was a "frivolous firebird," he predicted that the day would come when someone would declare him to be a "rigid moralist kicking sin" and "assigning power to tenderness, talent, and pride" (*SO*, 193). Not only did Nabokov's prediction come true, but critics continue to discover new facets of the writer's legacy to highlight and explore. As a result, it has become clear that the man and his work evince enormous complexity. The facile labels applied to Nabokov early in his career – the "cool aesthete," "impassive gamester" – have been replaced by other labels (if not "rigid moralist," then "highly ethical" writer, metaphysician, philosopher). Yet all of these labels are proving to be simply one-dimensional; the full depth of Nabokov's talent has yet to be plumbed. Indeed, in recent years, new aspects of Nabokov's formidable intellectual legacy, such as his research as a lepidopterist, have begun to receive serious notice.

The present collection does not attempt to be encyclopedic in scope or coverage. Nabokov and his artistic legacy have too many dimensions to receive comprehensive treatment in a volume such as this. Instead, a group of distinguished Nabokov scholars has been asked to provide the interested reader with some new critical pathways into Nabokov's rich creative landscape. Readers with some familiarity with Nabokov's work will encounter thought-provoking treatments of Nabokov's art and its place in a variety of cultural contexts.

Beginning with the bare facts of Nabokov's peripatetic life, one gains a quick glimpse into the richness of the man's life experiences. Born into a wealthy, aristocratic Russian family, only to lose his patrimony after the Russian Revolution, Nabokov moved to England to enter Cambridge University. After his father was killed by an assassin's bullet in 1922, Nabokov settled in Berlin and began a difficult struggle to earn a living as a writer. Although he ultimately emerged as one of the leading lights of Russian émigré literature, Nabokov found himself in the late 1930s faced

▷ Context

with the rise of Nazi fascism and the need to start over again, writing in a new language and moving to a new country. A renewed period of economic hardship and arduous work resulted in the unexpected yet immense success of *Lolita*. Financially secure at last, Nabokov returned to Europe, where he spent his last years writing new works in English, translating and revising his earlier Russian-language works, and overseeing the translation of both sets of works into other languages. All of these experiences made for an intense and colorful biography, and Brian Boyd's meticulous reconstruction of this biography encompasses two large volumes.[1]

When Nabokov himself contemplated the seismic shifts he experienced over time, he tended not to see them as random, disparate, or disjointed. On the contrary, he preferred to view his life in aesthetic terms. Indeed, one of the most important, recurring images in his fiction is the notion of life as a "text." The widowed narrator of the short story "Ultima Thule" writes: "in moments of happiness, of rapture, when my soul is laid bare, I suddenly feel . . . that everything – life, patria, April . . . is but a muddled preface, and that the main text still lies ahead" (*Stories*, 520–21). In *The Real Life of Sebastian Knight*, the narrator V. sums up the subject of his half-brother's last book with a bold declaration: "The man is the book," he writes (175 [ch. 18]), and he then continues: "The answer to all questions of life and death, 'the absolute solution' was written all over the world he had known: it was like a traveler realizing that the wild country he surveys is not an accidental assembly of natural phenomena, but the page in a book where these mountains and forests . . . are disposed in such a way as to form a coherent sentence" (178–79 [ch. 18]). In *Pale Fire*, the poet John Shade includes the following lines in his autobiographical poem: "Man's life as commentary to abstruse / Unfinished poem" (*PF*, 67 [lines 939–40]). When writing a memoir of his own, Nabokov explicitly announces his intention to describe his life the way one might discuss a novel. Speaking of the "match theme" in his life, he declares: "The following of such thematic designs through one's life should be, I think, the true purpose of autobiography" (*SM*, 27). In adopting this approach, Nabokov emulates the way his fictional character Fyodor Godunov-Cherdyntsev treats the historical figure N. G. Chernyshevski in *The Gift*. After pointing out a number of themes – the theme of "writing exercises," "nearsightedness," "angelic clarity," "pastry shops," "officers" – Fyodor comments: "the motifs of Chernyshevski's life are now obedient to me – I have tamed its themes" (*Gift*, 236 [ch. 4]).

In the essay that opens the present volume, Zoran Kuzmanovich picks up on the concept of design and patterning in Nabokov's artistic presentation of his own life, and he focuses on several significant images in Nabokov's work that provide clues as to how the writer tried to shape his inquisitive readers' understanding of his life experience. Noting that Nabokov's life was marked by devastating losses and heartening gains, Kuzmanovich uses the poem "Restoration" to reveal how the writer created a structured response to these momentous changes in his life. The expansion of consciousness, a resistance to the commonplace, a receptivity to the ever-present possibilities of sudden bliss – these are the enduring elements in Nabokov's appreciation of the world through which he passed.

These elements are also incorporated into the art of Nabokov's story-telling, as Brian Boyd skillfully demonstrates in the second essay of this volume. Boyd, who has long been one of Nabokov's best interpreters, provides a stimulating guide to the strategies and techniques Nabokov deployed to provoke certain responses from his readers. Concentrating on elements such as character, scene staging, plot structure, and shifts in point of view, Boyd reminds us that Nabokov "challenges and questions and refreshes every aspect of narrative," thereby becoming a kind of "personal trainer in mental flexibility." Through a close analysis of the openings of two novels written at the opposite ends of Nabokov's career, *Mary* and *Transparent Things*, Boyd highlights the fundamental freedom embedded in Nabokov's imaginative exercises, his rejection of dull convention, and his desire for the reader to participate in the invigorating joy of discovery.

One of the characteristic features of Nabokov's work that strikes even the first-time reader is the significant role that Nabokov gives to the world of literature in his texts. His fiction is replete with literary allusions, either overt or hidden, and one senses the writer's sensitivity to the artistic efforts of a multitude of other authors, stretching from the distant past to the present day. Alexander Dolinin's essay offers a fresh examination of Nabokov's attitude toward the impressive heritage of Russian literature to which Nabokov himself was now contributing, and which he wished to shape for personal reasons of his own. Dolinin's prior work on the role of literary allusion in Nabokov's fiction puts him in the perfect position to analyze this dimension of Nabokov's art, and the conclusions he draws are deeply illuminating and original. What Dolinin brings out is that Nabokov was keenly aware of his place in the Russian literary tradition and that far from remaining aloof from the literary quarrels that often preoccupied his fellow émigrés, he was a "lively troublemaker" who persistently battled his contemporaries to assert his primacy in a literary tradition he was striving to define. What is more, Dolinin goes on to explain why it was that when Nabokov translated his Russian-language novels into English, he toned down or eliminated many of the allusions to Russian literature that they had originally contained, and replaced them with allusions to such Western writers as Shakespeare and Edgar Allan Poe. As Dolinin sees it, Nabokov did this not merely because he felt that these allusions might be lost on the Anglo-American reader; rather, Nabokov wished to transcend his status as a "Russian" author and to replace that status with a new image as a "cosmopolitan" or "trans-national" author.

It is at this point that Susan Elizabeth Sweeney takes up the tale, focusing on Nabokov's transformation into an "American" writer. Starting with Nabokov's efforts to downplay the importance of a writer's nationality (SO, 63), and his own affirmations that "his best work was done in English" (SL, 454), Sweeney delves into Nabokov's complex creative approach to his new home and the numerous guises it assumes in his work. Sweeney makes the argument that Nabokov's adopted country stood in for his lost homeland, of course with varying distortions, adjustments, and substitutions. As she tracks the changing vision of America, real and invented, that Nabokov inscribed into his English-language novels, Sweeney asserts that Nabokov's American works compensate for his state of exile "by 'some sleight of *land*' – that is, by transposing one country with another." While recognizing Nabokov's precise knowledge of the *realia* of American life (which is especially evident in *Lolita*), Sweeney charts the varying degrees to which Nabokov's novels depict stylized versions of America – "Terra the Fair" – in which human experience, both blissful and agonizing, stand out in haunting relief. Sweeney closes her sweeping study of the American novels by pointing out that not only did Nabokov transform America in his fiction, he transformed American culture too. The words "nymphet" and "Lolita" now have special meaning in the American lexicon, and a host of writers exhibit "Nabokovian" features in their work.

Continuing the exploration of Nabokov's relation to the literary currents of his day, John Burt Foster, Jr. comments on the writer's complex views on European modernism (or, to be more precise, modernisms). Foster examines three aspects of this broad topic: Nabokov's response to English-language "high" modernism, his reaction to what may be called the "modernism of underdevelopment" in his native Russian literature, and the internationalist vision of "modernist fiction" that Nabokov adopted as a result of his experience living and writing in several countries after his departure from Russia in 1919. Outlining Nabokov's rejection of the mythical method that some of the high modernists espoused, Foster explains how Nabokov favored parody and cultural multiplicity to counter any movement that would reduce the individual to the level of stereotype. Nabokov's antipathy toward fixed stereotypes also led the writer to downplay the status some Western critics gave to Dostoevsky in their account of the development of Russian modernism. In place of Dostoevsky, Nabokov advanced Pushkin and Tolstoy as key figures in this development. Foster's essay concludes with an insightful summary of Nabokov's interest in (and revision of) the literary practices he observed in the work of Proust, Joyce, and Kafka.

Having delineated several of the literary contexts in which Nabokov's art may best be viewed, the present collection shifts focus to examine several distinct stages in Nabokov's development as a writer. Nabokov entered literature as a poet, and Barry Scherr provides a detailed overview of Nabokov's poetic career, commenting on the structural characteristics of Nabokov's verse output and tracing the evolution of the central themes of this body of work. Of particular interest to those who know Nabokov primarily as a writer of prose fiction may be Scherr's observation that Nabokov's poetry became increasingly profound and original over the course of his career, even as he was writing less of it due to his growing output in prose. While Nabokov's youthful poetry deals with personal themes that are not so evident in the early prose, the late poetry offers unusual transformations or distillations of the central concerns of the prose he was working on in those later years.

As Nabokov evolved from poet to novelist, his creative energies led him into the realm of the short story, and by the time he finished his last short story in 1951, Nabokov had written over sixty short stories and sketches. This body of work manifests the writer's predilection for innovation and experimentation, thus presenting fertile terrain for exploration. In her essay on the short fiction, Priscilla Meyer arranges the stories thematically and thereby encourages the reader to discern how Nabokov's treatment of central themes evolved over time. Meyer also notes Nabokov's use of the short stories as preliminary sketches for the more capacious novels. Into these short works he often introduced ideas that would receive more extensive elaboration in his subsequent novels.

Of the seven novels that Nabokov originally wrote in Russian, I have chosen to focus on the last three – *Despair*, *Invitation to a Beheading*, and *The Gift* – and in the essay I prepared for this volume, I have delineated the development of a seminal theme in these three works. Each of these novels provides a unique treatment of the creative impulse, and, in particular, of the attitude an imaginative protagonist takes toward the surrounding world. In Hermann Karlovich, the narrator and protagonist of *Despair*, Nabokov introduces a narcissistic figure who aggressively projects his solipsistic fantasies onto the world around him. That world, however, resists such a dictatorial approach, and the narrator finds his selfish fantasies rudely overturned by a reality that is more independent and autonomous than he conceives. In *Invitation to a Beheading* Nabokov depicts the inverse of this situation, and he now features a protagonist who must learn to trust the promptings of his creative spirit and to reject the conformist pressures of the world that imprisons him. Finally, in *The Gift*, Nabokov's longest and most intricate Russian novel, Nabokov unveils a middle path, and he centers his narrative on a young writer who learns to avoid the temptation of overwhelming the precious individuality of the people around him with personal projection, and who learns at the same time to trust his own creative instincts as well. Through this novel Nabokov reveals his own discoveries about how to cope with loss and how to transform the evanescent experiences of life into the lasting monuments of art. The complex relationship to the Russian literary tradition discussed in Dolinin's essay also emerges as a vital element in this masterful, multilayered novel.

With the completion of *The Gift*, Nabokov had reached a turning point in his life. Facing the political uncertainties of a world on the brink of war, and realizing that the audience for his works was ever shrinking, Nabokov made the difficult decision to abandon his native tongue and to adopt a new language as the primary vehicle for his artistic expression. Neil Cornwell's essay focuses on this pivotal period in Nabokov's career, a moment of something akin to trilingual hesitation, as Nabokov seemed to hover between choosing French or English as the next language in which he would begin to write. After commenting on Nabokov's linguistic aptitude and training, Cornwell examines the principal works that Nabokov wrote in French, the sketch "Mademoiselle O" and the speech composed in preparation for the 1937 centenary of Pushkin's death. Moving to Nabokov's early efforts in English, Cornwell concentrates on *The Real Life of Sebastian Knight*, which itself addresses issues of linguistic facility and the transition from Russian to English. Cornwell also remarks upon the last substantial works Nabokov wrote in Russian – the novella *The Enchanter*, and two remnants of an unfinished novel – "Solus Rex" and "Ultima Thule." Cornwell sifts through these late works to find the seeds of Nabokov's new identity as an English-language author.

When one considers the fact that in the late 1930s Nabokov was weighing the possibilities of radically reshaping his identity as a writer, one might not be surprised that a clear interest in the genre of biography (and autobiography) surfaced at this time. Galya Diment investigates Nabokov's idiosyncratic approach to biographical writing, using *The Gift* as the focal point of her discussion. What she finds in this investigation is that not only do the biographies of real and imagined others embedded in *The Gift* (Nikolay Chernyshevski and Konstantin Godunov-Cherdyntsev) shed insight into Nabokov's views on the form and practice of biographical writing, they also provide compelling glimpses into important experiences in Nabokov's own life. Diment's analysis underscores the crucial role that "sympathetic imagination" plays in the creative laboratory of the biographical project.

Imagination also stands at the center of Ellen Pifer's essay on the *Lolita* phenomenon. In her discussion of Nabokov's most famous novel, Pifer meticulously dissects the distortions and misdirections woven into Humbert Humbert's emotional narrative about his obsessive desire for one Dolores Haze, aka Lolita. With acute sensitivity to Humbert's aspirations and anxieties, Pifer skillfully guides the reader through the dense layers of parody, fantasy, and projection from which Humbert constructs his world and his narrative. She reminds us of the real damage Humbert has done to the girl he claims as his immortal love, and she underscores the paramount fact that despite some assertions to the contrary, aesthetics and ethics are inextricably intertwined in Nabokov's artistic world. Pifer also demonstrates how vital and relevant Nabokov's once-sensational novel has proven to be over the five decades since its original publication, citing Azar Nafisi's inspiring discussion of the novel in the memoir *Reading Lolita in Tehran*. The meaning that Nafisi and her students found in *Lolita* as they read and discussed it in secret in the Islamic Republic of Iran represents impressive testimony to the power and strength of Nabokov's artistic legacy.

Turning to the novels Nabokov wrote late in his career, Michael Wood singles out a theme that seems to grow ever more persistent in this period: a sensation that strikes Nabokov's characters that beyond their own world lies another world and, what may be even more unsettling, that some other being – similar, but perhaps more powerful, more competent, and even more authentic – looms behind their backs. Wood's interest here, however, is not so much the otherworldly per se, as the characters' own sense of wonder (or anxiety) over what may exist in this shadow realm. It is in their very belief – that the world around them is not the only possible world – that Wood detects a reasonable definition of what fiction itself "does and is." By encouraging his readers to wonder what might happen to his characters as the books they inhabit come to an end, Nabokov encourages those very same readers to wonder about their own fates, and about other possible worlds to come.

This *Cambridge Companion* closes with two essays that delve into aspects of Nabokov's work which have received some attention in discussions of specific texts, but which deserve a fresh look. Leona Toker's essay touches upon a number of topics of interest to Nabokov's readers – aesthetics, ethics, metaphysics, and politics – but it is perhaps the elusive subject of Nabokov's metaphysical concerns that has generated the most lively response in recent years. What makes Toker's discussion of this topic so valuable is the diachronic perspective she brings to the debate. Toker argues that Nabokov's speculations on what might exist beyond the horizon of one's death seems to have evolved considerably over time. The close readings of key texts that she conducts here will make a major contribution to a little understood but intriguing dimension of Nabokov's art.

In the final essay of the volume, Barbara Wyllie addresses the role that cinema plays in Nabokov's life and art. Although Nabokov was obviously a verbal artist, Wyllie shows how significant the genre of film was to his writing. To clarify this point, Wyllie examines the role of cinema from three angles – the considerable interest in film that Nabokov displayed throughout his life, whether he was panning or praising a given film; his professional activities in the field, including his work on the screenplay for the film version of *Lolita*; and his extensive use of cinematic elements in his works, from tricks of perspective to allusions to well-known (and not so well-known) films. Wyllie detects great ambivalence in Nabokov's treatment of film, but she finds in this very ambivalence a dynamic source of energy, depth, and complexity. Thus we arrive once again at one of the most fundamental characteristics of Nabokov's art – its enormous complexity, richness, and depth. A protean writer, Nabokov created a dazzling legacy that promises to attract and enchant readers for decades to come.

NOTE

1. See Brian Boyd, *Vladimir Nabokov: The Russian Years* (Princeton: Princeton University Press, 1990) and *Vladimir Nabokov: The American Years* (Princeton: Princeton University Press, 1991).

I
CONTEXTS

I

ZORAN KUZMANOVICH

Strong opinions and nerve points: Nabokov's life and art

I imagined, in bedtime reveries, what it would be like to become an exile who longed for a remote, sad, and (right epithet coming) unquenchable Russia, under the eucalipti of exotic resorts. Lenin and his police nicely arranged the realization of that fantasy . . .

Vladimir Nabokov, *Strong Opinions*, 177

[S]ome part of me must have been born in Colorado, for I am constantly recognizing things with a delicious pang.

Vladimir Nabokov to Edmund Wilson, July 24, 1947 (*NWL*, 218)

More than any other twentieth-century writer whose travel agents inadvertently included Lenin and Hitler, Vladimir Vladimirovich Nabokov was concerned with discerning thematic designs in his life and encoding across his works "the fantastic recurrence of certain situations" (*Pnin*, 159 [ch. 6]). Once *Lolita* made him a celebrity, he used his public prose to direct his readers toward those prescient designs and to suggest that historical exigency was merely a tool for the materialization of his fantasy. His interviews, prefaces, postscripts, letters to various editors, and responses to his critics always strike me as pre-emptive and corrective, at once recapitulative and predictive. They chide, they nudge, they set the story straight, and they do so not by informing but by evoking. They deepen the mystery of Nabokov's talent, while, with phrases such as "right epithet coming," they create a sense of qualification, a momentary reversal in, or rest from the inexorable forward movement while simultaneously speeding readers on their way to the always receding solution of that mystery of presence rendered through absence. Following the American publication of *Lolita*, this was a very successful strategy, simply because it set Nabokov's readers, usually academics, to work. Nabokov is the lone example of an exiled writer who by staying just slightly ahead of the twentieth century's political barbarities not only survived multiple linguistic dislocations but also made an artistic virtue out of his transcendental homelessness. That his works should have found a home with the reader is all the more surprising given Nabokov's contention that an author "clashes with readerdom because he is his own ideal reader and those other readers are so very often mere lip-moving ghosts and amnesiacs. On the other hand, a good reader is bound to make fierce efforts when wrestling with a difficult author, but those efforts can be most rewarding after the bright dust has settled" (SO, 183).

I understand this to mean that the writer is always trying to perpetuate his own discourse while the reader tries to appropriate it, evade it, ignore it, forget it, or deny it, thus creating "the bright dust," the excitement and the pathos of the reader's and writer's simultaneous pursuit and evasion of the other's narrative. But, despite that pathos, as Nabokov guardedly observed of Pushkin, "As so often happens with well-studied lives, an artistically satisfying pattern appears" (EO, III:201).

At the time of his death in 1977, the trajectory of Nabokov's life was already fairly well known. He was the first surviving son born into a distinguished and liberal family; initially a sickly child, he enjoyed a precocious and toy-bright, tutored, multilingual childhood. He developed insomnia (in adulthood to be controlled by composing chess problems), synaesthesia, and an interest in lepidoptery. Then came a considerable inheritance in his teenage years, a flurry of adolescent erotic pursuits and verse-making, removal to Western Europe just ahead of the Bolshevik guns that brought the idyllic life to an end and made exile the native idiom of the author. There followed the Cambridge years, the adoption of Sirin as a pseudonym, the accidental assassination of Nabokov's beloved father by Russian fascists, return from Cambridge to Berlin, broken engagement, the marriage to a Jewish émigré Véra Slonim, slow ascent to literary pre-eminence among quarrelsome, cultured, and dwindling émigré groups (many of whom saw his work as un-Russian), a period of what he called "my golden poverty," the birth of Dmitri, a brief affair accompanied by psoriasis, the move to Paris just ahead of Hitler's anti-Semitic frenzy, writing in a bathroom, the change from Russian to English, the arrival in United States just ahead of Word War II. The American period includes: an academic career at Wellesley and Cornell, butterfly-hunting cross-country trips where he would write parts of *Lolita* in a Buick, a second period of anxiety about economic prospects, the monumentally erudite translation of *Eugene Onegin*, the monumentally scandalous success of *Lolita*, both of which had something to do with Nabokov's declaring Edmund Wilson a "former friend" (SO, 219). *Lolita*'s financial success obviated the need for annual shows of finding Austen's "dimples" (LL, 58, 59), Joyce's "synchronizations" (LL, 289, 304, 309) and Dickens's "soot" (LL, 78, 79, 80) for Cornell's literature students, and Nabokov was able to return to Europe, this time to an old-fashioned Edwardian luxury hotel in Montreux, Switzerland, on the shores of Lake Geneva. From those shores, with his "purple plumed sunset" years upon him, he would eventually declare himself "as American as April in Arizona" (SO, 98) while reminding his readers that having been a Russian writer once he was now an American one who just happened to have been educated in England where he studied French literature, before spending fifteen years in Germany (*SO*, 26). By 1967, this polyglot and cosmopolite saw himself as an "ageless international freak" (*SO*, 106), and by 1968 gloried in his "freakish" uniqueness: "I don't seem to belong to any clear-cut continent. I'm the shuttlecock above the Atlantic, and how bright and blue it is there, in my private sky, far from the pigeonholes and the clay pigeons" (*SO*, 115–16).

This cagey self-image comes out of the September 3, 1968 interview with Nicholas Garnham for the BBC. As usual, Nabokov had had the list of questions sent to him and then responded to the questions in writing, insisting on his complete answers being quoted. In doing so, Nabokov used his status as a celebrity to change the terms of an interview to those of correspondence. Thus literary chit-chat, discussions of influence, and the inevitable handicapping of literary reputations often turned into a lesson, usually a lesson on reading Nabokov. He had sacrificed spontaneity and simultaneity, distancing himself from his interlocutors while making sure that what he said was remembered and that those quotable bits moreover were linked by some undercurrents of internal logic across a number of topics and occasions. Despite Nabokov's efforts at controlling the interview process, some critics of *Strong Opinions*, Nabokov's collected interviews, concluded that although Nabokov "composes his answers, they are not always composed."[1] John Updike, an astute reader of Nabokov, found the whole of Nabokov's work not only composed but in fact so composed as to give "the happy impression of an *œuvre*, of a continuous task carried forward." In 1964 he declared Nabokov "the best writer of English prose at present holding American citizenship" as well as "a solid personality" expressing itself in the "intensity of its intelligence and reflective joy," a performance "scarcely precedented in American literature." No mean stylist himself, Updike concluded that Nabokov writes ecstatic prose whose "every corner rewards inspection."[2] By using the term ecstasy, Updike locates Nabokov's prose outside Nabokov. Moving in the opposite direction, Joyce Carol Oates complains that Nabokov's prose is a habit through which "Nabokov empties the universe of everything except Nabokov."[3] Where Updike finds "the autobiographical elements . . . cunningly rearranged and transformed by a fictional design,"[4] Oates complains that a Nabokov-filled universe is "only sterile, monomaniacal, deadening to retain for very long in one's imagination."[5]

With Nabokov, there is no middle ground, so one must decide whose intuition to follow. Though Nabokov was eventually to disagree with Updike's readings of *Ada*, given Updike's sensitivity and Oates's seeming oversusceptibility to the contagion that is Nabokov's style, Updike's evaluation should be taken more seriously if for no other reason than Nabokov's high opinion of Updike's own writing, a hint that Updike was one of the readers Nabokov, for all his professed indifference to readers, cultivated as an audience: "I write mainly for artists, fellow-artists and follow-artists" (*SO*, 41). Another reader whose opinions Nabokov respected was his editor at *The New Yorker*, Katharine White, and an excerpt from a letter Nabokov wrote to her evinces the strain of Nabokov's efforts at creating his readers by instructing them what not to omit, ignore, or misread. In response to White's copy-editing of "Portrait of My Uncle," later reprinted as chapter 3 of *Speak, Memory*, Nabokov wrote: "I do not think I would like my longish sentences clipped too close, or those drawbridges lowered which I have taken such pains to lift." Nabokov pointed out that his sentences convey "a certain special – how shall I put it – sinuosity, which is my own and which only at first glance may seem awkward or obscure" (*SL*, 76–77). When one considers that Nabokov even in the postscript to *Lolita* bemoaned his American readers' lack of familiarity with his Russian works, it is fairly safe to assume that Nabokov saw his English writing as another phase in his work as an auteur, flowing under the drawbridges of English grammar, full of hidden depths, from which his migratory, echoing, and self-replenishing themes would not divulge themselves without the reader's knowledge of all his works. One should follow Updike's advice, then, and look again at every corner of Nabokov's sinuous edifice even though it is clear from that shuttlecock image that Nabokov tries very carefully to avoid being cornered.

In his study of Nabokov's prefaces and afterwords, Charles Nicol had observed a certain uniformity of process. Nicol lists the ten or so steps Nabokov takes, including a report on his personal situation at the time of the writing as well as an "elliptical" commentary on the book being introduced.[6] Nicol concludes that prefaces and afterwords are yet another of Nabokov's means for leaving "delicate markers." Readers who see Nabokov's indulgences in the elliptical as being of sufficiently "high order" are free to treat those markers as indispensable aids for revealing what one must know in order to read Nabokov properly, that is, read his plots, themes, and images as functionally synonymous.[7] If (along with arcs, circles, spirals, folded magic carpets, etc.) one does decide to treat Nabokov's self-images as "delicate markers" of the emplotted-ness threading Nabokov's life through his art, then historically that image of levitating shuttlecock Nabokov against the bright blue background seems quite out of place. There were not many trans-Atlantic crossings for the Nabokovs and even fewer airplane flights, none over the Atlantic. But the oddity dissipates if one remembers that to Nabokov's readers in 1968, the shuttlecock image would also call to mind less some kind of transcontinental badminton than the early Apollo/Saturn landing modules, featherless airy-somethings that situate their frail but heroic inhabitants on the brink of wonder, well beyond the reach of sniping critics. Even the fanciest-seeming of Nabokov's images usually has a basis in historical events. But it is history in the service of Nabokov's thematic designs. For example, that curious image of suspension or levitation may strike the unsympathetic or the uninformed readers as an act of self-mythologizing, a protective device that invites the right kind of attention, keeping all eyes on one's lofty self-positioning within a celebrity culture but closing oneself off to the gazes of pigeonholers.

To someone who has read and re-read Nabokov's works, the shuttlecock image as an image of levitation casts its shadow onto both a line of prior images and a line of those that Nabokov would not even write down for another few years. Looking backwards, one focuses, for example, on Ganin's imitating Japanese acrobats by walking on his hands in *Mary*, Alexandr Ivanovich tasting the icy air from his window ledge at the end of *The Defense*, Cincinnatus slipping out of "senseless life" into "elastic air" and, against all odds, briefly remaining "transfixed" there (*IB*, 96–97 [ch. 8]), all three leading to the moment in *The Real Life of Sebastian Knight* when V. describes how an author by "an incredible feat of suggestive wording" makes the readers feel as "if we discovered that by moving our arms in some simple, but never yet attempted manner, we could fly" (178 [ch. 18]). The image of levitation or engine-less flying reappears with Nabokov's father being tossed up by peasants celebrating his release from prison in *Speak, Memory*, and that same line of imagery will be continued, almost thirty years after *The Real Life of Sebastian Knight*, with John Shade's opening meditation in *Pale Fire* on flying and dying, Hugh's pitiful achievements at levitation in *Transparent Things*, and Van's more spectacular efforts in *Ada*. Nor should one forget that Nabokov chose for his pen name, Sirin, the word designating another fabulous flier, Slavic mythology's firebird of paradise.

When one adds flying or levitation to the bright blue background, Nabokov's seemingly fanciful off-the-cuff response to a question about his position in the literary stock market also points to a 1952 poem, "Restoration," unremarkable as a lyric but composed almost entirely out of what would have served as "nerve points" in other Nabokov texts. Its intersecting motifs have a density found only in parts of *The Gift*, *Speak, Memory*, and *Lolita*. When connected, these motifs form a pattern that points to restoration as a concept and conceit with a distinctly Nabokovian watermark which seems to require of Nabokov's readers that they know everything in order to know anything about him and his work.[8] Nabokov had cautioned the "wise readers" of his translated Russian works against "avidly" seeking in his American works "duplicate items or kindred scenery" (*Glory*, xiv

["Foreword"]). Phrased in such a way, the interdiction acts as an invitation to find what the previous readings missed. At the risk of psychoplagiarizing or confirming Nabokov's maxim that "mediocrity thrives on ideas," I would like to advance the idea of restoration not only as a uniting thread between Nabokov's life and art but also as a concept descriptive of Nabokov's method of creating "the inner weave" of his works and, by extension, as a reading tactic and goal Nabokov wished to impress upon his readers. Let us start with the poem:

Restoration (1952)

To think that any fool may tear
by chance the web of when and where.
O window in the dark! To think
that every brain is on the brink
of nameless bliss no brain can bear,   5

unless there be no great surprise
as when you learn to levitate
and, hardly trying, realize
– alone, in a bright room – that weight
is but your shadow, and you rise.   10

My little daughter wakes in tears:
She fancies that her bed is drawn
into a dimness which appears
to be the deep of all her fears
but which, in point of fact, is dawn.   15

I know a poet who can strip
a William Tell or Golden Pip
in one uninterrupted peel
miraculously to reveal,
revolving on his fingertip,   20

a snowball. So I would unrobe,
turn inside out, pry open, probe
all matter, everything you see,
the skyline and its saddest tree,
the whole inexplicable globe,   25

to find the true, the ardent core
as doctors of old pictures do
when, rubbing out a distant door
or sooty curtain, they restore
the jewel of a bluish view.   30

The poem's speaker stumbles through the three syntactically challenging fragments of lines one through ten, apostrophizing a "window in the dark," suggesting that in fact it is not possible to articulate in complete sentences the unbearable lightness of being on the brink of brain-flooding bliss when our weight is shed so that our pseudo-psychological agreements with ourselves and the pseudo-physiological ones with the world no longer hold. "[N]ameless bliss no brain can bear, / unless there be no great surprise" suggests that at least one brain could bear the bliss provided that this brain is not surprised to find its housing in the act of levitation. A brain not surprised to find itself in a levitating body would seem quite unlike "every brain." Because the phrasing is "every brain," not "every other brain," we must conclude that this is another one of the double negative circumspect constructions Nabokov tended to use when contemplating a mode of existence not restricted by gravity or mortality. That moment of epistemological and emotional evasion of gravity (and its long-term consequences for human bodies) is then compared in lines eleven through fifteen to a child's waking out of a nightmare, a daily surprise and resurrection no less impressive or welcome than levitation from the sleeper's point of view but perfectly ordinary to the fully awake, conscious, mind. Lines sixteen through twenty-one compare the act of waking/levitating/shedding weight to a poet's deft stripping of literal and figurative apples. Lines twenty-one through thirty apply these transformative activities to the efforts of the poem's speaker, apparently another poet, who explores all matter in order to reverse the effects of time upon it, remove the dust, and thus palliate into being a particularly precious view much as skilled craftsmen do in restoring old paintings.

Explained in this way, the poem does not amount to much. Yet by treating levitation as a trope for restoration and its accompanying mid-flight images as a set of keys to Nabokov's fictional world of incremental and auto-referential repetition, one may very well touch upon some of the "nerve points" that plot the thematic, formal, and therefore emotional designs in Nabokov's life and art. Of course one cannot look at such plots without noticing that Nabokov positions his re-readers where they feel as if their activity of purposeful decipherment of those nerve points will reveal the "inner weave" of his works all at once and thus produce in the reader the sensation of having "slipped the surly bonds of earth." Nabokov desired such slippages into atemporality, insisting that "if a book could be read in the same way as a painting is taken in by the eye, that is without the bother of working from left to right and without the absurdity of beginnings and ends, this would the be the ideal way of appreciating a novel, for thus the author saw it at the moment of its conception" (LL, 380). While such an ideal way of reading may not be possible with a single novel, inspiration at work may be glimpsed across a writer's entire œuvre and his well-studied life.

Any fool may tear

Born into a rich, prominent, talented, articulate, landed aristocratic St. Petersburg family, the older exiled Vladimir repeatedly imagined or remembered, in "a radiant shiver," the young and indulged Vladimir's "veritable Eden of visual and tactile sensations" (SM, 24 [ch. 1]) in a family circle where "Everything is as it should be, nothing will ever change, nobody will ever die" (SM, 77 [ch. 3]). Vladimir's April 23, 1899 birth followed the stillbirth of the Nabokovs' first son, and the precocious Vladimir quickly became and remained the most adored of the five Nabokov children. Shuttling between the stimulating elegance of St. Petersburg and the always dappled summer playgrounds on his relatives' estates, strolling on leafy avenues seen through sun-drenched stained glass and always promising something more than merely a walk in the woods, looking for bright and shiny things on glossy sun-set beaches of the Adriatic and the Mediterranean, young Vladimir stored up cherished impressions of objects, people, and places that would later leave him with a "hypertrophied sense of lost childhood" (SM, 73 [ch. 3]).

And that childhood was indeed a peculiar one. Born while Queen Victoria was still on the throne, Nabokov claims in Speak, Memory that he became a sentient being in August 1903. He was eighteen when his self-designed instruction in the verse of Russian Symbolists was interrupted by what would in fact be a very real change in the nature of his life. The rise of the Bolsheviks tore a hole in the web of family security and in young Vladimir's sense of entitlement, ending his father's outstanding political and journalistic life in Russia but also ending Nabokov's erotic and romantic life on his estate as well as his imagined future – that of a great Russian poet. Such a calamity was not without its compensation: "I would submit that, in regard to the power of hoarding up impressions, Russian children of my generation passed through a period of genius, as if destiny were loyally trying what it could for them by giving them more than their share, in view of the cataclysm that was to remove completely the world they had known. Genius disappeared when everything had been stored" (SM, 25 [ch. 1]).

In one important sense, then, Nabokov's art is the cataloging and re-arranging of what had been stored before fleeing the torn-apart Russia. But it was not only the artistic son who had stored up his cherished Russia and taken it with him. One of Speak, Memory's most moving images is of Nabokov's mother, Elena Ivanovna Rukavishnikov, a talented and mysti-cally inclined woman who was also the first audience for Nabokov's poetic efforts. Nabokov presents his mother in the context of his mediation on death as a "shameful family secret" (*SM*, 50 [ch. 2]). Another family secret was synaesthesia, a condition in which one type of stimulation evokes the sensation of another, so that the sequence of letters "*kzspygv*" meant "rainbow" in the contiguous perceptual dimension created by the mother's and the son's shared colored hearing. Nabokov's mother, too seems to have possessed the genius of a Shakespearean subconscious that would enable her to cope with cataclysmic tears in the fabric of her life: "A soapbox covered with green cloth supported the dim little photographs in crumbling frames she liked to have near her couch. She did not really need them, for nothing had been lost. As a company of traveling players carry with them everywhere, while they still remember their lines, a windy heath, a misty castle, an enchanted island, so she had with her all that her soul had stored" (*SM*, 49–50 [ch. 2]).

O window in the dark!

Lighted windows in Nabokov's work are often metaphors for the work of consciousness, at once a barrier and an opening, a brink. Apparently, from the time he conceived of human consciousness as a series of spaced flashes "between two eternities of darkness" (*SM*, 19 [ch. 1]), young Nabokov feared sleep. In *Speak, Memory*, he tells us that on doctor's orders, he slept in a room with a door cracked open to let the light in from the governess's room. Even as an adult, he imagined sleep as a "black-masked headsman binding me to the block." His "routine terrors of sleep" included the "familiar ax . . . coming out of its great velvet-lined double-bass case." An insomniac's wakeful consciousness then is the only defense against the "nightly betrayal of reason, humanity, genius" (108–9 [ch. 5]). In "Restoration" the daughter's tearful dawn-time nightmare is one such betrayal, though it is surprisingly reversible. Nabokov's insomnia and images of sleep as death are woven into the plot and the texture of *Invitation to a Beheading* and *Bend Sinister*, and each book is saturated with sensations of slumbering and sinking. Each ends with the image of some barrier dissolving, Cincinnatus's "gloom fleeted" in *Invitation to a Beheading* (223 [ch. 20]) while in *Bend Sinister* gloom and terror disappear "like a rapidly withdrawn slide" to reveal a better and different and more comfortable realm, with fellow humans inhabiting it. To a man who dies every night, waking up must be a surprise and a restoration of considerable magnitude. Waking consciousness's lucid life with its familiar voices thus reverses the slippage and sinking into sleep's death-like "heart-rending softness" and "black dazzling depths" (*BS*, 232 [ch. 18]).

Brain. Brink. Bliss.

Nabokov's thinking about webs of time and space, chance, and coincidence is always fragmentary, circumspect, metaphorical, and oracular. Neither in "Restoration" nor his novels does Nabokov reveal just what happens when the web of space and time, our particular tension film of reality, our belief or suspended disbelief is torn up to reveal a "contiguous realm." The two contiguous worlds have been identified by critics in a large number of ways, such as paradise and exile,[9] this world and a beneficent traffic-directing otherworld,[10] or average reality and true reality,[11] but they could just as easily be defined as fiction and autobiography,[12] Russian "human document" realism and glittery but exhausted European modernism,[13] or Sirin's English and Nabokov's Russian. Brian Boyd and Gennady Barabtarlo expand the number of worlds to three: outer, inner, and other, all moved by love;[14] Michael Wood chooses to look at three Nabokovs: the wise fool, the haughty mandarin, and the great, doubting magician.[15] Significantly, in the realm of this world the occasionally triune Nabokov came to regard "the objective existence of all events as a form of impure imagination" (*SO*, 154). But to act in any world, we must have both a mental representation of that world as well as a representation of ourselves in it, a fact that makes of the relation between the self and the world (however impure) something recursive and dizzying, a linguistic vertigo created when consciousness is investigated with consciousness. To Nabokov, the mind can grasp the world and its place in it only "with the assistance of creative fancy"; conversely, human reason cannot help but distort perception: "the shadow of the instrument falls upon the truth."

Surprise

Precisely because human reason struck Nabokov as a distorting and "garrulous dragoman who always runs ahead" and "prompt[s] us with explanations" (*Gift*, 331 [ch. 5]), he does not seem to have had complete faith in the intellectual faculties by which humans pursue truth or knowledge about "the whole inexplicable globe." Reason in the end is faith in the intelligibility of the world, and Nabokov did not feel the world to be intelligible in a strictly scientific way, for complete explicability makes surprise impossible and reading a routine activity. And reading Nabokov is anything but routine. D. Barton Johnson has observed that "the hallmark of Nabokov's style is an intricate integration of theme, plot, and motif."[16] Such integration takes place even at sentence level; his fiction surprises by mimicking departures from the veneer of immediate reality, reality being for Nabokov always a matter of layers of passionate and precise knowing, not a resting place for commonsensical consciousness. Such mimicry involves delayed perception: "Both men entered at the same moment. They looked at one another and – there was a great outburst of cheering as the puck was shot into the Swedish goal" (*Laugh*, 170 [ch. 20]). The second chapter of *The Gift* delays as long as possible the fact that Fyodor is not in Russia but on a Berlin tram. At other times, Nabokov will call attention to such delays by changing the tense of the action and suffusing the recalled image with frictionless liquid and sibilant consonants that mime the bounding arrival of the playful wet dog: "And now a delightful thing happens . . . I try again to recall the name of Colette's dog – and, triumphantly, along those remote beaches, over the glossy evening sands of the past, where each footprint slowly fills up with sunset water, here it comes, here it comes, echoing and vibrating: Floss, Floss, Floss!" (*SM*, 151–52 [ch. 7]). But the idea of life as a surprise for those who know how to look for it works in geographical as well as temporal terms: For the Nabokovs, the removal to America was, as Brian Boyd put it, "an awakening from a nightmare to a glorious new dawn."[17] Olga Krug would specify the nature of America as a glorious surprise in similar "Restoration"-like terms: "Elation, delight, a quickening of the imagination, a disinfection of the mind, *togliwn ochnat divodiv* [the daily surprise of awakening]!" (*BS*, 30 [ch. 3]). No wonder Nabokov felt as if parts of Colorado restored the landscape of his youth. How much America delighted Nabokov is clear from the fact that for the American portion of *Ada*'s Antiterra, he selected the America of the 1940s. If the loss of Russia had torn something in the fabric of Nabokov's life, America has offered a surprising mend, so much so that after the bombing of Pearl Harbor he was willing to volunteer to fight on America's behalf.

More importantly for Nabokov's work than for his life, surprise as wonder occasioned by something common but nonetheless unanticipated also functions at the level of plot: "'What nonsense. Of course there is nothing afterwards,'" proclaims a character in *The Gift*. "He sighed, listened to the trickling and drumming outside the window and repeated with extreme distinctness: 'There is nothing. It is as clear as the fact that it is raining.' And meanwhile outside the spring sun was playing on the roof tiles, the sky was dreamy and cloudless, the tenant upstairs was watering the flowers on the edge of her balcony, and the water trickled down with a drumming sound" (*Gift*, 312 [ch. 5]). Even such initially heartening surprises, however, can be undercut. To Kinbote's question "Who is the Judge of life, and the Designer of death?" *Pale Fire*'s poet John Shade responds with a simple and cryptically hopeful: "Life is a great surprise. I do not see why death should not be an even greater one" (*PF*, 225). Yet, such a comment has to be weighed against other pronouncements issued on the eve of his death, brought about by a bungled assassination attempt: "I am reasonably sure that I / Shall wake at six tomorrow, on July / The twenty-second, nineteen fifty-nine, / And that everything will probably be fine" (*PF*, 69). Shade's reason lets him down, but at the same time his theory of life as a surprise is spectacularly confirmed.

The deep of all her fears

Nabokov's childhood was a charmed life seemingly free of all grievances, with only an occasional worry about the consequences of his father's political and journalistic activity. Vladimir Dmitrievich Nabokov, one of the leading liberals in the Czar's government, had a public and parliamentary presence that often put him at odds with the Czarist policies and resulted in his forced resignation as a professor of law, loss of court title, loss of political rights, threat of a duel, even a three-month prison sentence. Nabokov's stories and memoirs register some of that fear as well as a filial love one generally does not find sons according to fathers in twentieth-century literature written in English. To realize the degree of such accord, one need only remember that for a Cambridge debate against a Bolshevist apologist, young Nabokov, always particular about his words, chose not to write his own speech but instead learned by heart one of his father's, "Soviet Rule and Russia's Future" (*SM*, 179 [ch. 9]).

On March 28, 1922, while Nabokov was on his Easter break, two Russian assassins attempted to kill Pavel Miliukov, a political opponent of Nabokov's father within the Kadet Party. Protecting Miliukov by attacking and holding down one assassin, V. D. Nabokov was shot and killed by the other thus creating the second major tear in the weave of Nabokov's life. The shock, grief, and absence of the father had some profound consequences for Nabokov's life. After taking second-class honors at Cambridge, Nabokov returned to Berlin, uncharacteristically started joining literary groups, and became engaged to Svetlana Siewert, a young woman whose parents would soon break off the engagement over Nabokov's lack of economic prospects. The lack of economic prospects would reflect itself as a concern only briefly in *The Gift*, so on the evidence of his major novels, one should take Nabokov at his word when he declares that it was not the loss of banknotes but the loss of Russia he grieved for quite physically. In Nabokov's art, the father's death would register in a number of disguises, first in the poems "Death" ("Smert'," 1924) and "Execution" ("Rasstrel," 1928) and then again in the mistaken murder of the poet John Shade in *Pale Fire*.

While it is the father's absence in *The Gift* that preoccupies Fyodor, in most of the other books, including *Lolita*, it is the death of the child that

Nabokov would find the most poignant, with the death of the son in the short story "Christmas," of David Krug in *Bend Sinister*,[18] of Lolita, her child, and the barber's son in *Lolita*, Hazel in *Pale Fire*, Lucette in *Ada*, and the possible death of the son in "Signs and Symbols" standing out as some of the better realized scenes in world literature. Although one could theorize some simple psychological displacement of grief to account for this inversion of the father's death for the death of fictional children, this is not the place to do it. Nabokov's reaction to the death of his father included yet another key image of restoration. In a 1925 letter to his mother, Nabokov wrote: "I am so certain, my love, that we will see him again, in an unexpected but completely natural heaven, in a realm where all is radiance and delight. He will come towards us in our common bright eternity, slightly raising his shoulders as he used to do . . . Everything will return."[19] One cannot fail to be moved by Nabokov's tenderness to his mother. But one should not forget that when he revisited his father's death in his autobiography, Nabokov envisioned him as a flying "paradisiac personage" whose levitation ends with a fall into an open coffin, an image that trades the comfort of a "completely natural heaven" and "our common bright eternity" for the terror and pathos of dying alone: Cincinnatus's "fear, [that] never halting, rushes through me with an ominous roar, like a torrent, and my body vibrates like a bridge over a waterfall" (*IB*, 192 [ch. 18]) and Humbert's sensation of his post-Lolita life: "a side door crashing open in life's full flight, and a rush of roaring black time drowning with its whipping wind the cry of lone disaster" (*Lo*, 253–54 [pt. 2, ch. 25]). While Nabokov's critics are certainly warranted in connecting the bungled, mistaken death of Nabokov's father with the executions in his works from "Death" to *Pale Fire*, on at least one level, it is only where sleep as the extinguishing of consciousness (a phenomenon quite familiar to all readers) meets with the bungled execution theme (death as randomness) and the death of children (death as inconceivable horror) that masterpieces are born.

Revolving on his fingertip

The moment we are aware of the recursion within the efforts of consciousness to know the world and to contemplate its own extinction, we too stand on the brink of a potentially blissful revelation while realizing over and over that we, or our reasoning faculties, construct the walls in which that window may be mounted.[20] Thus creative consciousness becomes a window both into time and out of it. In his moments of poetic optimism, Nabokov declared that he did not believe in time. While explaining the role or non-role of time in poetic composition, he saw time as "an instantaneous and transparent organism of events," yet *Speak, Memory* begins with the somber contention that "the prison of time is spherical and without exits" (*SM*, 20 [ch. 20]). Many of his more substantially drawn characters, whether they are "favorites" or lukewarm villains, often seem to labor under the same recursive burden in the narratives they inhabit. Like their author, these lucid loners seek just such an exit, seek to tear a hole in the fabric of time and escape to some contiguous realm, some more satisfying past time in the presence of people they loved and lost, or a vantage point from which they can at least glimpse or dream of some heartening design behind the gloomy tenderness and "topsyturvical coincidence" of their lives. Sometimes, like Adam Krug, they are vouchsafed a suspicion that "a nameless, mysterious genius [. . .] took advantage of the dream to convey his own peculiar code message which has nothing to do with school days or indeed with any aspect of Krug's physical existence, but which links him up somehow with an unfathomable mode of being, perhaps terrible, perhaps blissful, perhaps neither, a kind of transcendental madness which lurks behind the corner of consciousness" (*BS*, 64 [ch. 5]).

If readers read with the idea that the text is a dreamlike experience behind which they glimpse the finger of the author pointing them towards blissful atemporal wakefulness, they will put up with the possibility of transcendental madness or "referential mania" in order to secure a kind of vicarious faith, faith by proxy in the explicability of the well-authored rather than a whim-governed world, a faith justified by nothing but the intuition that goodness is more primordial than evil and that consciousness is an instrument of love, a way of embracing the universe. The competing intuition yields only the fear that the universe is a tool in the hands of the cruel, the careless, and the foolish. Given that the act of reading fiction requires us to read events forward and meaning backwards, we are bound to consider the possibility that our bare, factual material existence becomes meaningful, transmissible, and accessible to us as *human* existence only through the spinning and understanding of spun narratives. Nabokov wrote in *Nikolai Gogol*, that "bare facts do not exist in a state of nature, for they are never really quite bare . . . I doubt whether you can even give your telephone number without giving something of yourself" (119).

Skyline and its saddest tree

What we create for ourselves through all human linguistic interaction is a story-shaped world: what we give of ourselves acquires significance precisely because only narratives have the capability for surprising yet meaningful closure. In Nabokov's fictions, the anticipation of surprising closure makes madness flirt with revelation and transcendence with insanity, but the fictions are executed so as to convey, at least for the duration of the reading, the time-suspending sensation not only that "Life, love, libraries, have no future" (*Ada*, 559 [pt. 4]), but that they do not need one either. What contributes "robust joy and achievement" to those three entities creates for Nabokov "the highest terrace of consciousness" when "mortality has a chance to peer beyond its own limits, from the mast, from the past and its castle tower. And although nothing much can be seen through the mist, there is somehow the blissful feeling that one is looking in the right direction" (*SM*, 50 [ch. 2]). From this elevated if not quite levitating vantage point where past, mast, and mist echo, repeat, and succeed each other, even nature's "saddest tree" will appear to be in the service of transcendence, wonderment, restoration: "when the old trance [the onset of inspiration – ZK] occurs nowadays, I am quite prepared to find myself, when I awaken from it, high up in a certain tree, above the dappled bench of my boyhood" (*SM*, 223 [ch. 11]). Sometimes, as in "The Shadow'" (1925), "The Ballad of Longwood Glen" (1957), and the end of *The Gift*, the trance does not culminate in the waking up but in the magical disappearance of the levitating dreamer from the page into its "skyline": "Every great writer is a great deceiver, but so is that arch-cheat Nature. Nature always deceives. From the simple deception of propagation to the prodigiously sophisticated illusion of protective colors in butterflies or birds, there is in Nature a marvelous system of spells and wiles. The writer of fiction only follows Nature's lead" (*LL*, 5). Only against such premises should we understand Nabokov's conclusion that "language is found in nature."[21] Language is the restoration or translation of nature into art only for someone fully conscious of exposed deception as a seeing through "to the ardent core" where "the inner texture of life is also a matter of inspiration and precision" (*LL*, 381). The joy one feels in being magically and elaborately deceived is presumably offset by the delight of seeing through disguises, seeing, as in chess problems or biological mimicry, the performance of something pretending not to be there. And like Lucette in *Ada*, we love to see magic tricks repeated, even if the trick is no more complex than turning an apple into a snowball by stripping the apple in a single peel, an achievement presumably within everyone's reach (*Ada*, 209 [pt. 1, ch. 33]). Peeling of an apple in a single strip is Nabokov's figure for the kind of art he both created and appreciated:

> "You see," [Fyodor] explained to Zina, "I want to keep everything as it were on the very brink of parody. You know those idiotic '*biographies romancées*' where Byron is coolly slipped a dream extracted from one of his own poems? And there must be on the other hand an abyss of seriousness, and I must make

my way along this narrow ridge between my own truth and a caricature of it. And most essentially, there must be a single uninterrupted progression of thought. I must peel my apple in a single strip, without removing the knife."

(Gift, 200 [ch. 3])

They restore

From the brink of his ridge, one side of which is built on the parody or partial restoration of hunted down motifs and stylistic signatures from Russian, European, and American writers, Nabokov in fact routinely slipped his dreams into his works, dreams of recapturing and restoring, first on note cards and then in a book, the original flash of inspiration complete not only with trains of thought but their scintillating shadows as well:

> From the very beginning the image of his planned book had appeared to him extraordinarily distinctly in tone and outline, he had the feeling that for every detail he ran to earth there was already a place prepared and that even the work of hunting up material was already bathed in the light of the forthcoming book, just as the sea throws a blue light on a fishing boat, and the boat itself together with this light is reflected in the water. (Gift, 200 [ch. 3])

But Nabokov was not satisfied just to paint the blue flash of the original inspiration; he also tried to render for the reader the task of hunting down, materializing that flash:

> Suddenly he stopped short. Somewhere in his memory there was a hint of motion, as if something very small had awakened and begun to stir. The word was still invisible, but its shadow had already crept out as from behind a corner, and he wanted to step on that shadow to keep it from retreating and disappearing again. Alas, he was too late. Everything vanished, but at the instant his brain ceased straining, the thing stirred again, more perceptibly this time, and like a mouse emerging from a crack when the room is quiet, there appeared, lightly, silently, mysteriously, the live corpuscle of a word. . . . "Give me your paw, Joker." Joker! How simple it was. Joker.
>
> ("The Reunion" [Stories, 311])

Joseph Frank had concluded from Nabokov's lectures on literature that Nabokov wanted his students to learn to read novels as if they were spatial or synchronous phenomena, paintings, in fact,[22] but it seems to me that Nabokov occasionally animates his "paintings" with "live" corpuscles that, like Floss, Joker, and praying mantises pretending to be twigs, by a "hint of motion," transform to reveal something not seen before.

The jewel of a bluish view

Novels are devices used by the novelist to explore some pressing themes through experimental selves called characters and thereby, in a quasi-religious act, reconcile some contradictory elements of the novelist's existence. Nabokov's most memorable narratives are staged as confessions, and theorists of the confessional, from St. Augustine to Foucault tell us that confessions are verbal exercises by which one authenticates and restores oneself in the process of revealing oneself to God (Augustine) or (re)constitutes oneself in a perpetual hermeneutics for producing truth (Foucault).[23] Thus for both early Christians and Foucault, a successful hermeneutic presupposes readers transformed in the image of the spirit they set out to find in the confessions they perform or witness. Confession is thus an objectification of the self, a peeling off of one's drab past, as Shade puts it, to present it, over and over, not only as a knowable but as an invaluable object uniting the confessing and the confessor.

Invited to confess in his interviews, Nabokov used the opportunity to plant images of himself in his public prose that not only echo lines from "Restoration" but also give some clues to his images of himself caught up in creating the bejeweled shimmer of his details. Before he was finished with his first novel, Nabokov would comment to his mother: "We are translators of God's creation, his little plagiarists and imitators."[24] Creation of novels thus turns out to be translation or restoration of what for believers is the original speech act – the turning of dust into a living soul. But while in each novel Nabokov invites us to see that his textual performance is only a reflection or imperfect translation of some other/prior/forgotten/repressed/ineffable/"untrammeled" reality, he often relies on the confessional mode to secure from the reader a knowledge of that uncanny reality, that, like sin or bliss, is both at once inexpressible and very familiar. In delivering not only the "nerve point" image but tracing its mysterious arrival Nabokov tries to make palpable the return of the repressed/forgotten/painful, but as an anti-Freudian, he does not dwell on the pain of repressed traumas over abrupt loss. Rather, instead of mourning dwindling prospects, he puts the focus on memory's palpable achievement of conscious and joyful restoration. Happiness, Kundera tells us, is precisely desire for repetition, and Nabokov mimes that desire frequently. The erasure of figurative soot in "Restoration" and across Nabokov's works gives the lie to the "dust to dust" tropism and re-renders it instead as "dust to jewel," in the process making the rubbing out of millions of years necessary to turn dust into blue jewels no less simple than the rubbing out of a sooty door.[25] Nabokov had spoken of inspiration as a two-step process of rapture and recapture, and in one sense, writing is always the performance of "recapture" or the restoration of the inspired view of life. That his public prose ended up functioning as a self-elegizing blurb for his inspired art and that his characters thus end up dying into the blurb is less his fault than history's.

Nabokov warned that "it is pretty useless to deduce the life history and human form of a poet from his work; and the greater the artist the more likely it is for us to arrive at erroneous conclusions" (*Song*, 78–79). Any effort to tell the story of Nabokov's life, to explain the connection between that story and the story of his works in a few pages is doomed to grotesque reduction and facile oversimplification. Brian Boyd's judicious story of Nabokov's life required almost 1,400 pages and still gives the impression that there is much of Nabokov's life and art that is beyond biography. Nonetheless, tracing a single motif across Nabokov's life and work remains, for both novices and experts, a necessary process and fairly rewarding way of reading his work. And with that awareness, one cannot help but conclude on another (though hardly last) link in the chain of imagery Nabokov used to describe and pre-scribe himself: "[A]cross the dark sky of exile, Sirin passed, to use a simile of a more conservative nature, like a meteor, and disappeared, leaving nothing much else behind him than a vague sense of uneasiness" (*SM*, 288 [ch. 14]). Even here Nabokov seems to have anticipated and chuckled at his biogra-phers' uneasiness about that "conservative" image of himself as a meteor. Of course, he knew he was leaving us with much more than the uneasiness: meteors leave conclusive and precious evidence of their makeup in their dusty craters. The shadows cast by "Restoration"'s levitator and Nabokov's lungs filling with fluid on July 2, 1977 make it clear that the "levitating" Nabokov could not exempt himself from death and escape completely the curvature of the earth he saw reflected even in the nature of human thought (see "Ultima Thule" [*Stories*, 513]). While his total achievement is still being evaluated, Nabokov's future anterior chuckle at our uneasiness with his cheerful arro-gance, however, reminds us that with *The Gift, Lolita,* and *Speak, Memory* he had almost made the case for having learned the secret of levitation. As Updike finally put it in *Hugging the Shore,* Nabokov "saw from a higher attitude, from the top of the continents he had had to put behind him."[26]

NOTES

I am very grateful to my colleagues Suzanne Churchill and Felix Carroll, both of Davidson College, and to Anastasia Lakhtikova of St. Louis University for their careful consideration of two troublesome paragraphs of this essay.
1. Richard Brickner, "Strong Opinions," *New York Times Book Review* (November 11, 1973): 37.

2. John Updike, "Grandmaster Nabokov," *Assorted Prose* (New York: Knopf, 1965), 318–19.
3. Joyce Carol Oates, "A Personal View of Nabokov," *Saturday Review of the Arts* 1 (January 1973): 37.
4. Updike, "Grandmaster Nabokov," 320.
5. Oates, "Personal View," 37.
6. Charles Nicol, "Necessary Instruction or Fatal Fatuity: Nabokov's Introductions and *Bend Sinister*," *Nabokov Studies* 1 (1994): 115.
7. Ibid., 116, 121.
8. That image of levitation which migrates from novel to autobiography to poetry and back again, turns up, this time parodically, fourteen years after "Restoration" in a chatty (and later regretted) interview Nabokov gave to Penelope Gilliatt of *Vogue* right after his curative bath in a spa at the Engadine: "I discovered the secret of levitation. One puts the flat feet braced against the end of the bath and rises covered with bubbles like fur. I felt like a bear. A memory of a former state" (*Vogue*, 148.10 [December 1966]: 242; reprinted in *Three-Quarter Face: Reports and Reflections* [New York: Coward, McCann, and Geoghegan, 1980], 239–49).
9. Aleksandr Semochkin, *Nabokov's Paradise Lost: The Family Estates in Russia* (St. Petersburg: Liga Plus, 1999); Danilo Kiš, "Nabokov ili nostalgija," *Gradac* 13–14 (May–August, 1987): 28–30.
10. William Woodin Rowe, *Nabokov's Spectral Dimension* (Ann Arbor: Ardis, 1981); Véra Nabokov, "Predislovie," in V. Nabokov, *Stikhi* (Ann Arbor: Ardis, 1979); Vladimir Alexandrov, *Nabokov's Otherworld* (Princeton: Princeton University Press, 1991).
11. Ellen Pifer, *Nabokov and the Novel* (Cambridge, MA: Harvard University Press, 1980).
12. Herbert Grabes, *Erfundene Biographien: Vladimir Nabokovs englische Romane* (Tübingen: Niemeyer, 1975); *Fictitious Biographies: Vladimir Nabokov's English Novels* (The Hague: Mouton, 1977).
13. Georgii Adamovich, "Vladimir Nabokov," *Odinochestvo i svoboda* (New York: Izd. imeni Chekhova, 1955), 211–28 (translation by Irene Etkin Goldman may be found in *Twentieth-Century Russian Literary Criticism*, ed. Victor Erlich [New Haven: Yale, 1975], 219–31).
14. Brian Boyd, *Nabokov's Ada: The Place of Consciousness* (Ann Arbor: Ardis, 1985; rev. edn, Christchurch, NZ: Cybereditions, 2001); Brian Boyd, *Nabokov's Pale Fire: The Magic of Artistic Discovery* (Princeton: Princeton University Press, 1999); Gennady Barabtarlo, "Nabokov's Trinity (On the Movement of Nabokov's Themes)," in *Nabokov and His Fiction: New Perspectives*, ed. Julian W. Connolly (Cambridge: Cambridge University Press, 1999), 109–38.
15. Michael Wood, *The Magician's Doubts: Nabokov and the Risks of Fiction* (London: Chatto and Windus, 1994).
16. D. Barton Johnson, *Worlds in Regression: Some Novels of Vladimir Nabokov* (Ann Arbor: Ardis, 1985), 7.
17. Boyd, *Vladimir Nabokov: The American Years* (Princeton: Princeton University Press, 1991), 11.
18. While Nabokov was writing *Bend Sinister*, he learned of the death of his brother Sergei in a German concentration camp. Most critics of Nabokov do not view this

death as another major tear in the fabric of Nabokov's life; I do not see why it should not be. See, Zoran Kuzmanovich, "Suffer the Little Children," in *Nabokov at Cornell*, ed. Gavriel Shapiro (Ithaca: Cornell University Press, 2003), 49–58. The simple fact is that in Nabokov's works plotlines that include the death of children multiply greatly after Sergei's death. Véra's rumored miscarriages in the 1930s may also have had a role in this motif. See Stacy Schiff, *Véra* (New York: Modern Library, 2000).

19. Boyd, *Vladimir Nabokov: The Russian Years* (Princeton: Princeton University Press, 1990), 239.

20. Writing in 1988, Priscilla Meyer squarely identifies the window with "the passageway from life to death" and back for Nabokov's father (*Find What the Sailor Has Hidden* [Middletown, CT: Wesleyan University Press, 1988], 106).

21. Vladimir Nabokov, "Professor Woodbridge in an Essay on Nature Postulates the Reality of the World" [review of Frederick K. E. Woodbridge, *Essay on Nature*], *New York Sun* (December 10, 1940): 15.

22. Joseph Frank, "Lectures on Literature," in *The Garland Companion to Vladimir Nabokov*, ed. Vladimir Alexandrov (New York: Garland, 1995), 236.

23. Michel Foucault, *History of Sexuality*, vol. I, trans. Robert Hurly (New York: Random House, 1978), 59.

24. Boyd, *Russian Years*, 245.

25. In a very different sense, "the jewel of a bluish view" may be read prophetically and without irony as granting immortality. Nabokov did in fact capture another patch of immortality by way of a blue jewel – Nabokov's Blue (*Lycaeides idas nabokovi*). See John H. Masters, "A New Subspecies of *Lycaeides argyrognomon* (Lycaenidae) from the Eastern Canadian Forest Zone," *Journal of the Lepidopterists' Society* 26.3 (1972): 150–54.

26. John Updike, "Vale, VN," in *Hugging the Shore* (New York: Knopf, 1983), 245.

2

BRIAN BOYD

Nabokov as storyteller

In the quarter century since his death, much has been made of Nabokov as a thinker, as a metaphysician and moralist. We have learned a great deal, but D. Barton Johnson has recently challenged readers of Nabokov by asking, wouldn't we still be fascinated by his work even without his ideas?[1] Although Nabokov would write differently in all sorts of ways if his metaphysics and ethics were thinner and poorer, Johnson surely is right, we would still read Nabokov without them.

Why would we? The obvious first answer is style. Nabokov is widely and justly regarded as a high-water mark of literary style. But although we admire the style of *Speak, Memory*, or Nabokov's forewords and afterwords, or even *Strong Opinions*, we would not be drawn back to Nabokov again and again if there were just style and no story in his work. The dazzling detail, the inventive imagery, the patterned prose, the sinuous sentences, the thrill of the thought are all very well – very, very well – but even they are not enough.

Nabokov famously declared that "There are three points of view from which a writer can be considered: . . . as a storyteller, as a teacher, and as an enchanter. A major writer combines these three – storyteller, teacher, enchanter" (*LL*, 5). In his own terms, his metaphysics and ethics fall within his role as teacher, and his style within his role as enchanter, which he himself ranks highest in his holy trinity. Perhaps, but as a species we are so shaped as to be especially entranced by stories. We follow the fates of others, real or invented, far more readily and for far longer than we follow either pure ideas or pure expression. Nabokov attracts us in the first place, and keeps us returning, by his power as a storyteller.

But for that very reason, how can we describe him as a storyteller without saying what we have all known from the start? And how can we describe him as a storyteller without referring to his style, or without referring to the ideas that shape his way of telling stories?

Or how can we describe him as a storyteller when one of his hallmarks is that his strategies can be so different from work to work, when he could

31

write his most fantastic novel, *Invitation to a Beheading*, in the midst of his most densely realistic, *The Gift*? Austen, Dickens, and Tolstoy have each a narrative manner common throughout their respective canons. Joyce is even more different than Nabokov from work to work, but in his case he steadily matures, to the point of overripeness, even, in *Finnegans Wake*, whereas Nabokov makes deliberate choices from work to work so that even at similar times (*Ada* and *Transparent Things*) or with similar themes (Zoorland and Zembla) one of his works can be deeply unlike another.

Much of course has been written about Nabokov as storyteller, and much has been written about narrative and narratology in general, over the last forty years.[2] But can we describe Nabokov as a storyteller in a way that keeps close to the *feel* of his work, that doesn't trap the telling of tales in a tangle of terminology? Can we also do this in a way that doesn't move too quickly from description to explanation?

The nature of Nabokovian narrative

Let me first set out in stark, almost tabular form, Nabokov's features as a storyteller, and then compare the openings of novels from each end of his career to see how these characteristics play out in particular cases.

Nabokov is a master of language, but like late (and unlike early) Shakespeare, his aims as a storyteller predominate over detachable delights of style.

Unlike other major modernist novelists, Nabokov did not disparage **plot**; although he rarely offers formal stories within stories, in the manner of Cervantes, Fielding or Barth, he likes to offer hints of or vistas on other stories, or even a second main story concealed behind the first.[3] For all his compulsive originality, he relies on the salient events of story that arise out of the biological necessities of reproduction and survival: love or death, or both: intense, consuming, sometimes perverse passion; and murder, suicide, execution, assassination, violent death by fire, water, or air.

Like many writers from Sterne and Austen on, Nabokov drives stories by means of **character** rather than plot. But his stories are unique in their intense focus on *one* character. Nabokov respects individual experience as primary, as all that any of us can know from the inside. Each of his novels highlights the centrality and isolation of the consciousness of the hero. Usually there will be a marked disparity between the individual and his (it is almost without exception *his*) environment. The environment itself, whether as real as Fyodor's Berlin or as fanciful as Kinbote's Zembla, will be superbly evoked, but the hero will have a tragic or comic or tragicomic disjunction from it. He will usually be driven by an obsession – love, chess, art, murder, a real or imagined lost homeland – which gives an urgency to the story and an edge to the irony of the disjunction between the individual and his world.

Nabokov evokes **scenes** as few can do. His scenes are tightly consistent, exact, literal, specific, surprising, economical, evocative, quickly set up and often quickly dismissed. Nabokov uses detail with a naturalist's, a photographer's, a painter's, and a poet's eye: visual, natural, social, locomotory, and gestural particulars, seen from the outside but also felt from the inside. But despite his precision, he is sparing. He operates not by steady accumulation of detail but by swooping and swerving in ways that catch our attention, stir our imagination, and prod our memory, for the detail is highly selective, highly open-ended, highly diverse, highly correlated. And despite his focus on one central consciousness, he *peoples* his scenes with characters limned with the same quick exactness and surprising individuality as everything else, and evaluated for their capacity to see their world for themselves and to imagine it from the point of view of others.

But while Nabokov evokes scenes and people from without and within, he can also **shift** readily at any point *from* the scene. He may establish scenes almost as vividly as Tolstoy, but he can glide away from them at any moment in ways Tolstoy never does: to a metaphor or an abstraction, to another time or place or mind, real or imagined, within the story or elsewhere, to the mind evoking the scene in words, or to the mind of the reader recreating it. His scenes are always saturated by mind, by the hero's, or briefly, by another character's, by the narrator's or author's or reader's, able to move with grace and speed within or behind or away from the scene.

Beyond the scene, Nabokov handles stories with an inventive and critical awareness of narrative convention and possibility. He challenges and questions and refreshes every aspect of narrative, from *exposition* of new material, *preparation* for later developments, *transition* from one element to another, to the *conclusion* of stories.[4]

He does not impose technical innovations for their own sake, but nor will he accept a convention like first- or third-person narration simply because it exists *as* a convention. When one of his first-person narrators tells his own story, Nabokov will always supply him with a motive, a means, an occasion, and an audience, and the relationship between the telling and the tale will transform both. As his œuvre expands he resorts increasingly rarely to third-person narration, but if he does he will question or complicate it according to the needs or opportunities of the story.

Nabokov pays especially close attention to what both his characters and his readers can know at a particular point in the story. He has a superb command of *anticipation* and *recapitulation*, so central to the traditional impetus and impact of story, and heightened in his work by the hero's often obsessive quest after a goal. Because his stories focus on a single life, there are rarely secrets to be unearthed à la *Oedipus* or Dickens or Ibsen, or any reason for multiple narrators or disjoined narratives, à la Faulkner or Erdrich or De Lillo. To Nabokov, such devices falsify the unfolding of individual experience, and in his stories, the *siuzhet* (the events in the order they are related) therefore largely follows the sequence of the *fabula* (the events in the order they happen). But Nabokov explores time from many sides and knows how present experience may be modified by what we *have* lived and *will* live through, and he can add time's details and designs in many ways, internally (through a character's recollection or discovery) or externally (through a narrator's disclosure), overtly or covertly, smoothly or joltingly, in advance or arrears, in a trickle or a deluge, without the least anxiety that this will dispel the force of the current scene.

Nabokov rethinks story, scene, structure, and narrative situation out of an impatience with convention, a desire for artistic originality, a search for a singular way of revealing the singular circumstances of a new story, and a unique sense of both the scope and the limits of consciousness that inspires him to make the most of the gaps and the links between character, reader, and author. And because the human mind's capacity to represent, or metarepresent, is central to its power,[5] and because he is always preoccupied with the relationship between the inner (the individual consciousness) and the outer (the world outside the individual consciousness), Nabokov also incorporates in his stories an extraordinary number and variety of metarepresentations of the story, of parts that reflect the whole.

While it engages our curiosity and emotions as a story, a Nabokov novel always intimates that the narrative is also something else, a strategy as much as a story: an image, or a metaphor, a joke, a problem, a design, a playful puzzle, or a series of interlocking puzzles prepared by the author for us somehow to solve. The riddling strategy nevertheless arises out of the particular circumstances of the story, out of some special constraint or situation *in* the story, rather than being imposed on it arbitrarily, and is therefore different from work to work.

All the way through his stories, from the local to the global level, Nabokov attends to what we and his characters can know at a particular point, and to the difference between the characters' knowledge and what we as readers might be able to infer from our position outside their world. He stokes our expectations and rewards our capacity to notice, imagine, infer, recall. He becomes a kind of personal trainer in mental flexibility, his novels workouts that stretch our capacity for attention, curiosity, imagination, and memory, not to *stress* our limits, as so often in twentieth-century literature, but to *extend* them.

Family likenesses

Nabokov's stories may resemble others in their timeless preoccupation with love and death, and they may be different from each other, because of the special strategy he devises for each, but they also have a family likeness that sets them apart from other fiction.

A recurrent plot structure can identify an author's key concerns. In Austen, for instance, it is the difficult and potentially dangerous choice of marriage partner, because in her world nothing matters more than people reading other people with maximum care, and never do we need to read others more carefully than when considering the commitment of marriage. In Dickens, it is a legacy, contested, denied, or imposed, because he senses that the world's real riches are so often cruelly hoarded from those who deserve them. As we follow the characters' approach to a more equitable redistribution of life's bounty at the end of the novel, Dickens's exuberant invention dispenses for *us* imaginative riches to match those he finds in his world.

In Nabokov the key structure is the hero's obsession. On the one hand, it fires up an invaluable private intensity in the protagonist; on the other, it keeps him apart both from his immediate world and from the world of freedom and fulfillment he compulsively imagines – and here lies the source of so much of the humor, poignancy, and irony of Nabokov's fiction, and the emotional charge of his unreliable narrators.

Partly because of the dominating role of the hero's obsession, Nabokov's stories tend to avoid what we think of as a "dramatic" development of plot, plot advancing through conflict, through the clash of character actions, reactions, and interactions. Precisely because conflict catches our attention so easily, Nabokov feels, it has become a convention and a trap for storytelling. It generates a false picture of life as a series of forced moves leading to an inescapable outcome. And it seems to imply that our lives are shaped by our engagement, and especially our clashes, with others, when for him there is so much more to the mind's involvement in and detachment from its world.

Instead of the standard drama of action and reaction, Nabokov's plots tend to show the accumulating pattern of a single life, the whole distinctive pattern of a hero's past, the unique rhythms of his "fate," the special design of a person's individuality that extends through a life and often into the moment of death. His stories are not biographies; they do not attempt to cover the whole of a life with the same consistency; they tend to focus on a key time, often not short enough to be a crisis, usually not long enough for a lifetime.

In Nabokov's fiction each life follows its own distinct pattern, undiscernible in advance, ever clearer in retrospect, but certain moves recur again and again. First, *the myth of return*: the futile attempt to return to or relive the past. Next, *the myth of arrival*: the futile attempt to foresee or control the future. Third, *the surprise of the ending*, a new possibility that undercuts what we and the heroes have foreseen, but in a way that sends us, and perhaps them, back to the beginning. The ending may mark the failure to reach a coveted past, or a coveted future, or both at once. Often, it can crack the solid surface of the work's world, yet it may also send us spinning back to the beginning, returning to all that accumulates in the course of the hero's life, but with an answer to the puzzle of the whole perhaps somehow nearer, and a way of closing the gap between character, author, and reader somehow more possible.

Mary: zoom in on opening

How does Nabokovian narration operate at the local level? Let us focus on two opening scenes, the first chapter of Nabokov's first novel, *Mary* (1926), Ganin and Alfyorov stuck in the elevator, and the first two chapters of his second-to-last novel, *Transparent Things* (1972), Hugh Person hailed by the narrator as he arrives at a hotel in a Swiss mountain resort. These examples of Nabokov's very early and very late work are not his strongest stories, and have little of the force of *The Defense* or *Pnin*, let alone *Lolita* or *Pale Fire*, but much of what is true here should therefore be true a fortiori elsewhere in Nabokov.

Uncharacteristically, *Mary* starts with direct speech: "Lev Glevo. Lev Glebovich? A name like that's enough to twist your tongue off, my dear fellow" (*Mary*, 1 [ch. 1]). Ganin's tongue-twister name is funny, of course, and Nabokov's humor will never be far from his storytelling. But beneath the immediate humor lies more.

Stories, Aristotle says, must have beginnings, middles and ends, and the beginnings of stories need **exposition** to orient us. Exposition had become stylized and slick on the stage, as Nabokov knew well. He writes in "The Tragedy of Tragedy":

> A more sophisticated form of the French "dusting the furniture" exposition is when, instead of the valet and the maid discovered onstage, we have two visitors *arriving* on the stage as the curtain is going up, speaking of what brought them, and of the people in the house. It is a pathetic attempt to comply with the request of critics and teachers who demand that the exposition coincide with action, and actually the *entrance* of two visitors is action. But why on earth should two people who arrived on the same train and who had ample time to discuss everything during the journey, why must they struggle to keep silent till the minute of arrival whereupon they start talking of their hosts in

the wrongest place imaginable – the parlor of the house where they are guests? Why? Because the author must have them explode right here with a time-bomb explosion.

The next trick, to take the most obvious ones, is the promise of somebody's arrival. So-and-so is expected. We know that so-and-so will invariably come.

(USSR, 334–35)

Mary's ending overturns that last expectation, and its beginning radically reworks the "dusting the furniture" exposition-through-dialogue: the dialogue does takes place, but comically, in the dark, with neither participant able to see the other, and it involves an effusive Alfyorov whose very cheerfulness and garrulity irritate the peevish Ganin still further. The situation in the lift, with time to kill and with Alfyorov happily prattling away, introduces on the very first page the name of his wife Mary, due to arrive in six days' time. And since the scene, although it records the speech of both, clearly focuses on Ganin and his perceptions and thoughts, since it therefore identifies him as the likely protagonist, and since the novel is called *Mary*, we are primed to expect that some relationship will link Ganin and Alfyorov's wife.

Nabokov's economy, his comic inventiveness of situation, his critical attitude to narrative convention even in this exposition, his ability to rework exposition by way of the personalities and moods of the two characters, are all already in evidence, long before we discover how the story's ending undermines the expectation that a novel called *Mary* and the announcement of her arrival in its exposition will lead to her arriving as it were "on stage." Nabokov's attention to exposition and preparation, and the wit with which he reworks them, already operate at a high level.

Nabokov pays keen attention to what characters and readers can know at a particular point: his epistemology is very much present in the texture of his telling. The second paragraph of *Mary* is this, in response to Alfyorov's comment that Ganin's name is a tongue twister:

> "Yes it is," Ganin agreed somewhat coldly, trying to make out the face of his interlocutor in the unexpected darkness. He was annoyed by the absurd situation in which they both found themselves and by this enforced conversation with a stranger. (*Mary*, 1 [ch. 1])

Nabokov does not spell out at once *what* the absurd situation is, but offers us a little challenge and lets us have the pleasure of deducing, if not immediately, then within a few lines, that what has caused this "unexpected darkness" must be a stalled elevator. At the same time, he is true to Ganin's inability to see Alfyorov, to know what he looks like, and *in* being true to this, he cheerily toys with the expectation that a novelist will describe characters as they step on stage, and he shows that the self-contained Ganin has paid no heed, before they found themselves stuck in the elevator together, to this newcomer to his *pension*.

Nabokov attends not just to what the characters can know but also to what we as readers cannot yet know but might be able to infer from our position outside the characters. We cannot know, as soon as Ganin and Alfyorov do, that they are stuck in an elevator, but, as soon as Mary is mentioned, we can see that in a novel entitled *Mary* she will somehow connect these two men. He primes us to read closely by offering such constant hints and hooks for our attention.

But despite this superb opening, *Mary* settles in its second chapter into a rather conventional description of the *pension* and Ganin's situation within it. A finely observed report of a Russian émigré milieu, with Nabokov's naturalist's eye and artist's hand working closely together, it sketches a revealing picture of Ganin's dissatisfied life, but it is the sort of thing many writers could have managed or come close to. Nabokov has not yet quite become the unique writer he soon would be.

Transparent Things: zoom in

By the time of *Transparent Things*, Nabokov had long been a nonpareil. The novel opens:

> Here's the person I want. Hullo, person! Doesn't hear me.
>
> Perhaps if the future existed, concretely and individually, as something that could be discerned by a better brain, the past would not be so seductive: its demands would be balanced by those of the future. Persons might then straddle the middle stretch of the seesaw when considering this or that object. It might be fun.
>
> But the future has no such reality (as the pictured past and the perceived present possess); the future is but a figure of speech, a specter of thought.
>
> Hullo, person! What's the matter, don't pull me. I'm *not* bothering him. Oh, all right. Hullo, person . . . (last time, in a very small voice).   (*TT*, 1 [ch. 1])

So far as we can make out, this is not one character speaking to another, but the narrator trying to speak to a character, although why the character should be hailed in that clumsy "Hullo, person!" fashion is quite unclear, nor is it clear why the person doesn't hear, nor why the sudden shift to this interesting philosophical discussion of the future should occur here, nor what the relationship between "Persons" in the second paragraph might be to the "person" hailed in the first, nor who it is who doesn't want the speaker or narrator to bother this person or why. Here we cannot make out, even though we want to, speaker, addressee, bystanders, setting, situation, although we *can* sense that these are all present, if only we knew how. The "exposition" exposes little but our uncertainty about where we are.

Never before has Nabokov pushed quite so far, and he's too much of a storyteller not to know that we couldn't stand much of this, that we need a story. He gives us one, at the start of the second chapter:

> As Hugh Person extricated his angular bulk from the taxi that had brought him to this shoddy mountain resort from Trux, his eyes went up to check the aspect of the Ascot Hotel against an eight-year-old recollection. A dreadful building of gray stone and brown wood, it sported cherry-red shutters which he remembered as apple green.

Here is storytelling as we know it: an identifiable character named and described, performing an identifiable action in a recognizable world, in a setting described and named. What, then, is so special about Nabokovian storytelling, even late Nabokov storytelling, after the disconcerting chapter 1?

What's special is everything I have omitted. Here's how chapter 2 of *Transparent Things* actually begins, with all the Nabokovian peculiarity reinstated:

> As the person, Hugh Person (corrupted "Peterson" and pronounced "Parson" by some) extricated his angular bulk from the taxi that had brought him to this shoddy mountain resort from Trux, and while his head was still lowered in an opening meant for emerging dwarfs, his eyes went up – not to acknowledge the helpful gesture sketched by the driver who had opened the door for him but to check the aspect of the Ascot Hotel (Ascot!) against an eight-year-old recollection, one fifth of his life, engrained by grief. A dreadful building of gray stone and brown wood, it sported cherry-red shutters (not all of them shut) which by some mnemoptical trick he remembered as apple green. The steps of the porch were flanked with electrified carriage lamps on a pair of iron posts. Down those steps an aproned valet came tripping to take the two bags, and (under one arm) the shoebox, all of which the driver had alertly removed from the yawning boot. Person pays alert driver. *(TT, 3)*

Earlier I contrasted Nabokov the stylist with Nabokov the storyteller. It may be an artificial distinction, certainly not an absolute one, but it is true that a story's needs may be at odds with sheer style. This is high-energy prose, yet it will never appear in any anthology of fine flourishes: it's no "Lolita, light of my life, fire of my loins," or "The cradle rocks above an abyss." This is what I mean by saying that Nabokov, like late Shakespeare, subordinates style to story. Shakespeare was an immeasurably more sophisticated dramatic storyteller in his late play *Cymbeline* than in his youthful *Romeo and Juliet*. He had to write with more compression to achieve more complex aims, but where the *Oxford Dictionary of Quotations* includes phrases from *Romeo and Juliet* as early as the play's first speech, and then from scene after scene, it cites nothing of *Cymbeline* until almost a thousand lines into the play. Like Shakespeare, Nabokov can exude eloquence but subdues it to the local needs of his story. His language works wonders *in situ* but does not necessarily seem stylish *out* of its situation.

"As the person, Hugh Person (corrupted 'Peterson' and pronounced 'Parson' by some)" would be off-putting as an isolated line of prose but is beguiling in context. We notice with surprise, amusement, and relief the echo of the "person" of "Hullo, person" in chapter 1: this is presumably the person whom the disembodied voice was addressing, and his *name*, absurdly, is actually Person. The parenthetical aside about Person as a surname is comically clumsy pedantry, when the protagonist and his name have just been introduced, but it proves of a piece with the clumsiness of "Hullo, person" in the first line of the novel or "Easy, you know, does it, son" in the last, or Mr. R.'s awkward and pedantic introduction of his editor Mr. Person and his secretary Mr. Tamworth. We can eventually discover, therefore, that that ungainly parenthesis is one more clue that the unidentified speaker or narrator at the start of the novel is none other than the ghost of Mr. R.

A crucial and unique aspect of Nabokov's storytelling, especially in a tale like this, is that the **strategy** is as important as the story, that in this case the riddle of who tells the tale is as important as the role of the hero. It's crucial too that the strategy nevertheless *arises out* of the story, that this is a story of someone finding his way out of a life of mounting frustration when he is welcomed across the threshold of death by perhaps the only person in his recent life who had taken an interest in him and who cares enough now to tell his story. And it's crucial too, as so often in Nabokov, that there is a story behind the story – although Nabokov, with his love of surprise, of posing new *kinds* of problems in novel after novel, begins *Transparent Things*, paradoxically and unprecedentedly, with the story *behind* the story ("Hullo person. Doesn't hear me"), and in *this* case the immediate riddle the novel poses is to discover that the speaker in the story *behind* the story was a character *in* the story while he was alive.

But long before we can see that, we see long-limbed Hugh clambering out of the taxi.

Nabokov renders the scene vividly. He attends, as always, to human movement, seen from the outside but also felt from the inside, here in the irritation of "an opening meant for emerging dwarfs" that infects the narrating voice. He attends to visual detail, not that there's much of it – Hugh's "angular bulk," the driver's "helpful gesture," the hotel's "gray stone and brown wood," "cherry-red shutters," and "electrified carriage lamps on a pair of iron posts" – just enough to render in full color and movement the scene of arrival and the pseudo-chalet setting; but he also attends to the character registering the details, to Hugh's distaste for the town, his effort in emerging, his recoil at the "dreadful" building, his memory of the shutters as green.

Not that the narration confines itself to Hugh's perspective. Although visually alert to the outer details of the scene, and alert to Hugh's mind within the scene, at all sorts of levels (his larger context, "one fifth of his life, engrained by grief"; his current mood of distaste for "this shoddy mountain resort"; his bodily ungainliness, which will prove so unfortunately important; his sudden perception of a misrecollection), although it pays such attention to the outer and inner within the scene, the paragraph also shifts easily *from* the scene, to an aside on etymology, or to highlight its own verbal surface ("the aspect of the Ascot Hotel," "cherry-red shutters (not all of them shut)": and in this second case, notice how the visual attention to the scene and the verbal attention to the sentence do not at all exclude each other).

The long first sentence moves effortlessly back and forth from outer to inner, from locomotion to perception, from scene to language, from the long-term ("one fifth of his life") to the immediate and even the instant (the sudden snort of derision in that parenthetical "(Ascot!)" – presumably at the inappropriateness of the name's social pretensions for an alpine hotel). The sentence renders the scene, but even as it does so, it draws attention to the mind of Hugh within the scene, the mind of the narrator recording the scene, the mind of the reader registering the scene both with and beyond Hugh, and with and yet somehow behind the narrator, but able to catch up.

In the sentence that follows, what "mnemoptical trick" causes Hugh to remember the cherry-red shutters as apple-green? It doesn't matter, it's amusing in itself, the complementary color, the contrasting fruit; but two pages later the person introduced as "an aproned valet" will be described slightly more fully as "the apple-green-aproned valet," and we can recognize with more amusement what has caused Hugh's confusion and what a game of attention Nabokov is playing with his audience, what rewards he can hide behind any detail.

We have to keep attention up across a gap like this, but we have to exercise attention even within the sentence: the aproned valet came tripping down those steps "to take the two bags, and (under one arm) the shoebox, all of which the driver had alertly removed from the yawning boot." Are we alert enough to notice the *alert* driver versus the *yawning* boot, or the *shoebox* removed from a *boot*?

As an observer, a naturalist, and an artist, Nabokov renders the scene of Hugh's arrival in Witt with precision – the milieu, the occasion, the activity, the character as he takes in the scene or moves his awkward body within it or imposes his temperament and mood on it – but what makes it so uniquely

Nabokovian is that at the same time as he renders the inner and outer scene so sharply, he can shift *from* the scene to the mind evoking it in words, or to the mind of the reader, engaged with the scene seen from outside Hugh and seen and felt from within him, engaged with the unseen storyteller behind the words, and engaged with the words seen on the page. That multiplicity of levels we already sense here will only be compounded when we become aware both of the layers of Hugh's past that fold over onto this moment and of exactly what level of being the transparent things observe him from.

Every mature Nabokov novel is a demanding but exhilarating workout in what Fyodor in *The Gift* calls "multilevel thinking." What especially distinguishes Nabokov's stories, on small scale and large, is that they are saturated by mind, the hero's, the narrator's, the author's and the reader's. Nothing could be further from Hemingway's presentation of a story through objective actions and utterances that only *imply* the subjective.

Hemingway was writing partly *against* the fashion, by the early 1920s, for the deep representation of mind in the moment, in the stream of consciousness of a Dorothy Richardson, a Joyce, a Woolf. Nabokov too differs markedly from the stream of consciousness, but in another direction. He is interested not chiefly in the mind within the moment, although he gives this its due (Hugh's surprise as he looks up at the Ascot Hotel), not so much *that*, as minds able to transcend the moment, the mind of a character, a narrator, an author or a reader, able to flash or soar beyond a scene through a sudden shift of thought or perspective, consciousness able either to enfold or escape a scene.

Transparent Things is an extreme example of Nabokov as storyteller. In his previous novel, *Ada*, he had created a whole new world, a long, passionate, rapturous and tragic story amid bright settings and brighter characters. In *Transparent Things*, despite the cherry-red shutters and the apple-green aprons, we enter a grey and gloomy world where not much happens to poor Hugh except that he strangles the woman whom for some reason he loves, no matter how little she deserves it, then loses his own life in a pathetic attempt to revisit the scene of his first humiliations with her, which are all he has left. Nabokov can sweep us up in the emotions of his characters, as in the case of Van's enthusiasm for Ada, or Kinbote's for Zembla, or even, to our discomfort, Humbert's for Lolita, but he deliberately leaves us unmoved by Hugh's love for Armande or Hugh's pilgrimage back to his past, and he has to use all his virtuosity as a storyteller to make this story on the brink of a death come to life.

But the storytelling skills so concentrated even in the uneventful opening scene of *Transparent Things* can help suggest what is special about Nabokovian narrative.

Mary and *Transparent Things*: zoom out

How do *Mary* and *Transparent Things* reflect Nabokov as storyteller at the large scale rather than the small? In terms of **plot**, each novel focuses on love – indeed love compounded by adultery – and death: Ganin's love for Mary, and his planned elopement with her from Berlin, an adultery anticipated, assumed, but left untried, and placed in pointed counterpoint with Podtyagin's planned escape from Berlin, which will be thwarted by his approaching death; Hugh's abject love for Armande, despite her flagrant infidelities, and his strangling her in his sleep, not because of but despite her unlovableness, and *his* death by fire on his pathetic pilgrimage to the scene of his past with her.

Each novel is **driven by character**: *Mary*'s plot depends on Ganin's love, his self-enclosed nature, his arrogance, his restlessness, and although neither the strangling of Armande nor his own suffocation in a hotel fire are Hugh Person's choices, the plot of *Transparent Things* depends on his abjectness, his frustration, his doggedness, his misplaced sentimentality.

Each hero is **obsessed**, to the point of disjunction from his world, and in a uniquely Nabokovian way that maximizes the tension between obsession and freedom. Although Ganin chafes at his room in a cramped pension, his obsession with Mary lets him exult in his capacity to roam Berlin streets while inhabiting his spacious past, until to his surprise and ours he walks away from Mary and memory into an open future. The much less happy Hugh, as soon as he is released from prison for killing his wife in a dream, makes the free decision to return across the Atlantic to where Armande first obsessed him, but although in Witt he still seems trapped by inimical space and oppressive time, his chance death there liberates him at last into the ampler dimensions of his future.

Each novel deploys **anticipation and recapitulation** in new ways, and each exposes the myths of return to the past and arrival at the future. The numbered doors from April 1 to April 6, the countdown from Sunday to the Saturday of Mary's advent, provide a stark and insistently unilinear means of stalking the expected climax of Nabokov's first novel. In *Transparent Things* the anticipation of the future is much more multichanneled, saturated with apparent foreshadowings of Hugh's imminent death, from the failed warning of the opening chapter, and even the narrators' "perhaps if the future existed," through the throng of images, real, fictional, and dreamed, of deaths, fires, and falls.

In *Mary* **recapitulation** plays a key structural role, as the novel alternates present time, the days marking Mary's approach, with Ganin's memories of their past, again in rather rigid linear form, the memories proceeding with a chronological neatness that serves the novelist's needs rather than his hero's psychic reality.[6] In *Transparent Things*, recapitulation takes flamboyant form at the hands of narrators who can trace a mere pencil back centuries to the tree from which its wood was made. The story folds into Hugh's present trip to Switzerland, an account of his first trip, and his father's death, and his first whore, and on top of *that* past scene, a bravura recollection of a writer who enjoyed a whore in the same room almost a century earlier, and on top of *that* Hugh's second trip, to meet the novelist R., when he also found himself face to face with Armande.

Ganin thinks he can **return to his past** with Mary, or resume where he left off. But the central surprise of the novel's plot, the essential twist of the novel's **strategy**, is that the title character does not arrive, despite the steady countdown. When Ganin realizes that he *has* his past with him in memory, and need not return to it, he heads away from Mary toward an open future. The novel's title seemed to guarantee her arrival, but as the novel ends it is left unrealized and no longer matters.

Hugh feels less sanguine about returning to *his* past with Armande, especially as it was so often torment at the time, yet he feels compelled to try to revisit the first and only summer of their "love." But his foray through space in search of lost time fails dismally, to the point where the narrator taunts: "What had you expected of your pilgrimage, Person? A mere mirror rerun of hoary torments?" (*TT*, 94 [ch. 25]).

If *Transparent Things* mocks **the myth of the return** to the past, it undermines **the myth that we can know the future** we will arrive at. As readers, outside Hugh's world, and aware of the narrators' failed attempt to divert him from the hotel where he plans to stay, we can see images of death, fire, and falling that appear to signal that Hugh will die by jumping to escape a fire that the narrators have already seen in the making. But because of a last-minute change of room, his death does not happen as so insistently foreseen. Hugh does die in the fire, but by suffocation, and he is welcomed, in a dizzying and unexpected final scene, onto the level of being of the spectral narrators, especially the ghost of R., whom he had been visiting when he first met Armande. Again the novel as strategy depends on **the surprise of the ending**: not a plunge into death but a heady dance of imagery that leads Hugh to a threshold beyond the story and onto the level of its tellers.

Since adultery, planned or performed, sets the tone for both *Mary* and *Transparent Things*, one might expect it to result in the clash of wills so familiar in story from Agamemnon and Clytemnestra to Anna and Karenin and beyond. But Nabokov writes in "The Tragedy of Tragedy"

> The idea of conflict tends to endow life with a logic it never has. Tragedies based exclusively in the logic of conflict are as untrue to life as an all-pervading class-struggle is untrue to history. Most of the worst and deepest human tragedies, far from following the marble rules of tragic conflict, are tossed on the stormy element of chance. (*USSR*, 340)

For Nabokov, conflict is a convenient but conventional trap for story, and one that he springs open again and again. Ganin plans to take Mary from her husband, but neither Alfyorov nor Mary will ever know, after Ganin quietly slips away, having changed his mind, with no one but himself the wiser. Hugh Person kills Armande, not as a consequence of her infidelities, for which he has never reproached her, but only in the throes of the dream of someone who has always been as lurching and lumbering in sleep as in waking life.

In "The Tragedy of Tragedy" Nabokov envisages "the higher form of tragedy" – but it could in fact be the higher form of plot, whether tragic or not or theatrical or not – as

> the creation of a certain unique pattern of life in which the sorrows and passions of a particular man will follow the rules of his own individuality, not the rules of the theatre as we know them . . . a writer of genius may discover exactly the right harmony of . . . accidental occurrences, and . . . this harmony, without suggesting anything like the iron laws of tragic fatality, will express certain definite combinations that occur in life. (*USSR*, 341)[7]

In his own work Nabokov does not impose the character's individual mark with the stark irony of Hardyesque fate, but with a delicacy that it can often take the eye of sensitive retrospection to spot, in a pattern that once seen, cannot be unseen, like Ganin in stasis and then suddenly moving again, or Hugh awkwardly emerging to cross a new threshold.

In *Mary* Nabokov establishes a stiff rhythm to Ganin's existence as he alternates between the present and recollections of the past, but in fact he fails to provide Ganin with much of a past beyond his love for Mary, much of a present beyond his reminiscences of her and plans for escape with her, much of a future except his no longer needing Mary to help him cope with the present and beyond. These are not deliberate decisions, like Tolstoy's refusal to give his characters background lives, but simply youthful inexperience. As early as the Franz of his next novel, Nabokov will use backfill and infill to build up the patterns of a life that can extend even into the moment of death. In Hugh's case, the aggressive overtness and humiliating insistence of the patterns, from his unhappy years as a youthful somnambulist to his waking to death by fire, disturb us, as does so much about the novel. The overt patterning of time here stands in stark contrast to the complex, covert, cel-ebratory layering of past on past in Nabokov's immediately previous novel, *Ada*.[8] The difference reflects the gulf between Van's character, his love, his triumphant fate, and his role as fond retrospector, with Ada, of the past he shares with her, and Hugh's character, his love, his sad fate, and the power the narrators of his story have to search his past with a more than human, indeed quite inhuman, freedom.

The implied worlds of Nabokovian narrative

Because he rejects determinism, because he refuses to see life in terms of action and counteraction meshing like teeth on interconnecting cogs, Nabokov's stories minimize the conflict that ticks its way through so much of story. He constructs *his* stories to reflect the unique, unpredictable rhythm of an individual character's life.

He also shapes his stories so that each poses an overarching problem where the force of characters' moves and countermoves often seems less significant than their combining into an artfully playful and puzzling authorial design. He famously explains this by analogy with chess problem composition (*SM*, 288–93 [ch. 14]), and some chess-problem aficionados indeed feel that in his problems he is too ingenious, that he does not maximize the tension between black and white, but instead focuses too much on the tension between prob-lemist and solver, between the solver's expectations and the problemist's radical inventiveness. In the same way, resistant readers of his fiction prefer the simpler rhythm of action and reaction – the powerful clash of character and character, which, after all, our ancestors evolved to notice even before they were hominids or humans – to Nabokov's focus on the subtle tension between author and reader.

As plot became less central to literary storytelling in the twentieth cen-tury, there was a general tendency, at least early in the century, to pay less attention to the clash of characters over time and to focus instead on the inner experience of the mind within the moment. But Nabokov rejects that too as a primary focus, because he is interested in the mind as much *beyond* as *within* the moment or the self. What makes his work unique at the local level is his capacity to be true to the details of a scene but also to shift within or beyond the scene, and to take responsive readers with him.

He does not eschew situations in the here and now, and in fact he can render them, a stalled elevator, a taxi outside a hotel door, with stunning immediacy, not by the sheer accumulation of detail, but by catching our imaginations off guard. He knows that attention fades if we habituate to stimuli, so he refreshes and provokes it by shifting it from one point to another within a scene: not by shifting from one character's mind to another, since life rules that out, but by retaining a focus on one mind, yet freely sliding or soaring this way, aside or ahead, to another scene, another time, another plane, as smoothly or abruptly as he chooses, and expecting the reader can do so too.

Nabokov's storytelling allows a free choice at every moment, a perpetually open series of surprises, and his innovative subjects, structures, and stratagems, in works like *The Gift*, *Lolita*, *Pale Fire*, *Ada*, *Transparent Things*, anywhere at all, really, even as early as *Mary*, show him again and again opening up new dimensions of possibility, and inviting us to enter and explore these strange new spaces. But his very desire for freedom, on the small scale and the large, at the level of the sentence, the life, and the work, means that his imagination is present and active everywhere. Some readers resist what they feel as his imposing himself throughout his fictional worlds. Others appreciate his work as inviting both readers and characters, in line after line and life after life, into something freer than even the ample and opulent prison of space, time, and the self.

Unlike so many serious storytellers of the twentieth century, Nabokov can give us the pleasures of extraordinary characters and events: Luzhin, and the madness that impels him to his suicide; Humbert, and the obsession that drives him to abduction and murder; Kinbote, and his fantastic relocation of a thoroughly realistic poem; Van and Ada, and their eighty-year-long forbidden love. But even without extraordinary events, in the quiet worlds of a Ganin or a Hugh Person, Nabokov tells his stories with so much imaginative mobility and surprise that he gives us a new confidence in what *our* imaginations can do to apprehend our world and to step right outside it. In a sense, he tells the same story each time, since each life leads from a similar beginning to a similar end, but he also ensures, as life does, that it could not be more different each time.

NOTES

1. D. Barton Johnson and Brian Boyd, "Prologue: The Otherworld," in *Nabokov's World*, vol. I: *The Shape of Nabokov's World*, ed. Jane Grayson, Arnold McMillin, and Priscilla Meyer (Basingstoke: Palgrave, 2002), 19–25. Among work on Nabokov's metaphysics, see Boyd, *Nabokov's Ada: The Place of Consciousness* (Ann Arbor: Ardis, 1985), and 2nd edn. (Christchurch, New Zealand: Cyber-editions, 2001); D. Barton Johnson, *Worlds in Regression* (Ann Arbor: Ardis, 1985); Pekka Tammi, *Problems of Nabokov's Poetics* (Helsinki: Suomalainen Tiedeakatemia, 1985); Boyd, *Vladimir Nabokov: The Russian Years* (Princeton: Princeton University Press, 1990); and Boyd, *Nabokov's* Pale Fire: *The Magic of Artistic Discovery* (Princeton: Princeton University Press, 1999) (I regard Vladimir Alexandrov's *Nabokov's Otherworld* [Princeton: Princeton University

Press, 1991] as flawed, after its fine introduction). Among work on Nabokov's morals, see Ellen Pifer, *Nabokov and the Novel* (Cambridge, MA: Harvard University Press, 1980); Boyd, *Nabokov's Ada*; Leona Toker, *Nabokov: The Mystery of Literary Structures* (Ithaca: Cornell University Press, 1989); and Richard Rorty, "The Barber of Kasbeam: Nabokov on Cruelty," in *Contingency, Irony, and Solidarity* (Cambridge: Cambridge University Press, 1989), 141–68.

2. For a particularly comprehensive and subtle but uninvitingly formalistic analysis of Nabokovian narrative, see Tammi, *Problems of Nabokov's Poetics*.

3. Letter to Katharine White, March 17, 1951: "Most of the stories I am contemplating (and some I have written in the past . . .) will be composed on these lines, according to this system wherein a second (main) story is woven into, or placed behind, the superficial semitransparent one" (*SL*, 117).

4. For Nabokov's brief but important references to preparation and transition as items in the storyteller's toolkit, see his "Commentary to *Eugene Onegin*," *EO*, III:80; *Song*, 10; *LL*, 151; *LRL*, 73.

5. See Josef Perner, *Understanding the Representational Mind* (Cambridge, MA: Bradford/MIT, 1991), and *Metarepresentations: A Multidisciplinary Perspective*, ed. Dan Sperber (Oxford: Oxford University Press, 2000).

6. Dieter E. Zimmer argues that the ordered sequence of Ganin's recollections of Mary reflect a psychological truth in line with F. C. Bartlett's 1932 demonstration of memory as "constructional" ("Mary," in *The Garland Companion to Vladimir Nabokov*, ed. Vladimir E. Alexandrov [New York: Garland, 1995], 354–55). But this seriously misreads Bartlett. The mind does reconstruct memories as they emerge into consciousness, rather than upload exactly from a veridical databank, but memory does not and could not suppress details as they emerge to consciousness in order to recollect them only in the correct sequence. Nabokov does explain Ganin's deliberate private reconstruction of his past with Mary, in order to motivate the narrative sequence (*Mary*, 33 [ch. 4]), but he carries on the orderly retelling of Ganin's past even unprompted by Ganin's memory (*Mary*, 99–102 [ch. 15]), only then to provide an after-the-fact motivation in terms of memories that are explicitly *not* orderly: "All this now unfolded in his memory, flashing disjointedly, and shrank again into a warm lump when Podtyagin, with a great effort, asked him 'How long ago did you leave Russia?'" (*Mary*, 102 [ch. 15]).

7. The text should read "passions," as here, not "passing" as in the published version.

8. See my analysis of this layering of past on past in the Afterword to *Ada* (London: Penguin, 1999).

3

ALEXANDER DOLININ

Nabokov as a Russian writer

In 1950 Vladimir Nabokov, then an aspiring American author, wrote in chapter 14 of *Conclusive Evidence, a Memoir*, about his Russian literary career of the 1920s and 1930s as if he and Sirin (Nabokov's Russian pen name) were two different persons:

> the author that interested me most was naturally Sirin. He belonged to my generation. Among the younger writers produced in exile he turned out to be the only major one. Beginning with the appearance of his first novel in 1925 and throughout the next fifteen years, until he vanished as strangely as he had come, his work kept provoking an acute and rather morbid interest on the part of critics . . . Russian readers who had been raised on the sturdy straight-forwardness of Russian realism and had called the bluff of decadent cheats, were impressed by the mirror-like angles of his clear but weirdly misleading sentences and by the fact that the real life of his books flowed in his figures of speech, which one critic has compared to "windows giving upon a contiguous world . . . a rolling corollary, the shadow of a train of thought." Across the dark sky of exile, Sirin passed, to use a simile of a more conservative nature, like a meteor, and disappeared, leaving nothing much else behind him than a vague sense of uneasiness. His best works are those in which he condemns his people to the solitary confinement of their souls. His first two novels are to my taste mediocre; among the other six or seven the most haunting are *Invitation to a Beheading* which deals with the incarceration of a rebel in a picture-postcard fortress by the buffoons and bullies of a Communazist state; and *Luzhin's Defense*, which is about a champion chess player who goes mad when chess combinations pervade the actual pattern of his existence.
>
> (CE, 216–17)

This jocular split into two personae (conspicuous by its absence in the Russian version of the autobiography) was more than just a private literary hoax played on American readers who were unaware of Sirin's identity. In a sense Nabokov's self-portrait reads like a self-obituary declaring the end of his "real life" in Russian literature. With the beginning of World War II and Nabokov's flight to America, the world to which he had belonged – in his words, "the general atmosphere of exile culture, with its splendor, and vigor, and purity, and reverbarative force" (*SO*, 36–37) – vanished, and on the "other shores" across the Atlantic Nabokov shedded, together with his nom de plume and "infinitely rich and docile Russian tongue" (*SO*, 15), the created persona and public image of the writer Sirin. His coming to America was hence not a continuation of the European exile, a mere geographical transference, but, so to say, the expatriation of the second order.

In an interview Nabokov complained that his "complete switch from Russian prose to English prose was exceedingly painful – like learning anew to handle things after losing seven or eight fingers in an explosion" (*SO*, 54). However, the metaphor of dismemberment conceals a deeper and bitterer truth: along with impaired verbal agility, the switch involved the exile from his mastered territory and, therefore, from his former identity. Once again Nabokov lost his native land – the homestead of Russian literature in which he had enjoyed all the prerogatives of the heir apparent – and had to reinvent himself, to transmute the new painful loss and rupture into an aesthetic gain. Like the narrator of *The Real Life of Sebastian Knight*, a Russian who creates himself and his English book out of the life and writings of his dead half-brother who seems to watch over and control the quest, he fashioned his English "unreal estate" out of Sirin's heritage. The American writer Nabokov superseded Sirin, who remained unread and unknown for twenty years. Nabokov did not exaggerate when he wrote in 1956: "None of my American friends have read my Russian books and thus every appraisal on the strength of my English ones is bound to be out of focus" (*AnL*, 316 ["On a Book Entitled *Lolita*"]).

Only in the 1960s, when the sensational success of *Lolita* stirred interest in his Russian novels and all of them eventually appeared in English, did Nabokov get an opportunity to resurrect Sirin and introduce him to the American and West European audience. However, he worked out a peculiar strategy of presenting his earlier writings as inferior "outlines" or "dress rehearsals" for his English masterpieces. In regard to Sirin, Nabokov took a posture of a supreme aesthetic authority, an omnipotent and omniscient Master who condescendingly albeit fondly reviewed and revised his flawed albeit talented juvenilia. His verdict was strict: "Not all of that stuff is as good as I thought it was thirty years ago" (*SO*, 88). As he remarked self-confidently:

> The ecstatic love of a young writer for the old writer he will be some day is ambition in its most laudable form. This love is not reciprocated by the older man in his larger library, for even if he does recall with regret a naked palate and a rheumless eye, he has nothing but an impatient shrug for the bungling apprentice of his youth. (*Des*, xii ["Foreword"])

In the forewords, introductory notes, and interviews "the older man" Nabokov would hint at obvious or hidden faults of his Russian works (with the notable exception of *The Defense* and *Invitation to a Beheading*) which are clear only to him, "the sole judge in this case and court" (*Mary*, xiv ["Introduction"]). Having reread *King, Queen, Knave,* for example, he finds that it "sagged considerably more than [he] had expected" and repudiates "many lame odds and ends" (*KQK*, ix ["Foreword"]); he disdainfully refuses "to make things too easy for a certain type of reviewer" and "to point out the faults" in *Glory* (*Glory*, x–xi ["Foreword"]); he regrets that in *The Gift* "here and there history shows through artistry" and that he "did not have the knack of recreating Berlin and its colony of expatriates as radically and ruthlessly as I have done in regard to certain environments in my later, English, fiction" (*Gift*, n. p. ["Foreword"]). At the same time Nabokov never misses a chance to sneak in a favorable reference to his English writings and to subtly pit them against their Russian counterparts. Discussing the defects of *Glory*, he adds that in the final chapters "it soars to heights of purity and melancholy that I have only attained in the much later *Ada*" (*Glory*, xi), which sets the level of excellence achieved in the English novel as a yardstick for evaluating (and devaluating) the Russian one. He grudgingly admits that Hermann, the narrator of *Despair*, is a precursor of *Lolita*'s Humbert Humbert but again implies that the mastery of the later book is superior: "Hermann and Humbert," he states, "are alike only in the sense that two dragons painted by the same artist at different periods of his life resemble each other" (*Des*, xiii ["Foreword"]).

It is by maintaining the artistic inferiority of some Russian texts that Nabokov justified his idiosyncratic method of rewriting them in English. He relished what his private lexicon defines as "to abridge, expand, or otherwise alter or cause to be altered, for the sake of belated improvement, one's own writings in translation" (*IB*, 6–7). Three of his Russian novels – *King, Queen, Knave*; *Kamera obskura* (*Laughter in the Dark*); and *Despair* – are known to English readers in drastically amended redactions, unfaithful to the original in many important aspects; innumerable minor cuts, additions, and substitutions mark off all of his self-translations.[1] Of course, Nabokov's urge to improve upon his earlier writings was genuine and in certain cases his alterations did "permit a still breathing body to enjoy certain innate capacities which inexperience and eagerness, the haste of thought and the sloth of word had denied it formerly" (*KQK*, ix). Yet, to use Nabokov's metaphor, rejuvenating a "still breathing body" of an earlier text sometimes involved total blood transfusion. Beside purely artistic considerations, he was driven by a desire to recontextualize his Russian writings – to suppress or obliterate their vital ties with contemporary literary and historical contexts, especially Russian ones; to redirect their polemic or/and parodic currents and undercurrents towards new targets better suited to Nabokov's later transnational image; to adjust their style to the canon of *Lolita*, *Pale Fire*, or *Ada*. According to Nabokov, his "natural idiom" was connected to the heritage of Russian literature by a nexus of the "*implied associations and traditions*" (*AnL*, 316, emphasis added). However, it is these allusions that Nabokov now and then replaces in his translations with self-referential wordplay after the fashion of his later works, divesting the originals of rich intertextual undercurrents binding them to the national heritage. A single example should suffice.

As Julian W. Connolly remarked, Nabokov's revision of his second (and far from the best) novel *King, Queen, Knave* "brings out the power and the presence of the author in high relief . . . Nabokov charges the English version . . . with veiled autoreferences: the photographer who captures Dreyer's image on film is anagrammatically named Vivian Badlook (153), while a certain Blavdak Vinimori appears (complete with wife and butterfly net) as a guest at the hotel where Martha plots Dreyer's murder."[2] These obvious angrams à la *Lolita* or *Ada* are absent in the Russian original where the last name of an authorial representative is Porokhovshchikov, which refers to Nabokov only obliquely as it belonged to his distant relatives.[3] At the same time, thanks to its etymology (it derives from Russian *pórokh*, i.e. gunpowder) and sound, the name brings to mind two classical Russian texts.

Firstly, it alludes to Dostoevsky's character Ilia Petrovich Porokh (Gunpowder), a brazen officer in *Crime and Punishment* who unexpectedly appears at the police station when Raskolnikov finally comes there to confess his crime:

> "Aha-a-a! Fee, fi, fo, fum, I smell the smell of a Russian man . . ." a familiar voice cried out suddenly.
> Raskolnikov shook. There stood Gunpowder; he walked out suddenly from the third room. "This is fate itself," Raskolnikov thought. "Why is he here?"[4]

Secondly, the very sounds of the name Porokhovshchikov suggest a echo of *pokhorony* (funeral) and *pokhoronshchik* (undertaker) which, in its turn, alludes to Pushkin's tale "The Coffinmaker" (*Grobovshchik*) – a comic story of the caretaker Adrian Prokhorov,[5] another phonetic shadow of Porokhovshchikov, who moves his shop from a Russian neighborhood to a German one and in a dream is visited by the dead, his former customers. Like Pushkin's coffinmaker, Nabokov's representative enters the German world to dispatch the villainous heroine to her grave; like Dostoevsky's Gunpowder, he personifies "fate itself" punishing the criminal. Nabokov seems to deliberately juxtapose Dostoevsky's psychological portrayal of the murderer with Pushkin's playful treatment of Gothic themes in order to underscore his overall literary strategy in the novel: he transposes *Crime and Punishment* in a Pushkinian key, playing games with his characters (and, of course, his readers, too) and having the last laugh.

This rich allusiveness, however, is almost completely lost in the English translation, for Nabokov, rewriting *King, Queen, Knave*, chose to either obliterate its most important subtexts or replace them with his stock references to *Madame Bovary*, *Anna Karenin*, and Hollywood movies, which he had repeatedly used, if not overused, in his later American novels. In view of such losses, typical not only of *King, Queen, Knave* but of all the other Nabokov self-translations, it is impossible to agree with Elizabeth Beaujour who holds English versions to be definitive replacements of the Russian texts "to all intents and purposes."[6] At least in the realm of Russian literature (to which Sirin's novels, after all, belong), the originals remain unchallenged and unreplaced by their English paraphrases that downplay and suppress Nabokov's vital literary origins.

In a sense, the Russian writer Sirin fell victim to the tricky mythmaking and playacting Nabokov indulged in during his later years. Like those unhappy expatriates who leave their native country in search of a better life and then are doomed again and again to prove to themselves that their decision was right, Nabokov had to justify his emigration from his native language and literature to their acquired substitutes. For this purpose, he would argue that "the nationality of a worthwhile writer is of secondary importance" (*SO*, 63) and present himself as a born cosmopolitan genius who has never been attached to anything and anybody but his autonomous imagination and personal memory. To support the image, Nabokov now and then disguised and retouched his Russian past, denying the existence of meaningful ties with contemporary contexts. Contrary to the facts, for example, he claimed that he had had no German, had been "completely ignorant of modern German literature" and therefore his portrayal of Berlin was a "pure invention" while, as numerous echoes and allusions show, it polemically responded to both German and Russian writings about Berlin of the 1920s.[7] He invented dumb émigré reviewers who allegedly had distinguished a "Kafkaesque" strain in his *Invitation to a Beheading* or "the influence of German impressionists" in *Despair*[8] but never mentioned important Russian subtexts of these very novels, some of which had been identified by émigré critics. He pretended that he had always stood apart from literary battles and discussions of the day though his Russian works abound in topical parodies and polemics.

Nabokov's portrait of himself as an olympian young artist, a "Solus Rex" in the making, was so convincing that it could affect even some memoirists. One of them, Hélène Iswolsky who in the 1930s was a member of the

"Circle," a club of émigré writers and intellectuals, testified that Nabokov had never attended their meetings held at the apartment of Ilia Fondaminsky, the club's founder and Nabokov's personal friend:

> During his visits to Paris, young Nabokov stayed at Fondaminsky's, but did not mingle with the writers of the "Circle." I would see him as he hurriedly traversed the entrance hall, to find a refuge in the only spare room not invaded by our crowd, a slender, sprightly figure, the pale face with an ambiguous smile of a man wiser and sadder than his age.[9]

It does sound very Nabokovian but if we check Iswolsky's testimony against the published minutes of the "Circle" meetings, we'll see that she, whether consciously or unconsciously, distorts the truth: during his stay in Paris in February 1936 Nabokov twice was present at the meetings of the club when the famous Russian philosophers Berdiaev and Fedotov gave their talks.[10] Indicative of the writer's interests and concerns in his Russian years, such episodes, however, are rarely mentioned in Nabokov scholarship. It seems that memoirists, biographers, and critics alike tend to fall under the spell of Nabokov's own inventions, evasions, exaggerations, and half-truths and perpetuate his mythmaking game by sticking to its rules.

At the center of the Nabokov myth lies the very idea of his life in art as an uninterrupted path, a continuous ascension, to use the images of his poem "We So Firmly Believed" (*PP*, 89) from the "damp dell" of promising juvenilia up to the "alpine heath" of faultlessly crafted masterpieces, a history of triumphant emergence unimpeded (and maybe even furthered) by the painful switch to a different language. It is clear that this scenario automatically, by definition, sends all Nabokov's Russian writings down-hill, relegating them to a secondary role of immature, imperfect antecedents. True, Nabokov publicly mourned the loss of his native language – "my natural idiom, my untrammeled, rich, and infinitely docile Russian tongue" that, in his words, he "had to abandon . . . for a second-rate brand of English" (*AnL*, 316 ["On a Book Entitled *Lolita*"]; see also *SO*, 15) but this all too obviously unfair, tongue-in-cheek belittling of his celebrated virtuosity in English undermined the purport of these lamentations. Characteristically, Nabokov led his English readers and critics into believing that the switch to English was a necessity, an unavoidable stage of the evolution rather than a free choice ("I *had to*") and that, albeit psychologically painful, it did no harm to his artistic powers ("my *private* tragedy" with a stress on the second word). "What matters, surely, is that Nabokov . . . had found, through his very loss, a fabulous, freaky, singing, acrobatic, unheard-of English which (probably) made even his most marvellous Russian seem poor," asserts Michael Wood in the preface to his well-meaning and well-received book

The Magician's Doubt, and adds whimsically: "Perhaps one cannot *love* two languages."[11]

Wood's italics inadvertently lay bare a crack in his thesis. What he misses is that Nabokov's relations with the two languages were, in fact, as different as different kinds of love, *eros*, on the one hand, and *agape* and *philia*, on the other. His love for the English language was, no doubt, erotic and self-serving; as his own metaphor goes, he carried on a love affair with it. For Nabokov, English, a semi-foreign language, remained like a beautiful, desired *other* whom a suitor tries to charm, to seduce, to possess but can never fully attain; he reinvented it like a lover who endows the object of his passion with perfections no one else can see. Whatever the merits of Nabokov's "fabulous, unheard-of English," they result from his position outside the language and the desire to conquer it.

As for Russian, the exile taught Nabokov to thrive *within* it, to draw sustenance from it, and to love it selflessly like a believer who responds to the divine grace and thanks a "Person Unknown" for the life-giving and soul-giving gifts. To quote and paraphrase his poems of the late 1930s and the 1940s written before he created a new persona for himself, the native language was Nabokov's only possession ("all I have: my own tongue") and to give it away means to be drained of blood and to be crippled; it is only in Russian that he becomes "an idol, a wizard / bird-headed, emerald-gloved" who builds an "aerial viaduct" to "the flame-licked night of my native land" while English is an absolutely alien tongue that leaves an unpleasant aftertaste of anise-oil in the mouth (*PP*, 96–97, 105–109). Uprooted, displaced, and dispossessed, he found in his beloved Russian language and literature his only haven and home, and his swift, almost miraculous development from mediocre poetry to incomparable, masterful prose fully corroborated the observations of Joseph Brodsky, another great Russian expatriate:

> one more truth about the condition we call exile is that it accelerates tremendously one's otherwise professional flight – or drift – into isolation, into an absolute perspective: into the condition at which all one is left with is oneself and one's language, with nobody or nothing in between. Exile brings you overnight where it would normally take a lifetime to go . . . For one in our profession the condition we call exile is, first of all, a linguistic event: he is thrust from, he retreats into his mother tongue. From being his, so to speak, sword, it turns into his shield, into his capsule. What started as a private, intimate affair with the language in exile becomes fate – even before it becomes an obsession or a duty.[12]

If English served Nabokov as a sword, a wonderful tool and plaything, then his Russian was his shield and protective capsule – his salvational haven.

That is why it would be wrong to surmise that his Russian writings are stylistically "poorer" than their English counterparts and to follow Nabokov in downgrading them to the rank of apprenticeship. In fact, Nabokov's Russian œuvre is no less an accomplishment than the English one and each of them deserves to be regarded in its own right – not diachronically but synchronically, as two parallel realities like Terra and Anti-Terra in *Ada*.

By all criteria, the achievement of Nabokov as a Russian writer is at least commensurate with that of any major Russian novelist of the twentieth century. Actually none of his contemporaries, both inside the Soviet Union and in emigration, managed to stay at the top of their form for such a long time and to produce so much extraordinary work as Sirin. For instance, two other prominent writers who, by a strange coincidence, were born in the same year as Nabokov, Yury Olesha and Andrei Platonov, gained their worldwide fame on the strength of a few novels and short stories written at the end of the 1920s and the beginning of the 1930s; Bulgakov's *Master and Margarita* was the only significant novel written in the USSR during the period when Nabokov published, one after another, his Russian masterpieces; after the success of their first books, neither Gaito Gazdanov nor Nina Berberova, the rising stars of émigré letters, could fulfill their promise. By the end of the 1930s Sirin's reputation as the best Russian writer of his generation became indisputable. "All of us were shocked and charmed by his books, these merciless panoramas of existence devoid of any moralizing and didacticism," recalls an émigré poet Valery Pereleshin.[13] Even his literary enemies had to concede his eminence. Thus Georgy Adamovich, notorious for his persistent attacks against Sirin, stated in 1939: "I have written about Sirin's work a lot of times – always with surprise but not always with praise. Now I am happy for an opportunity to give him his due and to fully recognize his extraordinary, 'incomparable' (as they say about actors) talent."[14]

At the time, Nabokov recognized and assumed his responsibility for the destiny of Russian literature; like his alter ego, Fyodor Godunov-Cherdyntsev in *The Gift*, he firmly believed that he was chosen to save it from extinction. Closely following the works of Soviet writers and mocking their trendy innovations and ideological enslavement, Nabokov accused them of leading Russian literature into the quagmire of parochialism and thus betraying its great past. To use his favorite metaphors, the keys to the unfinished edifice of the national heritage passed to him and other free-thinking artists in exile whose mission was to continue the great tradition. In a Russian newspaper article written soon after his arrival in America Nabokov argued:

The very term "émigré author" sounds somewhat tautological. Any genuine writer emigrates into his art and abides there. As for Russian writers, they have always loved their motherland nostalgically even without leaving it in reality. Not only Kishinev or the Caucasus but Nevsky Prospect seemed like a faraway exile to them. For the last twenty years when it was developing abroad, under the impartial European sky, our literature moved along the thoroughfare while its counterpart inside Russia, having no rights of inspiration and sorrow, cultivated sunflowers in the backyard of spirit. An "émigré" book relates to a "Soviet" one as the metropolitan compares to the provincial. They don't hit a man when he is down, so it would be a sin to criticize literature that provides a backdrop against which an oleographic picture, a shameless historical daub looks like a masterpiece. For other, peculiar reasons I also find it improper to dwell upon our metropolitan literature. Yet I can say one thing for sure: thanks to the purity of its intentions, self-discipline, and ascetic, sinewy strength and despite the scarcity of first-rate talents (though when exactly were they aplenty?), it is worthy of its past. The poverty of everyday life, the difficulties of publication, the unresponsive readers, the barbarian ignorance of the average émigré rabble – all this was recompensed by an incredible opportunity, never before tried in Russia, to be free of any censorship, whether by the state or the public opinion.[15]

Yet for Nabokov, to be worthy of the past did not mean to preserve it from change through nostalgic cloning but rather, as he put it in the afterword to *Lolita*, "to transcend the heritage in [the artist's] own way" (*AnL*, 317 ["On a Book Entitled *Lolita*"]).[16] He shared the convictions of his older friend and ally Vladislav Khodasevich who condemned the sterile reactionary traditionalism of most prominent émigré writers and stated that Russian literature could survive in exile if, and only if, it sustained the incessant inner movement and change of forms and ideas:

The internal life of literature takes a form of recurrent flashes and explosions . . . The spirit of literature is the spirit of eternal explosion and eternal renewal. In these conditions, to preserve the literary tradition is to watch that the explosions occur in a rhythmical, purposeful way and do not destroy the mechanism. Thus literary conservatism has nothing to do with literary reactionism. Its aim is not to put down minor explosions and revolutions by which literature is set into motion but, on the contrary, to maintain the conditions for such explosions to take place with a purpose, freely and uninterruptedly. A literary conservative is an eternal incendiary: a keeper of the fire rather than a fire extinguisher.[17]

Khodasevich's paradoxical idea of literary conservatism as a kind of disciplined, restrained subversion beautifully fits Nabokov's position in respect to Russian literature. Contrary to the views of his opponents and detractors among the émigré literati who claimed that the very tradition based on aesthetic values of harmony and beauty lost its bearings in the chaos of modernity and had to be destroyed, Nabokov believed in its inviolability and saw himself as a "keeper of the fire," an "archaist-cum-innovator" protecting the continuum through "purposeful explosions." As early as 1926, the year of his first novel, he described Russian literature in organic metaphors: its wonderful, vigorous childhood has passed and, in the modernist excesses of Soviet writers, it is experiencing all the frustrations of sorrowful adolescence; however, it can look forward to its glorious, fascinating youth when some new mentors of Russian Muse continue the mission of their predecessors. "These writers of the future would be forged by the miracles of exile and return," foretold the young Nabokov,[18] preparing himself for the princely role.

Of course, Nabokov's idea of continuity involved disputation, controversy, debunking, reinterpretation; he reveled in overthrowing a "false idol" (such as Chernyshevski in *The Gift*), ridiculing a stale cliché or trendy device, shattering a convention. Yet what really matters is the constant presence of an intertextual dimension in his Russian œuvre that positions and defines itself against the Russian literary tradition, whether positively or negatively treated. Not only *The Gift*, an overtly metaliterary novel whose "heroine," to quote Nabokov's foreword, "is Russian literature" (*Gift*, n. p.) but all his other major Russian writings, starting with *Mary*, stand in relation to certain literary antecedents and precedents that establish a contextual framework for a text and serve as its foils. Among Nabokov's minor characters one can always find a Russian writer or a poet – Podtiagin in *Mary*, Luzhin senior in *The Defense*, Segelkranz in *Kamera obskura*, Roman Bogdanovich in *The Eye*, Bubnov in *Glory*, Herman's nameless Russian rival in *Despair*, an anonymous author of *Quercus* in *The Invitation to a Beheading*, to say nothing about a whole bunch of émigré authors in *The Gift* – all of whom represent certain trends in contemporary letters; literary tastes of heroes and heroines denote boundaries of their minds; the books themselves decree "correct" codes for reading and decry the "wrong" ones; multiple allusions, quotations, parodic echoes reveal clusters of subtexts that usually embrace several authors and periods at once – for example, Nikolai Gogol and Aleksandr Pushkin together with Fedor Dostoevsky, Andrei Bely, Leonid Andreev, and Ilia Erenburg in *Despair*. If in his American years Nabokov preferred reacting to and against a select international group of classics as their peer or superior, and pitting, say, Flaubert against Dostoevsky, or Shakespeare against Edgar Allan Poe, his Russian prose interacted predominantly with the national tradition from its origins up to the latest movements: it constructed its own literary geneology and at the same time asserted itself on the battleground of contemporary letters. That is why I think it is not enough to call Sirin a self-conscious writer and to postulate, as Khodasevich did, that his theme was the "life of the artist and the life of device in the consciousness of the artist."[19] In no lesser degree was he *tradition-conscious* and his theme – the life of Russian literature and the life of genres, styles, and themes within its framework. Moreover, these two sides of his art are interdependent and complement each other.

Nabokov's preoccupation with the fate of Russian literature went more or less unnoticed by the émigré criticism. A hostile group of Paris writers headed by Georgy Adamovich and Georgy Ivanov denounced his early novels as glib imitations of some unidentified German and French models and accused Nabokov of indifference to the national heritage and apostatic "non-Russianness."[20] Defending Nabokov from these attacks, his friend and supporter Gleb Struve admitted that Sirin's attention to formal precision and his disdain for humanistic and religious concerns set him apart from the mainstream of Russian literature associated with Dostoevsky and Tolstoy, but he claimed that in Sirin's yearning for form, measure, and order he was actually very close to Aleksandr Pushkin.[21] Because a kinship with the most revered, almost sacred figure in the national canon would legitimize Nabokov's position as a Russian writer and undermine the idea of his alienation, Adamovich countered Struve's claim with the assertion that Sirin's only Russian literary forefather was Gogol, whose "insane," sterile, cold, and inhuman traits he had inherited.[22] Several years later Petr Bitsilli in his insightful article "The Revival of Allegory" wrote that "Sirin's closeness to Gogol is indisputable" and presented some evidence of stylistic similarities between the two writers.[23] In his view, however, "the deathly weirdness and grotesque deformity" of Nabokov's images were even closer to Mikhail Saltykov, a marginal genius of Russian prose, whose wry portrayals of deformed minds and their empty, illusionary worlds foreshadowed *Despair* and *Invitation to a Beheading*.[24]

What contemporary Russian critics, even the most astute ones, didn't notice was Nabokov's intent to reshuffle the Russian classical canon, to reconsider the accepted criteria of selection, and thereby to construe his own literary lineage. He believed that a modern Russian writer should incessantly test the whole tradition, debunking stale notions and developing potentialities that for some reason have been overlooked or untried. Thus his paradigmatical émigré author Fyodor Godunov-Cherdyntsev in *The Gift* begins his literary evolution under the influence of Symbolist poetry but very soon rejects it and tries to create his own neoclassical style that stresses visual ingenuity and derives mostly from Russian pre-modernist poetry and prose as well as Ivan Bunin's colorful descriptive language. Then Fyodor discovers Pushkin's prose and, inspired by its "divine stab," sets to write his own narrative, a biography of his beloved father, a great naturalist and explorer, in which he actually demonstrates that Pushkinian "accuracy of the words and the absolute purity of their conjunction" were not completely superseded by the Russian nineteenth-century novel but lay dormant for a long time feeding mostly non-fictional genres (travelogues, memoirs, letters) and could be revived and elaborated in the modern context. His next step is the study of Gogol's imagery and devices that Fyodor uses in his iconoclastic *Life of Chernyshevski* – a bombshell directed against the utilitarian approaches to art that were common in Russian criticism after Pushkin. Having exorcized the evil spirit of Russian literature, he is ready to tackle a new challenging task – to write "a classical novel, with 'types,' love, fate, conversations" (*Gift*, 349), that is to venture out into the territory of Dostoevsky, Tolstoy, and Turgenev. In a sense *The Gift* itself is such a novel but with an ironic, subversive twist at every point: socio-historical "types" are presented as individual minds undetermined by environment, class origins, or historical situation; instead of a "declaration of love" the hero tells his girlfriend that he has found an idea for a remarkable novel; fate acts as a cunning artist playing little tricks on characters in order to bring them together; long conversations of two gifted writers suddenly turn out to be imaginary.

The story of Fyodor's literary education unveils Nabokov's multifaceted intertextual strategy with regard to Russian literature. Like his hero, he finds his roots in Pushkin (both as a poet and as a prose writer) and in what he called the Pushkinian "long, life-giving ray" in Russian poetry – from Baratynsky, Tiutchev, and Fet to Gumilev and Khodasevich. That is why it is predominantly classical and neoclassical poetry (plus Pushkin's poetical prose) that serves as Nabokov's main source of subtexts. An image, a combination of words, a recurrent motif in his novels and short stories would echo, whether directly or obliquely, nineteenth-century poetic topoi though in a new, unexpected context. Nabokov likes to construct his narratives as prosaic variations of some old poetic themes (for example, the theme of an imprisoned poet in *Invitation to a Beheading* or that of the ineffable in "Cloud,Castle, Lake"), modifying them almost beyond recognition but maintaining a connection to their origins through subtle intertextual references.

On the other hand, his attitude towards great Russian prose writers of the nineteenth century is different as it involves a competitive edge. He tends to appropriate their plots, characters, narrative techniques and then turn them around, subsuming them into a modernist structure and investing them with new meanings and functions. For example, in *The Eye* Nabokov develops upon a startling innovation first tried in Dostoevsky's tale "The Dream of

a Ridiculous Man" – the first-person account of a seemingly successful suicide committed by a humiliated loser – and creates a psychologically plausible character of a narrator-as-ghost only to reveal in the end that the hero
actually stayed alive but convinced himself that he had experienced physical
death and became invisible and invulnerable. While Dostoevsky's "ridiculous
man" forewarns the reader that he "fell asleep without being aware of it"
and had an uncanny dream of the suicide and afterlife, his counterpart in
The Eye believes (or wants to believe) he is dead, which creates a complex
narratorial riddle solved only in the finale of the novel. Similarly, tackling
a theme of fatal sexual attraction in *Kamera obskura* Nabokov plays with
the plot of Lev Tolstoy's tale *The Devil*, stripping it of its moralistic purport;
in *Despair* he "improves" upon Dostoevsky's *The Double* and *Notes from
Underground*, and in a number of short stories he "rewrites" Chekhov and
Bunin.

The closer to the modern literary scene, the more polemical and partial
Nabokov gets. His favorite weapons in dealing with contemporary Russian
writers were parody and caricature. Positioning himself as a champion of
Pushkin's heritage, he would persistently lampoon those émigré writers, critics, and poets with whom, in his words, "soul-saving came first, log-rolling
next, and art last" (*SM*, 213–14): Georgy Adamovich, Georgy Ivanov, Petr
Pilsky, Yury Felzen, Boris Poplavsky, Zinaida Gippius, Vasily Yanovsky, and
others. When Mark Aldanov, a prominent novelist, reproached him for a
mocking parody of Georgy Adamovich in *The Gift*, Nabokov replied that he
had been "guided not by an urge to laugh at this or that person . . . but solely
by a desire to show a certain order of literary ideas, typical at a given time."[25]
For the émigré literary scene of the 1930s, such an "order" presupposed the
dominance of existential anxiety and religious quests expressed in sincere
"human documents," "remedial lyricism" (*SO*, 224), or "Proustinianized"
discourse, and Nabokov's pastiches often blend different authors and trends
to reveal their common aesthetic fallacies. At the same time, he would
not spare the most conspicuous tendencies of the current Soviet literature,
especially those connected to modernist and avant-garde poetics, parodying, for instance, the stylistic mannerisms of Andrei Bely and his followers,
Viktor Shklovsky's montage techniques, Ilia Erenburg's meta-fictional experiments, Yury Tynianov's biographical narratives, or the very concept of the
"literature of the fact."[26] Nabokov's quick visceral reactions to all the challenges of contemporary Russian literature prove that his writings of the
period were pollinated and sustained by the cultural and literary contexts of
the 1920s and 1930s in which he, contrary to what Michael Wood thinks,
was not "the haughty mandarin" whom we meet in his "prefaces and class-
rooms and sundry truculent pronouncements about literature and life"[27] but

a cocky rookie fighting his way up to the top – a lively troublemaker who engaged in literary wars with his contemporaries to assert his primacy in the Russian literary tradition.

Nabokov's three-tier intertextual strategy – continuation (of classical and neoclassical poetic idiom), amelioration (of the nineteenth-century realist novel), and mocking parody (of influential contemporary trends) – makes him the most literary-minded Russian prose writer of the twentieth century. Yet it is a far cry from postmodernist inclusiveness as Nabokov does not mix up and equalize various discourses but rather presents literary tradition as a hierarchy and insists upon the importance of its preservation. In an outline of the finale of the second volume of *The Gift* (a project he began in 1939 and eventually aborted soon after settling in America), Fyodor Godunov-Cherdyntsev loses his wife when she is killed in an accident, and he looks for a way to express his feelings of grief and remorse and to find an anchor in the hostile, dark world where everything is coming apart. Instead of giving vent to his despair and fear he writes his continuation of Pushkin's unfinished drama *Rusalka* (*The Water-Nymph*) and during a German air raid in Paris reads it to his friend Koncheyev, a great Russian poet in exile. When Koncheyev is taking his leave Fyodor suddenly confounds him with a strange question: "Donesem?" (literally: "Shall we carry it through?"). Contrary to what Koncheyev thinks, it refers not to their chances of physical survival in the war but to their obligation as Russian writers to keep alive the legacy of Russian literature bequeathed to them by their fathers and to pass it on to the next generations of writers. Fyodor's own attempt to complete Pushkin's unfinished work in a time of personal and social disasters is the ultimate symbolic gesture, an avowal of filial loyalties that Nabokov himself later chose to forsake. Yet, even though it was aborted, Nabokov's dialogue with Russian literary tradition was powerful enough to sustain its fire for decades to come.

NOTES

1. On Nabokov's technique of self-translation, see: Jane Grayson, *Nabokov Translated: A Comparison of Nabokov's Russian and English Prose* (Oxford: Oxford University Press, 1977); and Elizabeth Klosty Beaujour, "Translation and Self-Translation," in *The Garland Companion to Vladimir Nabokov*, ed. Vladimir E. Alexandrov (New York: Garland, 1995), 714–24.
2. Julian W. Connolly, "*King, Queen, Knave*," in Alexandrov, *Garland Companion*, 212.
3. See the genealogical chart composed by Vadim Stark in *Nabokovskii vestnik 2: Nabokov v rodstvennom okruzhenii* (St. Petersburg: Dorn, 1998), 31–33.
4. Fyodor Dostoevsky, *Crime and Punishment*, trans. Richard Pevear and Larissa Volokhonsky (New York: Vintage: 1993), 527.

5. As David Bethea and Sergej Davydov noticed, Adrian Prokhorov is given the initials of his creator Aleksandr Pushkin and in some aspects ironically mirrors the poet's persona. See their "Pushkin's Saturnine Cupid: The Poetics of Parody in *The Tales of Belkin*," *PMLA* 86 (1981): 8–21.

6. See Elizabeth Klosty Beaujour, "Translation and Self-Translation," 721.

7. See, for example, Omri Ronen, "Puti Shklovskogo v 'Putevoditele po Berlinu'," *Zvezda* 4 (1999): 164–72.

8. Nabokov seems to respond to a remark of Gleb Struve who in his 1956 book *Russian Literature in Exile* wrote that émigré critics of the 1930s had "spoken much about the influences of contemporary foreign authors upon Sirin," specifically mentioning Proust, Kafka (in Struve's view, "too much in *Invitation to a Beheading* was Kafkaesque"), German expressionists, Giraudoux, and Céline; see Gleb Struve, *Russkaia literatura v izgnanii: Opyt istoricheskogo obzora zarubezhnoi literatury*, 3rd edn (Paris–Moscow: YMCA-Press/Russkii put', 1996), 192.

9. Hélène Iswolsky, *No Time to Grieve: An Autobiographical Journey* (Philadelphia: Winchell, 1985), 209.

10. See *Novyi grad* 11 (1936): 139–42.

11. Michael Wood, *The Magician's Doubts: Nabokov and the Risks of Fiction* (Princeton: Princeton University Press, 1995).

12. Joseph Brodsky, *On Grief and Reason: Essays* (New York: Farrar, Straus, and Giroux, 1995), 32.

13. V. Pereleshin, *Russian Poetry and Literary Life in Harbin and Shanghai, 1930–1950*. (Amsterdam: Rodopi, 1987), 44.

14. Georgii Adamovich, "Literatura v *Russkikh zapiskakh*," *Poslednie novosti* (February 16, 1939), 3.

15. Vladimir Nabokov, "Opredeleniia," Library of Congress Nabokov Archive, box 8, folder 7. It was probably published in the New York Russian newspaper *Novoe Russkoe Slovo*, but the issue has never been identified.

16. In the Russian translation of the afterword Nabokov renders "the heritage" as *nasledie ottsov*, i.e. "the heritage of the fathers" (Vladimir Nabokov, *Lolita*, trans. V. Nabokov [Ann Arbor: Ardis, 1976], 295).

17. Vladislav Khodasevich, "Literatura v izgnanii," in his *Literaturnye stat'i i vospominaniia* (New York: Izd. imeni Chekhova, 1954), 262; the essay was originally published in *Vozrozhdenie* in 1933.

18. I paraphrase the final part of Nabokov's paper on contemporary Soviet literature that he read in Berlin – "Neskol'ko slov ob ubozhestve sovetskoi belletristiki i popytka ustanovit' prichiny onogo" (A Few Notes on the Deformity of Soviet Fiction and an Attempt to Indicate Its Causes). See my annotated publication of the paper in *Diaspora II* (St. Petersburg: Feniks, 2001), 7–23.

19. Vladislav Khodasevich, "O Sirine," *Vozrozhdenie* (February 13, 1937): 9. I quote Michael H. Walker's translation in *Nabokov: Criticism, Reminiscences, Translations and Tributes*, ed. Alfred Appel, Jr. and Charles Newman (Evanston, IL: Northwestern University Press, 1971), 100.

20. See, in particular, Adamovich's disparaging review of *The Defense* in *Poslednie novosti* (October 31, 1929): 2, and Ivanov's infamous article in the first issue of the Paris journal *Chisla* (1930): 233–36. A useful though not unflawed selection of early Russian criticism can be found in *Klassik bez retushi: Literaturnyi mir*

o tvorchestve Vladimira Nabokova, ed. N. G. Mel'nikov and O. A. Korostelev (Moscow: Novoe literaturnoe obozrenie, 2000).

21. [Gleb Struve], "Vladimir Nabokoff-Sirine, l'amoureux de la vie," *Le Mois* 6 (June–July 1931): 141–42.

22. See Georgii Adamovich, "Sirin," *Poslednie novosti* (January 4, 1934): 3; "*Sovremennye zapiski*, kn. 55-ia, Chast' literaturnaia," *Poslednie novosti* (May 24, 1934): 3.

23. See Petr Bitsilli, "Vozrozhdenie allegorii," *Sovremennye zapiski* 61 (1936) (translated as "The Revival of Allegory" in Appel, Jr. and Newman, *Nabokov: Criticism, Reminiscences, Translations and Tributes*, 102–88); and Bitsilli's review of *Priglashenie na kazn'* and *Sogliadatai* in *Sovremennye zapiski* 68 (1939). In a letter to his first American translator Petr Pertsov, dated April 23, 1943, Nabokov praised Bitsilli as the most intelligent critic of his writings among émigrés; see Maxim Shraer, ed., "Pis'ma V. V. Nabokova P. A. Pertsovu," *Kontrapunkt* 4 (1999): 134.

24. Bitsilli, "The Revival of Allegory," 108–9.

25. Vladimir Nabokov to Mark Aldanov, letter of February 3, 1938, quoted in Brian Boyd, *Vladimir Nabokov: The Russian Years* (Princeton: Princeton University Press, 1990), 480.

26. On Nabokov's parodies of Soviet literature in *The Gift* and *Despair* see Alexander Dolinin, "Tri zametki o romane Vladimira Nabokova 'Dar,'" in *V. V. Nabokov: Pro et contra* (St. Petersburg: Izd. Russkogo Khristianskogo gumanitarnogo instituta, 1997), 697–740; Alexander Dolinin, "Parody in Nabokov's *Despair*," in *Hypertext Otchaianie / Sverkhtekst Despair: Studien zu Vladimir Nabokovs Roman-Rätsel*, ed. Igor Smirnov, *Die Welt der Slaven*, no. 6 (Munich: Sagner, 2000), 15–42.

27. Wood, *Magician's Doubts*, 6.

4

SUSAN ELIZABETH SWEENEY

"By some sleight of *land*": how Nabokov rewrote America

Nabokov the American

That Nabokov is an American writer seems both a marvelous conceit and an unavoidable fact. Twenty years ago, in my first published essay – provoked by an announcement that course work on *Lolita* couldn't count toward an American Civilization major – I suggested that while Nabokov might not wholly belong to the American literary tradition, some of his novels did.[1] Today, the case for his Americanness seems more conclusive, whether one considers his knowledge of American culture, his effect upon it, his publications, his audience, or his citizenship. It is true, of course, that Nabokov grew up in Russia, studied French and Russian writers at Cambridge, and published nine Russian novels as an émigré author in Europe. But he was also raised in a cosmopolitan family, became fluent in English early, and steeped himself in American literature – especially after 1940, when he came to the United States.

In *Bend Sinister*, the first novel he composed in his adopted country, Nabokov saluted America's most exuberantly patriotic poet with a strange new adjective: "waltwhitmanesque" (95 [ch. 6]). His fiction, letters, and interviews demonstrate comparable familiarity with other American literary figures, whether he admired or derided them, including Poe, Emerson, Hawthorne, Melville, James, Eliot, Pound, Frost, Fitzgerald, Hemingway, and Faulkner. He embarked on a close friendship with novelist Edmund Wilson and influenced younger writers as disparate as R. M. Koster, Edmund White, and Erica Jong. Nabokov addressed an American readership, too. He began his first English novel in 1938, preparing for eventual immigration to America; he depicted American culture in later works set in the United States;[2] and he published all his English books there, even as earlier Russian ones were translated and reprinted for his growing audience. "It is in America that I found my best readers," he explained (*SO*, 10). Nabokov remained an American citizen even after settling in Switzerland, where he followed national politics, celebrated the moon landing, contemplated moving to California, and paid US taxes.

"American" seems like an odd adjective to describe his career, however. Aleksei Zverev – after questioning Nabokov's affinity for the United States, familiarity with its literature, and influence on its writers – remarks that he "was more like a foreigner in relation to American culture than its own permanent property."[3] But Nabokov still fits within the country's literary tradition, either as immigrant or expatriate. John Updike tried to resolve matters by naming him "the best writer of English prose at present holding American citizenship."[4] Nabokov himself felt that his nationality was somewhat irrelevant: "The writer's art is his real passport." Nevertheless, he called himself "an American writer" (SO, 63) and recommended that libraries catalog all his books as "American Literature," since "his best work was done in English" (SL, 454).

Transpositions

Nabokov's American works do reflect the fact that America was not his original home. Indeed, his peripatetic history produced a strangely bifurcated literary career. He saw his life as a spiral in which "Twirl follows twirl, and every synthesis is the thesis of the next series": twenty years in his native Russia, twenty-one years of European exile, and twenty years in his adopted country – leading, in turn, to almost twenty more as an expatriate (SM, 275 [ch. 14]). Nabokov's life also suggests two allegiances: "The Russian Years" and "The American Years."[5] Finally, it is a tale of two authors, progressing from "V. Sirin," his Russian pen name, to "Vladimir Nabokov," the name under which his first English novel appeared. These experiences as émigré, immigrant, and expatriate profoundly affected Nabokov's writing. Some critics discuss his lifelong "art of exile," in Ellen Pifer's phrase,[6] while others, such as Michael Siedel, analyze his "exilic projection of America," in particular. Defining an exile as "someone who inhabits one place and remembers or imagines the reality of another," Seidel explains that this situation "creates a special imaginative effect, a splitting of vision," which Nabokov's American novels reproduce in their narrative designs.[7] Paul Giles adds that those texts use "alienation from America" to depict exile more poignantly, combining "metafictional labyrinths with a mordant, plangent mood of insufficiency and ironic absence."[8] I argue, more precisely, that Nabokov's American works compensate for his exile "by some sleight of land" – that is, by transposing one country with another (Ada, 18 [pt. 1, ch. 3]).

How does he accomplish such a feat? Consider, to begin with, this very phrase's verbal dexterity. Manipulating terms like "sleight of hand," to wrest new meanings from them, is among Nabokov's distinctive stylistic gambits. Here, the original expression refers to a deception created by nimble fingers and misleading gestures – the manual equivalent of *trompe l'oeil* – or to tricks requiring that skill. Nabokov often identifies showmanship with literary achievement, from the jugglers, acrobats, and magicians inhabiting his novels to the claim that "a great writer is always a great enchanter" (*LL*, 5). His tales use various maneuvers to deceive readers, and his prose style, as he obliquely admits, deploys "the mirrorlike angles of . . . clear but weirdly misleading sentences" (*SM*, 288 [ch. 14]). Nabokov associates his own literary legerdemain with having to abandon Russian "for a second-rate brand of English, devoid of any of those apparatuses – the baffling mirror, the black velvet backdrop, the implied associations and traditions – which the native illusionist, frac-tails flying, can magically use" (*Lo*, 316–17 ["On a Book Entitled *Lolita*"]). He suggests, moreover, that true conjuring involves sleight of hand, not mechanical aids (*Ada*, 173 [pt. 1, ch. 28]). At any rate, an alien illusionist who lacks those props – to continue Nabokov's metaphor – must demonstrate extraordinary skill to enthrall his readers. Nabokov's own prose, which is hardly "second-rate," is a case in point, and is hardly inferior: as Michael Wood explains, "he found, through his very loss, a fabulous, freaky, singing, acrobatic, unheard-of English which (probably) made even his most marvelous Russian seem poor."[9] Indeed, successful conjuring depends on such ingenious transpositions.[10]

If "sleight of hand" evokes his own verbal magic, then Nabokov's prestidigitation with this phrase exemplifies his self-reflexivity. Elsewhere, he transforms it into a description of adaptive mimicry: "sleight-of-wing" (*SO*, 153). In *Ada* – where it becomes "sleight of *land*" – his wordplay is even more telling. By replacing "hand," he emphasizes that word's association with authorship, composition, style, and signature. By replacing it with the rhyming, italicized "*land*," in particular, he implies that writing can transpose countries as easily as letters. The phrase's manipulation becomes more significant within its immediate context: a statement about the absurd notion of Terra, a planet where "Russia" – rather than being an American province – is actually "the name of a country, transferred as if by some sleight of *land* across the ha-ha of a doubled ocean to the opposite hemisphere" (17–18 [pt. 1, ch. 3]). Substituting "*land*" for "hand" not only reinforces the apparent change in names, regions, and landmasses; it also parallels *Ada*'s mind-boggling introduction of a worldview that cannot imagine Russia and America on separate continents. Nabokov's verbal transposition thus duplicates complex shifts in geographical, cosmological, and narrational perspective.

Nabokov's American texts often transpose Russia and the United States. With varying distortions, adjustments, and substitutions, his adopted country stands in for his lost homeland – an elegant arrangement, echoing the topsy-turvy paradoxes of "Time and Ebb" or "The Visit to the Museum," because America once seemed as far away as Russia eventually became. (Nabokov hunted butterflies, as a child, in a bog that his family called "America" because of its fabulous remoteness.)[11] Matters grew more complicated when he moved to Switzerland, and America became distant again. "[T]rying to develop, in this rosy exile, the same fertile nostalgia in regard to America" that he had cultivated for Russia, Nabokov now imagined it blending even more fantastically with his native land (*SO*, 49). His American works constantly correlate the two countries through such stratagems – especially by depicting distorted reflections, scrambled pictures, unfinished maps, visionary paintings, or miniature models of one world inside another.[12]

Looking backward

Nabokov's American literary career began with his first English novel, *The Real Life of Sebastian Knight*. True, this account of a narrator's search for his dead half-brother's "real life" takes place in Europe and was composed in Paris over a year before Nabokov came to America. Nevertheless, it was first published, in 1941, in the United States.

Sebastian Knight is a metaphysical detective story, a mock biography, a Doppelgänger tale, and a farewell to Nabokov's identity as a Russian author. Most of his earlier works are set in the Russian émigré community, and some even imagine returning to Russia; this novel, however, traces a writer's efforts to jettison that past. Sebastian – half-English and half-Russian – fled revolutionary Russia, abandoned the Russian language, and became a British novelist. Nevertheless, his half-brother seeks to prove that Sebastian longed for "the country where he had been born and bred" (27 [ch. 3]). The narrator begins his quest by interviewing their former governess (who resembles "Mademoiselle O," Nabokov's subject in an earlier autobiographical essay). "Mademoiselle" is one of several "old Swiss women who had been governesses in Russia before the revolution" (*RLSK*, 21 [ch. 2]). There they had yearned for Switzerland; but when they returned home after the revolution, "they found themselves complete strangers in a changed country, so that by a queer trick of sentiment – Russia (which to them had really been an unknown abyss, remotely rumbling beyond a lamplit corner of a stuffy back-room with family photographs in mother-of-pearl frames and a water-colour view of Chillon castle), unknown Russia now took on the aspect of a lost paradise" (21–22 [ch. 2]). Unfortunately, the narrator cannot prove that his half-brother ever felt such homesickness: although Sebastian remarked "that one of the purest emotions is that of the banished man pining after the land of his birth," and even considered writing about it, he found the subject banal (26 [ch. 3]). Nabokov, of course, shared neither Sebastian's disdain for nostalgia nor Mademoiselle's obliviousness to her surroundings. In his American works, however, he continually explored the "queer trick" whereby exile from one place leads to alienation in another; and in his own life, he eventually left his adopted country for Mademoiselle's native Switzerland.

Bend Sinister was the first novel Nabokov actually composed in America. Like his earlier Russian novel *Invitation to a Beheading*, it portrays a fantastic dystopia; but while *Invitation* describes a completely imaginary place, *Bend Sinister* caricatures real political systems and mentions actual countries, including America – a land of swimming pools, soda fountains, football games, and "technicoloured" campuses to which the hero seeks escape (188 [ch. 16]). In *Bend Sinister*, the problem of shifting from one literary tradition to another – illustrated, in *Sebastian Knight*, by a Russian narrator recounting, in English, the life of his half-Russian, half-English half-brother – takes the form of musings on translation. The previous novel's sibling relationship metamorphoses into the friendship between Krug, a widowed East European philosopher, and Ember, whose English rendition of Krug's latest book became an American bestseller that led to an American lecture tour.

Nabokov spent five years on *Bend Sinister*; by 1946, when it was completed, he had become an American citizen. During this period, he also taught at Wellesley (comparative literature, elementary Russian, intermediate Russian, and Russian literature in translation) and curated Lepidoptera at Harvard's Museum of Comparative Zoology. If Nabokov's efforts to teach Russian while writing in English account for this novel's emphasis on translation, then his long hours at the microscope may explain how it represents one world's manifestation inside another – as a miniature vista teeming with life. *Bend Sinister* associates Krug's troubled country, in fact, with a tiny piece of the American landscape: a puddle on the pavement.

Bend Sinister opens with the view from a hospital window. The narrator focuses, in particular, on an "oblong puddle inset in the coarse asphalt . . . a spatulate hole through which you can see the nether sky" (1 [ch. 1]). Nabokov points out that the "plot starts to breed in the bright broth of [this] puddle" as the narrator gazes at it (xiv ["Introduction"]). Accordingly, the "vortex of ripples creas[ing]" the puddle's brightness, on the first page, becomes "crumpled ripples" on the face of the first character to speak once the action begins (1, 5 [ch. 1]). Its agitated surface also emphasizes the novel's title, which Nabokov glosses as "a distortion in the mirror of being" (xii ["Introduction"]). And its oblong shape, he explains, reappears "as an ink blot in Chapter Four, an inkstain in Chapter Five, spilled milk in Chapter Eleven, the infusoria-like image of ciliated thought in Chapter Twelve, the footprint of a phosphorescent islander in Chapter Eighteen, and the imprint a soul leaves in the intimate texture of space in the closing paragraph" (xiv–xv ["Introduction"]). That last paragraph actually returns to the original puddle. The narrator, disclosing his authorial identity, notes that from the bedroom where he has just finished *Bend Sinister*, he can glimpse "a special puddle (the one Krug had somehow perceived through the layer of his own life), an oblong puddle invariably acquiring the same form after every shower because of the constant spatulate shape of a depression in the ground" (240 [ch. 18]). Nabokov confirms that it represents "a rent in [Krug's] world leading to another world of tenderness, brightness, and beauty" – Cambridge, Massachusetts, where *Bend Sinister* was composed (xv ["Introduction"]).

In May 1947, a month before the novel's publication, a similar puddle appeared in Nabokov's most famous short story. "Signs and Symbols" features a Russian émigré couple whose institutionalized son, suffering from the delusion "that everything happening around him is a veiled reference to his personality and existence," longs "to tear a hole in his world and escape." Forbidden to see him because of his recent suicide attempt, they return home to several wrong numbers and a final telephone call of unknown significance. (The story's ending prompts readers to worry about encoded information, too.) Earlier, when the parents leave the hospital, the narrator describes "a tiny half-dead unfledged bird . . . helplessly twitching in a puddle." That puddle – evoking "glass surfaces and still pools" that supposedly reflect their son's thoughts, as well as the "hole in his world" that he seeks (*Stories*, 595) – recalls the one in *Bend Sinister*. Presumably, it mirrors an actual depression in the pavement outside 8 Craigie Circle, in Cambridge, where Nabokov wrote both novel and story.[13]

In the summer of 1947, even as he published *Bend Sinister* and composed "Signs and Symbols," Nabokov started writing *Conclusive Evidence*. Dating that autobiography is difficult, however. He had begun his memoirs a dozen years earlier, writing "Mademoiselle O" in French and drafting an unfinished autobiography in English. The new work incorporated his governess's portrait but took other forms as it evolved: several *New Yorker* essays in the late 1940s; *Conclusive Evidence* itself in 1951; *Drugie berega*, a Russian version, in 1954; and an expanded English version, *Speak, Memory: An Autobiography Revisited*, in 1966. Like *Bend Sinister*, Nabokov's autobiography explores separate realms that are nonetheless interlinked, as in this description of magic lantern slides: "translucent miniatures, pocket wonder-lands, neat little worlds of hushed luminous hues! In later years, I rediscovered the same precise and silent beauty at the radiant bottom of a microscope's magic shaft" (*SM*, 166 [ch. 8]). It focuses on "the legendary Russia of his boyhood" (119 [ch. 6]), but also reflects the author himself remembering, composing, and narrating in the United States, decades later. The book concludes with Nabokov's first glimpse of the ship that would allow him, his wife, and their son to escape from wartime France to America:

> There, in front of us, where a broken row of houses stood between us and the harbor, and where the eye encountered all sorts of stratagems, such as pale-blue and pink underwear cakewalking on a clothesline, or a lady's bicycle and striped cat oddly sharing a rudimentary balcony of cast iron, it was most satisfying to make out among the jumbled angles of roofs and walls, a splendid ship's funnel, showing from behind the clothesline as something in a scrambled picture – Find What the Sailor Has Hidden – that the finder cannot unsee once it has been seen. (309–10 [ch. 15])

This final sentence exemplifies both Nabokov's theme of transposed geographies and his usual strategy – describing some sort of visual puzzle – for conveying it to readers. Indeed, he constructed his memoir as a backward glance that draws on retrospective knowledge, as in this passage, to perceive and reproduce an overall design. *Speak, Memory* ends, therefore, by looking toward his future in America – and toward an unwritten sequel, *Speak On, Memory*, which would have shown how his American experiences recapitulated his Russian origins and European exile.

Driving ahead

Nabokov first surveyed his adopted country in *Lolita*, which was originally published in France because, in 1955, no American publisher would touch it. John Haegert calls it "his only 'American' novel."[14] Nabokov said it was the most difficult to write, since it required "inventing America" (*Lo*, 312 ["On a Book Entitled *Lolita*"]). Certainly, it is his most detailed depiction of the United States. He not only studied American customs but actually composed the novel during cross-country butterfly-hunting expeditions that his family took in 1951, 1952, and 1953, as soon as his responsibilities at Cornell (where he was now professor of Russian literature) had ended for the summer. As a result, *Lolita* provides an incisive account of American culture, including advertisements, jukeboxes, roadside attractions, movies, comics, and so on. Some readers describe this national portrait as condescending, satirical, or eye-opening, while others argue that it extends native literary traditions.[15]

Nabokov himself, explaining that he had meant to attack "philistine vulgarity" in general, denies that *Lolita* is "anti-American" (*Lo*, 315 ["On a Book Entitled *Lolita*"]). It differs from his other novels, at any rate, because it never alludes to a fantastic realm – except "that intangible island of entranced time where Lolita plays with her likes" (17 [pt. 1, ch. 5) – but concentrates on the United States. Indeed, once Nabokov's protagonist begins to explore that country, he stops searching for "a Kingdom by the Sea, a Sublimated Riviera, or whatnot" (167 [pt. 2, ch. 3]).

Even before Humbert arrives in the land "of rosy children and great trees, where life would be such an improvement over dull dingy Paris" (27 [pt. 1, ch. 8]), he finds it overwhelming. Wood points out that although Humbert literally comes to America because of an uncle's bequest, he metaphorically does so

> because the weather in a picture breaks into his supposedly three-dimensional life. "These burst," Humbert says of the thunder clouds in an American print in a shop in the rue Bonaparte, "a splendid, flamboyant, green, red, golden and inky blue, ancient American estampe – a locomotive with a gigantic smokestack, great baroque lamps and a tremendous cowcatcher" . . . But then Nabokov makes the apparently incidental illustration into the very scene of his novel, pull[ing] America out of his stylistic hat like a magician.[16]

As Wood's imagery suggests, the novel's initial depiction of America constitutes another "sleight of *land*." It is significant that Humbert first encounters the country in a picture, too, because he repeatedly describes the American landscape as a map, painting, or model in a vain effort to control and comprehend it.

Soon after coming to America, meeting Dolores Haze, and becoming her mother's lodger, Humbert finds inside the *Young People's Encyclopedia* "a map of the States that a child's pencil had started copying out on a sheet of lightweight paper," ending with an "unfinished outline of Florida and the Gulf" (51 [pt. 1, ch. 11]). This chart anticipates Humbert and Dolores's initial road trip – forming zigzags, "wiggles," and "whorls" across the United States (154 [pt. 2, ch. 1]) – as well as their second, which she plans ahead of time, "marking laps and stops with her lipstick" (248 [pt. 2, ch. 23]). For Humbert, such peregrinations prove as ineffectual as that unfinished map, with the first journey "petering out" in a return to the East, the second interrupted by Dolores's escape, and the third – a "harrowing recapitulation" of the second – ending without him identifying her lover (154 [pt. 2, ch. 1], 252 [pt. 2, ch. 24]). Although Humbert introduces their travels by cataloging everything they encounter – reveling in the "royal fun" (146 [pt. 2, ch. 1]) and "Flaubertian intonation" of the phrase "We came to know . . ." (145 [pt. 2, ch. 1]) – he later concludes that they never knew America at all: "We had been everywhere. We had really seen nothing. And I catch myself thinking today that our long journey had only defiled with a sinuous trail of slime the lovely, trustful, dreamy, enormous country that by then, in retrospect, was no more to us than a collection of dog-eared maps, ruined tour books, old tires, and her sobs in the night" (175–76 [pt. 2, ch. 3]). Humbert also contrasts their journey with a map that *he* studied as a child, which "had 'Appalachian Mountains' boldly running from Alabama up to New Brunswick, so that the whole region they spanned – Tennessee, the Virginias, Pennsylvania, New York, Vermont, New Hampshire and Maine, appeared to my imagination as a gigantic Switzerland or even Tibet . . . That it all boiled down to a measly suburban lawn and a smoking garbage incinerator, was appalling" (209–10 [pt. 2, ch. 16]).

Comparing the American landscape to paintings proves equally ineffective. Initially, it appears to fulfill his childhood imaginings:

> By a paradox of pictorial thought, the average lowland North-American countryside had at first seemed to me something I accepted with a shock of amused recognition because of those painted oilcloths which were imported from America in the old days to be hung above washstands in Central-European nurseries, and which fascinated a drowsy child at bed time with the rustic green views they depicted. (152 [pt. 2, ch. 1])

This "paradox of pictorial thought" evokes other distorted reflections and scrambled pictures connecting separate geographies. Humbert's "shock of amused recognition," for example, echoes Nabokov's satisfaction at spotting that America-bound ship at the end of *Speak, Memory*. More important, the source of this sense of familiarity – long-ago depictions of faraway places – recalls Nabokov's description of such a painting in his own nursery (*SM*, 86 [ch. 4]). As a child, he imagined stepping onto its winding forest path, a fantasy that becomes the central motif of *Glory*. His American novels associate such pictures with escaping to America, in particular: in *Bend Sinister*, Krug arranges to purchase a painting entitled "Escape" (178 [ch. 14]); in *Pale Fire*, the king flees through a secret passage marked by the faded portrait on a closet door (121–22 [note to l. 130]).

Humbert's seeming recognition of the American landscape is misleading, however:

> the models of those elementary rusticities became stranger and stranger to the eye, the nearer I came to know them. Beyond the tilled plain, beyond the toy roofs, there would be a slow suffusion of inutile loveliness . . . and Claude Lorrain clouds inscribed remotely into misty azure with only their cumulus part conspicuous against the neutral swoon of the background. Or again, it

might be a stern El Greco horizon, pregnant with inky rain, and a passing glimpse of some mummy-necked farmer, and all around alternating strips of quick-silverish water and harsh green corn, the whole arrangement opening like a fan, somewhere in Kansas.   (*Lo*, 152–53 [pt. 2, ch. 1])

Although Humbert describes scenery in terms of European paintings – by Lorrain and El Greco, who flourished at the time of America's discovery – the comparison seems meaningless. Even as he associates the American landscape with such pictorial representation, it keeps flowing past him, remote, mercurial, and stubbornly unfolding in three dimensions rather than two.

Accordingly, Humbert next tries to comprehend it in three-dimensional terms, describing distant towns as if they were toy villages or architectural models. On their second journey – near Pisky, Dolores's birthplace, a name that suggests "pixie" – they stay in a motel room whose window reveals a road winding toward a "pretty town, which looked singularly distinct and toylike in the pure morning distance. One could make out an elf-like girl on an insect-like bicycle, and a dog, a bit too large proportionately, all as clear as those pilgrims and mules winding up wax-pale roads in old paintings" (*Lo*, 212–13 [pt. 2, ch. 16]). Although Humbert still identifies the landscape with childish imaginings and "old paintings," he now describes it in spatial terms. He no longer perceives America as a linear map or painterly composition, but as a three-dimensional scene – albeit in miniature. Upon entering the scene, however, he realizes that these perceptions are also mistaken: the elfin child is actually "a plain plump girl," the dog "a huge St. Bernard" (213 [pt. 2, ch. 16]).

This scene prefigures another description of a toy village with an enchanted name. Humbert characterizes Elphinstone, where Dolores finally escapes, as "a very cute little town. It was spread like a maquette, you know, with its neat green-wool trees and red-roofed houses . . . its model school and temple and spacious rectangular blocks" (246 [pt. 2, ch. 22]). But its miniaturization occurs in retrospect: by this point, Humbert has already located Elphinstone "on the flat floor of a seven-thousand-foot-high valley" and encountered its school, temple, and "wastelike block[s]" at full size (239, 241 [pt. 2, ch. 22]). Describing the town as "cute" and "little" implies a backward glance, as it recedes in his rear-view mirror, at the place where Dolores disappeared.

Such diminutive imagery reappears in another passage at the end of *Lolita* – one of "the subliminal co-ordinates by means of which the book is plotted" (316 ["On a Book Entitled *Lolita*"]) – when Humbert evokes, from memory, a "last mirage of wonder and hopelessness." Years earlier, after Dolores's disappearance, he had seen a town from a mountain road: "One could make out the geometry of the streets between blocks of red and gray roofs, and green puffs of trees, and a serpentine stream, and the rich, ore-like glitter of the city dump, and beyond the town, roads crisscrossing the crazy quilt of dark and pale fields" (307 [pt. 2, ch. 36]). This passage apparently provides one last glimpse of Elphinstone, with its miniature red roofs, "green-wool" trees, and roads "criss-cross[ing] drowsy rectangular shadows" (246, 241 [pt. 2, ch. 22]). Now, however, in a typical Nabokovian device, that visual memory becomes animated by sound:

> But even brighter than those quietly rejoicing colors . . . was that vapory vibration of accumulated sounds that never ceased for a moment, as it rose to the lip of granite where I stood . . . What I heard was but the melody of children at play, nothing but that, and so limpid was the air that within this vapor of blended voices, majestic and minute, remote and magically near, frank and divinely enigmatic – one could hear now and then, as if released, an almost articulate spurt of vivid laughter, or the crack of a bat, or the clatter of a toy wagon. (307–8 [pt. 2, ch. 36])

Indeed, this passage recreates one of Nabokov's own encounters with the American landscape. In his essay on the novel, he mentions "the tinkling sounds of the valley town coming up the mountain trail (on which I caught the first known female of *Lycaeides sublivens* Nabokov)" (*Lo*, 316 ["On a Book Entitled *Lolita*"]); in a letter, he describes the actual spot (outside Telluride, Colorado) in similar terms: "the town and its tin roofs and self-conscious poplars lying toylike at the flat bottom of a cul-de-sac valley . . . all you hear are the voices of children playing in the streets – delightful!" (*NWL*, 265).

The same experience of "magically near" remoteness makes Humbert realize how deeply he has wronged Dolores: "I stood listening to that musical vibration . . . and then I knew that the hopelessly poignant thing was not Lolita's absence from my side, but the absence of her voice from that concord" (*Lo*, 308 [pt. 2, ch. 36]). Haegert reads the passage as an account of America's lost innocence, too: "Worthy of comparison with Huck Finn's 'lonesome' eloquence on the river or even with Nick's imaginative reconstruction of the legendary Dutchmen at the end of *Gatsby*, [it] comprises one of [American literature's] rare aboriginal moments – usually pastoral and invariably elegiac."[17] Although this American vista – unlike the earlier unfinished maps, picturesque paintings, and toylike models – does finally come to life with sound, emotion, and temporal awareness, it reveals only how much Humbert has missed.

Nabokov's next book, *Pnin*, traces a similar journey. The hero, a naturalized citizen and visiting Russian professor at Waindell University, resides in one secondhand property after another – just as Nabokov did while writing this novel in the mid-1950s. The first chapter finds Pnin on the wrong train; the second, seeking new lodgings; the third, requesting a library volume he has already borrowed; and so on. Finally, after losing his job, Pnin returns to the American road's endless possibilities: in the last sentence, his car disappears into "the soft mist where hill after hill made beauty of distance, and where there was simply no saying what miracle might happen" (191 [ch. 7]). The novel's design is protean, too: it began as a series of stories, employs an episodic structure, and features an omniscient narrator who gradually becomes a first-person character and then "Nabokov" himself.

Despite the book's comic tone, Pnin is a poignant figure. He pictures dead friends and relatives among his audience at a lecture, and conflates scenery in an American park with wallpaper in his childhood nursery. Nevertheless, he remains hopeful: when planning to buy a house, for example, he muses "that had there been no Russian Revolution, no exodus, no expatriation in France, no naturalization in America," he might have owned a similar home in Russia (144 [ch. 6]). The novel's most striking transposition occurs, however, when another character mistakenly places New England at the same latitude as northern Russia: "Consequently the sight of a hummingbird in probing flight, or a catalpa in ample bloom, produced upon Varvara the effect of some unnatural or exotic vision. More fabulous than pictures in a bestiary were to her the tremendous porcupines . . . the elegant, eerie little skunks" (120 [ch. 5]). Like Pnin, she experiences this disjunction as a source of visionary wonder, not irreparable loss.

Since *Pnin* is both a story collection and a novel, focusing on a single chapter seems appropriate. Chapter Four, originally published in the *New Yorker* as "Victor Meets Pnin," establishes Pnin's avuncular relationship with his ex-wife's son. It begins by describing Victor's recurrent fantasy about an exiled king, which alludes to Nabokov's earlier unfinished novel, *Solus Rex*, and anticipates *Pale Fire*. Victor's daydream also reflects various adventure stories and family anecdotes about exile, thus initiating another series of displacements. Victor arrives for his visit a day late, for example. Meanwhile, Pnin buys him two gifts that backfire unexpectedly: *The Son of the Sea Wolf*, by "celebrated American writer Jack London" (100 [ch. 4]), which Victor mistakes for a Russian novel; and a soccer ball, which Pnin confuses with American football and discards after learning that Victor dislikes that sport. Despite these mishaps, however, they like each other immediately.

Victor is a fledgling artist whose formal experiments – representing objects through various media – resemble the mirror-like puddles in his daydream. He paints a car, for example, by reproducing reflections on its surfaces, "making the scenery penetrate the automobile"; and he discovers that a comb, placed upright behind a glass of water, yields "beautifully striped liquid, a zebra cocktail" (97, 99 [ch. 4]). This aesthetic culminates in the chapter's ending, which occurs after the characters retire for the night and includes Pnin's dream of being "fantastically cloaked, fleeing through great pools of ink under a cloud-barred moon from a chimerical palace," thus replicating Victor's fantasy (109 [ch. 4]). The last sentence describes a "display in the empty street" that no one sees because everyone is asleep: the "breeze wrinkl[ing] a large luminous puddle, making of the telephone wires reflected in it illegible lines of black zigzags" (110 [ch. 4]). That crumpled mirror in the American pavement – which recalls the puddles of *Bend Sinister* and "Signs and Symbols," and anticipates others that are "neon-barred" or "tinkl[ing] with Muscovy glass" in *Pale Fire* (47 [line 398], 75 [note to line 12]) – accords with Victor's earlier reflections and distortions. Indeed, his art of displacement exemplifies the novel's many transpositions in genre, structure, plot, narration, characterization, and setting.

Both sides now

After *Lolita*'s eventual success – as measured by bestseller lists and movie rights – Nabokov left American universities to devote himself to novels and butterflies. By 1961, he and his wife had settled in Montreux, Switzerland, while their son embarked on a European operatic career. From this vantage point, he depicted a new series of fantastic realms: an invented country, an imaginary planet, and various versions of America.

Pale Fire repeats Nabokov's earlier transposed geographies, but in a more stylized fashion. It juxtaposes two texts: "Pale Fire," a poem by American poet John Shade; and Charles Kinbote's commentary on it, another fantasy about an exiled king. The novel conflates two settings, as well: New Wye, the American university town where Shade and Kinbote meet; and Zembla, the "distant northern land" from which Kinbote's alter ego, King Charles the Beloved, has recently fled (98 [note to line 62]). "Pale Fire" introduces such transposed worlds in an opening couplet that encapsulates the plot of the entire novel:

> I was the shadow of the waxwing slain
> By the false azure in the windowpane.
>
> (33 [lines 1–2])

Kinbote's commentary speculates that this image "refers to a bird knocking itself out, in full flight, against the outer surface of a glass plane in which a mirrored sky . . . presents the illusion of continued space" (73 [note to lines 1–4]). Unlike most reflecting surfaces in Nabokov's American works, however – the distorted puddle in *Bend Sinister*, the "distended" planes of

Victor's car in *Pnin* (97 [ch. 4]) – the window's "feigned remoteness" forms a perfect optical illusion (*PF*, 37 [line 132]). It anticipates later instances of cosmic duplication in the poem: another windowpane, which seems to place interior objects outside in a "crystal land," and a "paperweight / Of convex glass enclosing a lagoon," which evokes the poet's ability to preserve a landscape "reproduced and glassed / In [him] as in a paperweight" (33 [line 12], 36 [lines 92–93], 115 [note to line 92]). It also anticipates Kinbote's descriptions of seemingly faraway Zembla: a "famous Glass Factory," "stained glass" windows, and endless reflections in "a really fantastic mirror, signed with a diamond by its maker" (120, 121 [note to line 130], 111 [note to line 80]).

Such crystalline imagery reinforces the remoteness and artificiality of the novel's setting. If Zembla recalls earlier realms – the nowhere of *Invitation to a Beheading*, the totalitarian state of *Bend Sinister* – America now seems invented as well, judging by locations like "Utana," "Idoming" (*PF*, 180 [note to line 286]), and "New Wye, Appalachia" (13 ["Foreword"]). More important, Kinbote's "fabulous kingdom" (85 [note to lines 47–48]) never dissolves into the author's world, as in those works, even if he does imagine appearing on another American campus disguised as "an old, happy, healthy, heterosexual Russian, a writer in exile" (300–301 [note to line 1000]). Instead, Zembla and America remain distinct yet interdependent, as do the novel's corresponding parts – poem and commentary – with each claiming precedence over the other. Each part, in fact, describes two distinct worlds. Shade's poem traces his efforts, following his daughter's death and his own near-death experience, to imagine escaping from earthly existence to an afterlife; Kinbote's commentary recounts the king's physical flight from Zembla to America. Each man tries to gain a new world without losing the old one but discovers that he can achieve such "sleight of *land*" only through Shade's poetry. It is fitting, then, that Kinbote calls "Pale Fire" a "sudden flourish of magic": Shade "put a pack of index cards into his hat – and shook out a poem" (28 ["Foreword"]).

The novel's extensive wordplay replicates that skillful conjuring trick. Consider the index, in particular. It illustrates the invented game of word golf, which gradually transforms one word into another; demonstrates Kinbote's disguised identities; and tries to hide the crown jewels within an endless circle of q.v.'s, despite another telltale entry naming a place "of difficult access and no importance . . . not in the text" (310 ["Index"]). The answer to such mysteries, Shade explains, is "not text, but texture" (63 [line 808]). Indeed, although critics have proposed various solutions to *Pale Fire*'s metafictional puzzles, its separate worlds are reducible only to the "[p]lexed artistry" of the novel as a whole (63 [line 814]).

In Nabokov's next novel, *Ada*, these intricate convolutions mutate into Van Veen's incestuous romance with Ada Veen, who seems to be a cousin or half-sibling but is actually his sister. The generic shape-shifting continues, too: Nabokov's last major novel is a family chronicle, love story, science fiction, and philosophical treatise. Meanwhile, the interconnected realms of earlier works become oddly duplicated countries, continents, and planets. *Ada* is "set in a dream America" (*SO*, 116), or, more precisely, a "tessellated protectorate still lovingly called 'Russian' Estoty," where various immigrants "enjoy a halcyon climate under our Stars and Stripes" (*Ada*, 3 [pt. 1, ch. 10]). Some locations – "New Cheshire," "Mayne" (4 [pt. 1, ch. 1]) – evoke actual cities and states, as in *Pale Fire*. However, this America exists on another planet. From the perspective of Antiterra, Earth itself seems imaginary, a "distorted glass of our distorted glebe" (18 [pt. 1, ch. 7]). Earth's geography becomes "configurations . . . solemnly purported to represent a varicolored map of Terra," and its history "a more complicated and even more preposterous discrepancy . . . in regard to time" (17, 18 [pt. 1, ch. 8]).

Such "sleight of *land*" duplicates Van's performance of card tricks, too. His prestidigitation leads, in fact, to "maniambulation," or handwalking – a form of locomotion that parallels the novel's geographical transpositions. Van even associates Terra with the upside-down realm that he navigates. When carpeting stains his palms with "peacock blotches," for example, he considers them "reflections of a richly colored nether world that he had been the first to discover" (185 [pt. 1, ch. 30]). He performs, moreover, as "Mascodagama," a "thespionym" alluding to Vasco da Gama, who first sailed from Europe to Asia (181 [pt. 1, ch. 3], 516 [pt. 3, ch. 8]). Mascodagama's acrobatic performance culminates in apparently inverting himself, then revealing that he is actually upright but was upside-down before – a "magical reversal" that brings down the house (184 [pt. 1, ch. 3]).

Van delights in handwalking because it involves standing "a metaphor on its head not for the sake of the trick's difficulty, but in order to perceive an ascending waterfall or a sunrise in reverse: a triumph, in a sense, over the ardis of time" (184–85 [pt. 1, ch. 3]). His pursuit of such spatial and temporal reversals also leads him to Terra. Van accepts Terra only as "a state of mind" – believing in its existence, after all, is a sign of insanity – but devotes his life to exploring it (264 [pt. 1, ch. 38]). As a clinician, he specializes in "terrological" psychiatry and conducts research at a "Department of Terrapy" (219 [pt. 1, ch. 35], 365 [pt. 2, ch. 5]). As a philosopher, he investigates "problems of space and time, space versus time, time-twisted space, space as time, time as space – and space breaking away from time" when death occurs (153 [pt. 1, ch. 24]). As an author, he first writes *Letters from Terra*, "a philosophical novel" about interplanetary exploration

(338 [pt. 2, ch. 2]), and then a "novella in the form of a treatise on the Texture of Time," which grades into the text of *Ada* itself (562–63 [pt. 4]).

To show how humans "build models of the past and then use them spatiologically to reify and measure Time," Van's treatise describes "a quaint old town" on one side of a Swiss river that was preserved, despite gradual modernization (544 [pt. 4]), by its "subtle reconstruction" in a replica "extrapolated onto the other side." This three-dimensional replica recalls Humbert's model villages in *Lolita*. The Swiss town's reconstruction, however, represents explicitly a temporal distance that was only implied by Humbert's last glimpse of Elphinstone. As Van explains, it cannot be placed on either side of the river but "shimmers in an imaginary space": a more conceptual version of all the distorted reflections, scrambled pictures, unfinished maps, evocative paintings, and toy models that represent transposed worlds in Nabokov's earlier novels (545 [pt. 4]).

Given Van's emphasis on such imagined places, it seems appropriate that at the end of their romance he and Ada "die, as it were, *into* the finished book," while the novel itself dissolves into a blurb praising the scenery of its "dream-bright America": "a misty view descried from marble steps; a doe at gaze in the ancestral park; and much, much more" (587, 588, 589 [pt. 5, ch. 5]). This disappearing act continues in Nabokov's last two novels, *Transparent Things* and *Look at the Harlequins!*, which explore time and space in various European and American settings on an increasingly private, remote, stylized version of Terra.

America the Nabokovian

Nabokov also transformed America itself – and not just its fictional representation – largely because of *Lolita*. He once observed: "*Lolita* is famous, not I. I am an obscure, doubly obscure, novelist with an unpronounceable name" (*SO*, 107). Almost three decades after his death, *Lolita* is more influential than ever. It has spawned two film adaptations, a Broadway musical, a play, and a host of pastiches, ranging from short pieces like Steve Martin's "Lolita at Fifty" to novel-length riffs including A. M. Homes's savage *The End of Alice*, Donald Harington's tricky *Ekaterina*, and Lee Siegel's playful *Love in a Dead Language*.[18] It has prompted countless writers to look askance at American culture – leading the way for postmodernist fiction in the 1960s and 1970s – and recently inspired similarly jaundiced storytelling in films like Todd Solondz's *Welcome to the Dollhouse* and *Happiness* or Sam Mendes's *American Beauty*.[19]

Lolita has changed the English language, too. "Nymphet" entered the lexicon almost immediately, both delighting and exasperating Nabokov:

composers of dictionary entries defining "nymphet" as "'a very young but sexually attractive girl,' without any additional comment or reference, should have their knuckles rapped," he complained (*SO*, 131). The name "Lolita" appears in dictionaries less often, but carries the same meaning and enjoys wider currency: a Google search turns up as many porn sites as textual citations. Since 1989, the *Oxford English Dictionary* has defined this word as "referring to the title of Nabokov's novel about a precocious schoolgirl seduced by a middle-aged man" and "used to designate people and situations resembling those in the book."

Although Nabokov claimed that *Lolita* was better known than he, the most ubiquitous allusion to the novel – in a rock song – identifies it by author rather than title: "Just like that old man in / That book by Nabokov."[20] Indeed, he remains a powerful presence in American culture. Nabokov influenced many writers who began publishing in the 1950s and 1960s, particularly John Updike, Thomas Pynchon, and John Hawkes. Another generation, in the 1970s, 1980s, and 1990s, acknowledged him more explicitly by imitating his lapidary style, revising his plots, and invoking him as a magisterial figure. Steven Milhauser's first novel, *Edwin Mullhouse*, pays tribute to Nabokov's fictitious biographies and his evocation of American childhood in *Lolita*.[21] Nicholson Baker's *U and I*, an account of Baker's largely imaginary association with Updike, reflects those mock biographies as well as Nabokov's influence on Updike.[22] Roberta Smoodin goes even further in *Inventing Ivanov*: she spins a tale inspired by Nabokov's relationship with an actual biographer, Andrew Field, while acknowledging his reality beyond her fiction.[23] Recently, such references have begun appearing outside serious adult literature. One of Lemony Snicket's books for children introduces a minor character, Mr. Sirin – an allusion to Nabokov's Russian pseudonym – as "a lepidopterist, a word which usually means 'a person who studies butterflies.'"[24] Neil Pollack's *Anthology of American Literature*, a collection of parodies, gently mocks Nabokov's persona in "The Pollack–Wilson Letters."[25]

Nabokov was remarkably successful at transcending contingencies of time and space to define himself as "American" – even as he redefined the meaning of that word. He often manipulates adjectives denoting nationality, placing "British" in quotation marks, for example (*BS*, 56 [ch. 4]; *Lo*, 68 [pt. 1, ch. 16]). Accordingly, his American novels sometimes describe characters' identities, gestures, clothing, or facial expressions as "American," but render that adjective in another language – creating an effect of both familiar observation and ironic distance. Thus Humbert, in *Lolita*, arrives in the United States thanks to a bequest from his "*oncle d'Amérique*" (27 [pt. 1, ch. 8]). Thus Pnin crosses his legs "*po amerikanski* (the American way)" and, when appearing in sport shirt and windbreaker at the wheel of a car, seems like "*nu pryamo amerikanets* (a veritable American)" (*Pnin*, 33 [ch. 2], 121 [ch. 5]). Pnin already is a US citizen, of course – even if others chuckle at his being "taken as an American" (37 [ch. 2]). Thus, in *Ada*, Lucette turns up the corners of "her sad mouth, *à l'Américaine*," although she too already is American, at least in Antiterran terms (382 [pt. 2, ch. 5]). Nabokov sums up his novels' ironic deployment of such adjectives with the warning, "*Ménagez vos américanismes*," which he dryly glosses as "Go easy on your Americanisms" (127 [pt. 1, ch. 20], 595 ["Notes to *Ada*"]). Accounts of his own citizenship, in interviews, make the meaning of "American" even more ambiguous: "my weight went up from my usual 140 to a monumental and cheerful 200. In consequence, I am one-third American"; "I am as American as April in Arizona"; "I feel American, and I like that feeling"; "I see myself as an American writer raised in Russia, educated in England, imbued with the culture of Western Europe" (*SO*, 27, 98, 131, 192). Deftly, he applies this seemingly straightforward adjective to a measurement of weight, a month, a location, a sensation, and even a transnational literary identity.

Nevertheless, Nabokov was an American writer – as well as an author who rewrote America on his own terms. His influence on the country's cultural landscape is exemplified by a word often found in book reviews and in academic journals devoted to his work: "Nabokovian." As the latest edition of the *Oxford English Dictionary* explains, this eponymic adjective usually denotes his artful prose: "Of or relating to Vladimir Nabokov; resembling or characteristic of his writing, esp. its ironic, witty, or erudite style." Eponymy, in fact, is a hallmark of that style. He devises numerous diminutives and sobriquets for characters even as he turns their names into nouns or adjectives – such as "Lolita," which variously designates a hurricane (*PF*, 58 [lines 679–80]), a skirt, and a town (*Ada*, 16 [pt. 1, ch. 2], 77 [pt. 1, ch. 13]), or "Pninian," which modifies Pnin's own speech, dress, habits, and tastes. Given Nabokov's mastery of such verbal conjuring, it is appropriate that his contributions to American literature ultimately transformed his own "obscure," "unpronounceable" Russian surname into a brand-new English word.

NOTES

1. Susan Elizabeth Sweeney, "The Classification of Genus *Nabokov*," *Massachusetts Studies in English* 9.3 (1984): 25–30.
2. In "The Road to *Lolita*, or the Americanization of an Emigré," *Journal of Modern Literature* 4 (1974): 3–31, Alfred Appel, Jr. examines Nabokov's early representations of American popular culture. In my essay, "'April in Arizona': Vladimir Nabokov as an American Writer," *American Literary History* 6.1 (1994):

325–35, I point out that *Lolita* and *Pnin* "portray exiles from embattled Europe who find in America a means to return to their childhood," while *Pale Fire* and *Ada* extend "the fantasy of an America that might, somehow, recapitulate [one's] own lost country" (331–32). Michael Wood, in "The American Nabokov," *Nabokovian* 38 (1997): 26–30, reads *Lolita*, *Pnin*, and *Pale Fire* as an "American trilogy": "Pnin finds a freedom that Humbert doesn't want and Kinbote couldn't recognize; and he finds it in an America of moral possibility" (30). Paul Giles, in "Virtual Eden: *Lolita*, Pornography, and the Perversions of American Studies," *Journal of American Studies* 34.1 (2000): 41–66, explains that *Lolita* and *Pnin* share "an elusive state of in-betweenness: both homely and unhomely, American and alien, sublime and abject" (54–55).

3. Aleksei Zverev, "Nabokov, Updike, and American Literature," trans. Anna K. Primrose, in *The Garland Companion to Vladimir Nabokov*, ed. Vladimir E. Alexandrov (New York: Garland, 1995), 547.

4. John Updike, "Grandmaster Nabokov," in *Assorted Prose* (New York: Knopf, 1965), 318.

5. Brian Boyd, *Vladimir Nabokov: The Russian Years* (Princeton: Princeton University Press, 1990); *Vladimir Nabokov: The American Years* (Princeton: Princeton University Press, 1991).

6. Nabokov's displacement from his homeland produces "a more intense and evocative relationship with that environment," Pifer remarks in "Nabokov's Art of Exile," in *Critical Essays on Vladimir Nabokov*, ed. Phyllis A. Roth (Boston: G. K. Hall, 1984), 220. Examining Nabokov's "double exile" – from the Soviet Union as well as Russia – Zinovy Zinik notes his "spectral co-habitation of two worlds: Russia inside the mind, and a foreign land outside, a novelistic device that follows the Cartesian dichotomy between mind and body" and initiates a new genre of émigré fiction, in "The Double Exile of Vladimir Nabokov," in *Nabokov's World*, vol. I: *The Shape of Nabokov's World*, ed. Jane Grayson, Arnold McMillin, and Priscilla Meyer (London: Palgrave, 2002), 198.

7. Michael Seidel, "Nabokov and the Aesthetics of American Exile," *Yale Review* 75.2 (1985): 233, 224, 225.

8. Giles, "Virtual Eden," 53–54.

9. Michael Wood, *The Magician's Doubts: Nabokov and the Risks of Fiction* (Princeton: Princeton University Press, 1994), 5.

10. Literally, "transposition" denotes a change in position, as in palming cards; figuratively, it describes a shift in location, transformation from one state to another, translation, alternation in established order, or way of writing differently – all meanings applicable to Nabokov's art.

11. Boyd, *American Years*, 4.

12. This argument is indebted to, but distinct from, D. Barton Johnson's account of "Nabokov's two world cosmology" in *Worlds in Regression: Some Novels of Vladimir Nabokov* (Ann Arbor: Ardis Publishers, 1985). Although Johnson notes that this ontological device "becomes increasingly prominent in the late English work," he does not link it to Nabokov's émigré, immigrant, and expatriate experiences (155).

13. In captioning a photograph, Boyd identifies the view described in the novel's opening pages with that from Nabokov's apartment (*American Years*, 226–27).

14. John Haegert, "Artist in Exile: The Americanization of Humbert Humbert," *ELH* 52.3 (1985): 777.

15. Humbert resists the country's "standardizing pressures" with his "aesthetic re-invention of America," according to Dana Brand in "The Interaction of Aestheticism and American Consumer Culture in Nabokov's *Lolita*," *Modern Language Studies* 17.2 (1987): 18, 15, and portrays it as a "kitschy, culturally debased, infinitely comic source of entertainment," David Castronovo explains in "Humbert's America," *New England Review* 23.2 (2002): 34. Zverev claims that *Lolita* revealed, for the first time, American culture's inanity – a theme that influenced later fiction but led to exaggerations of Nabokov's American-ness ("Nabokov, Updike," 541). And yet Martha Banta, in "Benjamin, Edgar, Humbert, and Jay," *Yale Review* 60 (1971): 532–49, shows that *Lolita* simply traces the corruption of an American dream (derived from both Franklin's self-made man and Poe's transcendent fantasy), just as *The Great Gatsby* does. Haegert finds these same "competing drives" represented in the novel's setting – as often happens in American literature – and calls Humbert a typical "American ethnic hero, albeit a very sorry one" ("Artist in Exile," 788, 780). Giles even speculates that *Lolita* reflects the "classic texts of American Studies that helped to invent and define the field" ("Virtual Eden," 41).

16. Wood, "American Nabokov," 26 (cf. *Lo*, 27, 26 [pt. 1, ch. 8]).

17. Haegert, "Artist in Exile," 792.

18. Steve Martin, "Lolita at Fifty," in *Pure Drivel* (New York: Hyperion, 1998), 93–99; A. M. Homes, *The End of Alice* (New York: Scribner's, 1986); Donald Harington, *Ekaterina* (New York: Harcourt Brace, 1993); Lee Siegel, *Love in a Dead Language: A Romance* (Chicago: University of Chicago Press, 1999).

19. Todd Solondz, dir., *Welcome to the Dollhouse* (Sony Pictures, 1995), and *Happiness* (Trimark, 1998); Sam Mendes, dir., *American Beauty* (Universal Studios, 1999). For Nabokov's influence on American culture, especially the literary scene of the 1960s, and his afterlife in the American popular press, see D. Barton Johnson, "Nabokov and the Sixties," and Suellen Stringer-Hye, "Vladimir Nabokov and Popular Culture," in *Discourse and Ideology in Nabokov's Prose*, ed. David H. J. Larmour (London and New York: Routledge, 2002), 139–49, 150–59.

20. Sting (pseud. Gordon Sumner), "Don't Stand So Close (to Me)," in *The Police: Zenyatta Mondatta* (A & M Records, 1980). The song's delivery indicates, how-ever, that many English speakers still mispronounce Nabokov's surname, which he advised his students to rhyme with "gawk of" (*SO*, 302).

21. Steven Milhauser, *Edwin Mullhouse: The Life and Times of an American Writer, 1943–1954, by Jeffrey Cartwright* (New York: Knopf, 1972).

22. Nicholson Baker, *U and I: A True Story* (New York: Random House, 1991).

23. Roberta Smoodin, *Inventing Ivanov* (New York: Atheneum Press, 1986).

24. Lemony Snicket (pseud. Dan Handler), *The Hostile Hospital: Book Eight in a Series of Unfortunate Events* (New York: HarperCollins, 2001), 169.

25. Neal Pollack, *The Neal Pollack Anthology of American Literature* (New York: McSweeney's Books, 2000), 95–99.

5

JOHN BURT FOSTER, JR.

Nabokov and modernism

Modernism – or as Peter Nicholls has emphasized, "modernisms"[1] – was a tangled web of international but mainly Western movements of literary innovation in the early twentieth century, especially from 1900 to 1930. Nabokov himself rarely used the term, which only came to dominate English-language criticism around 1960; and any account of his affinities with modernist attitudes in literature must begin by allowing for his resistance to all such historical labels. Sweeping generalizations about periods and styles were, after all, a stock-in-trade of Soviet literary policy as it promoted "socialist realism" from the 1930s onward. This doctrine routinely led to attacks on Nabokov's "top favorite" novelists from abroad (notably Flaubert, Joyce, Kafka, and Proust), and also resulted in the official exclusion of his own writings from Russia until Gorbachev and the glasnost of the 1980s. Even worse, these cultural policies blocked the careers and ruined the lives of many twentieth-century Russian writers, especially (for Nabokov) Osip Mandelshtam (1891–1938). This gifted poet graduated from the same progressive school in St. Petersburg that Nabokov later attended, and his death in a Siberian labor camp warned of the novelist's own probable fate had he not left for the West in 1919. Both Nabokov's intense dislike for literary "-isms" and the Soviet background for this hostility burst forth in one of his "strong opinions" of the 1960s, in which he expressed "helpless shame" at the thought of Mandelshtam having to write "under the accursed rule of those beasts" (*SO*, 58).

Ironically, despite the "accursed rule" of *this* historical term, one of socialist realism's foremost adversaries in a cold war battle of the books that lasted during Nabokov's entire career was none other than modernism. Predictably vilified in the *Great Soviet Encyclopedia* (1955) as the "designation of various decadent currents in bourgeois art and literature in the epoch of imperialism,"[2] the modernisms that Nabokov admired could be acquitted on every count in this indictment. The great modernist writers, in his eyes, resisted cultural decline, at least as found in ready-made, stereotypical brands of fiction; were uncomfortable if not downright alienated in the bourgeois societies of their time; and undermined the grandiose claims of imperial power with various linguistic and literary subversions. On this last, perhaps least obvious point, we might recall Joyce's judgment of an Englishman's English as "his language, so familiar and so foreign,"[3] the satire of Austrian imperial institutions that forms one strand in Kafka's fiction, or the harsh, quasi-dictatorial currents of feeling in Proust's salons. As a result, if modernism is taken, not in the prescriptive Soviet sense that Nabokov detested, but, more tentatively and pluralistically, as the starting point for inquiry into alternative or unacknowledged perspectives on cultural history, it can give valuable insights into the shape of his career and his place in twentieth-century literature.

Three such insights, each tied to a distinct geographical and cultural sphere familiar to Nabokov, will be explored in this chapter. First, and in most detail because it spotlights Nabokov's differences from modernism as widely understood in England and the United States (and as portrayed in the *Cambridge Companion to Modernism*[4]), I will examine the extent and significance of his rejection of English-language "high modernism." This once dominant notion of modernism was personified and canonized by Ezra Pound and T. S. Eliot; and it also included James Joyce and, more loosely, William Butler Yeats, as well as novelists like Joseph Conrad and Virginia Woolf. I will then raise the issue of Nabokov's emphatic but understudied response to what has been called a "modernism of underdevelopment" in his native Russian literature, left unstudied mainly because by Soviet lights modernism could not possibly have existed among the Russian classics. Finally, I will describe the international vision of "modernist fiction" that Nabokov adopted as a result of having lived and written in Germany, France, and Switzerland as well as England and the United States in the course of his long displacement from Russia.

Differing from Anglo-American high modernism

The term "modernism," with the sense of major, tradition-shattering cultural innovation, emerged as a word to conjure with quite late in English. It appears to have originated within the Romance languages, though not in French where, as Michel Décaudin has pointed out, at least since Baudelaire the term of choice had been "modernité."[5] Instead, the word had referred to doctrinal controversy in the Roman Catholic Church and, more narrowly, to poetry in Spanish beginning in the 1880s.[6] But just before World War I, the word began to acquire powerful implications in English thanks to Pound's success as a propagandist and impresario for "making it new." As a result, the loosely knit group of writers that had begun to make an impact during Nabokov's first period in the English-speaking world (his Cambridge years, 1919–1922) would gain canonical status by 1940, when he came to the United States, having already begun to write in English in the late 1930s. In addition to Joyce, whose *A Portrait of the Artist as a Young Man* first appeared with Pound's assistance in 1914–1915, and Eliot, about whom Pound exclaimed around the same time that "he has actually trained himself *and* modernized himself *on his own*,"[7] this constellation of modernists has often included William Butler Yeats. Yeats was almost fifty and already a well-known Anglo-Irish poet when Pound became his secretary in 1913 only to tell him, with notable cheek, that he really needed to change his style. Yeats had also been an influential, though not always uncritically admired predecessor for Joyce and Eliot.

In 1922, less than a decade after this initial coalescence of personalities, when *Ulysses* was published in February and *The Waste Land* (dedicated to Pound to credit his help in editing the poem) in the fall, "high modernism" achieved a "miracle year" to rank with Wordsworth and Coleridge's 1798 collaboration on *Lyrical Ballads*. Yet although Nabokov remained in England as a college student until June 1922, and at the time still thought of himself as a poet rather than a fiction writer, his autobiography makes it clear that he remained mainly interested in *Russian* poetry. The leading figures here were Pushkin, the late Romantic Tiutchev (*SM*, 265 [ch. 13]), and the five "B's," as Nabokov playfully once called them, who represented various symbolist and early modernist currents in Russia's so-called "Silver Age" from 1890 to 1920: Balmont, Briusov, Bely, Blok, and Bunin (*Gift*, 86 [ch. 1]). To the extent that he paid attention to the English scene, he preferred the so-called Georgian poets, like Rupert Brooke and A. E. Housman (*SM*, 265 [ch. 13]), who came right before the modernists. Much later, when interviewers canvassed his tastes, Nabokov dismissed Eliot as "not quite first-rate" and Pound as "definitely second-rate" (*SO*, 43), showing his lack of any real interest in these masters of high modernist poetry. Nor does either poet figure in *The Real Life of Sebastian Knight* (1941), Nabokov's first novel in English, even though this book consists of the fictional biography of a strikingly innovative English novelist whose career flourishes from 1925 to 1936, just after high modernism's glory years.

However, although Nabokov rarely comments on Yeats directly, *The Real Life of Sebastian Knight* does include a typically ingenious oblique tribute to the poet. Nabokov completed this novel in January 1939, at the very time that Yeats died in Roquebrune, while wintering on the Riviera. The Anglo-Russian writer-protagonist of this novel, who has grown up separated from his English mother, eventually learns that she too died in Roquebrune, but that it was "the other Roquebrune, the one in the Var" (*RLSK*, 18 [ch. 2]).

The hero, however, only discovers the mistake after a special memorial visit to the "wrong" Roquebrune, the town on the Riviera that contemporary English-language readers would have identified with Yeats. This moving yet misdirected communion with a dead parent (and also with the fictitious writer's "English connection") suggests neither full acceptance (unlike Yeats, the mother did *not* die on the Riviera) nor total denial (despite being in the wrong place, the son *did* commune with his memories). Instead, it suggests that in Yeats's case Nabokov felt an unexpected sense of affinity within difference.

For one thing, to begin with the motif of communion with the dead, Yeats's strong interests in the occult, inspired in part by Russian sources by way of Madame Blavatsky, correspond to Nabokov's more skeptical and teasingly indefinite evocations of "the other side," recently emphasized by Alexandrov and Boyd.[8] For another, though both writers are best known for their poetry and fiction respectively, they did devote a lot of time and energy to writing and rewriting their memoirs, and their fascination with life writing spills over into many novels and poems. With Nabokov, *The Real Life of Sebastian Knight* is itself a case in point, as the title makes clear. Yeats and Nabokov both diverge in this regard from the doctrines of poetic impersonality that were famously asserted, if not in fact practiced, by Eliot and Pound. On this issue Nabokov also diverges from Franz Kafka, whom he ranks second only to Joyce as a writer of twentieth-century prose (*SO*, 57). But when he specifies that Kafka's masterpiece is *Die Verwandlung* (*The Metamorphosis*), one of the few longer works published in the author's lifetime, he downplays the significance of the famous unfinished novels as well as of the many letters and diaries that have by now been accepted into the Kafka corpus. For Nabokov there is a sharp distinction between this more directly autobiographical understanding of life writing and his own preference for the memoir, which avoids the explicitly personal and confessional to focus, as Yeats also does, on careful portraits of people whom he knew as family members, close associates, or teachers. However, since these portraits are in the end self-reflexive, and thus serve to bring out some aspect of the author's own life and personality, they are at least indirectly personal, and to that extent at odds with high modernist doctrine.

As for the "English connection," the Anglo-Russian heritage of Nabokov's invented novelist chimes with Yeats's own hyphenated status. The implication is that Nabokov, writing now as an English-language author, will add to the already substantial cross-cultural impact of writers like Turgenev, Tolstoy, Dostoevsky, and Chekhov, all of whom come from a tradition outside the English mainstream on the model of Yeats's involvement with the

Celtic Revival and the Irish National Theatre. This sense of distance from an English cultural center carries over to the two writers' somewhat distanced relationship to the high modernists who were, of course, themselves not English. Here there is a generational factor that correlates with a widely shared sense of important stylistic differences: Yeats (born in 1865) and Nabokov (born in 1899) were separated by a half generation on either side from Pound, Eliot, and Joyce who were all born in the 1880s. As a result, neither of their long, fifty-year careers fits easily into accounts of modernism that take their bearings from the high modernists; Yeats is commonly held to have begun as a late Romantic or symbolist (thus paralleling several of Nabokov's "five B's" in Russian poetry), and Nabokov is often read as a pre-postmodernist alongside Borges and Beckett.

Above all, however, both writers showed their affinity-with-a-difference in the distinctive ways that they identified with the same imagery of spirals and helixes in the course of evoking a modernist sense of vanishing centers and broken continuities. Thus Yeats's much-cited image of the "widening gyre"[9] expresses more regret at the loss of a fixed cultural reference than does Nabokov's intensely personal autobiographical emblem, the "rainbow spiral in a glass marble" (SM, 152 [ch. 7]). The twists and turns, colorful variety, and smoothly rounded outer limits of this spiral inside a sphere can be understood to represent Nabokov's complex yet finally successful itinerary, despite wars and revolutions, through several distinct cultures. The sphere (to be sure) is centered, probably as an emblem of full artistic mastery; but the rainbow spiral of his life – which is in fact probably a helix – revolves around a continuously moving center whose mobility contrasts with Yeats's assumption of a fixed point of origin.

High modernist fiction – unlike its achievements in poetry – was much more congenial to Nabokov, of course, and by 1922 he clearly had some knowledge of Ulysses (SM, 272 [ch. 13]). He would eventually make a point of asserting that this novel held first place among "my greatest masterpieces of twentieth-century prose" (SO, 57). In this spirit, when he ends the searing scene of David Krug's death in Bend Sinister (1947) with a glimpse of the boy's battered body (BS, 224 [ch. 17]), he includes details that recall the moving description of Leopold Bloom's dead son Rudy at the end of the "Circe" chapter. Nonetheless, Nabokov's admiration for Joyce was neither all-inclusive nor unconditional. Thus he was not especially enthusiastic about Portrait, and in his own novel about a youthful artist (The Gift of 1937–1938, his most ambitious and finest Russian work), the hero clearly achieves a higher level of artistic and human maturity than Joyce's Stephen Dedalus. Similarly, though Nabokov shared Joyce's fascination for multilingual wordplay, he had serious doubts about Finnegans Wake.

Even his high praise for *Ulysses* left room for major reservations. Most notably, the witty parallels between the eighteen chapters in Joyce's novel and various episodes in Homer's *Odyssey*, which Eliot had saluted in 1923 as an epoch-making breakthrough in literary technique with the slogan of "the mythical method,"[10] left Nabokov cold, for reasons to be discussed in a moment. Also, despite some specimens of stream-of-consciousness writing in *Bend Sinister*, he generally avoided what he called "incomplete, broken, rapid wording" (*LL*, 289) in the manner of Leopold Bloom's interior monologues in *Ulysses*. On the other hand, he did admire Joyce's remarkable virtuosity as a stylist, which appears with increasing gusto as the book moves to its crescendo in the "Sirens" episode, with its elaborate musical effects. A similar virtuosity marks Nabokov's own career, and not just in *Lolita*, which first brought this affinity home to English-speaking readers. Consider his own willingness to "make it new" in the 1930s in the series of Russian novels that opens with the romantic glamour of *Glory*, shifts to the stripped-down simplicity of *Kamera obskura* (later translated into English as *Laughter in the Dark*), then turns to the sardonic subversions of *Despair* and the nightmarish fantasy of *Invitation to a Beheading*. Yet in these very years Nabokov is also working on *The Gift*, with its much happier evocation of developing talent. Especially Joycean in its stylistic method is *Despair*, with its exuberant parodies of the Dostoevsky crime novel (or, as Alexander Dolinin has argued, of Dostoevsky's twentieth-century Russian imitators[11]), parodies that recall Joyce's tongue-in-cheek reworkings of sentimental mass fiction in the "Nausicaa" chapter, or of nationalistic bombast in "Cyclops."

In distinguishing among the varied options for modernist fiction to be found in *Ulysses*, Nabokov saw the key issue to be the contrast between parody and myth. Even as he delighted in parody – which he could define as a "springboard for leaping into the highest region of serious emotion" (*RLSK*, 70) – he rejected the priority that Eliot's praise for *Ulysses* had given to myth, a priority reinforced by Eliot's own practice in *The Waste Land*. A similar attitude underlies Nabokov's consistently harsh rejections of *Death in Venice*, which for Thomas Mann had represented a personal breakthrough into the literary use of mythical material, one that incidentally had anticipated *Ulysses* and *The Waste Land* by a decade. Not that Nabokov himself always excluded mythical parallels from his fiction. A notable, though isolated, example appears in *The Defense* where his ungainly and unconventional chessmaster hero Luzhin, on deciding to propose to his future wife, meets a Cupid figure in the form of a pebble-shooting boy (*Def*, 114 [ch. 7]; cf. *Def* 102 [ch. 6]). Still closer to *Ulysses*, perhaps, would be the allusions to

Carmen that pepper Nabokov's writings from *Bend Sinister* onward, which, if not as systematic as Joyce's use of Homer, do exploit the resonances of a well-known story, which in this case has the status of a modern, not a classical myth.

On the whole, however, Nabokov rejected myth as a form-giving device for modern fiction. Besides its connections with Freud and psychoanalysis, to be touched on later, the mythical outlook tended to value free-floating generalities over concrete specificities. As a result, it threatened to replace individuals with stereotypes in a reductive manner of thought and perception utterly foreign to Nabokov. By contrast, parody in this context does not amount to a sterile take-off on previous writing that is essentially parasitic and unoriginal. Instead, it is a brilliant stylistic balancing-act that succeeds in giving a fresh twist and valuable new meanings to the conventional or already expressed. In short, parody is innovative; it is modernist rather than decadent. Luzhin's Cupid, after all, sets the stage for a marriage proposal that is unique in its touching oddity, while for Nabokov Carmen is reincarnated as Lolita, Hispanic not by way of Seville but of her American parents' Mexican honeymoon, and a gypsy in the special sense of wandering the American highways. In the process she does not manipulate men so much as she is exploited by Humbert Humbert and Clare Quilty, both of them "car-men" in the sense of using automobiles to advance their careers as sexual predators.

In responding to English-language high modernism, then, Nabokov favors parody, cultural multiplicity, a richly textured novelistic prose, and a guarded receptivity to life writing. He rejects the mythical method, fixed cultural centers, poetry made new in the manner of Pound, and the doctrine of authorial impersonality. He thus participates, in his own way, in the drift away from what comparatist Astradur Eysteinsson has described as the Eliotic vision of modernism that reigned between World War II and Eliot's death in 1965, the very years of Nabokov's second, American period in the English-speaking world.[12] Eysteinsson goes on to suggest that since the 1960s the decline in Eliot's centrality as both a poet and a critic was accompanied by the growing authority of certain of his contemporaries who had been closer to the disasters of central European history from 1914 to 1945, especially Kafka as creative writer and Benjamin as critic/theoretician. As an exile from both Soviet Russia and Nazi Germany, of course, Nabokov had his own direct experience of those disasters, though he has sparked no equivalent revisionary trend. However, even as Nabokov refused to accept high modernism as *the* summit of early twentieth-century literature, he repeatedly attempted to publicize a Russian alternative. This other, more diffuse expression of modernist attitudes grows out of a Russian tradition that I shall call, echoing an insight advanced two decades ago by political theorist Marshall Berman, the "modernism of underdevelopment."[13]

Responding to the Russian modernism of underdevelopment

Berman did not coin this phrase with the intent of devaluing the brilliant achievements of Russian artistic, intellectual, and scientific life in the century before the Bolshevik Revolution. On the contrary: it refers to the intensification of modernist attitudes that could result, even before the modernist period itself, from Russia's cultural situation in relation to the West. With the massive importation of Western intellectual and artistic forms into Russia, these items could create in this new environment a sense of cultural rupture that exceeded any shock from their status as innovations within Western traditions themselves, due simply to their perceived difference from Russian traditions, a situation that has since been replicated in many Third World or postcolonial settings.[14] Perhaps the most famous example of this effect is Bazarov in Turgenev's *Fathers and Sons* (1862), who personifies the Russian tendency of the time to radicalize early positivism and its enthusiasm for scientific method by giving this trend the culturally more ambitious and threatening name of nihilism. Berman's topic, however, lies elsewhere, with Peter the Great's foundation of Petersburg in 1703 to replace landlocked Moscow as Russia's capital, thus giving the nation a real window on the West. One consequence was the literature, from Pushkin through Gogol and Dostoevsky in the nineteenth century to Andrei Bely and Mandelshtam in the twentieth, that focuses on this city and its utter novelty in the Russian context. This tradition has of course been studied from many angles; Berman's originality lies in his insight that, given Russian social conditions, the Petersburg setting could itself foster an intensely modernist sensibility.

Nabokov, whose life in Russia centered on Petersburg and its nearby countryside, displays a complex attitude of acceptance and rejection toward the writers associated with this theme. Pushkin and Gogol in his view were early-nineteenth-century authors of startling originality, whom he made extraordinary efforts to explain to English readers. Though not explicitly modernist themselves, they were obviously worthy of being compared to modernist masters, to Proust's art of memory for example in Pushkin's case (*EO*, III:227–29) or to Flaubert's sardonic treatment of human mediocrity in Gogol's (*NG*, 57, 70). Andrei Bely (1880–1934) was an actual contemporary of the high modernists; and his novel *Petersburg*, which appeared in three different versions between 1912 and 1922, even used the word "modernist" in one key passage.[15] The young Nabokov had become fascinated with Bely's writings just after the Bolshevik Revolution, while he and his family were living in the Crimea in 1918,[16] and he later ranked *Petersburg* as third only to *Ulysses* and *Die Verwandlung* among twentieth-century prose masterpieces (*SO*, 57). If the name Sirin, his pseudonym as a Russian writer, came from a siren-like creature in Russian folklore and thus mainly served to express Nabokov's dedication to art, it is important to realize that it was also the name of the publishing house that brought out Bely's works as well as those of other Silver Age figures.

Among the writers associated with the Petersburg tradition, Nabokov objected only to Dostoevsky, whose affinities with the modernist temperament were widely and enthusiastically recognized by Western readers throughout the early twentieth century. Whether there remained some deeper indebtedness between the two novelists is open to debate, but one Dostoevsky work did clearly earn Nabokov's unstinting praise. That is the short novel *The Double* (1846), the youthful novelist's second work and a relative failure in its time despite his great hopes for it. In the early twentieth century, however, it became a defining example for the Russian formalist theory of parody,[17] and as a model for parody it figures in Nabokov's own parodic novel *Despair*. Thus when Hermann, the murderer turned unreliable narrator in this novel, tries to pick a title for his manuscript, he can reflect, with comical lack of insight, "What should I call my book then? 'The Double'? But Russian literature possessed one already" (*Des*, 201 [ch. 11]). Here Dostoevsky functions as Joyce's predecessor in demonstrating the importance of parody for innovative fiction, but otherwise Nabokov dissents sharply from international veneration for Dostoevsky as a pre-eminent novelist-thinker, even a prophet. Not only does he contend that the ideas are bogus – whether they are political, psychological, ethical, existential, or religious – but ideas as such, he insists in the spirit of Dostoevsky's close contemporary Flaubert, have no place in fiction. The novel, to fulfill its potential as art, needs above all to be polished in style, rigorous in structure, and vividly concrete in content. As a result, though in effect Nabokov agrees with Bakhtin on *The Double*'s key role within Dostoevsky's entire œuvre, he cannot agree with Bakhtin's basic thesis, that the double-voicedness of style that produced the parodies in this early work prepares for the "great dialogue" of multifaceted ideological debate in the major novels written following Dostoevsky's return from Siberia.[18]

Ironically, therefore, Bely's *Petersburg*, with its poetic richness of style, its hallucinatory images, and its many imaginative parodies of Pushkin, Gogol, and Dostoevsky himself (identified for English readers in Maguire's and Malmstad's notes) comes closer to the kind of longer novel that Nabokov would have liked from Dostoevsky after *The Double*. Even more telling is the fact that the encyclopedic recapitulation of the Petersburg tradition in Bely's novel also pulls Tolstoy's *Anna Karenina* into the orbit of the "modernism of underdevelopment." Thus Senator Ableukhov, one of Bely's three main characters, is a high government bureaucrat whose wife has left him and whose career has reached an impasse; he clearly updates the situation of Anna's husband, though Bely ultimately softens Tolstoy by introducing a marital reconciliation. Or, in a comic subplot, Lieutenant Likhutin manages to botch an attempt at suicide even more completely than Anna's lover Vronsky. It is intriguing as well to think of Ableukhov's son Nikolai, another main character, as a projection forward in time of Anna's abandoned son, Seriozha, who in some respects was an *alter ego* of Tolstoy himself. Nabokov had once planned to do an English translation of *Anna Karenina* (which he preferred to *War and Peace*) with the same care that he had lavished on Pushkin's *Eugene Onegin*, but these plans fell through. Still, he does agree with Bely's implied point, that some aspects of Tolstoy could be mobilized in the interests of a modernist project. By pointing out, for example, that *Anna Karenina* can rival Proust in its manipulation of time (*LL*, 220–21), that it anticipates Joyce's stream-of-consciousness technique (*LRL*, 183), and that its descriptive details can be powerfully imagistic (thus appropriating a term popularized by Pound [*LRL*, 147, 200]), Nabokov contests standard views of Tolstoy as the supreme nineteenth-century realist, and nothing more. It is worth recalling that Tolstoy lived a decade into the twentieth century (learning about his death is a key moment in Nabokov's autobiography [*SM*, 207–8 (ch. 10)]), and that Nabokov included Tolstoy in a seminar on Russian modernism at Cornell, on a rare occasion when he is known to have actually used the term.[19]

Thus, in Nabokov's response to the Russian modernism of underdevelopment, it was *not* Dostoevsky who counted most, although it was Dostoevsky who had broadcast that tradition's exacerbated sense of rupture throughout the Western world. It was Bely instead, whose exuberant will to stylistic experiment was truer to the example set by *The Double*, and who must also have appealed to Nabokov because he had a more liberal social vision than Dostoevsky. Behind Bely, however, loomed the more compelling figures of Pushkin and Tolstoy. Indeed, we might say that for Nabokov it was not Raskolnikov in *Crime and Punishment*, the ax-murderer and would-be Napoleon, who best expressed the shock of the new in classic Russian literature. It was instead the inexorable ticking of the terrorist bomb in *Petersburg*, along with its less stridently apocalyptic but artistically more polished forerunners. Consider the government clerk hounded by Peter the Great's statue in Pushkin's masterful long poem *The Bronze Horseman*; or Vronsky's restless aping of foreign fashions such as English horse-racing, Italian painting, or modern estate management; or especially Anna Karenina's fatal leap beneath the wheels of a train – a passage with such power for Nabokov that in his lectures on Russian literature he would simply quote it verbatim (*LRL*, 187–88).

Promoting international modernist fiction

Thus far, in the course of reviewing Nabokov's attitudes toward modernism in both Anglo-American and Russian contexts, we have considered his responses to Joyce and Bely, two of the four writers on his shortlist of twentieth-century masterworks. The other two are Kafka, placed second as already indicated, and Marcel Proust, whose *A la Recherche du temps perdu* (*In Search of Lost Time*) comes last. As with Kafka, here too Nabokov prefers finished work, so he singles out just the first half of Proust's seven-volume novel, due to the author's death before making final corrections on the second half. Taken together, Nabokov's four masterworks suggest a vision of international modernist fiction that replaces the miracle year of English-language high modernism with a miracle decade from 1913 to 1922, featuring authors from all four language areas in which Nabokov spent his life. The decade opens with Kafka writing *Die Verwandlung*, with Proust finding a publisher for the first volume of the *Recherche*, with Joyce still seeking one for *Portrait of the Artist*, and with Bely finishing the first version of *Petersburg*. By the decade's end, not only has *Ulysses* finally appeared in book form, though in France rather than England due to threats of censorship; so has the final third version of Bely's novel. Meanwhile Proust dies in the midst of correcting the fourth volume of the *Recherche*; and Kafka, already seriously ill with tuberculosis, drafts his never-to-be-completed *Das Schloss* (*The Castle*). Just three years later Nabokov, having turned his attention from poetry to prose, would write his first novel.

Besides separating Joyce from Eliot and Pound or substituting Bely for Dostoevsky, Nabokov's sense of international modernist fiction is polemical in three major ways. Simply as a triad of Western novelists from the British Isles, France, and Germany, "Joyce, Kafka, Proust" should be seen as a 1960s revision of an earlier modernist triad of "Joyce, Proust, Thomas Mann." In part, this shift reflects Kafka's ever-growing reputation, especially after World War II and the Holocaust, as well as Nabokov's personal literary preferences. But it also expresses his strong antipathy for Mann, whose myth-oriented *Death in Venice*, it so happens, had appeared in 1913, the same year that Kafka wrote *Die Verwandlung*. Nabokov's focus on Proust, meanwhile, does double duty. At one level it fends off the claims of several more recent French writers from the 1930s, like Sartre and Malraux, who were Nabokov's

JOHN BURT FOSTER, JR.

contemporaries but who greatly admired Dostoevsky. At another, it upholds a novelist-psychologist of memory whose views on the supreme value of art and on the role of conscious effort as well as chance inspiration in the creative process resonated strongly with Nabokov. Proust also countered the Freudian emphasis on myth, on the unconscious, and on psychosexual determinism.

Finally, as Nabokov recognized, all three writers harked back to Flaubert as the best nineteenth-century model for modernist fiction. In *Lectures on Literature*, he is careful to stress that "without Flaubert there would have been no Marcel Proust in France, no James Joyce in Ireland" (147), and later he makes a similar claim about Kafka (256). Nabokov himself shared this positive assessment of Flaubert, at one point seconding his father's opinion that *Madame Bovary* was "the unsurpassed pearl of French literature" (*SM*, 174 [ch. 9]). But Nabokov's own Flaubertian devotion to audacities in structure, style, and image includes a major loophole, for in his version of the often-attempted comparison between Flaubert's famous novel and *Anna Karenina*, Nabokov gives the last word to Tolstoy: "There is more melody in Flaubert's poem, one of the most poetical novels ever composed; there is more might in Tolstoy's great book" (*LRL*, 198). Left unspoken in this sentence, but surely implicit, is a second contention – that Pushkin's novel-in-verse *Eugene Onegin*, clearly *the* most poetic novel ever written, deserves even higher praise than *Madame Bovary*. Ironically, both Eliot and Pound were themselves great admirers of Flaubert, but what sets Nabokov's Flaubert-inflected vision of modernism apart from theirs is that neither of them, with their essentially Mediterranean sense of literary worlds outside English, would have considered further comparisons with Pushkin and Tolstoy.

Nabokov's initial contacts with Kafka and Proust, unlike those with Bely and Joyce, are hard to pin down. Given his combined major in Russian and French at Cambridge and his subsequent move to Berlin in 1922, it is conceivable that he already had some awareness of their significance before he began his own career as a novelist. However, direct allusions of a more than general nature do not appear until considerably later, to Proust in *Kamera obskura* (the 1932 predecessor of *Laughter in the Dark*) and to Kafka in "Solus Rex" (in a 1940 Russian anticipation of a more explicit reference in *Bend Sinister* [*BS*, 33–34 (ch. 3)]).[20] What Nabokov finds fascinating in Proust at this point is the possibility of an intricate interplay between fiction and autobiography, the eloquent complexity of Proustian images as they hover between descriptive precision and elaborate metaphoric implication, the ideal of artistic individualism that fosters an aesthetic cultivation of the self while avoiding the cruelty of egotism, and of course the famous

Proustian quest to recover lost time. Kafka evokes, by contrast, the primal terror of metamorphosis as regression, instead of the advance into a higher, more beautiful state of being with which Nabokov, as a passionate lepidopterist, was so familiar. The contrasting negative state results in a nightmarish dehumanization that extinguishes creativity and the very will to live, in a sinister counter-vision to Nabokov's normally more sanguine outlook. Yet it is one that certainly applies to the Germano-Slavic dictatorships that deeply affected his entire adult life, most drastically from 1917 to 1940.

The Proustian literature of memory has clear affinities with the life-writing model for fiction and poetry already noted in Nabokov and Yeats. In addition, despite the fact that Proust has been interpreted in psychoanalytical ways, from Nabokov's perspective there is a crucial difference between him and Freud. In particular, although Proust's doctrine of involuntary memory could suggest a dominance of unconscious mental processes, for Nabokov the emphasis should fall on the subsequent effort of will required to extract and develop the fortuitous spark of connection between buried past and oblivious present. It is not just the taste and smell of a madeleine pastry soaked in tea, corresponding exactly with the same sense impressions from many years before, that brings back the past with such overwhelming force in Proust. Equally important is the narrator's intense mental effort, returning again and again to those elusive impressions, that succeeds in filling out their contours so that a much more complete memory can rise to consciousness, like an anchor strenuously pulled from immense depths.[21] We should also remember in this connection that Proust's narrator's discovery of vocation depends on overcoming a debilitating sense of his own lack of willpower. On the much broader plane of the *Recherche*'s entire seven volumes, moreover, the unparalleled uniqueness, many-sidedness, and susceptibility to multiple interpretations of Proust's characters, which of course coexist with a certain effort to deduce "laws of behavior," contrast nonetheless with Freud's system-building ambitions, which from Nabokov's critical perspective effaced individuality and difference in favor of schematic generalities.

Never a slavish follower of writers whom he honored, Nabokov became especially touchy when critics likened *Invitation to a Beheading* to Kafka. The predicament of Cincinnatus C., as a hero with an initialed name who is put on trial for a mysterious crime before an all-powerful court, certainly has a Kafkaesque quality. But though Nabokov admired *Die Verwandlung* as a supreme example of pure fantasy in fiction, thus offering a telling rebuttal to literary realism, for him both Lewis Carroll and Gogol were just as crucial in driving this point home. What gave Kafka's story its unique power was the jarring contrast between its fantastic premise, a man transformed into a giant insect, and its utterly matter-of-fact treatment, with the result that "The limpidity of his style stresses the dark richness of his fantasy" (*LL*, 283). Thus, even though several nightmarish motifs in *Invitation* may recall Kafka, the stripped-down style of *Laughter in the Dark*, in concert with that novel's more realistic yet still horrific story line, could have represented for Nabokov the fruits of a more substantial Kafka lesson, one involving style as well as content.

Four masterworks, by Proust and Kafka as well as by Bely and Joyce – such is Nabokov's final, sharply focused vision of international modernist fiction. It is a vision that involves careful discriminations, ones that along with banishing writers like Mann who are *not* listed also excludes even these four authors' other, unnamed works. In the career that began soon after the decade of these prose masterpieces, Nabokov also continued to honor a certain poetic tradition. It is a tradition that will seem off-center if Pound and Eliot are the standards, one that hovers instead between symbolism and a modernist sensibility in the manner both of Silver Age Russian poetry and of Yeats. In addition, Nabokov would defend the broader sense of modernism implicit in the Russian "modernism of underdevelopment," but in his own heterodox way: he downplays Dostoevsky in favor of Bely, Tolstoy, and Pushkin. Given the cultural barriers of the cold war era, this emphasis on wider literary horizons was admirable, even if it has never taken hold to the same extent as similar efforts on behalf of figures denied recognition in the fascist and Nazi years. In the current era of "going global," what the reputation of Nabokov's Russian favorites might turn out to be, along a spectrum from "too Western" to "already postcolonial," is uncertain; but they certainly challenge ordinary time-bound and often geographically limited definitions of modernism. As for Joyce, once he had been freed from the clutches of Pound and Eliot, he could join Proust, Kafka, and Bely in guiding and reinforcing Nabokov's fifty-year quest for innovative fiction.

This was a quest that, despite Nabokov's distrust of labels, both broadens and deepens our sense of what modernism means for fiction and for literature in general. In varying proportions through the decades and across languages, Nabokov would pursue edgy stylistic experiments, especially parody, on the model of Joyce and Bely; plunge into surreal worlds of nightmarish distortion in the spirit of Kafka; and embark on a de-psychoanalyzed literature of memory and memoir in emulation of Proust. The results, to simplify a career that could shift approaches within a single work (witness *Lolita* or *Ada*), included exuberantly parodic novels like *Despair* or *Pale Fire*, harshly surreal ones like *Invitation to a Beheading* or *Bend Sinister*, and vividly detailed memory books like *The Gift* or the splendid autobiography *Speak, Memory*. In the process Nabokov steadfastly rejected the schematic generalities of "ideas" in the manner of Dostoevsky or Freud, favoring instead an artistic precision that harked back to Tolstoy and Flaubert and could do justice to its own truths of "curiosity, tenderness, kindness, ecstasy" (*Lo*, 317 ["On a Book Entitled *Lolita*"]). Accordingly, his "modernisms" amount to an international, multilingual synthesis that, even as it draws on the Anglo-American version so richly personified by Joyce, is able to look elsewhere as well. Thus Nabokov heeds Kafka's transfiguration of German expressionism and can absorb the long sweep of French "modernité" from Flaubert to Proust. But above all his innovative fiction gives much-needed attention to the neglected ferment of Russia's Silver Age and to the great originality of several of its nineteenth-century predecessors, most notably Pushkin, Gogol, and Tolstoy.

NOTES

1. Peter Nicholls, *Modernisms: A Literary Guide* (Berkeley: University of California Press, 1995).
2. *Bol'shaia Sovetskaia Entsiklopediia*, ed. B. A. Vvedenskii (n.p.: Gosudarstvennoe nauchnoe izdatel'stvo, 1955), 28:41.
3. James Joyce, *A Portrait of the Artist as a Young Man*, ed. Chester G. Anderson (New York: Viking, 1968), 189.
4. *The Cambridge Companion to Modernism*, ed. Michael Levenson (Cambridge: Cambridge University Press, 1999).
5. Michel Décaudin, "Being Modern in 1885, or, Variations on 'Modern,' 'Modernism,' 'Modernité,'" in *Modernism: Challenges and Perspectives*, ed. Monique Chefdor, Ricardo Quinones, and Albert Wachtel (Urbana and Chicago: University of Illinois Press, 1986), 25–32.
6. Matei Calinescu, *Five Faces of Modernity: Modernism, Avant-Garde, Decadence, Kitsch, Postmodernism* (Durham: Duke University Press, 1987), 69–80.
7. Ezra Pound, *Selected Letters 1907–1941*, ed. D. D. Paige (London: Faber and Faber, 1971), 40.
8. See Vladimir E. Alexandrov, *Nabokov's Otherworld* (Princeton: Princeton University Press, 1990); and Brian Boyd, *Vladimir Nabokov: The Russian Years* (Princeton: Princeton University Press, 1990) and *Vladimir Nabokov: The American Years* (Princeton: Princeton University Press, 1991).
9. From the opening line of "The Second Coming" (1920).
10. T. S. Eliot, "*Ulysses*, Order, and Myth," in *Selected Prose of T. S. Eliot*, ed. Frank Kermode (London: Faber and Faber, 1975), 178.
11. Alexander Dolinin, "Caning of Modernist Profaners: Parody in *Despair*," *Cycnos* 12.2 (1995): 43–54.
12. Astradur Eysteinsson, *The Concept of Modernism* (Ithaca: Cornell University Press, 1990).
13. See Marshall Berman, *All That is Solid Melts into Air: The Experience of Modernity* (New York: Simon and Schuster, 1982), especially "Petersburg: The Modernism of Underdevelopment," 173–286.
14. Berman, *All That is Solid*, 232.

15. Andrei Bely, *Petersburg*, trans. Robert A. Maguire and John E. Malmstad (Bloomington: Indiana University Press, 1978), 183. Compare Berman, *All That is Solid*, 266–67.
16. See Boyd, *The Russian Years*, 149–52.
17. Iurii Tynianov, "Dostoevsky and Gogol': Towards a Theory of Parody." The two halves of this essay have been translated separately, part one in *Dostoevsky and Gogol: Texts and Criticism*, ed. Priscilla Meyer and Stephen Rudy (Ann Arbor: Ardis, 1979), 101–7, and part two in *Twentieth-Century Russian Criticism*, ed. Victor Erlich (New Haven: Yale University Press, 1975), 102–16.
18. Mikhail Bakhtin, *Problems of Dostoevsky's Poetics*, ed. and trans. Caryl Emerson, intro. Wayne C. Booth (Minneapolis: University of Minnesota Press, 1984), esp. 78–100, 211–27, 237–51.
19. Brian Boyd, "Nabokov at Cornell," in *The Achievements of Vladimir Nabokov: Essays, Studies, Reminiscences*, ed. George Gibian and Stephen Jan Parker (Ithaca: Center for International Studies, Cornell University, 1984), 134.
20. For Proust, see Vladimir Nabokov, *Kamera obskura* (*Ssoch*, III:350 and 353); for Kafka, see "Solus Rex" (*Stories*, 525; *Ssoch*, V:88).
21. Marcel Proust, *Swann's Way*, trans. C. K. Scott Moncrieff and Terence Kilmartin, rev. D. J. Enright (New York: Modern Library, 1998), 61–63.

2
WORKS

6

BARRY P. SCHERR

Nabokov as poet

Nabokov's reputation rests to such a degree on his achievements as a prose writer that it is easy to overlook his entry into literature as a poet. In this regard he is reminiscent of two illustrious predecessors, Ivan Turgenev and Ivan Bunin, both of whom similarly began by writing poetry. Turgenev, though, quickly realized that his true talent was in prose and soon abandoned verse. Bunin, in contrast, was more similar to Nabokov in that he did not forsake poetry after turning to prose but continued to compose verse, albeit with decreasing frequency, throughout his career. However, as the recipient of the Pushkin Prize in 1903, Bunin had achieved some renown for his verse, while Nabokov, who expressed admiration for Bunin's poetry and was apparently influenced by it, would likely have remained a footnote in literary history had he not begun to write prose.

Nabokov's interest in poetry nonetheless figures prominently in his reputation as a major literary figure. In his translation of Pushkin's great novel in verse, *Eugene Onegin*, Nabokov purposely did not use rhyme or adhere to the iambic tetrameter of the original, asserting that to do so would mean sacrificing literal accuracy. He then attacked a rhymed and metrical translation by Walter Arndt that appeared at about the same time. The resulting intense debate over the relative merits of the two approaches continues to resonate. *Pale Fire*, among his best and most complex novels in English, begins with a 999-line poem in heroic couplets (iambic hexameter verse with each pair of lines rhyming). Bits of Russian poetry sometimes occur in his English novels; thus he inserts "Vliublennost'" ("Being in Love"), which in some ways resembles his own early love poetry, in the quasi-autobiographical *Look at the Harlequins!* (25 [pt. 1, ch. 5]), and parodies Anna Akhmatova and her imitators in *Pnin* (56 [ch. 2], 181 [ch. 7]). His last Russian novel, *The Gift*, includes more than two dozen poems or poetic fragments, most ostensibly written by the quasi-autobiographical protagonist.

Before the prose, though, there was just the poetry. In the eleventh chapter of *Speak, Memory* Nabokov describes the moment when he first experienced the poetic urge, inspired by a raindrop falling off a leaf after a storm. More of this passage, though, is devoted to outlining three traps for the beginning poet – traps which, as subsequent critics were to point out, he did not entirely avoid during the years that he attempted to mold himself into a poet. The most innocuous of these, perhaps, was the temptation to create verse lines according to a simple pattern in which Russian words seem to ease themselves comfortably and relatively effortlessly into the iambic tetrameter line: a short verb or pronoun at the beginning, a long adjective occupying the middle portion, and a short noun at the end (220–21). The result would be a perfectly good line of verse, and the critics all noted that the young Nabokov – or Sirin, the pseudonym under which he published his literary work beginning in 1921 – exhibited technical mastery and a precise if at times overly rich vocabulary.[1] However, formal brilliance alone does not make for true poetry. The second trap involves employing "pseudo-Pushkinian modulations" (224) and borrowings from numerous other poets as well, rather than developing a recognizable and different "voice" of one's own. Nor did the young Nabokov avoid a third trap, that of allowing banal and artificial feelings to substitute for genuine and original ideas: "It seems hardly worthwhile to add that, as themes go, my elegy dealt with the loss of a beloved mistress – Delia, Tamara or Lenore – whom I had never lost, never loved, never met but was all set to meet, love, lose" (225).

Such failings in a fifteen-year-old composing a first poem are hardly a cause for surprise, but his initial venture into published poetry bore the same weaknesses. Inspired by his love for Valentina Shulgina, who appears in *Speak, Memory* as Tamara and as the title character in *Mary*, he wrote poems to her regularly. In 1916 he privately published sixty-eight of these works, in a booklet simply titled *Stikhi* (*Poems*). Although one of the poems also came out in a prominent "thick journal" of the time, the collection as a whole reveals a limited and predictable range of topics. References to the night, to shadows, and stars abound; roses, lilies, chrysanthemums, and other flowers accompany the poet's love; the themes of anticipatory waiting and, especially, memory predominate.[2] Even the titles echo each other: "Osen'" ("Fall"), "Osennee" ("Fall-time"), "Osenniaia pesnia" ("A Fall Song"), "'Osennii den' ...'" ("'A fall day ...'"). The volume consists largely of immature love poetry by a young man who has read a lot of nineteenth-century Russian verse and has largely mastered its form but has little new to say. Some three decades later, in 1945, his sister Elena would rediscover the volume in a Prague library and copy out the poems for Nabokov. She found the poems "charming"; he said it was amusing to reread them, but that he had entirely forgotten them.[3] Recalling them in his autobiography, he would say that they "were juvenile stuff, quite devoid of merit and ought never to have been put on sale" (*SM*, 238 [ch. 12]). When compiling a definitive selection of his poetry (again titled *Stikhi* [*Poems*]) which appeared only posthumously, in 1979, he did not include a single work from this 1916 book.

A year later Nabokov prepared a more modest volume, *Dva puti* (*Two Paths*), with a dozen poems by himself and eight by Andrei Balashov, a schoolmate at the Tenishev School in Petrograd. One of these poems, "Dozhd' proletel" ("The Rain Has Flown"), was later republished at least twice by Nabokov (*PP*, 18–19; *Stikhi*, 7). His interest in this early work may well stem from its resemblance to that very first inspiration for a poem which he describes in *Speak, Memory*; the final lines describe a raindrop ("a pearl") falling from a leaf bent by the drop's weight. Nature figures prominently in *Two Paths*: two other poems describe the aftermath of rainstorms, as in the first collection there is a work titled "Fall," and two of the three sonnets are musings by the poet inspired by the woods. This handful of poems is largely freed from the adolescent romantic feelings that pervaded *Poems*, but there is little here which rises above the level of a neophyte's efforts.

However, this was far from the only verse that Nabokov wrote at the time. The years from 1917 through 1925 represent the period of his most intensive poetic activity, during which he wrote literally hundreds of poems. Exactly how many remains a mystery. When preparing his 1979 edition of *Poems* Nabokov reexamined the poems he wrote, rejecting many that appeared in previous volumes, but including some 170 poems that were not previously collected. Of those, forty-seven (all but a dozen of which are from 1925 or earlier) had never even been published,[4] and for copyright reasons have been omitted from all the numerous compilations of Nabokov's poetry that have come out in Russia since the time of glasnost. At least these works are known; how many may remain in his journals is an open question. Nabokov says that the thirty-nine Russian poems he included in *Poems and Problems* "represent only a small fraction – hardly more than one percent – of the steady mass of verse which I began to exude in my early youth, more than half a century ago, and continued to do so, with monstrous regularity, especially during the twenties and thirties . . ." (*PP*, 13). The 3,000 or more works implied by that statement would seem to be an exaggeration, but already in early 1918 Nabokov had composed something over 300 poems, all written since June 1916, from which he selected more than 200 for a never-realized collection; of all these works only "The Rain Has Flown" made it into the 1979 volume.[5]

Thus the earlier the verse, the more of it that Nabokov rejected in his later years. When his widow, Véra, writes in the preface to the 1979 *Poems* that the 247 works represent an "almost complete collection" of his poems, it would be more accurate to say that it is a collection of the items that he wished to have remembered. Even if the poetry found within his prose works and his translations is left aside, he still published over 500 poems in Russian along with nearly two dozen in English; fewer than half of these Russian poems are reproduced in the 1979 *Poems* – and that is not counting whatever may have remained in his journals. He preferred to forget nearly all the pre-1918 poetry, while he was to value the great majority of the verse he published from the late 1920s on, when he was coming to devote his chief attention to prose.

The poetry that falls in between those two periods – that written from the beginning of 1918 through the mid-1920s – was no longer mere *juvenilia*. The older Nabokov, however, retained a decidedly mixed feeling toward it, keeping fewer than a fourth of the poems from both *Grozd'* (*The Cluster*, 1922, containing poems largely written from mid-1921 through April of 1922) and *Gornii put'* (*The Empyrean Path*, 1923, though with poems written earlier than those in *The Cluster*, from early 1918 through mid-1921). These collections represent the first of Nabokov's post-revolutionary work, with some of it written in the Crimea, prior to his departure for England, some during his time as a student at Cambridge, and the remainder in Berlin, where his family had settled in 1920.

If the quality of these poems is mixed and the critics considered them to be mannered, weighted down by fancy words and an abundance of detail but often lacking in original ideas, they nonetheless contain the seeds of his mature manner. Both formally and thematically this work foretells what is to come, while the influences that shaped his poetic manner are clearly in evidence. In terms of his verse form, Nabokov evinces a striking conservatism. The early twentieth century was a time of great experimentation in Russian poetry, with poets developing new metrical forms, employing various kinds of approximate rather than exact rhyme, and often either creating complex new stanzas or resurrecting once popular traditional stanzaic forms (such as ottava rima, a stanza that originated in Italy and was later used by Byron in England as well as by a number of nineteenth-century poets). The iamb had long been the favored meter among Russia poets, but by the first decades of the twentieth century they were employing it in less than half their poetry, with perhaps a fifth of all their poems employing one of the newer, so-called "nonclassical" meters (those in which the number of syllables between the metrically stressed syllables is not constant, as in the anapest where two unstressed syllables separate those with stress, but varies within a certain range). Nabokov largely ignores the new trends. His first collection, the 1916 *Poems*, shows a metrical profile much like that of some poets from the late nineteenth century, with fewer iambic poems and a correspondingly large amount of ternary verse (dactyls, amphibrachs, and anapests). From 1917 through the late 1920s the choice of meters is even more conservative, with over two-thirds of his poetry iambic, a small amount (under 10 percent) in trochees, and most of the rest in ternaries. His rhymes also tend to be relatively old-fashioned, with the approximate rhyming that does occur largely clustered in a relatively small handful of texts. As for his stanzaic forms, he strongly prefers the quatrain, and among the quatrain types he favors the most standard form in Russian, with feminine rhyme (where the stressed rhyme vowel appears on the line's next-to-last syllable) and masculine (where the rhyme vowel is in the last syllable) alternating AbAb. Nabokov's traditionalist tendencies also appear among other émigré poets, for some of whom the more radical experiments in verse were associated with writers who stood to the left politically.[6]

Nabokov was prone to assert that prose and poetry differ little: "I have never been able to see any generic difference between poetry and artistic prose. As a matter of fact, I would be inclined to define a good poem of any length as a concentrate of good prose, with or without the addition of recurrent rhythm or rhyme" (SO, 44). Even if one agrees that poetry is only essentially a kind of concentrated prose, thematically at least there turn out to be significant variations between the two genres in Nabokov's œuvre. He includes in his poetry some themes not found in the prose, and, more often than not, even when the topics are similar the manner of presentation is more straightforward in the poetry, providing keys for interpreting certain motifs in the prose.

Perhaps most strikingly, the early poetry is marked by a religiosity that is generally absent from Nabokov's prose. Thus in the ten-poem cycle "Angely" ("Angels," 1918; *Stikhotvoreniia*, 134–41), the titles of the nine poems following the introductory text each correspond to one of the angelic ranks.[7] Religious visions appear in "I videl ia: stemneli neba svody . . ." ("And I saw: the vaults of heaven grew dark . . . ," 1921; *Stikhotvoreniia*, 95–96) and "Pavliny" ("Peacocks," 1921, *Stikhotvoreniia*, 154–55). Even the poem written shortly after his father's assassination, "Paskha" ("Easter," 1922; *Stikhotvoreniia*, 76) shifts from the reality of that death in the first stanza to the notion of miracle and resurrection in the second. In these instances, and others, Nabokov relies on religious texts for inspiration and makes use of Christian motifs in a more direct and open manner than in his prose. To be sure, *"potustoronnost'"* (the "other world" or the "hereafter") recurs throughout his prose work; according to his wife, this was the chief theme in Nabokov (*Stikhi*, 3). However, in the prose and some of the late poetry the notion seems linked more to the supernatural or to a metaphysical other realm rather than to Christianity. In these early, less circumspect works it is possible to see an early variant of the theme and a suggestion of its possible origins.

The notion of "two worlds" extends beyond *potustoronnost'* to other topics in Nabokov's verse; among these are the poet's distant homeland as opposed to his exile.[8] Here too there is a difference between the prose and the poetry, with the themes of nostalgia and loss more directly evident in the latter.[9] Typical in this regard is "V poezde" ("On a Train," 1921; *Stikhotvoreniia*, 83), where the narrator begins by noting "I left long ago, and a non-native evening / was glowing above the non-Russian plain" ("Ia vyekhal davno, i vecher nerodnoi / rdel nad ravninoiu nerusskoi"). The narrator falls asleep and dreams of the "suburban train stations" ("dachnye vokzaly") out of his past and briefly senses the landscape of his youth. But an instant later he realizes where he is, and "the road is black, without purpose or end" ("Doroga chernaia, bez tseli, bez kontsa"). Here and elsewhere, Nabokov juxtaposes the memory of an idyllic past that lives on in the imagination against the gloomy reality of the present. The motif of dreams or daydreams recurs throughout the poems on this topic, frequently along with the blurring of dream and reality. The topic of exile exhibits numerous variants.[10] Thus "Pesnia" ("A Song," 1923; *Stikhotvoreniia*, 276–77) simply describes the world left behind; the poem begins: "Believe it: everyone will return to the homeland" ("Ver': vernutsia na rodinu vse") and from there provides a recreation of the past. "Reka" ("A River," 1923; *Stikhotvoreniia*, 270–72), one of the more lengthy treatments of this topic, explores the complexity of what is remembered and the difficulty of conveying an image to others: "rivers, like souls, all differ" ("reki, kak dushi, vse raznye"). The memory may be clear, but words themselves are barely adequate to convey it. The titles of numerous works from this period indicate just how pervasive this topic was for Nabokov. Three individual poems as well as a set of three sonnets all bear the title "Petersburg." Three more are called "Russia," and others "To Russia." Similarly, "Homeland" ("Rodina") is the title of three poems, while some are addressed "To the Homeland." In the poetry, even more than the prose, it is possible to discern the degree to which Nabokov was haunted by his forced departure from Russia, by a sense of loss, and by an incessant desire to return to a world that was no more.

While the theme of memory frequently appears in association with Russia, he turns to it more broadly for a range of autobiographical poems both during this period and subsequently. "Detstvo" ("Childhood," 1922; *Stikhotvoreniia*, 130–34) is less concerned with the loss of Russia, though that is certainly hinted at in places, than with the recreation of the sights and experiences that he recalls from his youth. This narrative poem could be seen as an early attempt at autobiography, with its descriptions of his home, of the activities and objects that marked his typical day, and of his thoughts and dreams. An effort to recall a closer period occurs in "Krym" ("The Crimea," 1921; *Stikhotvoreniia*, 141–44), written in London less than two years after his family's evacuation from that peninsula just ahead of the advancing Bolsheviks. Employing the ten-line stanza characteristic of Russian odes from the eighteenth and early nineteenth centuries, Nabokov provides a series of distinct images, which, taken as a whole, capture the wondrous beauty of the peninsula. Unlike his poems that deal more with exile, here Nabokov concentrates on the landscape and the sense of place.

Much of "The Crimea" depicts various aspects of the natural world; nature was the topic of Nabokov's earliest poetic effort, and many of the shorter lyrics that he writes into the 1920s continue to describe specific scenes of the world around him. The seasons of the year, already a frequent subject in his first collection, now receive a more original and occasionally quite memorable treatment. For instance, "Zima" ("Winter," 1919; *Stikhotvoreniia*, 122) describes a frost-covered window that looks out into the woods, a shed to which firewood has been brought, and the crinkling of felt boots on the cold winter morning. In *The Empyrean Path* Nabokov has what amounts to an entire series of poems on trees: cypresses in one poem, birches in another, chestnuts in a third, apple trees in a fourth. Nabokov's lepidopterological interests find their reflection in poems that describe butterflies or moths. Here again the poetry tends to be more straightforward than his prose, where the references to them often tend to be metaphorical and elusive. In "Esli v'etsia moi stikh . . ." ("If my verse flutters . . .", 1918; *Stikhotvoreniia*, 101) he directly compares the efforts of a newly emergent butterfly spreading its wings to the care and precision with which he molds sounds into poetry. "Babochka" ("The Butterfly," 1921; *Stikhotvoreniia*, 160–61) bears the subtitle "Vanessa antiopa," a butterfly popularly known as the Red Admiral and mentioned on more than one occasion in Nabokov's works. Nabokov may have favored the more common iambic verse, especially iambic tetrameter, but during the period when he composed this poem he experimented several times with a meter from classical poetry, the elegiac distich, which gives a solemn tone to his glorification of this creature's beauty. His ability to turn scientific observation into poetry finds reflection in "Biology" (1921; *Stikhotvoreniia*, 167), written during his student years at Cambridge, where he describes the beauty that is found "in the science about the quivering of life." However, while the poem's narrator takes pleasure in his refined work, he also enjoys knowing that at home a volume of verse awaits him.

While Nabokov's poetry stands somewhat outside the mainstream of developments in Russian verse of the twentieth century, it reflects to some degree his reading of poets from his own era and the immediately preceding generation. His early love poems show evidence of his familiarity with the Russian Symbolists,[11] among whom he seems, at least for a while, to have been closest to Aleksandr Blok. A pair of poems in *The Cluster* were written on the occasion of Blok's death in 1921 (*Stikhotvoreniia*, 66–68). In one of these he uses some of Blok's own imagery and vocabulary to celebrate his achievement, and in the other he cites the four poets whom he sees as Blok's nineteenth-century predecessors: Pushkin, Lermontov, Tiutchev, and Fet. Other poems from this period reveal Blok's presence, including two works composed within a few weeks of each other in 1923: "Vstrecha," ("Meeting"; *Stikhotvoreniia*, 275–76), with an epilogue from Blok, and the previously cited "A Song," which borrows heavily from Blok's "Devushka pela v tserkovnom khore . . ." ("A girl was singing in the church choir . . ."). A later poem, "L'Inconnue de la Seine" (1934; *Stikhotvoreniia*, 203–04) shows the possible influence of Blok's "Neznakomka" ("The Stranger").[12] Nabokov gradually drifts away from Blok. Although this Symbolist poet also had visions of a realm beyond our own, his was simply set "above" the everyday world. Nabokov's notion of the "other world" is more complex, with this world and its counterpart mirroring each other and interacting in often unpredictable ways. Nabokov's changed attitude may also have resulted from the pro-revolutionary verse that appeared toward the very end of Blok's career; Nabokov's long unpublished poem "Dvoe" ("The Two") is a direct response and counter to "The Twelve."[13]

Ivan Bunin, a generation older than Nabokov, not only resembled the younger poet in following the path of moving from poetry to prose, but also in standing aside from the major movements of his day and in exhibiting a striking "conservativism" in his verse forms. Nabokov on more than one occasion claimed to prefer Bunin's poetry to the far better-known prose (e.g., in *SM*, 285 [ch. 14]). *The Cluster* includes an admiring poem entitled "To Ivan Bunin" ("Ivanu Buninu," 1922; *Stikhotvoreniia*, 68), and the critic Yuly Aikhenvald, in reviewing this collection, saw Nabokov as attempting to follow Bunin.[14] Since then critics have continued to see similarities with Bunin as well as with another émigré poet, Vladislav Khodasevich. In both cases, though, the relationship consists largely of Nabokov's esteem for their poetry and the tendency of all three to be closer to nineteenth-century than twentieth-century practice in the formal features of their verse.

A more complex relationship occurs with the poetry of Boris Pasternak. In a 1927 book review Nabokov unflatteringly compared Pasternak to the nineteenth-century poet Vladimir Benediktov, who in his day enjoyed enormous popularity but had since become regarded as a poet who largely pandered to popular tastes. Nabokov was later to express a strong dislike for Pasternak's *Doctor Zhivago*, and he wrote "Kakoe sdelal ia durnoe

delo" ("What Is the Evil Deed," 1959; *Stikhotvoreniia*, 227), which parodies a poem by Pasternak about his novel. Yet there were other times when
Nabokov expressed sincere admiration for Pasternak's poetry.[15] The dense
imagery and verbal play that characterize some of Nabokov's poems even
caused one critic to assert that he was the only émigré poet who both studied
Pasternak and learned from him.[16]

However, the poet to whom Nabokov felt closest may well have been
Nikolai Gumilev. He clearly admired this person who had been executed by
the Bolsheviks, seeing him as a martyr. A poem written in Gumilev's memory begins "You died proudly and serenely, you died as the Muse instructed"
("Gordo i iasno ty umer, umer, kak Muza uchila," 1923; *Stikhotvoreniia*,
261). He was equally attracted to Gumilev the poet, praising his technique:
"When reading him [Gumilev] you understand, among other things, that a
poem cannot simply be a 'construct,' a 'lyrical something,' an assortment of
chance images . . . A poem must above all be interesting."[17] On several occasions Nabokov employed distinctive titles that had been used by Gumilev,
and on others he wrote poems that were reminiscent of him in the way that
they derived from legends and knighthood.[18]

Ultimately, though, Nabokov remains very much an independent figure.
The very range of poets with whom he has been associated is telling: Blok,
Pasternak, and Gumilev were all associated with different and somewhat
opposing movements in twentieth-century poetry (Symbolism, Futurism, and
Acmeism, respectively), while both Bunin and Khodasevich harked back to
earlier eras. In some ways Nabokov's own comments on verse practice are
the most telling about his vision of poetry. "Poetu" ("To the Poet," 1918;
Stikhotvoreniia, 86), the opening poem in *The Empyrean Way*, has been
called programmatic.[19] He begins by calling on poets to "leave the marshy
swamps of mellifluous nonsense"; verse should be clear and powerful, with
precise words. He appears as well to attack some of the new, less regular
verse forms, looking instead for a purity and clarity in verse. In "Razmery"
("Meters," 1923; *Stikhotvoreniia*, 260) he describes each of the Russian
meters, while reserving pride of place for his beloved iamb. This strong
traditionalist bias continues to typify his outlook on the poetic craft.

The poetry discussed so far comes either from his early collections or
from the uncollected verse that he had written by the early 1920s. During
the mid-1920s and especially by the late 1920s he wrote less poetry. Thus
his next collection of verse did not appear until 1929; it consists of only two
dozen poems that were included in a volume of fifteen short stories entitled
Vozvrashchenie Chorba (*The Return of Chorb*). His next gap between collections was significantly larger: a collection called *Stikhotvoreniia 1929–1951*
(*Poems 1929–1951*) comes out in 1952, with just fifteen works. And finally,

Poems and Problems, the last collection to appear during Nabokov's lifetime, was published in 1970. It includes (a) thirty-nine Russian poems covering his career, from 1917 to 1967, accompanied by Nabokov's English translations; (b) fourteen poems that had been composed in English; and, (c) somewhat whimsically, eighteen chess problems (though he claims, in the introduction [*PP*, 15] that these last "demand from the composer the same virtues that characterize all worthwhile art"). Of the thirty-nine Russian poems, thirteen had not appeared in previous collections.

While the frequency of his poetry falls off sharply during the mid-1920s, he continues to write some original poetry, both in Russian and, after 1940, in English, to say nothing of his translations both into and from Russian. Nabokov never really abandons poetry; in fact, what he does write becomes ever more accomplished. Gleb Struve, author of the seminal study on Russian émigré literature, stated bluntly that "Rarely with any other poet has there been such a chasm between the early and the late period as is the case with Nabokov."[20] In part, Struve has in mind the formal features of Nabokov's poetry. If iambic meters, exact rhyme, and four-line stanzas typify his verse, then after 1923 he tends to vary his meters a little more, to "loosen" his tendency toward exact rhyme, and, in a handful of instances, to experiment with relatively unusual verse forms.[21] Struve's main point, though, is that, especially with the 1952 volume, Nabokov's poetry comes to exhibit a greater profundity and originality than it did during his early years.

In fact, the change was more evolutionary than revolutionary: the qualities evident by the 1930s and later had been prepared by the intervening poetry. The emphasis on love that dominates his earliest poems and that continues to appear into the early 1920s virtually disappears. In a 1927 review Nabokov had stated that plot was as essential to poetry as it was to prose,[22] and indeed even his lyric verse frequently displays a narrative rather than a purely descriptive quality: thus "Snovidenie" ("A Dream," 1927; *Stikhotvoreniia*, 191–92) describes the appearance of a murdered friend at a gathering, of a whispered but unheard explanation, followed by waking from the dream. An aura of mystery frequently pervades these poems, when Nabokov creates inexplicably porous borders between various realms: dream and reality, this world and the other world, past and present Russia, European exile and the Soviet Union.[23]

Equally varied and complex is the pervasive influence of Pushkin on his writing. Poems written from exile about Petersburg frequently contain references to Pushkin (see especially three works with the title "Petersburg" from 1921, 1922, and 1923); in 1924, with the sonnet "Smert' Pushkina" ("The Death of Pushkin," *Stikhotvoreniia*, 282–83) he clearly identifies with and exalts Russia's greatest poet.[24] His 882-line "Universitetskaia poema"

("A University Poem," 1927; *Stikhotvoreniia*, 310–36) pays homage to his great predecessor in a quite different way. While Pushkin's novel in verse, *Eugene Onegin*, consists of fourteen-line stanzas with the rhyme scheme AbAbCCddEffEgg, Nabokov, in a tour de force, turns that form upside down, composing stanzas with the rhyme scheme AAbCCbDDeeFgFg. He also inverts the plot. If Tatiana, the heroine of *Eugene Onegin*, who ultimately rejects the eponymous hero out of loyalty to the bonds of marriage, represents purity and a kind of feminine ideal, then Nabokov's Violeta has already had adulterous relationships while the poem's male hero has an affair with and then leaves her.[25] Nabokov's interest in Pushkin extends to his writing a conclusion for the unfinished verse drama *The Water-Nymph* (*Rusalka*, 1826–1832), which tells of a lower class woman who is seduced by a prince and is abandoned by him. She drowns herself, is turned into a water-sprite, and, at the point where Pushkin's manuscript breaks off, has sent her daughter to the riverbank to seek revenge on the prince. Nabokov's rather predictable ending has the prince submitting to his inevitable death (*Stikhotvoreniia*, 357–61). More interesting than the actual continuation was Nabokov's intention to have used it as the conclusion of a sequel to his last Russian novel, *The Gift*.[26]

That novel presents the odyssey of an émigré writer, Fyodor Godunov-Cherdyntsev, who, not unlike Nabokov, migrates from poetry to prose. Pushkin is similarly present in this novel, both as an influence on Fyodor ("Pushkin entered his blood," 98 [ch. 2]) and through the work's final lines (366), which, though written out as prose, in fact precisely follow the meter and rhyme of the Onegin stanza. The bulk of the poetry in the novel is ostensibly that of Fyodor, including some eighteen poems from his first collection of poetry, presented either in their entirety or in part. Of these, "Blagodariu tebia, otchizna . . ." ("Thank you my land . . ."), whose composition is described in some detail, has been termed the key to the novel.[27] The body of poetry is sufficiently large that it calls for its own analysis, and scholars have remarked that these poems seem to differ from the rest of Nabokov's verse in terms of their rhythm, overall structural qualities, and to some extent even thematics.[28] At the same time Nabokov claimed this poetry as part of his œuvre, selecting all the poems for his definitive collection (*Stikhi*, 1979) and referring to one of the poems in the novel "Lastochka" ("The Swallow") as his favorite among all his Russian poems (*SO*, 14). Interestingly, Fyodor, like Nabokov, is very much taken with Andrei Bely's highly idiosyncratic analysis of verse rhythm, which is said to influence Fyodor's poetic composition (150–52 [ch. 3]). Both at this time and later, in the extensive *Notes on Prosody* that were appended to the commentary accompanying his translation of *Eugene Onegin*, Nabokov referred only to Bely's interesting but outdated theories, and seemed blithely unaware of the extensive scholarship on Russian metrics.[29]

Already by 1945 Nabokov declared that his best verse, in Russian as well as in English, had been composed in America.[30] Two long poems from the early 1940s, written in Russian and later translated by him into English, stand out in particular: "Parizhskaia poema" ("The Paris Poem," 1943; *PP*, 114–25) and "Slava" ("Fame," 1942; *PP*, 102–13). In the former Nabokov reviews his Paris years, when he was in the midst of a Russian-speaking literary circle, which he terms in the poem the "Russian Parnassus." With its fragmentary narrative and disguised allusions to various figures and literary texts, the poem remains obscure for the general reader. It attracted, however, the curious attention of Nabokov's contemporaries and continues to intrigue literary sleuths. "Fame," similarly filled with frequently obscure references, consists of a dialogue between the lyrical "I" and an unnamed double. In this instance the focus is less on a specific literary milieu than on the nature of art and the uncertainty of recognition for those writing in exile.[31]

Once Nabokov had decided to write in English, he essentially stopped composing prose works in Russian, but the same was not true of poetry: he continued to dabble in Russian verse, as late as 1956 publishing a cycle of seven short poems which, taken as a whole, can be read as a commentary on his poetic art.[32] As for his English efforts, he had written several poems in that language as far back as the very beginning of the 1920s. but these were highly derivative. In 1941, he announced his (near) abandonment of Russian in "Softest of Tongues," a poem of sufficient merit to warrant publication in *The Atlantic Monthly*. After describing how he has had to say goodbye, in Russian, to many things in his life, he concludes the poem by noting: "But now thou too must go; just here we part, / softest of tongues, my true one, all my own ... / And I am left to grope for heart and art / and start anew with clumsy tools of stone." Over the next decade and a half he was to average about one poem a year in either that magazine or (more often) *The New Yorker*. The body of poetry is hardly vast, and Nabokov himself said that "they are of a lighter texture than the Russian stuff" (*PP*, 14). Granted, the English poems more often have a whimsical or sardonic tonality, but most are of more than passing interest. In "An Evening of Russian Poetry" (1945; *PP*, 158–63) a seemingly comic beginning gives way to serious comments about poetry and exile as the narrator answers questions from his American audience. In dealing with such topics as verse form and the subject matter of his poems, as well as with his sense of longing for things Russian, the narrator touches on some of the themes most central to Nabokov's Russian poetry. "The Ballad of Longwood Glen" (1957; *PP*, 177–79) tells of Art Longwood, who, on a family outing, climbs a tree and never comes down. The poem, with its rhymed couplets and wry commentary on the fate of Mrs. Longwood (who, "retouched," marries a photographer and returns to the glen with her new husband "like regular tourists"), has almost a jaunty air, but its casual mention of deaths (of the Longwood children) and its hints of the other world impart serious undertones. The abrupt removal of Art Longwood from his apparently comfortable and ordinary life into another realm raises questions that leave the reader pondering. Nabokov is not alone in regarding the poem as among his best achievements in English verse.[33]

Nabokov uses his English poetry as well for comments on translation. Thus in "On Translating 'Eugene Onegin'" (1955; *PP*, 175) he somewhat perversely composes a pair of Onegin stanzas, which follow precisely the meter and rhyme scheme employed by Pushkin, to explain that he essentially ignores both those features in his translation of *Eugene Onegin*. In 1952 Nabokov composed "Rimes," a rhymed poem that similarly describes how "The incorruptible translator / Is betrayed by lady rime."[34] Nonetheless, when Nabokov set out to translate poems by Pushkin, Lermontov, Tiutchev, Fet, and Khodasevich in the 1940s, he tried to follow both rhyme and meter precisely; his notions about concentrating on meaning rather than form took hold only after those efforts. The translations of his own poetry (in *Poems and Problems*, 1970) came after his work on *Onegin* and follow the same principle he developed for translating Pushkin's novel – sense and syntax are conveyed faithfully, while rhyme and meter appear only in isolated lines, when they happen to arise without distorting meaning. In contrast, for Nabokov's translations into Russian, where rhyme provides far less of a barrier than is the case with English, he tends to follow the form of the original quite closely. Among the handful of translations from English are the poetic passages in *Lolita* (for the Russian edition of that novel), and sonnets 17 and 27 by Shakespeare, along with some excerpts from *Hamlet*. He also translated the dedication to Goethe's *Faust* and several French poems.

Most would agree that if Nabokov's creative output consisted only of his poetry, he would hardly have become a famous writer. His verse was not widely discussed beyond reviews of his collections until the early 1990s, though since then it has received at least its share of critical attention.[35] Some voices continue to remind us that Nabokov's earlier poetry was uneven at best, with many lines and stanzas in even the better-known poems less than sparkling; it is not unusual for his prose to be cited as more poetic and more resourceful than his verse.[36] As many of his earliest reviewers noted, the formal virtuosity of his early poems was often mannered and not matched by an originality in his voice or his ideas. And yet, from the mid-1920s on, particularly as he turned to poetry with a stronger narrative structure, he was able to provide scope for his wit, his inventiveness, and his gift for parody. His poems come to read like miniature versions of his prose works, exploring many of the topics and even employing many of the same techniques. The best of his mature poetry, whether the Russian "The Paris Poem," or the English "Ballad of Longwood Glen," can stand on its own as a secondary yet notable achievement that enhances his reputation for verbal artistry and thematic creativity.

NOTES

1. For a survey of reactions to Nabokov's poetry, see Paul D. Morris, "Vladimir Nabokov's Poetry in Russian Emigré Criticism: A Partial Survey," *Canadian Slavonic Papers* 40.3–4 (1998): 297–310.
2. M. E. Malikova, "Zabytyi poet," in V. V. Nabokov, *Stikhotvoreniia*, (Novaia biblioteka poeta), (St. Petersburg: Akademicheskii proekt, 2002), 8–9. Hereafter cited as *Stikhotvoreniia* in the text.
3. Vladimir Nabokov, *Perepiska s sestroi* (Ann Arbor: Ardis, 1985), 10, 27.
4. D. Barton Johnson, "Preliminary Notes on Nabokov's Russian Poetry: A Chronological and Thematic Sketch," *Russian Literature Triquarterly* 24 (1991): 314–15.
5. Brian Boyd, *Vladimir Nabokov: The Russian Years* (Princeton: Princeton University Press, 1990), 142.
6. Gerald S. Smith, "Nabokov and Russian Verse Form," *Russian Literature Triquarterly* 24 (1991): 305. See the earlier portions of this article (271–305) for the comparative analysis on which my comments are based.
7. On this cycle, see N. I. Tolstaia, "'Sputnik iasnokrylyi'," *Russkaia literatura* 35.1 (1992): 188–92.
8. Julian Connolly, "The Otherworldly in Nabokov's Poetry," *Russian Literature Triquarterly* 24 (1991): 330.
9. Laurent Rabaté, "La Poésie de la Tradition: Etude du Recueil *Stixi* de V. Nabokov," *Revue des Etudes slaves* 57.3 (1985): 401.
10. For an extensive discussion of this topic, see Iurii I. Levin, "Bispatsial'nost' kak invariant poeticheskogo mira V. Nabokova," *Russian Literature* 28.1 (1990): 45–56.
11. György Zoltán Józsa, "Zametki k istokam nekotorykh motivov rannei liriki V. V. Nabokova," *Studia Slavica Academiae Scientiarum Hungaricae (SSASH)* 42.1–2 (1997): 1–2, 179–86.
12. D. Barton Johnson, "'L'Inconnue de la Seine' and Nabokov's Naiads," *Comparative Literature* 44.3 (1992): 232.
13. Boyd, *Russian Years*, 156–57.
14. *Rul'*, January 28, 1923, 13. The review was signed "B. K."

15. Robert P. Hughes, "Nabokov Reading Pasternak," in *Boris Pasternak and His Times: Selected Papers from the Second International Symposium on Pasternak*, ed. Lazar Fleishman (Berkeley: Berkeley Slavic Specialties, 1989), 154–56.
16. Georgij Adamovich, "Vladimir Nabokov," *Twentieth-Century Russian Literary Criticism*, ed. Victor Erlich (New Haven: Yale University Press, 1975), 227–30.
17. *Rul'*, May 11, 1927, 4.
18. E. P. Chudinova, "Poeziia Vladimira Nabokova," *Russkaia rech'* 24.3 (1990): 28–29.
19. See, for instance, Vsevolod Setschkareff, "Zur Thematik der Dichtung Vladimir Nabokovs (aus Anlass des Erscheinens seiner gesammelten Gedichte)," *Die Welt der Slaven* 25.1 (1980): 82.
20. Gleb Struve, *Russkaia literatura v izgnanii*, (New York: Chekhov Publishing House, 1956), 165.
21. On the range of his verse forms, see Thomas Eekman, "Vladimir Nabokov's Poetry," in *The Language and Verse of Russia: In Honor of Dean S. Worth on his Sixty-Fifth Birthday*, ed. Henrik Birnbaum and Michael S. Flier (Moscow: Vostochnaia literatura, 1995), 88–100. See as well Smith, "Nabokov and Russian Verse Form."
22. *Rul'*, August 31, 1927, 4.
23. Levin, "Bispatsial'nost'," 46–48.
24. S. Pol'skaia, "Sonet V. Nabokova 'Smert' Pushkina'," in *A. S. Pushkin i V. V. Nabokov: Sbornik dokladov nauchnoi konferentsii 15–18 aprelia 1999 g.*, ed. V. P. Stark (St. Petersburg: Dorn, 1999), 10–19.
25. A. A. Babikov, "Motivy 'Evgeniia Onegina' v 'Universitetskoi poeme' V. V. Nabokova," in Stark, *A. S. Pushkin i V. V. Nabokov: Sbornik dokladov*, 269.
26. Jane Grayson, "Rusalka and the Person from Porlock," in *Symbolism and After: Essays on Russian Poetry in Honour of Georgette Donchin*, ed. Arnold McMillin (Worcester, England: Bristol Classical Press, 1992), 162–85.
27. A. A. Dolinin, "Tri zametki o romane Vladimira Nabokova 'Dar'," in *Nabokov: Pro et Contra*, comp. B. Averin, M. Malikova, and A. Dolinin (St. Petersburg: Russkii Khristianskii gumanitarnyi institut, 1997), 697–710.
28. Smith, "Nabokov and Russian Verse Form," 286–90; M. Iu. Lotman, "A ta zvezda nad Pulkovym . . . : Zametki o poezii i stikhoslozhenii V. Nabokova," in *V. V. Nabokov: Pro et Contra*, vol. II, comp. B. V. Averin (St. Petersburg: Russkii Khristianskii gumanitarnyi institut, 2001), 219–21.
29. G. S. Smith, "*Notes on Prosody*," in *The Garland Companion to Vladimir Nabokov*, ed. Vladimir E. Alexandrov (New York: Garland, 1995), 561–66.
30. Nabokov, *Perepiska s sestroi*, 18.
31. For explications of both poems, see Andrew Field, *Nabokov: His Life in Art* (Boston: Little, Brown, and Co., 1967), 90–96.
32. Michael Meylac, "Intertextuality and (Meta)poesis: Some Enigmas of Nabokov's 'Seven Poems'," in *Nabokov's World*, vol. II: *Reading Nabokov*, ed. Jane Grayson, Arnold McMillin, and Priscilla Meyer (Basingstoke: Palgrave, 2002), 40–58.
33. Brian Boyd, *Vladimir Nabokov: The American Years* (Princeton: Princeton University Press, 1991), 303–5.
34. The poem is published in Malikova, "Zabytyi poet," 41–42.

35. A set of articles in *Russian Literature Triquarterly* (which included Smith, "Nabokov and Russian Verse Form"; Johnson, "Preliminary Notes on Nabokov's Russian Poetry"; and Connolly, "The Otherworldly in Nabokov's Poetry") helped bring Nabokov's poetry to wider attention. General studies of his poetry since then include Barry Scherr, "Poetry," in Alexandrov, *Garland Companion*, 608–25; Eekman, "Vladimir Nabokov's Poetry," and Malikova, "Zabytyi poet."
36. See for instance, Larisa Miller, "I drugoe, drugoe, drugoe . . . ," *Voprosy literatury* 39.6 (1995): 86–102.

7

PRISCILLA MEYER

Nabokov's short fiction

The first comprehensive collection of Nabokov's short fiction, containing sixty-five stories, was published eighteen years after his death. Nabokov had written the first fifty-five in Russian and later, together with his son Dmitri, translated them into English; he wrote the remaining ten in English after emigrating to America in 1940. Dmitri Nabokov compiled the 1995 volume from the four definitive English collections of thirteen stories each that appeared during his father's lifetime, *Nabokov's Dozen*, *A Russian Beauty and Other Stories*, *Tyrants Destroyed and Other Stories*, and *Details of a Sunset and Other Stories*, adding thirteen more, eleven of which had never before been translated into English. The unexpected discovery of an early story, "Easter Rain," raised the total number of stories in the 1997 Vintage edition to sixty-six.

Nabokov wrote his first story, "The Wood-Sprite," in 1921, when he was an undergraduate at Trinity College, Cambridge, and his last, "Lance," in 1951, when he was teaching literature at Cornell. During that period Nabokov was an émigré writer in Berlin and Paris, a lepidopterist at Harvard's Museum of Comparative Zoology, and a professor of literature, first at Wellesley and later at Cornell. He composed nine novels in Russian; the first novel he wrote in English was *The Real Life of Sebastian Knight* (1941), and his greatest American novels were written after he abandoned the short story. *Lolita* (1955), *Pnin* (1957), *Pale Fire* (1962), and the Russian version of his memoir, *Drugie berega* (1954), that became *Speak, Memory* (1966) in its final English incarnation, appeared in the following decade.

Nabokov called the short story a "small Alpine form" of the novel; while the stories have greater unity of time and action than the longer works, the same themes and methods appear in both genres, reflecting the eras of his life through the prism of his art.

The Nabokov family had to flee Bolshevik Russia in 1919, leaving behind the family house in Petersburg as well as their beloved Vyra estate that is the setting for Nabokov's earliest memories – of his parents, of the birth of his passion for butterflies, of his first love and first poem, as described in *Speak, Memory*. The loss of his perfect childhood, his country and his Russian language was made even more agonizing when Nabokov's father was killed trying to shield his friend Pavel Miliukov from an assassin's bullet on March 28, 1922 at a lecture in Berlin. In the stories written and published in émigré journals during his early years in Berlin, Nabokov tries to turn that intense pain into art.

Russia

The earliest stories are variations on the theme of the loss of Russia. In "The Wood-Sprite" ("Nezhit'," 1921) a figure from Russian mythology is forced into emigration because his forest is being cut down. The sprite comes to the writer of the story and reminds him of the "endless, irreplaceable happiness" they had romping together in the "old country."[1] "It is we, Rus', who were your inspiration, your unfathomable beauty, your agelong enchantment!" (5), the Sprite exclaims. The Russian for wood-sprite is "Leshii"; in his Russian novel *The Gift* (1937–1938), Nabokov names the hero's Vyra-like family estate "Leshino" – the loss of the enchantment of the estate's natural universe and attendant spirits, the *leshii* and the *rusalka* ("water-nymph"), is a recurring theme in his work. The ancient folk spirits connect the Russian natural universe and Nabokov's childhood experience of it to magic, enchantment, and the otherworld. These associations characterize the femme fatale Nina Rechnoi (meaning "of the river") in *The Real Life of Sebastian Knight* who draws the writer hero back from his English world to his native Russian element at his death.

But Nabokov sees the danger of giving in to the constant longing for Russia. In "Russian Spoken Here" (1923), a family of émigrés in Berlin captures a Soviet police spy from the GPU (the earlier name of the KGB) in their apartment and decides to keep him locked in their bathroom. Their desire for revenge on the Communists who have turned their country into a prison turns them into prison wardens themselves, obsessed with their captive for the foreseeable future. In "Razor" (1926) another Russian émigré in Berlin wreaks revenge on the officer who had once ordered his execution during the Civil War by terrorizing him in his barber chair. For a moment Razor himself almost becomes an executioner but is content to have caused the officer the same anguish of a death sentence that he himself experienced.

This constant preoccupation with Russia eclipses one's vision of the world. In "The Seaport" (1924), émigrés living in a town in southern France exist in their own Russian cocoon, and the hero mistakes a French prostitute for a Russian woman he knows, addressing her in the wrong language. In

"Easter Rain" (1925), Josephine, a Swiss governess (drawn from Nabokov's own, whose portrait he drew in "Mademoiselle O,") who has worked for twelve years in Russia, dyes eggs and, although she is coming down with pneumonia, brings them to some émigré acquaintances on Russian Easter. They are only irritated by her sentimentality and unwilling to share their private loss with her; yet she too lives in a lost Russian past and is almost absorbed into the otherworld by her fever. In her delirium she imagines that the statue of Peter the Great leaps off his bronze steed (as he does in Pushkin's *Bronze Horseman* and Andrei Bely's *Petersburg*) and kisses her three times in the Russian fashion. When she returns to consciousness at the end of the story, she sees her caretaker on the floor, retrieving the ball of black yarn that has rolled under the chest of drawers. The image of the ball rolling into and out of a confined space becomes an emblem of human existence, first entering the world we know from the otherworld and then returning to that otherworld. In the later novel, *The Gift*, the hero's set of poems is framed by "The Lost Ball" and "The Found Ball"; in *Invitation to a Beheading* (1935–1936) a ball rolls into, around, and then, improbably, out the door of the hero's prison cell. Josephine's illness has temporarily taken her out of human existence, but returns her to life. Awakening to a beautiful spring rainfall to find her caretaker squirming on the floor under the chest of drawers, Josephine "broke out in peals of laughter . . . feeling that she was resurrected, that she had returned from faraway mists of happiness, wonder and Easter splendor" (648). She has returned refreshed and restored from a dream Russia where she cannot read the "wondrous news" in a dream newspaper, to life in her homeland, after a six-day visit to the Russian edition of the otherworld.

By 1926 Nabokov began to let go of the theme of the émigré's obsession with a lost Russia but returned to it in a richer treatment years later in "The Visit to the Museum" (1939). The tale begins realistically and gradually becomes surreal; the hero of the story goes into a provincial museum in southern France in search of the portrait of his friend's grandfather and, lost among the exhibits, takes a surreal journey through history that becomes increasingly terrifying as he "escape[s] from the museum's maze" (284) into post-Revolutionary Petersburg, by then Leningrad: "Alas, it was not the Russia I remembered, but the factual Russia of today, forbidden to me, hopelessly slavish, and hopelessly my own native land" (285). The fantasy of return to Russia, accompanied by the fear of the real consequences for an émigré (who might not be able to get out again), haunts Nabokov's art and takes on the significance of a journey to the otherworld. The hero of "The Visit to the Museum" sees himself as a "semiphantom in a light, foreign suit . . . desperate to protect my fragile, illegal life" and incapable of shedding his "integument of exile" (285). For the émigré, a return to Russia can take place only in fantasy or in the otherworld; in Nabokov's art the two spaces overlap and death can be envisioned in terms of a return to Russianness, as it is for Sebastian in the novel written at the same time, *The Real Life of Sebastian Knight*.

In his progress through the museum, the hero of "The Visit to the Museum" goes through a long passage and enters a room full of musical instruments, in the center of which stands "a bronze Orpheus" (283). The Orpheus myth is an important emblem of Nabokov's experience. Orpheus was the greatest musician and poet in Greek legend. Apollo gave him a lyre and the Muses taught him to play it so beautifully that he could make the trees dance, tame wild beasts, soothe quarrels, and drown out the songs of the Sirens. He marries Eurydice, who dies when, walking in a meadow, she steps on a viper. Orpheus descends to the Underworld to bring her back, and charms Charon so that he ferries him across the Styx. Hades agrees to let Eurydice return on condition that Orpheus not look back at her until she reaches the light of the sun. She follows him, guided by his music, but he looks back before she has reached the sunlight and so loses her forever. In "The Visit to the Museum," the hero is returning to the Underworld in returning to Russia; by the end of the tale he has managed to escape the Soviet version of it, but not to bring back anyone or thing that he had loved there.

Orpheus

In the earlier "The Return of Chorb" (1925), Nabokov had used the Orpheus myth to structure the entire tale. Chorb's wife dies on their honeymoon in the south of France when she touches "the live wire of a storm-felled pole," the "impact of an electric stream" playing the role of the viper that kills Eurydice (148). Chorb thought that "if he managed to gather all the little things they had noticed together – if he re-created thus the near past – her image would grow immortal and replace her forever" (140). He retraces their journey from southern France back to the room in a disreputable hotel in Berlin where they had spent a chaste wedding night. "Thus Chorb traveled back to the very source of his recollections, an agonizing yet blissful test now drawing to a close. All there remained was but a single night to be spent in that first chamber of their marriage, and by tomorrow the test would be passed and her image made perfect" (152). To relive that first night, Chorb requires a stand-in for his wife and hires a prostitute to play the role. He brings her to the hotel room and immediately goes to sleep. She looks out the window at a statue of "a stone Orpheus" and then also goes to sleep.

"Her sleep lasted not more than an hour: a ghastly drawn-out howl roused her. It was Chorb screaming. He had woken up sometime after midnight, had turned on his side, and had seen his wife lying beside him. He screamed horribly, with visceral force. The white specter of a woman sprang out of bed . . . the ordeal was over" (153). Chorb has succeeded in leading his wife's spirit back from the moment of her physical death to the beginning of their wedded life, succeeding where Orpheus failed because Chorb is not concerned with his wife's mortal aspect. The story parodies mortal existence in the form of the prostitute whose province is only physical love, as well as in the description of the mundane vulgarity of Chorb's wife's parents, the Kellers, from whose offensive household the couple ran away on their wedding night. The Kellers appear as the prostitute runs out of the room and Chorb, sitting on a couch smiling a "meaningless smile," is confronted with the irrelevant demands of mortal life. The parents will be devastated when they learn of their daughter's death, but Chorb has immortalized her spirit and can commune with it in the otherworld.

Nabokov juxtaposes the "real" world to an otherworld throughout his work, rendering mortal life in various forms, as theater, as a house or prison from whose windows one can just glimpse the otherworld. The mortal world, associated with motifs of bodily life, like ham, furniture, teeth, is a parody of the unknowable but infinitely beautiful otherworld that lies just at the limit of our ken. Through art one can gain some intuition of that world, and Nabokov identifies with Orpheus in attempting to traverse the boundary between the two realms. Chorb screams when he reaches that boundary; his "meaningless smile" may mean either that he is now at peace or that the experience has rendered him mad, or both.

Nabokov's early stories depict the loss of a beloved, either of a wife or a son, transformations of his own loss in which he finds relief through the pleasure of his artistic vision. In the early "Gods" (1923), a man is able to bear the loss of his infant son because he believes the son can hear his fable. "Words have no borders" (49). Words can reach the otherworld in the form of immortal art. While his wife goes to the cemetery, he waits in a vacant lot: "At my feet, a squashed tin glints rustily inside a funnel of sand . . . There is no death. The wind comes tumbling upon me from behind like a limp doll and tickles my neck with its downy paw. There can be no death . . . You and I shall have a new, golden son, a creation of your tears and my fables" (50).

For Nabokov the Orpheus myth unites the quest for the lost land and dead beloved with the idea that both can be reached through art. In the novel *Pale Fire* Nabokov's theme of the quest for knowledge of the next world through art reaches its ideal state; the mad scholar Kinbote, who imagines he is the incognito King of Zembla, asks the poet John Shade to recreate his lost kingdom in his poetry, to translate it into art. In 1939 Nabokov began writing what was to have been a novel, *Solus Rex*, but finished only two chapters of it, published as the stories "Ultima Thule" (originally chapter one) and "Solus Rex" (which would have been chapter two) that contain the elements of *Pale Fire* in an early stage of evolution. The two chapters/stories are the intermediate stage of the development of the ideas in "The Return of Chorb" into their brilliant realization in *Pale Fire*. *Ultima Thule* was the Greek name of the northernmost point of the known world. In that story, Sineusov's wife has died, and he hopes to make contact with her in the otherworld, emblematized by *Ultima Thule*. The story is couched as his letter to her, written in the hope that consciousness survives bodily death. He tells her that one night in his hotel room on the Riviera, his former tutor, Adam Falter, somehow suddenly solved the riddle of life and death, and began to scream "like a woman in the throes of infinitely painful childbirth" (506). When Falter confides his knowledge to his psychiatrist, it causes the doctor to die of a heart attack. Sineusov tries to get Falter to tell him the "essence of things" that has been revealed to him, and Falter refuses. But Sineusov has told us that when his wife was dying, too weak to speak, she had written on a slate the things she loved most in life: "verse, wildflowers, and foreign currency" (510), and during their conversation, Falter slips in these words, speaking of "the poetry of a wildflower or the power of money" (515), and explaining "I act like a beggar, a versifier, who has received a million in foreign currency" (516). The story affirms the possibility of communication with the spirit of a beloved across the divide between life and death, the boundary Chorb and Falter attain around midnight in their hotel rooms. Falter denies Sineusov this access, so he is forced to resort to his art.

A "Swede, Dane – or Icelander" has commissioned Sineusov to illustrate his epic poem, *Ultima Thule*, written in a language unintelligible to him, about the political intrigues of some Northern king whose kingdom is on a remote island. Although the poet has never returned, and has left for America, Sineusov explains to his dead wife that he continues to illustrate the epic, hoping that "its spectral, intangible nature, the lack of aim or reward would lead me away to a realm akin to the one in which, for me, you exist, my ghostly goal" (511). "Solus Rex" is the tale of that distant Northern land, where Sineusov has become king in order to be reunited with his wife, now become Queen Belinda. Ultima Thule, like Charles Kinbote's Zembla in *Pale Fire*, is at once kingdom, fantasy, and artistic creation, a parodic version of an otherworld that can bring solace to the bereft. In John Shade's poem "Pale Fire," Shade finds some "faint hope" that he may find his daughter Hazel in an otherworld, while his neighbor Kinbote hopes to find his own lost otherworld, Zembla, immortalized in Shade's poem.

Variations on the fate of the poet

In his stories, Nabokov considers variations on the themes of the fate of the émigré, the artist, the bereft mate or parent, the lepidopterist. As an experiment, an exercise in gratitude, he bestows one of his own blessings on an otherwise limited character. In "The Aurelian" (1930) the elderly German shopkeeper Pilgram, a *wurst* and potatoes man, is, contrary to type, a dreamer with a secret passion for butterflies. Like Nabokov, he became infatuated with butterflies as a boy, but unlike Nabokov, he is "churlish," unkind to his wife, and "ignorant of the world" (250). Mentally, Pilgram visits the great lepidopteral sites and longs to travel. His chance finally comes when a rich amateur collector pays him 950 marks for a rare specimen that Pilgram has on commission from a lepidopterist's widow. Pilgram gives her 50 marks, buys a ticket to Spain, and leaves his wife a note: "*Off to Spain . . . Feed the lizards.*" But he stops in his shop to pick up some change, where "eyed wings stared at him from all the sides, and Pilgram perceived something almost appalling in the huge happiness that was leaning toward him like a mountain" (257). He drops his money pot, and dies of a heart attack when he stoops to pick up the coins. "Yes, Pilgram had gone far, very far. Most probably he visited Granada and Murcia and Albarracin, and then traveled further to Surinam and Taprobane . . . So, in a certain sense, it is quite irrelevant that some time later . . . Eleanor saw . . . her husband, sprawling on the floor with his back to the counter, among scattered coins, his livid face knocked out of shape by death" (258). Even an unkind mundane chiseler can be a passionate lepidopterist and achieve his dream in the world of the imagination that grades immediately (in his case) into the otherworld, leaving his mortal remains on the floor of his little shop.

A similar thematic principle obtains in "Torpid Smoke" (1935). An unappealing nineteen-year-old Russian émigré in Berlin, Grisha, shares Nabokov's passion for reading and writing Russian poetry and has one of Nabokov's novels, *The Defense*, on his shelf along with Gumilev's and Pasternak's verse. Unlike Nabokov, he lives with his unaffectionate, lackluster family; his mother is dead and his father has made him study political economy. Grisha goes to his father in the dining room to ask for cigarettes; the event of the story is Grisha's sudden realization that this sad moment of failed communication will become not only a painful memory but part of his creative process: "With terrifying clarity, as if my soul were lit up by a noiseless explosion, I glimpsed a future recollection; it dawned upon me that exactly as I recalled such images of the past as the way my dead mother had of making a weepy face . . . when mealtime squabbles became too loud, so one day I would have to recall, with merciless, irreparable sharpness, the hurt look of my father's shoulders as he leaned over . . . morose, wearing his warm indoor jacket powdered with ashes and dandruff; and all this mingled creatively with the recent vision of blue smoke clinging to dead leaves on a wet roof" (400). And Grisha returns to lie on his couch in his room, enlivened by the arrival of a new metrical line involving "a farther 'shore'" and classic northern chill, knowing that he is writing "puerile, perishable poems," but no matter, "I trust the ravishing promises of the still breathing, still revolving verse, my face is wet with tears, my heart is bursting with happiness, and I know that this happiness is the greatest thing existing on earth" (400). Despite the unhappy circumstances of family and exile, Grisha's art infuses him with joy. In the dining-room scene the narration moves from third person to first person: the duality of narrative voice conveys both Grisha's experience and his story about the experience, as it does in Nabokov's later novel, *The Gift*. He feels dissociation from his physical self in the beginning of the story: "He perceived himself (the pince-nez, the thin, dark mustache, the bad skin on the forehead) with that utter revulsion he always experienced on coming back to his body out of the languorous mist" (398). By the end of the story the feeling is put to creative use. Even such an unattractive character as Grisha may experience the bliss of artistic creation. The hero of *The Gift*, Fyodor Godunov-Cherdyntsev, is a far more attractive variant of this young Russian émigré poet in the throes of composition in his room in Berlin, closer to Nabokov himself: he has a loving mother with whom he grieves for his lost father. Grisha is designed as Fyodor's opposite – his life is even sadder, bereft of warmth and sympathetic genius, and yet his creative power can bestow absolute happiness.

Nabokov's love of lepidoptery and verse composition are given to inferior, limited characters in "The Aurelian" and "Torpid Smoke"; in "The Circle" (1936) a refraction of the blissful life on the family estate is shared by another "inferior": Innokentiy, the son of the village schoolmaster, had viewed the aristocratic Godunov-Cherdyntsev family at Leshino with class-conscious indignation. The story is constructed as a circle, beginning "In the second place . . ." (375), which by the final sentence is revealed to be part of a list of the reasons Innokentiy felt uneasy having met the Godunovs again in Paris after several years in exile. The first is that the daughter Tanya remained enchanting and invulnerable, the second that "he was possessed by a sudden, mad hankering after Russia" (375), and the third because he regretted the resentment and uncouthness of his youth. He recalls Tanya's sixteenth birthday party at which he sat at the non-aristocratic distant end of the table, and her indirect confession of love when she leaves for the Crimea. Written in the third person ostensibly from Innokentiy's point of view, the story nonetheless conveys Nabokov's vision of life at Vyra as described in

Speak, Memory and refracted through *The Gift*, a glorious life Innokentiy is shut out of and, by his own admission, too envious or self-conscious to join in when invited.

Thugs

In Berlin Nabokov, forced into exile by the Bolsheviks and lamenting the establishment of a totalitarian regime in Russia, found himself surrounded by the increasing tyranny of Nazi Germany. Although he scorned the idea that any true artist was responding to social conditions, the horrors of the period nonetheless are echoed in his stories of the late 1930s. The theme of the artistic personality hounded by thugs appears in "The Leonardo" (1933), "Cloud, Castle, Lake" (1937), "Tyrants Destroyed" (1938), "Lik" (1939), and "The Assistant Producer" (1943). In the first, Gustav, a furniture mover, and his unemployed brother Anton are irritated by Romantovski, a new lodger in their building, because he is different – he buys books, keeps odd hours, is unsociable. They bully him and finally kill him, knifing him in a street scuffle. They are amused to find out from the police that their victim was "a leonardo," a counterfeiter. The narrator of the tale who had assembled the scenery at the beginning laments: "My poor Romantovski! And I who believed with them that you were indeed someone exceptional, that you were a remarkable poet whom poverty obliged to dwell in that sinister district. I believed, on the strength of certain indices, that every night, by working on a line of verse or nursing a growing idea, you celebrated an invulnerable victory over the brothers." Then the set that the narrator assembled dissolves. "Everything floats away. Harmony and meaning vanish. The world irks me again with its variegated void" (367). The forces of mere materiality have killed the unique individual, an artistic type, however criminal. Gustav has been saving money to "marry Anna, acquire a sideboard, a carpet" (359). The details are part of the theme of life as a stage set, in which furniture is a sign of its temporary nature; the theme appears in Nabokov's novel, *Invitation to a Beheading*, when the hero is visited in his prison cell by members of his family who bring all their furniture with them for the brief visit. In further characterization of the thug as existing exclusively in the material world, Gustav has a face "the color of Westphalian ham" (366). The ham motif appears in several of the stories as an emblem of tawdry everyday life until it is given a starring role in *Pale Fire*, where it temporarily disrupts the approach of the assassin Gradus. Ham is the opposite of eternity in the mortal/immortal pairing because of the sound play in Russian of *vetchina* and *vechnost'*, ham and eternity. The thugs have their ham, the artists – their eternity.

"Cloud, Castle, Lake" tells a similar tale of the individual hounded by a group of German tourists. A Russian émigré wins a trip in a lottery and accepts reluctantly, hoping that this trip "would bring him some wonderful, tremulous happiness. This happiness would have something in common with his childhood, and with the excitement aroused in him by Russian lyrical poetry, and with some evening skyline once seen in a dream, and with that lady, another man's wife, whom he had hopelessly loved for seven years" (431). Although he is harassed on the train trip by the German tour group, who throw out his cucumber in favor of their own sausage, Vasiliy Ivanovich does find his happiness: the view, "in the inexpressible and unique harmoniousness of its three principal parts . . . was something so unique, and so familiar, and so long-promised, and it so understood the beholder that Vasiliy Ivanovich even pressed his hand to his heart, as if to see whether his heart was there in order to give it away" (435). He wants to stay there permanently, but the leader of the trip refuses to let him, tries to entice him with beer, but ends by taking him onto the train by force where "they began to beat him – they beat him for a long time, and with a good deal of inventiveness. It occurred to them, among other things, to use a corkscrew on his palms. The post-office clerk, who had been to Russia, fashioned a knout out of a stick and a belt, and began to use it with devilish dexterity . . . All had a wonderful time" (437). Again the foreign artistic sensibility is victimized by the German (and implied Russian) thugs, whose brutal group mentality is hostile to any individual, and immune to beauty.

Nabokov examines the mentality of these thugs in "Tyrants Destroyed" and takes revenge. The story's narrator examines the anatomy of a tyrant, the ruler of the fictional Zoorlandia, beginning from his early years, describing how a "limited, coarse, little-educated man . . . a pig-headed, brutal vulgarian full of morbid ambition . . . dresses up in godly garb" (440) and transforms his "wildflowery country into a vast kitchen garden" (441), "penetrating everywhere, infecting with his presence the way of thinking and the everyday life of every person, so that his mediocrity, his tediousness, his grey habitude were becoming the very life of my country" (442). The narrator considers killing him, but Hamlet-like, delays – "I don't know how to go about killing him" (454) – until he realizes that "[b]y killing myself I would kill him, as he was totally inside me" (457). Preparing for self-destruction, he is suddenly overwhelmed by the festivities taking place in honor of the tyrant's fiftieth birthday and undergoes "a strange, almost alchemic metamorphosis," understands his "sin against our great and merciful Master" (458), and repents his apostasy. But he is saved from this madness by laughter. "Having experienced all the degrees of hatred and despair, I achieved those heights from which one obtains a bird's eye view of the ludicrous . . . in my efforts to make him terrifying, I have only made him ridiculous, thereby destroying him . . . This is an incantation, an exorcism, so that henceforth any man can exorcize bondage. I believe in miracles" (459).

Nabokov later effected this same exorcism, there of the dictator Paduk, in his novel *Bend Sinister* (1947), again incorporating the analogy with *Hamlet* and also allowing that hero relief in madness. The imagery of the colored lights at the birthday celebration repeats that found in *Invitation to a Beheading*, an earlier, more stylized and philosophical vision of a modern tyranny. In *The Gift* Nabokov looks back to the origins of this "giftless" type in his biography of N. G. Chernyshevski (1828–1889), emphasizing the critic's blind materialism, limitedness, and lack of hygiene, in order to work out a "secret remedy against future tyrants" (460). In *Pale Fire* Nabokov distills his mockery of the type of thug-assassin into Kinbote's portrait of Gradus.

Ambiguity

Despite the potent forces provoking Nabokov to destroy the tyrant through artistic means, he was nonetheless simultaneously able to write playful and elegant stories full of ambiguity. In "The Admiralty Spire" (1933), the narrator addresses an indignant letter to a lady writer whom he accuses of having "kidnapped my past" (349). Her novel about the love affair between Olga and Leonid, written under a male pen name and taking its title – "The Admiralty Spire" – from Pushkin's *Bronze Horseman*, tells the tale of the narrator's romance with Katya in what he claims to be a terrible distortion of it. He deplores the inexactitude of detail, the inclusion of political discussions of revolutionary events, and conventional descriptions, especially of himself ("I shall leave on your conscience his Lermontovian lustreless eyes and aristocratic profile" [350]). He replies to her novel with his own memories of their love: "what bliss it was, without rising, still picking berries, to clasp Katya's warm shoulder and hear her soft laughter and little grunts of greed and the crunch of her joints as she rummaged under the leaves" (353). He concludes his tirade, "In spite of everything you were beautiful . . . so adorable that I could cry, ignoring your myopic soul, and the triviality of your opinions, and a thousand minor betrayals; while I, with my overambitious verse . . . and my breathless, stuttering speech . . . must have been contemptible and repulsive" (356). Then he drops his verbal disguise and addresses Katya directly, incensed by her version of their last meeting: "What a disgusting, senseless fabrication!" Both the reported tale and the narrator's memories are ludicrous; the reader is left to decide whose rendition is the more accurate, the lady novelist's or the poet-memoirist's. The implicit discussion of literary criteria mocks the idea that literary fiction must, or even can, mirror life, and by the end the very title of Nabokov's story has acquired three sets of quotation marks – Pushkin's, Katya's, and Nabokov's.

In "That in Aleppo Once . . ." (1943), written in English ten years later, the ambiguity is richer and more subtle, while employing the same device of the conflicting reports of the narrating man and the absent woman. Again a desperate character turns to a writer, a fellow Russian émigré called V. who is already established in New York when the narrator arrives there, to "clarify things for me through the prism of your art" (568). In the "apocalyptic exodus" from France, fleeing "something monstrous and impalpable, a timeless mass of immemorial horror" (the German invasion of France), the narrator has lost his newly-wed wife; the train he had gotten off briefly is gone, with his wife on it, when he returns. When he at last finds her again in Nice, she tells him she has betrayed him with a man she met on the train. He torments her violently, forcing her to tell him all the agonizing details over the days they spend getting the papers necessary to leave France. Suddenly she denies the entire story. "Perhaps I live several lives at once . . . Perhaps this bench is a dream and we are in Saratov or on some star" (565). They finally get exit visas and he dashes to Marseilles for boat tickets. When he returns there is nothing in their hotel room but a sugar pink rose in a glass on the table – his wife is gone. He goes to friends to find her and learns that she has told them an elaborate tale: "she had madly fallen in love with a young Frenchman, . . . had implored me for a divorce and I had refused; that in fact I had said I would rather shoot her and myself than sail to New York alone" (567) and "loads of other preposterous details" such as "her dog, that poor beast which you hanged with your own hands before leaving Paris." On the train south, his wife had started sobbing over this dog: "'I cannot forget the poor dog.' The honesty of her grief shocked me, as we had never had any dog. 'I know,' she said, 'but I tried to imagine we had actually bought that setter . . .' There had never been any talk of buying a setter" (562). He takes the boat to New York alone, but on board meets a doctor acquaintance who says he had seen her a few days before boarding and "she said that I would presently join her with bag and tickets" (567).

The reader must again resolve conflicting tales. The narrator says he is convinced that his wife never existed, yet describes the "tiny brown birthmark on her downy forearm" (561). The address of his wife's uncle in New York proves nonexistent, but a reliable source says the uncle and his wife have moved to San Francisco. Is the narrator delusional, his wife mad, or is it all V.'s fiction? The narrator concludes his letter: "It may all end in *Aleppo* if I am not careful. Spare me, V.: you would load your dice with an unbearable implication if you took that for a title" (568). In Shakespeare's

Othello, after the Moor has realized his error in killing his wife for her suspected unfaithfulness, he says: "Set you down this; / And say besides, that in Aleppo once, / Where a malignant and a turban'd Turk / Beat a Venetian and traduc'd the state, / I took by th'throat the circumcised dog, / And smote him – thus" (act 5, scene 2). That V. nonetheless does take the title for the story may mean that, like Othello, the narrator has killed himself, tormented by his own suspicion, his wife's possible infidelity, the wrong he has done her. It could equally suggest that V. has made an elegant tale of his friend's misfortune, relating it not only to Shakespeare, but aligning Othello, the Moor of Venice, with the great-grandson of the Moor of Peter the Great, Pushkin, who suspected his wife Natalie of infidelity and perished in a duel over insinuations about it. The narrator describes his wife as "not much younger than Natalie of the lovely bare shoulders and long earrings in relation to swarthy Pushkin," and as a poet, "finds pleasure in imitating the destiny of a unique genius (down to the jealousy, down to the filth, down to the stab of seeing her almond-shaped eyes turn toward her blond Cassio behind her peacock-feathered fan) even if one cannot imitate his verse" (561). That "blonde Cassio" killed Russia's greatest poet. Whatever solution the reader arrives at, Nabokov's story creates a three-layered tale of a husband's violent jealousy that destroys him: Othello's, Pushkin's, and his narrator's.

American gems

Nabokov's greatest stories, "Signs and Symbols" (1948) and "The Vane Sisters" (1951), were written in English. "Signs and Symbols" employs the device of "That in Aleppo Once . . .": the reader must make an interpretive decision, thereby participating in deciding the characters' fate, which places him in the role of co-author of the story. An old Jewish couple tries to visit their son in a mental institution, but when the two get there they are not allowed to see their son because he has again attempted to take his life, and the parents go home without giving their son the "innocent" birthday present of a basket of ten different fruit jellies in ten different jars. The son suffers from "referential mania," imagining that "everything happening around him is a veiled reference to his personality and his existence . . . Phenomenal nature shadows him wherever he goes. Clouds in the staring sky transmit to one another, by means of slow signs, incredibly detailed information regarding him. His inmost thoughts are discussed at nightfall, in manual alphabet, by darkly gesticulating trees" (599). While this is clearly insane, his mother's selective reading of the world through the prism of her own grief is also a distortion of reality. On the parents' way to the hospital "the underground train lost its life current between two stations" (598). Waiting for the bus on the way home they see "a tiny half-dead unfledged bird . . . helplessly twitching in a puddle"; on the bus a girl is weeping on an older woman's shoulder. The wife forgets to give her husband the keys while she shops and he is briefly locked out of their apartment. At home, the husband goes to sleep while the wife looks over her old photographs, and sees "Aunt Rose, a fussy, angular, wild-eyed old lady, who had lived in a tremulous world of bad news, bankruptcies, train accidents, cancerous growths – until the Germans put her to death, together with all the people she worried about" (601). At midnight, the husband gets up and they decide they will bring their son home. "We must get him out of there quick. Otherwise we'll be responsible. Responsible!" (602). With the decision their spirits rise. The telephone rings, terrifying the mother. A young girl asks for Charlie. They continue planning to move their son when the phone rings again, the same "toneless anxious young voice" asks for Charlie and the wife explains, "You have the incorrect number . . . you are turning the letter O instead of the zero" (602). They sit down to a festive midnight tea. The story concludes as the husband reads the labels of the jam jars: "apricot, grape, beech plum, quince. He got to crab apple when the telephone rang again" (603).

Is the third call from the hospital, reporting that the son has finally succeeded in committing suicide? Have the images of dying things that fill the story been symbols of impending doom? Should we try to find meaning in the sequence of jam types to resolve the ambiguity? Should we associate the possibility of three Os with Nabokov's motif of "all the nines turning to zeros," signifying a transition from one world to another? Does the phrase "when the telephone rang" echo the moment when Nabokov learned that his father was killed, on "the night of March 28, 1922, around ten o'clock . . . when the telephone rang" (SM, 49 [ch. 2])? If we answer yes to these questions, we participate in both the son's reading of the world as fraught with meanings referring to him and in the mother's selection of heart-rending detail in her view of daily life; we read the dead underground line and the twitching fledgling as legitimate symbols of death and thereby condemn the son to suicide. The son is insane, and the mother's flight from Russia and Nazi Germany give her all too legitimate reasons to understand life in terms of "the endless waves of pain that she and her husband had had to endure" (601). But Nabokov endorses neither the son's nor the mother's reading of the world; his stories are part of a struggle against a tragic view of life, an overcoming of the terrible cataclysms endured by so many, a refusal to give in to nostalgia and grief. Life cannot be read as if it were a work of fiction, and fiction should not consist of clumsy, determining symbols. And so we cannot know whether the phone call is from the young girl who has made a third mistake, despite the mother's careful explanation, or whether the son has finally "torn a hole in his world and escape[d]" (599).

"The Vane Sisters" answers the tragedies endured in "Signs and Symbols" with a joyful possibility: human consciousness survives death and continues to communicate with loved ones from beyond the grave. A professor of French describes a brilliant icy afternoon in the small hilly town where he teaches at a girls' college. He notices "a family of brilliant icicles dripdripping from the eaves of a frame house" and how "[t]he lean ghost, the elongated umbra cast by a parking meter upon some damp snow, had a strange ruddy tinge" (620). Following these visual delights, he finds himself in an unaccustomed street where he encounters the young, brash, married professor D. who had formerly taught at the college. D. had an affair with an undergraduate, Sybil Vane, who committed suicide when he broke it off. D. casually mentions that Sybil's sister Cynthia died the week before of heart failure.

The incident triggers the French professor's memories of the Vane sisters. In a narrative which gradually reveals him to be a supercilious snob, he recalls how he had brought Sybil's French exam containing her farewell to Cynthia, and "was impelled to point out to her the grammatical mistakes in it." He describes the black hairs on Cynthia's legs, her bitten, dirty fingernails, and her family with great condescension: "her mother's first husband had been of Slav origin, but otherwise Cynthia Vane belonged to a good, respectable family" (623). The one thing he admires is her paintings, of metallic things, and of "a windshield partly covered with rime, with a brilliant trickle (from an imaginary car roof) across its transparent part" (624). But he is dismissive of her "theory of intervenient auras": "For a few hours, or for several days in a row, and sometimes recurrently, in an irregular series, for months or years, anything that happened to Cynthia, after a given person had died, would be, she said, in the manner and mood of that person . . . The influence might be good or bad; the main thing was that its source could be identified. It was like walking through a person's soul, she said" (625). The professor describes Cynthia's experiments with spiritualism and her fondness for puns, logogriphs, and misshapen words. "And I wish I could recollect that novel or short story . . . in which, unknown to its author, the first letters of the words in the last paragraph formed, as deciphered by Cynthia, a message from his dead mother" (626). This is Nabokov's instruction to look for the acrostic he has hidden in the last paragraph of "The Vane Sisters," which goes unnoticed by the narrator. It reveals the source of his uncharacteristically vivid vision at the beginning of the story: "Icicles by Cynthia, meter from me, Sybil" (631). The narrator's "raw awareness" of the "transparent stalactites backed by their blue silhouettes" (619) and the parking meter's shadow was a gift from the generous sisters' intervenient auras.

"The Vane Sisters" provides a counter to "Signs and Symbols." Faith in the survival of human consciousness after death is the opposite of referential mania. The solipsistic madness where everything refers to self is a danger that Nabokov's art persistently alerts us to; dwelling on one's losses will blind us to the beauty of the universe and prevent our looking outwards for signs of tenderness from the beyond. The gift of artistic vision that the Vanes give the French professor is what spared Nabokov himself from feeling that he was at the center of a conspiracy – that took away his country, his father, his Russian language. The artist can reach beyond the boundaries of this life and both create and attain a world where "nobody will ever die" (SM, 77 [ch. 3]).

NOTE

1. *Stories*, 4. All further quotations from this collection will be indicated by a parenthetical reference containing the page number of the quotation.

8

JULIAN W. CONNOLLY

The major Russian novels

Of the nine novels that Nabokov wrote in Russian, the last three – *Despair* (*Otchaianie*), *Invitation to a Beheading* (*Priglashenie na kazn'*), and *The Gift* (*Dar*) – are arguably his finest. In them Nabokov explores the nature of the creative spirit and the relationship between artists and the subjects that inspire them. *Despair* offers a cautionary tale of creative solipsism with its depiction of a self-proclaimed artistic genius who shows little regard for the autonomy of the people whose lives he subsumes into his creative fantasy. *Invitation to a Beheading* presents the contrary position as Nabokov focuses on an imaginative individual who must work up the courage to trust his own creative vision and end his fealty to the conformist pressures of the surrounding society. *The Gift* provides the most sweeping portrait of the artistic personality, and it discloses in exquisite detail the transformative powers of a finely honed creative consciousness. What is more, each of these novels tackles its subject in a unique way. The resulting triptych testifies to the extraordinary range of Vladimir Nabokov's own imagination.

Despair

Although Nabokov had depicted aspects of the creative personality in his earlier works (particularly *The Defense* [*Zashchita Luzhina*] and *Laughter in the Dark* [*Kamera obskura*]),[1] *Despair* provides the first sustained treatment of the ethical implications of artistic inspiration and achievement. The narrator and protagonist Hermann Karlovich craves recognition as a great artist. As he puts it, "I longed, to the point of pain, for that masterpiece of mine . . . to be appreciated by men" (*Des*, 178 [ch. 10]). However, he has chosen an unconventional medium to demonstrate his talent: he decides to kill a man who he believes is his identical double and mislead the police into assuming that it is he, Hermann, who has been murdered. Once an insurance settlement has been paid to his wife Lydia, Hermann will rejoin the woman and the two will begin a new life of ease and comfort. Continuing the imagery of artistic achievement, Hermann smugly refers to the insurance payment as the "royalties" on his finished work (*Des*, 178 [ch. 10]).

Hermann's vision is profoundly self-absorbed and solipsistic, and Nabokov carefully structures his narrative to trigger within the reader a distinctive response to this solipsism. Since this narrative is conducted exclusively from Hermann's point of view, first-time readers of the novel find themselves seeing the world through his eyes, and thus they are led to adopt his limited, self-centered perspective. By the end of the work, however, the reader realizes that this perspective is grievously flawed. Press reports of the murder and a subsequent letter from Lydia's cousin, an artist named Ardalion, make it clear that Hermann's victim Felix bears no resemblance to Hermann at all. Once readers fully comprehend this fact, they look back over the preceding narrative and see clear signs that Hermann's assertions of identity were wrong. Even in Hermann's initial descriptions of Felix, one can find notes of equivocation and doubt. For example, he is perturbed by the fact that Felix does not seem to acknowledge the deep similarity he assumes is there. Handing Felix a mirror, he cries out: "Don't you see that we two – don't you see, you fool, that we are – Now listen – take a good look at me" (*Des*, 12 [ch. 1]). Again, returning to the reader, Hermann commands: "Look nearer: I possess large yellowish teeth; his are whiter and set more closely together, but is that really important?" (*Des*, 17 [ch. 1]). Later in the novel, Hermann amuses himself with the notion that if he occasionally shows his face to the reader, the reader will not know whether the face is Hermann's or Felix's: "Only by this method can I hope to teach the reader a lesson, demonstrating to him that ours was not an imaginary resemblance, but a real possibility, even more – a real fact, yes, a fact" (*Des*, 30 [ch. 2]). One senses that Hermann is trying to convince himself as much as the reader here. Finally, when Hermann meets up with Felix for a second time months later, he indicates his own concern that the resemblance he had earlier detected may have been only an illusion: "For a moment I had the impression that it had all been a delusion, a hallucination – that never could he have been my double, that gump . . . For a moment, as I say, he appeared to me as like me as any man. But then . . . his features fell back to their proper position, and I saw, once again, the marvel that had arrested me five months before" (*Des*, 74 [ch. 5]).

While these clues offer suggestive evidence that Hermann's assertions about his resemblance to Felix are not grounded in fact, they also bear witness to a more fundamental problem. As Ardalion tells Hermann: "You forget, my good man, that what the artist perceives is, primarily, the *difference* between things. It is the vulgar who note their resemblance" (*Des*, 41 [ch. 2]). Indeed, throughout his narrative Hermann reveals a penchant for descrying resemblances and recurrences that turn out to exist only in his mind, not in the world around him. At one point he enters a tobacconist's shop and sees "one of Ardalion's still-life pictures: a tobacco pipe, a green cloth, and two roses." When the clerk tells him that it was painted by her niece, he exclaims to himself: "Well, I'm damned! . . . For had I not seen something very similar, if not identical, among Ardalion's pictures?" (*Des*, 69 [ch. 4]). When he finally has the chance to check this resemblance, though, he discovers that the picture Ardalion had painted was "not quite two roses and not quite a pipe, but a couple of large peaches and an ashtray" (*Des*, 105 [ch. 6]). In other words, there was not very much similarity after all. What is more, Nabokov endows Hermann's egregious predilection for perceiving the similarities between things with an ironic sociopolitical overtone as he has his character praise the ideals of Soviet society: "Communism shall indeed create a beautifully square world of identical brawny fellows, broad-shouldered and microcephalous" (*Des*, 20 [ch. 2]; see also *Des*, 158 [ch. 9]).

Ardalion's assertion that a genuine artist perceives the "difference" between things points to a central flaw in Hermann's claim to artistic genius. Unlike an accomplished artist, Hermann is inattentive to *details*, to all those minute characteristics that lend individuality and uniqueness to people and things. This blindness not only results in the miscarriage of his scheme to fool the police into thinking that he himself has been murdered, it leads directly to his capture as well. When he first reads in the newspaper that the police did not see any resemblance between himself and the murdered man, Hermann still believes that the police cannot discover the dead man's identity and therefore cannot track Hermann down, since he had assumed that very identity. Yet a reference in the press story to an object disclosing the victim's identity leads Hermann to re-read the narrative he had just composed, and he is stunned to find that he had recorded a moment when Felix made a gesture with his walking stick, which was branded with Felix's name. Felix had left the stick in Hermann's car before the murder, and Hermann had forgotten to remove it when he left the scene.

Although Hermann castigates himself for his oversight in regard to the walking stick, he never acknowledges the more fundamental error of believing that Felix was his identical double. Of course, these errors in visual perception underscore a more serious error – a form of *ethical* blindness. Preoccupied with satisfying his own narcissistic desires, Hermann believes that his artistic genius gives him total license to ignore the wills and lives of those around him. Yet even as he mocks the nearsightedness and gullibility of those around him, he remains oblivious to the fact that these people live independent lives beyond his control. Thus he proudly tells the reader that to Lydia, he was "the ideal man" and that he loved her "because she loved me" (*Des*, 25 [ch. 2]). Even the most trusting of readers, however, will detect telling signs that Lydia is having an affair with Ardalion.[2] Similarly, Hermann shows Orlovius a letter ostensibly written by Felix and confidently assumes that he has convinced Orlovius that he, Hermann, is being blackmailed. He reacts with consternation, then, when the press reports that after the murder Orlovius asserts that Hermann was mentally unbalanced and "used to write letters" to himself (*Des*, 191 [ch. 10]).

As noted above, Hermann longs to be recognized as an artist of genius, and contrasts his own talent with the achievements of novelists in the past: "But what are they – Doyle, Dostoevsky, Leblanc, Wallace – what are all the great novelists who wrote of nimble criminals . . . what are they in comparison with me? Blundering fools!" (*Des*, 132 [ch. 7]). However, the very plan with which he hopes to establish his genius – the commission of murder in service of a higher idea – shows not that he is the original artist he claims to be, but rather that he is something of an imitative figure following in a long line of literary characters, from Rodion Raskolnikov in Fedor Dostoevsky's *Crime and Punishment* to Anton Kerzhentsev in Leonid Andreev's novel *The Thought*.[3]

The genuine artist in the novel is not, of course, Hermann Karlovich, but Nabokov-Sirin, and that author imprinted his indelible watermark onto the very text of Hermann's narrative, particularly in the original Russian version. In chapter 2, for example, one finds a description of one of Ardalion's paintings: "malinovoi siren'iu v nabokoi vaze" (*Ssoch*, III:415). In this passage, which literally translates as "raspberry-colored lilacs in a leaning vase," one can discern the shadow both of Nabokov's Russian pen name Sirin, and his real surname. The English version of the text has other forms of authorial patterning to which Hermann seems oblivious.[4]

Disappointed by the failure of the police and the press to appreciate the artistic mastery of his crime, Hermann turns to another, more conventional artistic medium, the written word, "to obtain recognition, to justify and save the offspring of my brain, to explain to the world all the depth of my masterpiece" (*Des*, 194–95). However, despite numerous assertions of literary expertise – "speaking of literature, there is not a thing about it I do not know" (*Des*, 45 [ch. 3]); "my self-control is perfect" (*Des*, 29 [ch. 2]) – his text reveals a pervasive lack of control, beginning with the opening paragraph of the text, in which he seems unable to settle on a single line of thought to pursue. Later he acknowledges that his "devices seem to have got mixed up a little" (*Des*, 45 [ch. 3]), and he has the recurring problem of adding wintertime details (snow, bare patches of soil) to descriptions of summertime scenes (*Des*, 37 [ch. 2]). At one point he wonders: "has perchance my pen mixed the steps and wantonly danced away?" (*Des*, 88 [ch. 5]). In reality, it is not that his pen has "danced away" of its own accord, but rather that it has been seized by the hand of his creator, Vladimir Nabokov. Unbeknownst to Hermann, Nabokov uses the very text that Hermann hopes will demonstrate his artistic genius to expose his character's irreparable shortcomings. Through his handling of Hermann's crime and of Hermann's attempt to redeem the failed scheme through the written word, Nabokov demonstrates how misguided and delusional Hermann's aspirations are. In his next novel, however, Nabokov would show how a genuinely creative personality might gain the ability to slough off conditions of constraint and find entrance into a new realm of artistic freedom.

Invitation to a Beheading

After completing *Despair*, Nabokov began making plans for his longest and most complex Russian novel, *The Gift*. Part of that project would be a biography of the nineteenth-century writer and critic Nikolay Chernyshevski. While working on that biography, Nabokov was suddenly seized with the idea for a new novel, and he quickly wrote down an initial draft "in one fortnight of wonderful excitement and sustained inspiration" (*SO*, 68). To a certain degree, the subject of the new novel represents an inversion of material in the Chernyshevski biography. Its protagonist serves time in prison, just as Chernyshevski did. But the new protagonist, Cincinnatus C., is a very different type of being from Chernyshevski. Whereas the latter was an ardent (if somewhat muddled) adherent of materialism, Cincinnatus senses beyond the boundaries of the everyday world a realm of more authentic and perfect beauty. The novel also inverts material in *Despair*. In place of a man who was so "cocksure about the power of [his] pen" (*Des*, 88 [ch. 5]) that he treated those around him as if they were his literary characters to be manipulated as he wished, *Invitation* features a character who possesses an original creative vision, but who does not initially trust his perceptions and who has been cowed into conforming to the dictates of the characters around him. Over the course of the novel, Cincinnatus learns to trust his own intuitions, thus finding a way to free himself from these oppressive constraints.

As the novel opens, Cincinnatus has been sentenced to be beheaded for the crime of "gnostical turpitude" (*IB*, 72 [ch. 6]). To put it more simply, however, Cincinnatus represents a threat to those around him because he appears to be a unique individual in a world of stylized, featureless beings. This world is a bizarre realm of pasteboard sets and shallow, theatricalized figures.[5] The novel's characters seem to dissolve or swap identities without rhyme or reason. Some of the background settings are badly drawn, like crude daubings on canvas. Nabokov's depiction of Cincinnatus's society suggests a grotesque state in which the creative capacities have atrophied or grown stagnant. As readers work their way through the text, they encounter events and scenes that contain odd inconsistencies or flaws. For example, a table that can be moved in one scene (*IB*, 28 [ch. 2]) is later described as having legs that "had been bolted down for ages" (*IB*, 30 [ch. 2]). It is worth noting that the narrative perspective on these events is of little help to the reader trying to make sense of what is being described. Those distortions or misreadings that cropped up in Hermann Karlovich's narrative have now become pervasive, and the overall effect is somewhat dreamlike or nightmarish. The novel's readers thus find themselves in Cincinnatus's position as they struggle to find meaning in a grotesque world of non-sense.

As Cincinnatus reacts with increasing dismay to the nightmarish quality of his surroundings, he senses that he is the only one in this world "who is alive" (*IB*, 52 [ch. 4]; cf. *IB*, 70 [ch. 6]). He carries within himself a vision of another, more authentic reality of which his present surroundings are only a shabby, vulgar copy: "It exists, my dream world, it must exist, since, surely there must be an original of the clumsy copy" (*IB*, 93 [ch. 8]). He continues: "*There, tam, là-bas*, the gaze of men glows with inimitable understanding. . . . *There, there* are the originals of the gardens where we used to roam . . . *there* everything strikes one by its bewitching evidence, by the simplicity of perfect good . . . *there* shines the mirror that now and then sends a chance reflection here" (*IB*, 94 [ch. 8]).[6] He surmises that he is here "through an error – not in this prison, specifically – but in this whole terrible, striped world" (*IB*, 91 [ch. 8]).

Having come to this conclusion, however, Cincinnatus must still find a way out of this "striped world." He senses that the impending execution might serve as a kind of awakening, but at the outset of the novel, the thought of execution causes him paralyzing fear. What is more, he has become deeply attached to this world, and particularly to his shallow, unfaithful wife Martha. He senses that he must withdraw his emotional investment in this world and cease giving credence to the reality of these tacky figures who surround him. As the narrator puts it, "by evoking" these other characters, "Cincinnatus allowed them the right to exist, supported them, nourished them with himself" (*IB*, 156 [ch. 14]). In other words, "he inspired the meaningless with meaning, and the lifeless with life" (*IB*, 155 [ch. 14]).

Most importantly, Cincinnatus must husband his own embryonic talents and activate his creative potential. He writes: "I know something. I know something. But expression of it comes so hard!" (*IB*, 91 [ch. 8]). He acknowledges that he has the "capacity" (or, in the Russian original, the "gift" [*dar*]) to conjoin all of his intuitions into a single point, but that "the secret is not revealed yet" (*IB*, 52 [ch. 4]). Through the sheer act of writing, however, Cincinnatus begins to hone his expressive potential. Whereas his first attempt at writing results in garbled phrases ("In spite of everything I am comparatively. After all I had premonitions, premonitions of this finale" [*IB*, 12–13 (ch. 1)], and he immediately crosses it out because he feels the watchful gaze of his jailer on his head, he gradually becomes more controlled and more eloquent in his writing. At the same time, he becomes more convinced that the world around him is a sham setting and that he must suspend his belief in its viability: "This is the dead end of this life, and I should not have sought salvation within its confines" (*IB*, 205 [ch. 19]). Significantly, it is the written word itself that suggests a path for escape. Near the end to the novel Cincinnatus writes: "Envious of poets. How wonderful it must be to speed along a page and, right from the page, where only a shadow continues to run, to take off into the blue" (*IB*, 194 [ch. 18]). As it turns out, this description of Cincinnatus's vision of escape anticipates the impending execution scene and thus, Cincinnatus presciently authors his own ultimate transcendence.

Cincinnatus's growing confidence and strength are signaled in his last written record. Summarizing his insights about the illusory world around him, he writes that he is almost fearless of "death," but then he crosses out that word and begins to think of more precise equivalents. As it turns out, he never returns to his writing, for, after encountering a fabulous moth that had escaped his jailer's grasp, he realizes that "everything had in fact been written already" (*IB*, 209 [ch. 19]). Moths and butterflies can serve in Nabokov's work as emblems of resurrection or the survival of the spirit after death (see, for example, the role of the moth in the story "Christmas"). Here, the escape of the live moth from destruction by the artificial spider serves to show (and may even facilitate) Cincinnatus's own transcendence of the sham world imprisoning him. After seeing the moth, Cincinnatus leaves behind on a single sheet of paper the graphic image of the word "death" crossed out.

This negation of a negative concept echoes the workings of a fabulous mirror described earlier in the novel by Cincinnatus's mother – the *nonnon* mirror – in which an artificially distorted object placed before an artificially distorted mirror results in the creation of a "marvelous thing": "minus by minus equaled plus, everything was restored, everything was fine, and the shapeless speckledness became in the mirror a wonderful, sensible image" (*IB*, 135 [ch. 12]). Here, however, the graphic image retains both the initial mention of death *and* its cancellation, and it thus serves as a potent foreshadowing of the remarkable conclusion to this remarkable novel.

In the final scene of the novel, Nabokov describes Cincinnatus's execution in such a way that he makes it appear *both* that Cincinnatus is beheaded *and* that he escapes whole and unscathed. What this scene suggests, then, is that one aspect of Cincinnatus – weak, frail, and credulous – has been extinguished, thereby releasing another, more essential element. Throughout the novel one finds repeated references to a "double" within Cincinnatus (and within everyone one, "doing what we would like to do at that very moment, but cannot" [*IB*, 25 (ch. 2)]). Amidst the collapsing stage setting and "flapping scenery," *that* Cincinnatus strides away "in that direction where, to judge by the voices, stood beings akin to him" (*IB*, 133 [ch. 20]). The image of "voices" may indicate that these kindred spirits are fellow creators, poets, writers. At last Cincinnatus no longer has to be "envious of poets," for he has joined their rank himself. At the same time, the image of the voice provides a link between Cincinnatus and his mysterious father, whom he had never met. Cecilia C., Cincinnatus's mother, tells Cincinnatus that she only heard the man's voice, and never saw his face. Some critics have detected in this tale of mysterious paternity an echo of the conception of Christ.[7]

The story of Cincinnatus's imprisonment and transcendence has been read as an expression of Gnostic philosophy, reenacting "the cosmic drama of Gnostic redemption."[8] Yet while it is evident that Nabokov draws on imagery found in Gnostic writings (the pearl, fire, masks, existence as a prison), it seems unlikely that he was seeking to create a work with such a narrow focus. While the Gnostic imagery adds drama and color to Cincinnatus's quest, an awareness of Gnostic teachings does not exhaust the rich potentiality of the text. Indeed, the novel carries multiple layers of significance, from the political (it was written the year after Hitler was appointed chancellor of the German government and during a time of increasing repression in Stalinist Russia),[9] to the metaliterary.[10] As Leona Toker has shown, Nabokov incorporated a high degree of indeterminacy into his text.[11] Such indeterminacy perhaps works to militate against any reductionist interpretation of the text, for such reductionism would reflect and perpetuate the very totalitarian impulses directed at Cincinnatus by his jailers. Unlike these jailers, who cannot tolerate that things that are ambiguous, elusive, and challenging (see *IB*, 120–22 [ch. 11]), Nabokov's ideal reader may find in these qualities something stimulating and extraordinary. Envisioning the effect of this novel on its intended audience, the writer declared: "I know (*je connais*) a few (*quelques*) readers who will jump up, ruffling their hair" (*IB*, 8 ["Foreword"]). This work, which Nabokov identified as his "dreamiest and most poetical novel" (*SO*, 76), continues to shimmer as a unique jewel in the author's extensive œuvre.

The Gift

Upon completing *Invitation to a Beheading* Nabokov returned to *The Gift*, and after considerable writing and revisions, he finished the novel in January 1938.[12] One can find several affinities between the two works: a focus on the nature of creative consciousness, the difficulty of artistic expression, concern with the mystery of death, intuition about a wondrous realm beyond the borders of everyday life. Yet Nabokov has set his novel not in a bizarre dystopian society of the future, but rather in Berlin of the 1920s, and the work is steeped in the realia of Russian émigré life. Even so, *The Gift*, like its offshoot, is a complex, multilayered work. It tracks the efforts of a young writer, Fyodor Godunov-Cherdyntsev, to develop and refine his creative abilities. The reader follows Fyodor through several stages: his reflection on his early poetry, his attempt to write a biography of his father, and his successful completion of a biography of the nineteenth-century writer and critic N. G. Chernyshevski.

In Fyodor's quest the reader notes reflections of Cincinnatus's condition. Like Cincinnatus, Fyodor feels himself to be "a special, rare and as yet undescribed and unnamed variant of man" (*Gift*, 163 [ch. 3]). Also like Cincinnatus, Fyodor senses that he has a special inner knowledge or orientation toward life that has been "mysteriously transmitted" from his father to himself (*Gift*, 119 [ch. 2]). The articulation of his inner knowledge, however, proves exceedingly difficult. The terms in which he describes his frustration at not being able to express what he sees with his artistic vision echoes terms used by Cincinnatus: "At times I feel that somewhere it has already been written by me . . . that I have only to free it part by part from the darkness and the parts will fall together of themselves . . . Sometime I shall read you at random disjointed and inchoate extracts from what I have written: how little it resembles my statuesque dream!" (*Gift*, 138 [ch. 2]). Like Cincinnatus too, Fyodor possesses two aspects: the Fyodor who lives in quotidian reality and a Fyodor who has access to another realm of inspiration and vision, as is evident in this description of the composition of a poem: "He was somnambulistically talking to himself as he paced a nonexistent sidewalk; his feet were guided by local consciousness, while the principal Fyodor Konstantinovich, and in fact the only Fyodor Konstantinovich that mattered, was already peering into the next shadowy strophe" (*Gift*, 55 [ch. 1]). Fyodor's returns from flights of inspiration have a similar effect to the end of a curious "criminal exercise" in which Cincinnatus indulged. Locked in his cell, Cincinnatus imagines disassembling his body and reveling in a sense of freedom and joy, but then the bolt of the cell door slams shut, and Cincinnatus regains all the weight that he had shed (*IB*, 32–33 [ch. 2]). Similarly, after finishing work on a poem, Fyodor "passed immediately from a world of many interesting dimensions into one that was cramped and demanding" (*Gift*, 157–58 [ch. 3]).

One of Fyodor's central concerns as an artist is the preservation of the fleeting experiences of mortal life. Fyodor's own life has been marked by a series of losses – the loss of Russia and the loss of his father, as well as numerous minor annoyances, such as the loss of keys to his apartment. Nabokov's novel asserts, however, that one does not have to be plunged into despair by such losses. For every frustration, life (or fate) provides some compensation, perhaps not on the material plane, but certainly in the realm of the mind and the spirit.

Two figures who play essential roles in this cycle of loss and recovery are Fyodor's father, a famous naturalist and explorer who never returned from his last expedition, but whose presence is mysteriously felt at times in the novel, and Fyodor's beloved Zina Mertz, a responsive soul who enters his life in the middle of the novel and who appears to be linked with the specter of Fyodor's father through a series of important images, such as rainbows and prismatic light effects. At the outset of chapter 2, for example, Fyodor describes how his father "entered the base of a rainbow – the rarest occurrence! – and found himself in colored air, in a play of light as if in paradise" (*Gift*, 77 [ch. 2]). When Fyodor encounters Zina in the hallway of their apartment building, he notes the presence of "a prismatic rainbow" on the wall. At that very instant, he feels "the strangeness of life, the strangeness of its magic, as if a corner of it had been turned back for an instant and he had glimpsed its unusual lining" (*Gift*, 183 [ch. 3]). This image of the "strangeness of life" connects Fyodor's meeting with Zina with his conception of his father. Trying to imagine what his father thought about when he was alone, he wonders if his father pondered "the strangeness of human life, a sense of which he mysteriously transmitted to me?" (*Gift*, 119 [ch. 2]). It is even possible that the spirit of Fyodor's father has somehow played a role in Fyodor's meeting with Zina.[13]

One potential way to recapture and preserve the evanescent experiences of life is to record them in a work of art, and much of the writing that Fyodor does in the novel has biographical and autobiographical significance. Nabokov's exploration of the biographical impulse here centers on an aspect of the genre that engaged the author's attention during the mid-1930s: the degree to which writing about the life of another (or even about one's own life) casts a patina of fiction over that life. In a seminal essay on Aleksandr Pushkin that Nabokov prepared for the upcoming centenary of Pushkin's death in January 1937, Nabokov asks: "Is it possible to imagine the full reality of another's life, to relive it in one's mind and set it down intact on paper? I doubt it: one even finds oneself seduced by the idea that thought itself, as it shines its beam on the story of a man's life, cannot avoid deforming it."[14]

Nabokov expands upon this insight in his treatment of Fyodor's first attempt at a biography – an account of his father's life. Although Fyodor's initial descriptions of one of his father's expeditions are conveyed from a position of external chronicler ("I now imagine the outfitting of my father's caravan" [*Gift*, 116 (ch. 2)]), as he becomes more involved in the recreation of this expedition in his imagination, he finds himself slipping into the scene. Thus he begins using the first-person plural pronoun "we" ("*our* caravan moved east"; "*We* saw" [*Gift*, 117 (ch. 2), emphasis added]). Finally, he seems to take on his father's personal perspective, and he begins using the first-person singular pronoun in such a way that he speaks from his father's position: "In Tatsien-Lu shaven-headed lamas roamed about the . . . streets spreading the rumor that I was catching children in order to brew their eyes into a potion for the belly of my Kodak" (*Gift*, 122–23 [ch. 2]). Eventually, however, he catches himself, and he recognizes the problem with this approach. As he writes to his mother to explain why he is not continuing the biography, he states: "If you like I'll admit it: I myself am a mere seeker of verbal adventures . . . I have realized, you see, the impossibility of having the imagery of his travels germinate without contaminating them with a kind of secondary poetization, which keeps departing further and further from that real poetry with which the live experience of these receptive, knowledgeable and chaste naturalists endowed their research" (*Gift*, 139 [ch. 2]). It should be noted here that Fyodor's penchant for projection is evident throughout the novel. Not only does he imagine the perspective of Alexander Chernyshevski brooding over the loss of his son to suicide (*Gift*, 33–35 [ch. 1]), he also creates an imaginary representation of a fellow writer named Koncheyev and conducts two imaginary conversations with this fictional construct.

Having erred on the side of personal projection in the unfinished biography of his father, Fyodor takes a very different approach in his next project, the Chernyshevski biography that forms chapter 4 of the *The Gift*. To convey the tenor of Chernyshevski's life and fate, Fyodor adopts an unusual stance: he treats Chernyshevski almost as if the historical figure were a literary character. Fyodor does not falsify or invent events, but he turns up subtle repetitions and connections in Chernyshevski's life and treats them as one would the "themes" found in fiction – the "theme of 'nearsightedness,'" "another theme – that of 'angelic clarity,'" etc. (*Gift* 214–15 [ch. 4]). Part of the way through his narrative, Fyodor declares: "the motifs of Chernyshevski's life are now obedient to me – I have tamed its themes, they have become accustomed to my pen" (*Gift*, 236; [ch. 4]).

The portrait of Chernyshevski that emerges from this treatment is complex. While Fyodor is unsparing in his criticism of the contradictions and confusion he finds in Chernyshevski's pronouncements on art, the reader also senses a certain degree of sympathy for Chernyshevski's consistent lack of good fortune in life. Indeed, one finds several aspects of Chernyshevski's biography that resonate with corresponding elements in Fyodor's life. To begin with, they share a birthday: July 12, 1828 for Chernyshevski, and July 12, 1900 for Fyodor. What is more, Chernyshevski possessed a "mysterious 'something'" (*Gift*, 264 [ch. 4]) that recalls a trait Fyodor had perceived in his own father: "In and around my father . . . there was something difficult to convey in words, a haze, a mystery . . . It was as if this genuine, very genuine man possessed an aura of something still unknown but which was perhaps most genuine of all" (*Gift*, 114 [ch. 2]). It is worth recalling that Cincinnatus too possessed this type of mysterious aura, and in both the case of Cincinnatus and Chernyshevski, this aura aroused fear and discomfort within the political authorities. As Fyodor puts it: "Magnetic and dangerous, it was this that frightened the government more than any proclamations" (*Gift*, 264 [ch. 4]). Then too, Chernyshevski's long years of exile and separation from his family may also have reminded Fyodor of his own father's absence. Finally, the difficult relationship Chernyshevski had with his son presents a dark counterpart to the deep love and respect Fyodor felt for his father.

Despite the nuances that Nabokov worked into this portrait, the generally irreverent tone of the piece led the editors of the journal *Sovremennye zapiski* to decline to publish the chapter when Nabokov submitted it to them, thereby emulating the reaction of a fictional editor in *The Gift* who terms Fyodor's work "reckless, antisocial, mischievous" and refuses to publish it (*Gift*, 207 [ch. 3]). As a marker of Fyodor's maturation, however, the Chernyshevski biography reveals the writer achieving a significant balance. He neither overwhelms the subject with elements of personal projection as he felt he was doing in the biography of his father (or, as Hermann Karlovich did throughout *Despair*), nor does he shy away from expressing his unique personal vision (as Cincinnatus feared doing in *Invitation to a Beheading*).

The reader of *The Gift* perceives a steady progression in Fyodor's creative efforts. From the early works which dealt exclusively with personal experiences (his poems about his childhood), Fyodor attempted to write a work about another person – his father – but he again found himself investing that account with too much personal projection. Eventually he was able to write an account of another person with more detachment, separated as he was from the subject by time and temperament. Now, having attained a precious equipoise between engagement and detachment, he has acquired the technical skills to return to the treasured material of his own life with the aim of preserving it in art.

A pivotal moment in this process occurs during an episode of sunbathing in the Grunewald. Having stripped naked, Fyodor submits himself to the sun's rays. He writes: "The sun licked me all over with its big, smooth tongue. I gradually felt that I was becoming moltenly transparent, that I was permeated with flame and existed only insofar as it did. As a book is translated into an exotic idiom, so was I translated into sun" (*Gift*, 333 [ch. 5]). Fyodor's description of his contact with the flaming rays of the sun invokes imagery used repeatedly by Cincinnatus to describe his perception of a higher, more authentic realm of being. For example, trying to characterize the feeling he gets when he imagines this more authentic reality, Cincinnatus compares it to lying supine on a gloomy day, when suddenly, "the gloom stirs . . . and you know that the sun has just come out from behind the clouds" (*IB*, 94 [ch. 8]); he compares his own nature to a top spinning "such tongues of flame, that to this day I occasionally feel . . . that first branding contact, the mainspring of my 'I'" (*IB*, 90 [ch. 8]). Cincinnatus later prefaces a recollection of a childhood experience of walking on air with a description of the "gliding sun, which would suddenly spill out passionate light" and which would be repeated "in the flaming glass of the open window" (*IB*, 96 [ch. 8]).

At this moment of contact with the sun, Fyodor experiences a sense of bifurcation similar to the doubling depicted in *Invitation to a Beheading*. One aspect of Fyodor's being, the "skinny, chilly hiemal Fyodor Godunov-Cherdyntsev" was as "remote" as a Siberian exile, whereas "[m]y personal I, the one that wrote books, the one that loved words, colors, mental fireworks, Russia, chocolate and Zina – had somehow disintegrated and dissolved" (*Gift*, 333–34 [ch. 5]). Fyodor, however, does not go that far ("One might dissolve completely that way"): he gets up and leaves the Grunewald. Nonetheless, one has the impression that Fyodor's sunbathing experience has brought him into contact with a higher plane of being, one that confirms his progress as an artist. Making his way through the Grunewald, Fyodor is struck with a series of recollections of death – the presumed death of his father, the suicide of a young man named Yasha Chernyshevski, and the death of Yasha's own father. Seized with a desire not to allow all these experiences "to . . . get lost in his soul's lumber room," Fyodor now realizes "There is a way – the only way" (*Gift*, 337 [ch. 5]).

This "way," of course, is art, and Fyodor soon tells Zina both that he is "black as a gypsy from the Grunewald sun" and that "[s]omething is beginning to take shape – I think I'll write a classical novel, with 'types,' love, fate, conversations" (*Gift*, 349 [ch. 5]). As if to validate this decision, Fyodor dreams of meeting his father, who signals his pleasure with his own travels and with his son's book about him, blessing, as it were, the path his son has chosen. The dream ends with Fyodor in his father's arms: "there swelled an ecstatically happy, living, enormous paradisal warmth in which his icy heart melted and dissolved" (*Gift*, 355). With this additional endorsement of the spirit, Fyodor outlines to Zina his ideas on a novel that would deal with the way that fate had brought them together. Zina cautions him that his plan would result "in an autobiography with mass executions of good acquaintances," to which Fyodor responds: "Well, let's suppose that I so shuffle, twist, mix, rechew and rebelch everything . . . that nothing remains of the autobiography but dust – the kind of dust, of course, which makes the most orange of skies" (*Gift*, 364 [ch. 5]).

Many critics regard the text of *The Gift* as that autobiography that Fyodor envisions, only "shuffled," "twisted," and "mixed," and the complex manipulation of first-person and third-person modes of narration in the work may lend support to this view. If one accepts the notion that to write about someone's life (even one's own) inevitably casts a patina of fiction over the treatment of that life, then it is understandable that the mature author responsible for the text of *The Gift* might regard his younger self from an externalized perspective, and would therefore treat this younger self as something like a literary character, a "he" as much as an "I."[15] Indeed, toward the end of the novel the reader senses a divergence between the narrating consciousness (which up until this point has mainly been associated with Fyodor) and the figure of Fyodor himself. First, the reader becomes aware of a crucial fact that the character Fyodor does not realize: that Fyodor and Zina are locked out of the apartment that they anticipate sharing for the first time alone. Then, in the very last lines of the novel, as Fyodor and Zina head off to that apartment, the narrative consciousness pulls away and cries out: "Good-bye, my book!" (*Gift*, 366 [ch. 5]), leaving the reader to wonder how Fyodor and Zina will handle their imminent discovery of the missing keys. The novel thus ends on an open note, and Nabokov's author asserts: "the shadows of my world extend beyond the skyline of the page, / blue as tomorrow's morning haze – nor does this terminate the phrase" (*Gift*, 366 [ch. 5]). Although the written text may have a finite ending, the created world lives on in the author's and reader's consciousness.

While presented in the form of a paragraph, the last lines of the novel can be rearranged to form the stanzaic structure used by Pushkin in his novel in verse, *Eugene Onegin*, and this evocation of Pushkin provides a fitting end to a novel about the nature of creative consciousness, growth, and the passage of time. What is more, Nabokov signals here his own allegiance to the Pushkinian tradition in Russian literature. Earlier in the novel, in preparation for the biography of his father, Fyodor had read Pushkin to "strengthen the muscles of his muse"; he "fed on Pushkin, inhaled Pushkin" to the point where "Pushkin entered his blood" and "Pushkin's voice" merged with "the voice of his father" (*Gift* 97–98 [ch. 2]). In fact, *The Gift* as a whole serves as a rebuttal to those in the émigré community who viewed Pushkin as an outdated relic and called for a literature that would give voice to the raw anguish of modern life.[16] In *The Gift*, however, Nabokov outlines an alternative direction for Russian literature: not to wallow in despair, but to take the best of what life has to offer and to pass it through the receptive filter of the creative consciousness to fashion new works of timeless grandeur and relevance.

In the sequence of novels from *Despair* to *The Gift* Nabokov fashioned a body of work displaying three variants of the creative personality. Beginning with one who suffers from an overinflated ego and who tries to impose his personal fantasies onto those around him, Nabokov went on to depict a character saddled with the opposite condition: he is so intimidated by the dictates of the unimaginative beings who surround him that he does not dare to trust the insights of his individual inspiration. Finally, in *The Gift* Nabokov portrayed an artist who managed to attain a fine balance between respect for the autonomy of others and the capacity to perceive, reshape, and arrange impressions derived from living experience to create new, unique works of art. In his later work, Nabokov would explore other variants of the creative personality. Thus far in his career, however, *The Gift* stands out as Nabokov's most concentrated celebration of the full richness and mystery of life, with its losses and disappointments as well as its joys and rewards, and of the capacity of art to record and immortalize that richness. It stands as a fitting capstone to Nabokov's brilliant achievement in Russian prose.

NOTES

1. In 1937 Vladislav Khodasevich made the famous (and only slightly overstated) declaration that "[t]he life of the artist and the life of a device in the consciousness of the artist – this is Sirin's theme, revealing itself to some degree or other in almost every one of his writings." Khodasevich, "On Sirin," trans. Michael H. Walker, ed. Simon Karlinsky and Robert P. Hughes, *TriQuarterly* 17 (1970): 100.
2. For a discussion of some of these signs, see William C. Carroll, "The Cartesian Nightmare of *Despair*," in *Nabokov's Fifth Arc: Nabokov and Others on His Life's Work*, ed. J. E. Rivers and Charles Nicol (Austin: University of Texas Press, 1982), 84–85.
3. For a discussion of Hermann's relationship to literary characters from the past, see Julian Connolly, "The Function of Literary Allusion in Nabokov's *Despair*," *Slavic and East European Journal* 26 (1982): 302–13; and Alexander Dolinin, "Caning of Modernist Profaners: Parody in *Despair*," *Cycnos* 12.2 (1995): 43–54.

4. See Julian Connolly, *Nabokov's Early Fiction: Patterns of Self and Other* (Cambridge: Cambridge University Press, 1992), 157–58.

5. For a discussion of the theatrical motifs in the novel, see Dabney Stuart, *Nabokov: The Dimensions of Parody* (Baton Rouge: Louisiana State University Press, 1978), 58–67.

6. For an illuminating discussion of the way Nabokov encodes the "here/there" ("tut/tam") dichotomy into the letters that make up the text of the novel, see D. Barton Johnson, *Worlds in Regression* (Ann Arbor: Ardis, 1985), 162–67.

7. Gavriel Shapiro discusses Christian iconography in the text in his *Delicate Markers: Subtexts in Vladimir Nabokov's* Invitation to a Beheading (New York: Peter Lang, 1998).

8. Sergej Davydov, "*Invitation to a Beheading*," in *The Garland Companion to Vladimir Nabokov*, ed. Vladimir E. Alexandrov (New York: Garland, 1995), 192. See also Robert Grossmith, "Spiralizing the Circle: The Gnostic Subtext in Nabokov's *Invitation to a Beheading*," *Essays in Poetics* 12 (1987): 51–74.

9. For an insightful analysis of the relationship between political totalitarianism and the destruction of art as disclosed in the novel, see Robert Alter, "*Invitation to a Beheading*: Nabokov and the Art of Politics," *TriQuarterly* 17 (1970): 41–59; reprinted in Alfred Appel, Jr., and Charles Newman, eds., *Nabokov: Criticism, Reminiscences, Translations and Tributes* (Evanston, IL: Northwestern University Press, 1971), 42–59; also reprinted in Julian W. Connolly, *Nabokov's* Invitation to a Beheading: *A Critical Companion* (Evanston, IL: Northwestern University Press, 1997), 47–65.

10. See Dale Peterson, "Nabokov's *Invitation*: Literature as Execution," *PMLA* 96 (1981): 824–36; reprinted in Connolly, *Nabokov's* Invitation to a Beheading: *A Critical Companion*, 66–92.

11. See Leona Toker, *Nabokov: The Mystery of Literary Structures* (Ithaca: Cornell University Press, 1989), 135–41.

12. Brian Boyd, *Vladimir Nabokov: The Russian Years* (Princeton: Princeton University Press, 1990), 446.

13. See Boyd, *Russian Years*, 473.

14. "Pushkin, or the Real and the Plausible," trans. Dmitri Nabokov, *The New York Review of Books* (March 31, 1988): 40.

15. Alexander Dolinin argues against the identification of "Fyodor" and the author of the text, asserting that the authorial "I" is separate from both the "he" and the "I" that are associated with Fyodor throughout most of the text. See his essay on *The Gift* in Alexandrov, *Garland Companion*, 163–65.

16. Ibid., 142–43.

9

NEIL CORNWELL

From Sirin to Nabokov: the transition to English

Between the ages of ten and fifteen in St. Petersburg, I must have read more fiction and poetry – English, Russian and French – than in any other five-year period of my life . . . In other words, I was a perfectly normal trilingual child in a family with a large library.

Vladimir Nabokov, *Strong Opinions*, 42–43

By the middle of the 1930s, Nabokov, writing since 1920 under the pen name "V. Sirin," had achieved an enviable reputation as the leading Russian émigré writer of prose fiction. Publication of *Dar* (*The Gift*, written 1933–1938) and *Priglashenie na kazn'* (*Invitation to a Beheading*, 1935–1936) was to put this beyond question. However, by late 1939, the Nabokovs were preparing for an imminent new life in the English-speaking world. In May 1940, as famously described at the close of *Speak, Memory*, they left Europe for New York, on what was to be the penultimate voyage of the liner *Champlain* – just before the fall of Paris. One meteoric career, that of the exiled Russian writer Sirin, was effectively over. A second and, in world terms, rather more explosive career, that of the American-English writer "Vladimir Nabokov," was about to be launched.

How did this all but unparalleled situation come about? The short answer is, as with Nabokov's flight from Russia: the intervention of history. A longer and somewhat more complex answer is founded in the Nabokovs' aristocratic cultural roots, and in our protagonist's personal and literary responses to the Russian émigré, as to the interwar European, artistic scenes. The present chapter, therefore, attempts to examine Nabokov's career in the second half of the 1930s, when he was writing in three languages (Russian, English, and French) and might conceivably have pursued his literary fortunes either in England or in France, rather than in the United States.

After a few preliminary remarks, the Nabokov of these last European years (at least of this stage of his career) will be surveyed in his personae as a budding French and then English writer – together with a glance at his last fictional productions in Russian. Relevant works will also be weighed as contributions toward Nabokov's subsequent career as a full-fledged English writer.

The trilingual development

The Nabokovs, at the turn of the twentieth century, were thoroughly steeped both in inherited wealth and in the Russian and European culture of the more enlightened Russian aristocracy. The first, of course, enabled the second: resident tutors and governesses of various nationalities were employed; extensive foreign trips were taken – to France, Germany, and the Austro-Hungarian Riviera. Russian aristocrats still spoke French (at least for social purposes) and often one or more other languages: Nabokov's parents were unusually well versed in English and V. D. Nabokov had good German. Vladimir Nabokov always stressed his "English" upbringing, which he liked to date virtually from the cradle: "I was bilingual as a baby" (*SO*, 5); "I was an English child" (*SO*, 81); "I was a perfectly normal trilingual child" (*SO*, 43). French was soon added to English and Russian (indeed the native tongue was the one soon enough deemed to require remedial attention, at least in its written form). By the time the October Revolution and civil war brought his idyllic and privileged world crashing down, the eighteen-year-old Nabokov was a highly educated published poet of formidable cultural sophistication.

In emigration, a few family jewels and a generous grant from émigré benevolent funds enabled the two elder Nabokov boys to study at Cambridge, where Vladimir read French and Russian literature (*not* English). The family had meanwhile moved on from London to Berlin. Vladimir settled in Russian Berlin, following graduation and the shocking assassination of his father, to eke out a living in circumstances similar to those described in, for instance, *Mary* and *The Gift*, throwing himself into émigré literary life. Poetry, translations, and soon stories and a succession of novels followed. "V. Sirin" quickly became the leading light of the younger generation of exiled Russian literati.

Ever the Russian at Cambridge, where he felt a need to preserve his native language, Nabokov in Berlin preferred to play the English card. In addition to "Sirin," early Nabokov publications appeared under such affectations as "Cantab" or "V. Cantaboff," while he even invented an English dramatist named "Vivian Calmbrood" (an early forerunner of the more famously anagrammatic "Vivian Darkbloom"), whose works he pretended to translate. Most of Nabokov's translation work of this early period was into Russian (from both English and French). While Nabokov came to know the English language, and its literature, with an almost incredible thoroughness, his spoken English, later taken in America to be "Cambridge English," retained an accented undercurrent of Russian (as revealed by extant recordings and television interviews). He would sometimes insist, however, that English had been "my *first* language."[1] All of these qualities are displayed, or played on, and replayed, in *The Real Life of Sebastian Knight* – in so many ways the key transitional text.

Despite living in Germany for fifteen years, Nabokov claimed never to have learned German. Although his mastery of German certainly never approached that of his three essential tongues, his professed ignorance of that language may well have been considerably exaggerated. This probably stemmed in part from a relative distaste for German life and culture – especially as experienced by the Russian emigration – and again revealed in the Berlin settings of the Russian novels. The rise to power of the Nazis made Germany even less congenial, and indeed dangerous, for the Nabokov family – Véra being of Jewish origin, and with Dmitri (born 1934) as a new addition.

In common with certain other bilinguals and polyglots, Nabokov often claimed not to think in any of his languages, but in images.[2] French had always been regarded as the third string to his bow, but in the 1930s, by which time the center of Russian émigré culture had in any case moved from Berlin to Paris, France called. "Though his French was first-rate," as Brian Boyd puts it, "he never felt it as supple or secure as his English."[3] Nabokov began traveling to give readings in Paris and Brussels and to initiate literary activities in both French and English: indeed, in January 1936, when he composed "Mademoiselle O" ("dashed off" – incredibly – "in two or three days"),[4] he had projects underway in all three of his languages. In January 1937, Nabokov left Berlin for the last time for a reading tour and to seek means of livelihood in France or England. Over the next few months he conducted an affair in Paris, visited England for readings, joined his family in Prague (where his mother still lived), and then brought Véra and Dmitri to the South of France – and subsequently to Paris.

The French Nabokov

Third language or not (and, astonishingly enough, he had translated Mayne Reid's *The Headless Horseman* into French alexandrines at the age of eleven),[5] Nabokov's French achieved a fair measure of literary exposure in the 1930s. He had considered a move to Paris as early as 1930 (when, according to Boyd, "in many ways France still seemed the natural goal").[6] The following year he published an essay treating "the idea of 'the contemporary': the individuality of each person's 'epoch,' and the magic our age's overlooked trifles will have in the eyes of the future."[7] Additionally, and even before settling in France, Nabokov had published his two main French works: the "story" "Mademoiselle O" and an essay on Pushkin. All of Nabokov's works in French, Elizabeth Beaujour has pointed out, have Russian subjects: collectively, moreover, they may be considered to represent aspects of *The Gift*.[8]

"Mademoiselle O," a work existing in a number of versions published by its author outstripping any other Nabokov text (five renditions spread over three languages) also had two precursors. These were the Russian short story "Paskhaln'nyi dozhd'" ("Easter Rain," 1925; *Ssoch*, I:75–81), long thought to have been lost, and fragments of autobiography, written in 1936 (and in English) which do remain lost. The early story features a – with hindsight, at least – very recognizable elderly Swiss governess (on this occasion named Josephine) who, on her return to a wet and gray Lausanne, feels a keen nostalgia for the Russia she had worked in for years. Motifs and passages from this work can be found in the later French and subsequent versions.[9] What happens, therefore, with the "Mademoiselle O" phenomenon, is the following sequence. The original personage (in fact one Cécile Miauton) first emerged from Nabokov's artistic consciousness in a fictional version (in Russian). The work was then recast as an autobiographical chapter (lost and in English), before reaching its fullest fruition in the version written in French. It was next translated into English (as a story), and then revised, again as a story (*Nine Stories*, 1947), but included as chapter 5 of the autobiography (*Conclusive Evidence*), transposed into its Russian counterpart (*Drugie berega*), and finally revised again in English for (the "autobiography revisited") *Speak, Memory*.[10] The whole literary process takes some forty years. Even that was not quite the end of the saga, as the intermediate English version appears again, posthumously, as a self-standing text in its own right, in *The Stories of Vladimir Nabokov* (1995).[11]

The status of "Mademoiselle O," as "cornerstone" of the future autobiography, is well established (*SM*, 8). This "memoir/story," it is claimed, "played a pivotal role in [Nabokov's] developing art of memory."[12] However, justification is needed for the suggestion that the French text may be regarded as, in some sense, "superior." The French "Mademoiselle O" is much the longest of its five versions (being, indeed, close to novella length). Nabokov's readings of it, to francophone audiences (initially, the Brussels Pen Club), were highly successful and soon led to publication in the periodical *Mesures*.[13] Subsequent translations or reworkings (summarized as comprising a reduction of the discursive to achieve concision, with a restructuring into sections and the consequent removal of "link" passages)[14] are viewed by the original version's principal champion, J. E. Rivers, as "variations, not replacements" of a "French text, which qualifies as a neglected masterpiece."[15]

Distinct from the long list of "governesses" in Nabokov's works,[16] Mademoiselle makes it a point of honour to be called "institutrice et non gouvernante" (*Mlle O*, 8). The "O" (retained only in the title of the "story" printings, but disappearing into "chapter 5" of the autobiographies) is insisted upon as the genuine surname (*Mlle O*, 9: "Je viens de l'appeler par son vrai nom").[17] Furthermore, Nabokov's French preamble contains the sentence: "So the idea came to me to save what is left of this image, all the more so because I have always wanted to revive for my own enjoyment, and also as a sign of posthumous gratitude, the exact nuance that the French language gave to my life as a Russian" (*Mlle O*, 8).[18] These points, made in the first couple of pages (and, like much else, not reproduced in the post-French versions), serve to establish a certain uniqueness for Mademoiselle. The first-person narrator here ("Easter Rain" had been told in the third person) confirms an "authenticity" for what will become the extraordinarily emblematic "O" of the dual title (of work and protagonist). The remarkable extrapolations of this process are elaborated in Rivers's masterly exposition of what he calls "an 'o' hologram."[19] The sentence quoted presents a declaration of intent as to the pursuit and re-creation of Mademoiselle's "image" and of the narrator's gratitude and affection – both toward Mademoiselle herself and toward the language imparted to him by this unique "instructress." The French Mademoiselle starts off dead ("signe d'une gratitude posthume" [*Mlle O*, 8]) and is brought to life by artistry.

These features are either completely missing or considerably downplayed in the subsequent versions, in which, it is generally agreed, the narrator's sympathy for Mademoiselle, for whatever reason, appears progressively to diminish. Moreover, the narrator's "confession" of his own feelings as an exile (see *Mlle O*, 14–15), juxtaposed with the situation just described of Mademoiselle, can only lead us to sense, in the French text, "an implied equation: 'Mademoiselle = me.'"[20] These points, and the ramifications of the allusive "O" (which include facets of shape, roundness, circularity, zero, a "world" and "orotundity") are only to be found – and indeed *could* only be found – in the original French version, in a work "written to be read aloud."[21] "Among Nabokov's three languages," Rivers explains, "only French has the natural, unforced orotundity that can be molded by his art into a hologram of Mademoiselle's 'image'" (Mademoiselle, logically enough, sounds at her best in her own language); the French "Mademoiselle O" gives the only clear idea of what Nabokov "would have sounded like if he had gone on" – as he might have done – as a French writer.[22]

Go on he did, but only to publish, in the following year, a literary essay. This time Nabokov had prepared "well in advance," a paper for French listeners, again in Brussels, that he called "a firework display of festive thoughts on the velvet background of Pushkin."[23] Further readings in Paris followed, including a singular occasion on which Nabokov, substituting for a

Hungarian woman writer, addressed an audience largely comprising James Joyce and family (brought along, to help make up the numbers, by mutual friends, Paul and Lucie Léon) and the visiting Hungarian football team.[24] Again, the spoken lecture was enthusiastically received and publication soon followed, this time in *La nouvelle revue française*.[25]

"Pouchkine ou le vrai et le vraisemblable" ("Pushkin, or the Real and the Plausible"), was a quirky Nabokovian extravaganza composed for the centenary of Pushkin's death. After a whimsical introduction to the topic of "fictionized biographies" ("biographies romancées" [364/39]), a subject currently being treated also by Nabokov in *The Gift* (in which, too, Pushkin is an important presence), he provides a few images toward "some nice fictionized biography" ("Voilà de la belle biographie romancée, ou je me trompe fort!" [369/40]).[26] He then proceeds to rescue Pushkin for a French readership by providing samples of his verse in rhymed French, and by including digs along the way at the "criminal mutilation" of Pushkin's texts for operatic purposes, and at the "vastly inferior" Dostoevsky (365/39, 372/41). The verse translations amount to "reasonably plausible Pushkin, nothing more: the true Pushkin is elsewhere" ("C'est du Pouchkine assez vraisemblable, voilà tout: le vrai est ailleurs" [375–76/42]). Nabokov concludes with a brief summary of his own artistic policy. In Nabokov's French writings, as well as in his Russian works of this period, one should perhaps not forget the "influence" of his acknowledged guru – the fictitious French philosopher Pierre Delalande.

Three of Nabokov's novels had already been translated into French and a fourth followed. However, from the period of his French residence onwards, he discontinued serious creative work in French, although he continued to use the language for other purposes. He supervised carefully later French translations (by others) of his English novels; and he did in fact himself translate one Russian story into French.[27]

The English Nabokov

Nabokov's French works were published, then, before he lived in France. Through nearly three years of French residence, he worked in Russian and in English. Indeed, as Beaujour has observed, "throughout Nabokov's career the dominant language of his literary expression was frequently *not* the ambient language of the place where he was physically located."[28] Writing to Gleb Struve in 1933, complaining of slow progress over the French publication of his novels, he declared, "my oldest dream is to be published in English." The following year, a London publisher agreed to take two novels. By 1935, Boyd writes, "the problem of having them translated to meet his standards would set him on the path to writing his fiction in English."[29] Although Nabokov achieved a certain respect in French literary circles, it was duly tempered with reserve. Andrew Field deems this to have been because "his manner was that of the English snob," while Véra Nabokov claimed: "There were no opportunities for a career for him there."[30] According to Lucie Léon Noël, "Volodia simply could not acclimate himself to the French way of life."[31]

Translations

Before leaving Germany, Nabokov had translated one of his two contracted novels into English. *Kamera obskura* (1932–1933), first translated by Winifred Roy, appeared (as *Camera Obscura*) in 1936.[32] Deeply dissatisfied with this translation, but anxious not to lose his first English publication, Nabokov agreed with some reluctance to its appearance. In order to avert a similar fate for *Otchaianie* (1934), the Nabokovs first tried to find their own translator, and then Nabokov proposed his own version of what would appear as *Despair*.[33] This process Nabokov found to be "a frightful business, looking over one's insides and trying them on like a glove and discovering the best dictionary to be not a friend but the enemy camp."[34] One of Struve's students checked the English, and *Despair* duly came out, to little commercial success, in 1937, under the inappropriately popular John Long imprint.[35] On hearing that an American publisher was offering a serious advance for the rights to *Camera Obscura*, however, Nabokov, by now in southern France, again abandoned work on *The Gift*, starting afresh to replace the Roy version with his own. He made a number of changes to the novel, in detail (such as the characters' names) and in substance (as he had done with *Despair*), before it was published in 1938 as *Laughter in the Dark*.[36]

As early as 1935, therefore, Nabokov was writing an autobiographical sketch in English, inquiring about a teaching job in England, and starting to translate his novels into English. Before taking up residence in France, he was in London for readings, revisiting Cambridge, and hearing from Struve that "academic prospects were bleak."[37] Returning to the continent, he moved his family to France, resumed work on *The Gift*, embarked on further novelistic self-translation, began turning his attention to employment possibilities in the United States – and began writing a novel in English: *The Real Life of Sebastian Knight* (*Sebastian Knight* for short). His own English background – linguistic, intellectual, and residential – and the still lingering desire for a career move to England must largely account for the deliberate "Englishness" of Sebastian Knight and his story. As Boyd puts it, to "already written autobiographical sketches of a Russian's early associations with England," Nabokov "spliced . . . his recent impressions of literary London."[38] For his first English (though in all his ninth) novel, composed in a non-English speaking country within an astonishing two months, Nabokov availed himself of linguistic assistance from Lucie Léon and as well, according to her biographer, Véra's "handwriting can be found all over the manuscript of *Sebastian Knight*."[39]

The Real Life of Sebastian Knight

The novel purports to be an attempted biography of the recently deceased writer Sebastian Knight (born 1899), written by his younger half-brother, who makes himself known to the reader only as "V." (*RLSK*, 69 [ch. 8]). This first-person narrator – V., a Russian émigré living in Paris – chooses to write this book in what he modestly terms his "miserable English" (32 [ch. 4]), for reasons that are never explained, and with "a complete lack of literary experience" (99 [ch. 11]). At the same time, he possesses sufficient artistic sophistication to warn the reader: "Remember that what you are told is really threefold: shaped by the teller, reshaped by the listener, concealed from both by the dead man of the tale" (50 [ch. 6]).

Sebastian (or in the rare Russian form "Sevastian" – with its possibly tell-tale "v": 189 [ch. 19]), whose English mother was named Virginia Knight, had acquired, by the time of his death (apparently from hereditary heart disease) in January 1936, a certain reputation as an English writer – the author of five books. The text of *Sebastian Knight* indeed is liberally laced, in the form of reference, quotation, and synopsis, with exemplary evidence of Sebastian's rather mannered and often preciously titled fiction. The father that Sebastian and V. supposedly shared had died in 1913, following a wound sustained in a duel fought over a festering affair of honor (wherein may lie a possible element of paternal doubt). Having left Russia in 1918, Sebastian studied at Cambridge, taking considerable pains to anglicize himself. Not least, he made what may be called the "knight's move" (chess imagery being significant in the novel) of adopting his mother's surname in preference to what V. obfuscates as "our simple Russian name" (56 [ch. 6]).[40] He has an English lover and muse-cum-amanuensis named Clare Bishop, and his contacts with V. are minimal. Sebastian's biography (if not his "real life") is suggestive of several largely inexact parallels, both with the real Nabokov and with several protagonists of Nabokov's Russian fiction.

The "present" of the novel, or its nearest approach in terms of action – interrupted by streams of reminiscence, flashback, reverie, quotation, and other seeming digressions – takes place in the weeks following Sebastian's demise, sometime in March 1936.

Why is the apparently unliterary V. so obsessed with his writer half-brother? Is there more to this than the expressed admiration for his books? And why is he so dismayed by Sebastian's apparent rejection of his Russian roots? The nearest we get to an answer comes through an important chronological displacement saved until the end. *Sebastian Knight* itself emerges, overall, as not so much a biography of its subject (whose "real life" remains unknown and unknowable), but rather an account of the stumbling attempts to approach and compile this would-be biography – or even an oblique "guide" to biographical methodology. It is a book that ultimately contrives to leave all the words in its title (including perhaps even "the" and "of") ultimately open to conjecture.

V. furnishes family background and boyhood reminiscence, before proceeding to his occasional adult meetings with Sebastian in emigration. The quest to uncover Sebastian's biography, sparked by the circumstances of his death (revealed only in the last chapter), leads V. to England. Here he visits Sebastian's London flat, traces his steps in Cambridge, and interviews close acquaintances. These include a certain Mr. Goodman, who has just dashed off an opportunistic and allegedly totally egregious biographical account of his own. However, V. allows himself to be deflected from a confrontation with Clare – surely his most vital witness – and even does the decent (but surely, for a biographer, disastrous) thing of respecting Sebastian's instruction to destroy two bundles of love letters. One of these is from Clare and another from an unknown Russian woman, Sebastian's last and secret love. Undaunted by these blunders, V. picks up the trail of the latter mistress by traveling to Blauberg, the location of Sebastian's ill-fated initial tryst. Here he again meets with failure but, through the chance agency of a mysterious investigator named Silbermann, obtains the names and addresses of four Russian women staying there at the time of Sebastian's 1929 sojourn.

The narrative, moving on to Berlin and Paris, assumes more of the traits of a spoof thriller (Sebastian's first novel, *The Prismatic Bezel*, seemingly belonged to this parodic genre), as apparently false leads may or may not mask the authentic track, and misidentifications mingle with missed clues. Retrospective reckonings and traps fallen into, as well as one set by him, lead V. to jump to, yet fail to verify, conclusions that are assumed by most commentators to be broadly correct – but may still be in error. The final relationship, vis-à-vis Sebastian and indeed each other, of Nina Rechnoy, Helene von Graun, and Madame Lecerf may or may not have been correctly determined by the accident-prone V. If Nina (sometime "de") Rechnoy, *née* Toorovetz (145 [ch. 15]: *tura* being the Russian word for the rook in chess), is really Madame Lecerf, then who is Helene von Graun (the second plausible

Blauberg visitor – other than a woman bearing the surname of one of Nabokov's ancestors, with an added "von")?

The action then flips back to Sebastian's last days. Responding to his brother's SOS letter, and an urgent telegram from a Doctor Starov, V. had undertaken a frustrating race against time, by train from Marseilles to a sanatorium in the environs of Paris – only to embark on a vigil beside the wrong man. Sebastian had already died. Nevertheless, V. claims to have experienced a bedside epiphany, striking a profound chord both with an ill-omened recent dream and a supposed concealed message in Sebastian's last novel. This is what had set V. on his obsessional biographical quest. He has intuited the revelation that "any soul may be yours, if you find and follow its undulations" (202 [ch. 20]). V. thus feels himself to have taken on the persona of Sebastian Knight "on a lighted stage." His culminating metaphor combines the theatrical with the metafictional: "try as I may, I cannot get out of my part: Sebastian's mask clings to my face, the likeness will not be washed off. I am Sebastian, or Sebastian is I, or perhaps we both are someone neither of us knows" (203 [ch. 20]).

Sebastian Knight has been read as a series of biographical approaches mirrored by (or mirroring) each of Sebastian's own fictional works – and there are indeed certain correspondences here.[41] Sebastian's final novel, entitled *The Doubtful Asphodel*, which V. considers to be "unquestionably his masterpiece" (172 [ch. 18]), deals with an unnamed dying man and is felt by V., somewhere within its pages, to contain some "absolute solution" to the mystery of life and death (176, 178). Along with Sebastian's other books, it also includes details or characters that somehow reappear within V.'s own narrative. Furthermore, Sebastian had himself planned to write a book in the form of (once again) a "fictitious biography" (38 [ch. 4]). This prompts some to posit Sebastian Knight himself as the author of "his" *The Real Life* – or final novel. Alternatively, V. is proposed as the "real" novelist, and therefore himself the inventor of Sebastian Knight. Nabokov critics strongly of the "otherworld" persuasion tend to favor a benevolent guiding hand from the deceased Sebastian, extending to V. inspiration and (albeit faltering) assistance.

More satisfying, perhaps, is an interpretation of the apparent final fusion of identity between Sebastian and V. in terms of an allegory of cultural mobility. Thus one can see reflected Nabokov's own choices and decisions at the end of the 1930s. The "English" Russian author Sebastian Knight has belatedly moved back towards his Russian roots, albeit in the tragic circumstances of an unhappy love affair (with, apparently, a Frenchified Russian woman) and a fatal heart condition. He corresponds now in Russian (with this lover and eventually with V.). He submits to treatment by a Russian doctor (Starov) in Paris (cultural capital of the Russian emigration), signing himself into the St. Damier ("chessboard") sanatorium under his Russian name (the place where Nabokov's uncle had died in 1916). And finally he turns again to his Russian half-brother. On the other hand, V., who had chosen France and a nonliterary career over an Anglophile life of letters, finds himself, having "mysteriously take[n] on much of his brother's literary identity" (as Foster persuasively argues), by the end of the book *himself* turning into an English writer (if not exactly that very, or "real," English writer).[42]

"I know, I know as definitely as I know we had the same father, I know Sebastian's Russian was better and more natural to him than his English," insists V. (82 [ch. 9]). It is far from clear within the text that this is indeed so, just as it was to become less obviously the case, in the longer run, in the cultural trajectory of Nabokov himself. Neither is it clear what V. "definitely" knows. "Who is speaking of Sebastian Knight?" is a question twice posed within *The Real Life of Sebastian Knight* (49 [ch. 5]; 63 [ch. 7]). No real answer is ever given; or rather, perhaps, the answers are several.

Rejected while its author still lived in Europe, the novel was published in the United States at the end of 1941 (some eighteen months after the Nabokovs' arrival).[43] Composed in haste, for a British literary competition, "not in his special Russian but in what he felt was a second-rate brand of English,"[44] and not generally accorded a high position in the Nabokov canon, this first English novel remains nevertheless an extraordinary achievement. Nabokov immediately demonstrated his potential as an English writer, producing, to say the least, an apprentice work of the highest order.

The Russian Nabokov

While working in French and English in the second half of the 1930s, Nabokov still produced Russian works as Sirin. In addition to completing his Russian masterpiece *The Gift* (Russian émigré censorship of the "Life of Chernyshevski" notwithstanding), during his French years he wrote poetry and stories, and returned to writing plays. Of greater interest, though, regarding his imminent career as an American author, are his last attempts at substantial prose fiction in Russian.

Mention should first be made of a late and longer Russian story, a comparatively rare foray into political fiction, "Tyrants Destroyed" ("Istreblenie tiranov"), written on the French Riviera and taking almost as long to write as his first English novel.[45] A composite of Hitler, Lenin, and Stalin (based on direct experience of Nazi Germany and indirect knowledge of Soviet Russia), Nabokov's dictator is "at first glance a third-rate fanatic and in reality a pigheaded, brutal, and gloomy vulgarian full of morbid ambition" who "dresses up in godly garb" (*Stories*, 440). Possibilities of liberation through "tyrannicide" (455) and suicide are rejected, in favor of destruction through (literary) ridicule. While this story may not be the most highly regarded example of Nabokov's shorter fiction, it clearly anticipates his second English novel, *Bend Sinister* (1947).

Toward the end of 1939, as plans for departure to America advanced, Nabokov began two Russian novelistic projects that were to be positively his last essays in Russian fiction. Both began as offshoots from *The Gift*, the common thread being that of bereavement (Zina being doomed in that novel's planned sequel).

The Enchanter

The principal Nabokovian antecedent to *Volshebnik* (*The Enchanter*) is indeed to be located within *The Gift*. Zina's stepfather suggests a synopsis for a novel in which "an old goat" marries a woman to get access to her daughter – who proceeds to remain cold and aloof, thereby creating "a kind of Dostoevskian tragedy" (*Gift*, 186 [ch. 3]). *The Enchanter* explores the earlier stages of such a saga. *Lolita*, of course, would take it much further. Both works introduce their own twists into the *Ur*-plot.

The protagonist of *The Enchanter* immediately reveals himself as a closet pedophile whose ambition is to inveigle, by means of cunning strategies, "like a chess player" (*En*, 38), a carefully chosen twelve-year-old girl into a protracted relationship of "enchantment," leading from seduction to sex-slavery. By this stage, he considers that "only a most fortunate combination of circumstances, a hand most inadvertently dealt him by fate, could result in a momentary semblance of the impossible" (24). However, he then immediately spots a suitable target, whom he cynically acquires as a stepdaughter by courting and marrying her dying mother. On the mother's demise, his plan for the child is "to take disinterested care of her, to meld the wave of fatherhood with the wave of sexual love" (49). His designs seem poised for fulfillment when he swiftly whisks the girl away on a trip South.

> We shall live far away, now in the hills, now by the sea, in a hothouse warmth where savagelike nudity will automatically become habitual, perfectly alone (no servants!), seeing no one, just the two of us in an eternal nursery, and thus any remaining sense of shame will be dealt its final blow. There will be constant merriment, pranks, morning kisses, tussles on the shared bed, a single huge sponge shedding its tears on four shoulders, squirting with laughter amid four legs. (72)

However, at the first hotel stop, his haste and the fates appear to conspire against him. A series of minor frustrations culminates in the terrified girl waking up at a crucial moment, and proceeding to scream the place down. The man panics, rushes out, and throws himself under a passing truck. The characters, with one minor exception, are all unnamed; in addition, time and place remain vague. According to Nabokov's 1956 recollection at least: "The man was a central European, the anonymous nymphet was French, and the loci were Paris and Provence" (12).

While *The Enchanter* is usually seen as merely an interesting forerunner to *Lolita*, its author regarded it as an independent work, and it does display qualities of its own. The novella opens with the thoughts, or interior mono-logue, of the protagonist and then continues as an omniscient third-person narrative, reflected through the protagonist's point of view, and extended to the very last moment of the deadly conclusion. It may therefore be consid-ered a disguised first-person narrative of dubious reliability; or, in Dmitri Nabokov's words, it shares with other Nabokovian works a quality of "the study of madness seen through the madman's mind" (111). Critics stress the recurrent fairy-tale motifs (and "enchanter" is in any case a significant word in Nabokov's vocabulary), the imagery of defloration at the beginning and the end, and the leitmotif of the talismanic gold chain.[46] The protagonist of *The Enchanter* has a keen eye for detail, and may in fact himself even be a jeweler, but he is oblivious to the pattern in which he is being enclosed, whatever may be its provenance. He – the enchanter – dies, as Ellen Pifer has observed, still "utterly enchanted, utterly in thrall to his monomania."[47]

The novella *The Enchanter*, then, was written in Russian in Paris during the autumn of 1939 and rejected (presumably for reasons of prudery) by the émigré press. Arriving in America, Nabokov presumed the text lost, or indeed destroyed. Some years later, the basic idea was to be transposed to an American setting and it grew "in secret the claws and wings of a novel" (*En*, 13), to become the much longer and far richer *Lolita*. However, in 1959 a typescript of the work did turn up. Nabokov reread it "with considerably more pleasure than I experienced when recalling it as a dead scrap during my work on *Lolita*," suggesting to his publisher that, as "a beautiful piece of Russian prose, [it] could be done into English by the Nabokovs" (16). At that time the idea was taken no further. However, the work's title did reappear on a later (and indeed final) penciled list of nine Russian stories, which Nabokov considered worthy of publication, and this included pro-posed English titles (all subsequently translated by Dmitri). The considerably longer *The Enchanter*, however (which *had* indeed been Nabokov's intended title), was published separately in 1986, nine years after its author's death (with two brief "Author's Notes," and a translator's essay). The original

Russian text (as *Volshebnik*) was published only in 1991 (reprinted *Ssoch*, V:40–81).

"Solus Rex"

Originally envisaged as a continuation of *The Gift*, what evolved into the proposed novel *Solus Rex* was mapped out by Nabokov late in 1939, and continued until the following April.[48] "Solus Rex," originally the novel's second chapter, though completed first, appeared as a story (by "Vladimir Nabokov") the month before its author's departure for the New World.[49] "Ultima Thule" (intended as chapter 1 of *Solus Rex*) had to wait until 1942, by which time the novel had been finally abandoned, for story publication in a New York émigré journal.[50] The fears of the Nabokovs that inspiration for the *Solus Rex* project might not survive trans-Atlantic upheaval proved well founded. A flavor of how this last Russian novel, which had "promised to differ radically" from all its predecessors, would have developed is conveyed by Nabokov some thirty years later, in a note to the eventual English translation of these two surviving "stories" (*Stories*, 657–58).

"Solus Rex," in its existing form, appears to bear only tangential connection to "Ultima Thule." It is of interest mainly for its anticipation of aspects of *Pale Fire*, and the imaginary northern kingdom of Zembla, though links have also been noted with *Bend Sinister*.[51] "Ultima Thule," however, as an independent work, is another matter. As a story, it may be considered "one of Nabokov's best."[52]

"Ultima Thule" is a first-person narrative, emanating from an artist named Sineusov and addressed to his recently deceased wife, whom he hopes somehow to contact, perhaps through the agency of his former tutor, Adam Falter. Falter appears as a moribund psychotic who, "having passed a hygienic evening in a small bordello" (*Stories*, 506), has stumbled upon a traumatic, supposedly the ultimate, metaphysical discovery. Unwary disclosure of this accidentally acquired "riddle of the universe" (509) to an Italian psychiatrist had immediately killed the latter with astonishment, and Falter ("butterfly" in German augments the English connotations), fearing further police meddling, refuses to reveal it to Sineusov. However, shortly before his own death, his obtuse line of casuistic argument in reply to Sineusov's questions is admitted inadvertently to include "two or three words" constituting "a fringe of absolute insight" (522). Critics usually identify echoes in his discourse of the things supposedly best liked by the deceased Mrs Sineusov ("verse, wildflowers and foreign currency" [*Stories*, 510]) as the significant words, thus demonstrating her afterlife survival and continued influence.[53] This sounds plausible but is also questionable, as this triad may be associated originally with a "strange Swede or Dane – or Icelander" (composer of an epic poem called *Ultima Thule*). Moreover, the implied contact with the beyond through a medium scarcely seems a notion quite as terrifyingly unimaginable as Falter's "superhuman discovery" (505) purports to be. And it could, anyway, be a narratorial or authorial plant. Falter's initial exclamation, upon hearing Sineusov's demand, of "Well, I'll be damned" (513) might be another candidate (though, once again, damnation – however frightening – hardly sounds original). Completion of the novel might have settled such matters but, as it stands, "Ultima Thule" may be considered a Nabokovian counterpart to Henry James's "The Figure in the Carpet." In the tradition of *Sebastian Knight*, it tantalizes the reader with a vital undisclosed secret. What D. Barton Johnson discerns as "the 'Ultima Thule' theme" (the riddle of the universe, or the meaning of death; limited versus unlimited consciousness) is seen as "central to much of Nabokov's mature fiction"; in particular, however, "*Solus Rex* is the incomplete center panel of a triptych," flanked on the left by *Sebastian Knight*, and on the right by *Bend Sinister*.[54]

The trilingual impact

Without examining the total output from the later 1930s, we can still see that period as a profusely prescient, as well as an extraordinarily innovative, stage in Nabokov's literary career. Principally, of course, he composed one of the great twentieth-century Russian novels, *The Gift*. Not only, as already noted, did this work inspire various immediate offshoots; as Boyd has remarked: "Almost all of Nabokov's major artistic projects for thirty years can trace their origins back to *The Gift*."[55] A supposedly subsidiary body of work, however, produced over an unsettled and unsettling five-year trilingual spell, laid the most effective foundations for the coruscating – and largely American – career that was to follow.

Translation of two Russian novels into English prepared Nabokov for tentative self-translations in the 1940s, followed by a much more intensive program fulfilled in the 1960s. Copious preparation of lectures facilitated not only an academic career (at Stanford, Wellesley, and Cornell), but the critical monograph *Nikolai Gogol* (1944), and further (posthumously published) lecture volumes. The Pushkin essay, and verse translations into French, opened the way for versions of Russian poetry into English (*Three Russian Poets*, 1945) and the later, vastly more ambitious (and theoretically distinct), *Eugene Onegin* project. "Mademoiselle O" was the acknowledged "cornerstone" of an eventual autobiography. *The Enchanter* engendered *Lolita*, while the *Solus Rex* chapters also achieved a degree of re-presentation in later English novels. *The Real Life of Sebastian Knight* had launched

Nabokov as an original English novelist. As Beaujour emphasizes, his English, even in the early "apprentice" novels, far from being "second rate," was "richer and more flexible than the language wielded by almost all of his monoglot contemporaries."[56]

Although he lamented the "loss" of his Russian tongue, Nabokov's career as a Russian writer was not entirely over. He planned to complete *Solus Rex*, at least, or even "to write my play about Falter," but never did.[57] He continued writing poetry in Russian; he published the first integral edition of *The Gift* (*Dar*, 1952), followed by the Russian version of his autobiography and a selection of favored stories – *Spring in Fialta* (*Vesna v Fial'te*, 1956) – which, incidentally, included "Tyrants Destroyed" and "Ultima Thule." In 1967 he "Russianed" his *Lolita* – to preserve it from the tender mercies of future Russian translators. Even his trilingualism was to achieve provocative reassertion within the parallel world of *Ada*.

If what is called "the 'Ultima Thule' theme" betokens, in whichever sense (metaphysical or metafictional), the bridging of two worlds, then the end of the 1930s was, for Nabokov, "simply the transition point" – between two continents, two languages, and the two careers which were ultimately to rejoin as one.

NOTES

1. Andrew Field, *VN: The Life and Art of Vladimir Nabokov* (London: Macdonald, Queen Anne Press, 1987), 127.
2. Elizabeth Klosty Beaujour, "Bilingualism," in *The Garland Companion to Vladimir Nabokov*, ed. Vladimir E. Alexandrov (New York and London: Garland, 1995), 37–43.
3. Brian Boyd, *Vladimir Nabokov: The Russian Years* (Princeton: Princeton University Press, 1990), 432.
4. Ibid., 422.
5. Ibid., 81.
6. Ibid., 432.
7. Ibid., 364. "Les écrivains et l'époque," *Le Mois*, no. 6 (June 1–July 1, 1931): 137–39. Nabokov reverted to his real name "only after he had accepted his destiny as a polyglot writer" (Beaujour, *Alien Tongues: Bilingual Russian Writers of the "First" Emigration* [Ithaca and London: Cornell University Press, 1989], 89).
8. Beaujour, *Alien Tongues*, 91.
9. Svetlana Polsky, "Vladimir Nabokov's Short Story 'Easter Rain,'" *Nabokov Studies* 4 (1997): 151–62.
10. For comparisons, see Jane Grayson, *Nabokov Translated: A Comparison of Nabokov's Russian and English Prose* (Oxford: Oxford University Press, 1977), 147–55; John Burt Foster, Jr., "An Archeology of 'Mademoiselle O': Narrative Between Art and Memory," in *A Small Alpine Form: Studies in Nabokov's Short Fiction*, ed. Charles Nicol and Gennady Barabtarlo (New York and London: Garland, 1993), 111–35. Foster also considers Nabokov's use of French

writers within the texture of (the French) "Mademoiselle O." His *Nabokov's Art of Memory and European Modernism* (Princeton: Princeton University Press, 1993), 110–29, is substantially identical.

11. The note in *Stories* (661), taken from *Nabokov's Dozen* (1958), is less informative than later reprintings of *Nabokov's Dozen* mentioning the "final text" of 1967 (e.g., Penguin, 1984, 175). Both acknowledge Hilda Ward's assistance with the first English version (*Atlantic Monthly*, 1943), erroneously citing French publication as "1939."

12. Foster, "An Archeology," 131.

13. Quotations from Vladimir Nabokov, *Mademoiselle O* (Paris: Julliard, 1982), 7–36 (hereafter cited as *Mlle O* in text).

14. Grayson, *Nabokov Translated*, 147–48.

15. J. E. Rivers, "Alone in the Void: 'Mademoiselle O,'" in *Torpid Smoke: The Stories of Vladimir Nabokov*, ed. Steven G. Kellman and Irving Malin (Amsterdam: Rodopi: 2000), 87. On translations as "replacements" of original texts, see Beaujour, "Translation and Self-Translation," in Alexandrov, *Garland Companion*, 714–24.

16. Rivers, "Alone," 95–96.

17. While untrue biographically, this is not impossible historically (Rivers, "Alone," 119). Kleist's very different *The Marquise of O* might also come to mind.

18. Translation from Rivers, "Alone," 117 (otherwise, the French original remains untranslated).

19. Ibid., 120ff.

20. Ibid., 103.

21. Ibid., 122: "orotundity," meaning "with round mouth" (*Webster's*), emphasizes the particularity of (French) vowels and the shaping of the mouth to produce them.

22. Ibid., 130, 88.

23. Boyd, *Russian Years*, 431.

24. Ibid., 432; *SO*, 86; Neil Cornwell, *James Joyce and the Russians* (Basingstoke and London: Macmillan, 1992), 71–79.

25. Vladimir Nabokoff-Sirine, "Pouchkine ou le vrai et le vraisemblable," *La Nouvelle revue française*, 25 (March 1937): 362–78; "Pushkin, or the Real and the Plausible", trans. Dmitri Nabokov, *The New York Review of Books* (March 31, 1988): 38–42. Quotations refer to French followed by English page numbers.

26. On Pushkin's impact on Nabokov, see Sergej Davydov, "Nabokov and Pushkin," in Alexandrov, *Garland Companion*, 482–96; Irena Ronen, "Nabokov the Pushkinian," in *Nabokov at Cornell*, ed. Gavriel Shapiro (Ithaca and London: Cornell University Press, 2003), 114–22.

27. "Musique" ("Muzyka," 1932), *Les Nouvelles littéraires*, 1959 (noted by Grayson, *Nabokov Translated*, 11–12). The translations were: *La Course du fou* (*The Defense*), 1934; *Le Guetteur* (*The Eye*), 1935; *Chambre obscure* (*Camera Obscura*), 1937; and *La Méprise* (*Despair*), 1939 (controversially reviewed by Jean-Paul Sartre).

28. Beaujour, *Alien Tongues*, 88.

29. Boyd, *Russian Years*, 407.

30. Field, *VN*, 193.

31. Beaujour, *Alien Tongues*, 213, n. 45.

32. Book publication: *Kamera obskura*, 1933; *Camera Obscura*, trans. Winifred Roy (John Long [an imprint of Hutchinson]: London, 1936).

33. Book publication: *Otchaianie*, 1936; *Despair*, trans. by the author (London: John Long, 1937). See Boyd, *Russian Years*, 419–20.

34. Nabokov to Zinaida Shakhovskaya (October 1935). See Boyd, *Russian Years*, 421.

35. Ibid., 430.

36. Ibid., 445. *Laughter in the Dark* (Indianapolis: Bobbs-Merrill, 1938); final revised edition, 1961. *Despair* was revised again in 1966 (Grayson, *Nabokov Translated*, 23–58; 59–82).

37. Boyd, *Russian Years*, 435.

38. Ibid., 495–96.

39. Ibid., 503; Stacy Schiff, *Véra (Mrs Vladimir Nabokov)* (London: Picador, 1999), 97.

40. The "knight's move" (or "gambit") in chess allows that piece to proceed "in an L-shaped move of two squares in one row and one square in a perpendicular row over squares that may be occupied" (*Webster's New Collegiate Dictionary*); or "two squares horizontally and one vertically or two vertically and one horizontally" (*Encarta World English Dictionary*). Nabokov, a composer of chess problems, was fond of the concept, as may be seen by his poem "The Chess Knight" ("Shakhmatnyi kon'," 1928) and the novel *The Defense* (*Zashchita Luzhina*, 1930). His use of the phrase in a literary sense (for example with reference to Jane Austen in his *Lectures on Literature*, referring to "Fanny's chequered emotions" [*LL*, 57]) may derive (unacknowledged) from Viktor Shklovsky's collection of essays entitled *Knight's Move* (*Khod konia* [Berlin, 1923]); and, according to G. M. Hyde, Carroll's *Through the Looking Glass* (see Hyde, *Vladimir Nabokov: America's Russian Novelist* [London: Marion Boyars, 1977], 87–90).

41. See J. B. Sisson, "The Real Life of Sebastian Knight," in Alexandrov, *Garland Companion*, 633–43; and, on Sebastian Knight and modernism, Foster, *Nabokov's Art of Memory*, 159–70.

42. Foster, *Nabokov's Art of Memory*, 165. Cf. Priscilla Meyer, "Black and Violet Words: *Despair* and *The Real Life of Sebastian Knight* as Doubles," *Nabokov Studies* 4 (1977): 37–60. Nabokov's relationship with his own brother, Sergei, may also be pertinent (Susan Elizabeth Sweeney: cited by Meyer, 36; 60).

43. *The Real Life of Sebastian Knight* (Norfolk, CT: New Directions, 1941).

44. Boyd, *Russian Years*, 496.

45. Ibid., 486–87. "Istreblenie tiranov," *Russkie zapiski*, August–September 1938; *Stories*, 438–60.

46. Gennady Barabtarlo, "Those Who Favor Fire (on *The Enchanter*)," *Russian Literature Triquarterly* 24 (1991): 89–112; Susan Elizabeth Sweeney, "*The Enchanter* and the Beauties of Sleeping," in Shapiro, *Nabokov at Cornell*, 30–45.

47. Ellen Pifer, "*Lolita*," in Alexandrov, *Garland Companion*, 315.

48. Boyd, *Russian Years*, 505, 516–17.

49. "Solus Rex," *Sovremennye zapiski* 70 (April 1940): 5–36; *Ssoch*, V:85–112; *Stories*, 523–45.

50. "Ultima Thule," *Novyi zhurnal* 1 (1942): 49–77; *Ssoch*, V:113–39; *Stories*, 500–22.

51. D. Barton Johnson, *Worlds in Regression: Some Novels of Vladimir Nabokov* (Ann Arbor: Ardis, 1985), 206–23.
52. Boyd, *Russian Years*, 518.
53. Field, *Nabokov: His Life in Art* (London: Hodder and Stoughton, 1967), 308.
54. Johnson, *Worlds in Regression*, 215.
55. Boyd, *Russian Years*, 520.
56. Beaujour, *Alien Tongues*, 105.
57. Brian Boyd, *Nabokov: The American Years* (Princeton: Princeton University Press, 1991), 13, 23.

10

GALYA DIMENT

Nabokov's biographical impulse: art of writing lives

"[T]he motifs of Chernyshevski's life are now obedient to me," Fyodor Godunov-Cherdyntsev tells his imagined reader in Nabokov's *Gift*. "I have tamed its themes, they have become accustomed to my pen; with a smile I let them go: in the course of development they merely describe a circle, like a boomerang or a falcon, in order to end by returning to my hand; and even if any should fly far away, beyond the horizon of my page, I am not perturbed; it will fly back . . ." (*Gift*, 236–37 [ch. 4]).

The Gift, written in 1935–1937, is a perfect, concrete place to ground our general discussion of major trends in Nabokov's art of biographical and autobiographical presentation, for the novel richly contains them all. In addition to the "real" biography of N. G. Chernyshevski, a nineteenth-century Russian writer, publicist, and political activist (chapter 4), it features an unfinished biographical sketch of Fyodor's father (chapter 2), which contains themes from the life of Nabokov's own father; and it also presents a "fictional" biographical exposé of Berlin émigré and Chernyshevski namesake, Yasha Chernyshevski (chapter 1). Furthermore, the novel as a whole is one of the classic examples of an autobiographical *Bildungsroman*, akin to Joyce's *A Portrait of the Artist as a Young Man*.

Writing lives of "real" others

In *Strong Opinions*, published almost forty years after the Russian version of the novel, which came out in *Sovremennye zapiski* (a Russian émigré literary periodical published in Paris) in the late 1930s, Nabokov would defend Fyodor's – and ultimately his[1] – life of Chernyshevski as authentic because it was based on "plain facts" and "the plain truth of documents" (*SO*, 156). His notion of authenticity, however, appears to have been different from that of many other biographers. We can definitely hear Nabokov's own objections when Fyodor condemns "those idiotic '*biographies romancées*'

170

where Byron is coolly slipped a dream extracted from one of his own poems" (*Gift*, 200 [ch. 3]), and yet, Nabokov himself was by no means a "purist" in any traditional sense.

Upon deciding to write the life of Chernyshevski, Fyodor tells his girlfriend, Zina: "I want to keep everything as it were on the very brink of parody . . . I must make my way along [a] narrow ridge between my own truth and a caricature of it" (*Gift*, 200 [ch. 3]). Chernyshevski's biography, however, comes to the very edge of the "brink," and, many would argue, often goes over the line. "As is invariably noted at the beginning of positively all literary biographies," the author tells us at the start, "the little boy was a glutton for books" (*Gift*, 213 [ch. 4]). About Chernyshevski's wife, Olga Sokratovna, we read: "How she used to fling the plates around! What biographer can stick the pieces together?" (*Gift*, 235 [ch. 4]). In a similar satirical vein, Ludwig Andreas Feuerbach is russified into "Andrey Ivanovich Feuerbach," while Georg Wilhelm Friedrich Hegel is transformed into "Egor Fyodorovich Hegel" (*Gift*, 243 [ch. 4]).

Chernyshevski was an easy target for caricature – an honest, often sentimental idealist with a messy personal life and a rather heavy-handed, inelegant writing style, he left enough "compromising" materials in his diaries and letters for any parodist worthy of his trade to hang him. And yet he was so much more. Imprisoned and exiled at the height of the harshest years of Nicholas I and his secret police, Chernyshevski spent nineteen years in Siberia, and when he was finally allowed to return to a Volga town, Saratov, where he had been born sixty-one years earlier, he was a sick and broken man who would only live another four months. Chernyshevski's utopian novel, *What Is to Be Done?*, may have been woodenly written, but due to its lofty ideas of democracy and women's emancipation it became the most influential literary work of its generation. That Nabokov largely ridiculed Chernyshevski's life, his work, and his sufferings in *The Gift* was so offensive even to Nabokov's peers in emigration that the otherwise tolerant editors of *Sovremennye zapiski*, where the novel was appearing in installments, went as far as to suppress chapter 4 altogether.

While Nabokov could not anticipate the fate of his biography in the hands of the editors, he did anticipate the general outrage it would cause in the reaction of the fictional critics to Fyodor's work: "to lampoon a man whose works and sufferings have given sustenance to millions of Russian intellectuals is unworthy of any talent" (*Gift*, 207 [ch. 3]). The critics – real, as well as fictional – came, of course, armed with a common assumption that biographies should be "fair and balanced," with no distortions and no exaggerations. It was not, however, an assumption Nabokov held. The narrow ridge Fyodor speaks of to Zina separates so much more than just seriousness and hilarity: it also separates "fact" and fiction and, as we will see below, "imagination" and "invention."

One does not have to go far to find instances of rather obvious fictionalizing in the life of Chernyshevski, beginning with the references to one of his other biographers, Mr. Strannolyubski ("Strangelove"), who turns out to be every bit as fictional as Fyodor. In a more general way, patterning of the themes, or as Fyodor puts it in the quote I started this chapter with, "taming" the themes to make them "obedient" (the device which is also so prominent in a later depiction of Nabokov's own life in *Speak, Memory*) is, of course, another technique we usually do not associate with biographies of "real" people.

When accused of "fictionalizing" his biographical and autobiographical accounts, Nabokov, as we saw earlier, would strongly deny it. He did so, I believe, mostly out of fear that if he gave any ground to his critics, they would fail to make a necessary distinction between his nuanced technique and the crude one of the authors of the "idiotic *'biographies romancées.'*" His technique appears to have been grounded in skillfully designing a very special creative space for himself which lies between the "invented facts" of fiction and the "real facts" of one's personal life, and which he himself called the "imagined facts."[2] The notion itself comes from *Nikolai Gogol*, yet another purely Nabokovian attempt at a biography of a famous Russian writer. There Nabokov explained Gogol's difficulty with writing the second part of *Dead Souls* by suggesting that "he was in the worst plight that a writer can be in: he had lost the gift of imagining facts and believed that facts may exist by themselves. The trouble is that bare facts do not exist in a state of nature, for they are never really quite bare . . ." (*NG*, 119 [ch. 4]).

The way the "bare" facts get transformed into something else in the Chernyshevski chapter has been well analyzed by Irina Paperno, a foremost scholar of Chernyshevski, who comes to the following conclusions when comparing Nabokov's narrative of Chernyshevski's life and the documentary sources Nabokov used in abundance: "Almost every scene of chapter four is based on collaging of 'deformed' material from several documentary sources . . . In his 'deformation' of the documentary material Nabokov consistently applies particular devices . . . The overall impression created is that Nabokov decorates and 'colorizes' the canvas of his documentary material."[3] Nabokov "decorates" his sources because he seems to trust Chernyshevski's contemporaries and "eyewitnesses" no more than he trusts his own critics, and, while using their otherwise helpful information, he makes it serve his larger purposes through a subtle process of transforming pseudo-bare facts of the documentary accounts into "imagined" facts of his artistic narrative.

If we accept Nabokov's dictum that one's talent as a writer is all about "the gift of imagining facts," then in order to fully appreciate his approach to the biography of Chernyshevski we need to cast a closer look at his particular brand of imagination and how it manifests itself there. Keats, who is often associated with the ultimate gift of "sympathetic imagination" in literature, liked to say that a true poet was but a "camelion . . . filling some other Body."[4] There is something of that chameleon in Nabokov as well, for he likes to get into his subject's very skin and to feel from within what makes him tick. Keats also said, however, that in order to become a chameleon, the poet has to abandon his own identity, and that is where, it seems to me, Keats and Nabokov part company. Unlike Keats, Nabokov appears to be incapable or unwilling to fill any body through an act of an intentional "self-negation," and since his "sympathetic imagination" does not necessarily go hand in hand with perfect sympathy for the subjects of his biographies, Nabokov often functions simultaneously as a "sympathetic" spirit and an unsympathetic judge. That is, I believe, what makes his work in this field of literary endeavor so unique.

It also leads to starkly opposite critical views of the biography of Chernyshevski: for every critic who condemns – or praises – it as demeaning to its subject, there is a critic who argues that it is nothing of the sort. Typical in this respect is a comment by L. L. Lee who suggests that "Fyodor's (Nabokov's) strikingly original work makes Chernyshevsky a truly sympathetic, if foolish, man and rescues him from politics in the sense that he becomes human and not a symbol."[5] Another critic, Maurice Couturier, sums up the overall effect of the biography as follows: "the man revives, the myth dies."[6]

This ambiguity of critical views is cleverly anticipated by a discussion which, in *The Gift*, precedes the publication of the biography. Fyodor there tells his audience that he is now "serious" about writing Chernyshevski's life:

> "But how did such a wild thought get into your head?" chimed in Mme. Chernyshevski. "Why, you ought to write – I don't know – say, the life of Batyushkov or Delvig, something in the orbit of Pushkin – but what's the point of Chernyshevski?"
> "Firing practice," said Fyodor.
> "An answer which is, to say the least, enigmatic," remarked the engineer Kern. (*Gift*, 196 [ch. 3])

Here, in a nutshell, are all the ingredients which Nabokov knew would keep his critics busy: his life of Chernyshevski is "wild," inasmuch as it is one of the strangest and most nontraditional biographies ever written; it is obviously "enigmatic" to outsiders; and it is definitely a "firing practice" for Fyodor – and Nabokov – both in the sense of a "warm-up" for later works, and, more importantly, in the sense of mastering shooting to kill.

It is not surprising that Nabokov's gift for sympathetically "imagining facts," his Keatsian ability to "fill" the body of the character and see him from the inside does make Chernyshevski appear to some as more "human," yet one should not be fooled. There is nothing "sympathetic" in the ultimate judgment Nabokov makes so palpable as to what Chernyshevski represents and why, for that reason, he is a proper target for condemnation rather than compassion. The biography of Chernyshevski is as cultural as it is personal, and it is the cultural aspect of it that Nabokov, no doubt, found to be its most authentic and serious quality. Nabokov's condemnation is utterly unambiguous, for he is as likely to spend his sympathy on Chernyshevski as he is on devout Bolsheviks, many of whom also had imprisonments and exiles in their past. "A hundred years ago, in Russia," Nabokov wrote in *Strong Opinions* about the 1860s which Chernyshevski inhabited and personified, "the most eloquent and influential reviewers were left-wing, radical, utilitarian, political critics, who demanded that Russian novelists and poets portray and sift the modern scene . . . That was half a century before the Bolshevist police not only revived the dismal so-called progressive (really regressive) trend characteristic of the eighteen sixties, but, as we all know, enforced it" (*SO*, 11–12).

"The Life of Chernyshevski" proved trend-setting in Nabokov's art of "real" biography. *Nikolai Gogol*, written nearly ten years after *The Gift* and this time with no fictional intermediaries, has a lot in common with Fyodor's biography. The first incarnation of *Nikolai Gogol* was even called "Gogol Through the Looking Glass," which slyly underscored the monograph's truly fanciful nature and its rejection of the existence of "bare facts." As was the case with the "Life of Chernyshevski," critics were quick to notice the seeming idiosyncrasy of the biography. Thus reviewing *Nikolai Gogol* for *The New Yorker* in 1944, Edmund Wilson chided his then friend for having done Gogol "a certain amount of violence" by making him appear more like a rather ridiculous fictional character in one of Nabokov's novels than the "real" writer of his own superb fiction.[7] Nabokov, in the best tradition of his invariable public denials of all such allegations, called his treatment of Gogol just "the innocent . . . little sketch of his life" (*SO*, 156). There is, however, a major distinction between the two biographies inasmuch as Lee's "sympathetic-if-foolish" formulation, which is inappropriate for "The Life of Chernyshevski," does fit *Nikolai Gogol*. We actually have something here Nabokov considers worthy for him – and us – to sympathize with: namely Gogol's genius as a writer.

Writing his own life in fiction and autobiography

When I say that Nabokov had his own special technique of writing biographies, including his own, I do not at all want to suggest that he had an elaborately worked-out theory applicable to all. His public pronouncements on the subject are, as we have seen, so contradictory as to make any theoretical consistency impossible. After all, he both dismissed the existence of "bare facts" *and* kept professing his belief in the existence of "plain facts," which he invoked not only in his defense of Fyodor's biography but also in his admonition to his own future biographers: "That, and only that, is what I would ask of my biographer – plain facts, no symbol-searching, no jumping at attractive but preposterous conclusions . . ." (*SO*, 156). Nabokov's appears to have been a rather instinctual and highly private system: he simply trusted himself with knowing when the line between "invention" and "imagination" was in danger of being crossed, and did not necessarily trust others. His own biographers were, therefore, strongly discouraged from attempting any balancing act which involved coming too close to the "brink."

One of the best indicators of Nabokov's core beliefs when it comes to how *he* could best achieve the authenticity and accuracy of a personal record, including his own, may be found in, among others, a comment he made about the portrayal of his relationship with Valentina (Liusia) Shulgina in his first novel *Mary* and in his subsequent autobiography, *Speak, Memory*: "I had not consulted *Mashenka* [*Mary*] when writing Chapter Twelve of the autobiography a quarter of a century later; and now that I have I am fascinated by the fact that despite the superimposed inventions . . . a headier extract of personal reality is contained in the romantization than in the autobiographer's scrupulously faithful account" (*Mary*, xiv). Leaving aside, for a moment, his statement that *Speak, Memory* is scrupulously faithful, "the very notion that one's personal reality" can be often better transmitted through fiction than nonfiction is quite striking here. At the very least, it does suggest that if the truthful rendering of such "personal reality" is the ultimate goal of a biographer or an autobiographer, then drawing too strict a line between fiction (of a proper kind, of course) and nonfiction in presenting personal material could be counterproductive.

It was probably for that reason that in a later-discarded introduction to the first version of his autobiography, *Conclusive Evidence*, Nabokov boldly defined his narrative as "the meeting point of an impersonal art form and a very personal life story."[8] He would also suggest in *Strong Opinions* that a deliberate "distortion of a remembered image may not only enhance its beauty with an added refraction, but provide informative links with earlier or later patches of the past" (*SO*, 143). Thus life, whether one's own or somebody else's, when imaginatively "distorted" (or "deformed," as Paperno puts it) and "refracted," rather than slavishly "recorded" in an unrealistic pursuit of "objectivity," is much fuller, more dimensional, and, in the long run, more truly "life-like."

The two accounts of Nabokov's relationship with Valentina Shulgina both have, in fact, a substantial amount of artful "distortion" and "refraction," notwithstanding Nabokov's characterization of the *Speak, Memory* rendition as "scrupulously faithful." Both feature fictional names for the heroines (Tamara in *Speak, Memory*); both heavily rely on "patterns," themes "tamed" to fit the larger designs of Nabokov's narrative. The same can be said about the "Father" chapter of *The Gift* and the "Father" chapter of *Speak, Memory* (chapter 9), a pair that I would like to examine more closely here. Both chapters were of immense importance to Nabokov for, as Georges Nivat suggests in *The Garland Companion to Vladimir Nabokov*, they may actually form "the central chapter" in their respective works because of the crucial role V. D. Nabokov played in his son's life.[9]

Alexander Dolinin makes the following connection between "The Life of Chernyshevski" and the largely unfinished biography of Fyodor's father: "*The Life of Chernyshevski* proves that a biography written by a real artist defames, exorcizes, scorches rather than extols, and, by implication, justifies Fyodor's decision not to write a biography of his father" (in Alexandrov, *Garland Companion*, 155). But the problem may be the opposite, and one can argue that Fyodor does not finish the biography of his father precisely because he, still a novice writer, does not trust himself to be a "real artist" yet and thus feels he is not ready to write a biography where sympathy colors not just his imagination but also his attitude. Nabokov, after all, undoubtedly a "real artist" by the time he sits down to write his autobiography almost fifteen years later, and then revises and amplifies it in the 1960s, does successfully complete a biography of his own father. This progression in the art of biography, from destructive ("firing practice") to constructive (reaffirmation of one's life), goes hand in hand with the progression in maturity and self-knowledge. It is, after all, so much easier to define yourself through what you are not (thus lampooning a stranger) than through what you are: in this case, your father's son.[10]

Ironically, however, it is in this later part – being one's father's son – that *The Gift*, like *Mary*, may actually have "a headier extract of personal reality" than *Speak, Memory*, and thus be very successful as Nabokov's autobiography even if as a biography of Fyodor's father it may fall somewhat short. While in *Speak, Memory* Nabokov *re-creates* his closeness with his father, in the novel he actually *creates* it. He does so by literally conflating his father and himself, letting his father retain his very recognizable personality and biographical traits but making him a passionate lepidopterist with a degree from Cambridge.[11]

But even as a pure biography of the writer's father, and though unfinished, chapter 2 is in some ways at least as "accurate" (in a larger sense) a portrait of V. D. Nabokov as the relevant chapter in *Speak, Memory*. The "bare" facts are changed, for the most part, but barely. While Fyodor's father is – and, importantly so, as I will discuss shortly – ten years older than Nabokov's (born in 1860, as opposed to 1870), his birthday also falls in July (even if the dates are not quite the same – July 8, as opposed to July 20),[12] he marries Fyodor's mother only a year after Nabokov's father marries Vladimir's mother (1898 as opposed to 1897), and the brides are pretty much the same age (twenty and twenty-one). The family summer estate, Leshino, is an obvious "twin" of the Nabokovs' estate in Vyra, and like Elena Nabokov, Fyodor's mother insists on meeting her husband alone on the days he comes on the train from St. Petersburg. Fyodor's father also shares with Vladimir's father long absences from home which made their sons long for their return and instilled in them a burning desire (which Fyodor fulfills in his narrative) to imagine being with their fathers in all their exciting journeys. The similarities in personalities between the two fathers were, in fact, so stark that, according to Brian Boyd, "Nabokov's mother later wrote in astonishment to her son how exactly Godunov captured her husband's every nuance."[13]

When the facts are less than "bare," there occurs "a delicate distortion of a remembered image" for the sake of greater authenticity of a biographical recreation. When Fyodor's mother sends her son a letter describing the early memories of her marriage to his father (like Vladimir's mother, who left Berlin for Prague after the death of her husband, she lives apart from her son, here in Paris), it unmistakably underscores significant touches of Nabokov's real father. The letter depicts Konstantin Godunov-Cherdyntsev as loving but resolute towards his young wife. When, soon after they were married, she decided to surprise him and naively followed him to Central Asia in her "English traveling costume with its short . . . checked skirt, with the binoculars over one shoulder and a kind of purse over the other" (*Gift*, 105 [ch. 2]), her husband immediately and ruthlessly sent her back home. Being eighteen years older than his wife, he often acted toward her like a benevolent but exacting father-figure, the role that Elizaveta Pavlovna seems to have accepted and even been grateful for.

From what we know, this was pretty much the role V. D. Nabokov – "a man of exacting standards sometimes bitingly expressed"[14] – played vis-à-vis his wife, even though they were just six years apart. This, apparently, became especially the case four years after their marriage when, in 1901, the 25-year-old Elena Nabokov lost both of her parents. The true nature of the relationship of the "real" parents is thus portrayed through purely fictional means – the invented personal letter from a mother to a son, and a three-fold increase in the couple's age difference which would make the husband's "fatherly" role toward his wife appear more natural.

Chapter 9 of *Speak, Memory*, which is an amplified version of chapter 9 in the first version of the autobiography, *Conclusive Evidence*, benefited from additional documents in his mother's Prague archive, and remembrances from his siblings which had not been available to Nabokov in the late 1940s. He officially calls what he presents in *Speak, Memory* the "short biography of my father" (*SM*, 173 [ch. 9]). There is an interesting reversal of the usual effect of fiction and nonfiction that can be easily detected when comparing the biography from *The Gift* and the one found here. Whereas in *The Gift* – "superimposed inventions" notwithstanding – we often get very personal and intimate glimpses of Nabokov's own father, his relationship with his wife, and the son's excruciating pain at losing him so early in both their lives, in *Speak, Memory* the account is more artistic and detached, even if the overall emotional impact on the reader is actually more profound. It is a classic example of what Nabokov had in mind when he first defined his autobiography as "the meeting point of an impersonal art form and a very personal life story."

The movement that this chapter follows is symbolic of its overall design and purpose. It starts with the enumeration of the mundane documentary sources of his father's life, similar in their nature to the ones Nabokov used in "The Life of Chernyshevski": "I have before me a large bedraggled scrapbook, bound in black cloth. It contains old documents, including diplomas, drafts, diaries, identity cards, penciled notes, and some printed matter, which had been in my mother's meticulous keeping in Prague until her death there, but then, between 1939 and 1961, went through various vicissitudes" (*SM*, 173 [ch. 9]). It ends with his father seen by Vladimir and us "[w]ith the opportuneness of dream arrangements" elevated "on the red-carpeted landing above" and next to a statue of a Greek goddess who is demoted here to "an armless Greek woman" because there is only one real "god" in this scene, and that is V. D. Nabokov (*SM*, 193 [ch. 9]).

In between, we learn some "bare facts" of the father's earthly life: his education ("he completed the Gymnasium . . . with a gold medal . . . studied law at the St. Petersburg University"); his marriage to Nabokov's mother ("On November 14 . . . 1897, he married Elena Ivanovna Rukavishnikov . . . with whom he had six children"); his political career and views ("he severed all connection with the Tsar's government and resolutely plunged into antidespotic politics . . . He was eloquently against capital punishment . . . In 1906 he was elected to the First Russian Parliament . . ."); his tastes in

literature, music and art ("he knew . . . the prose and poetry of several countries, knew by heart hundreds of verses . . . he must have heard practically
every first-rate European singer between 1880 and 1922 . . .") (*SM*, 175–79
[ch. 9]). More importantly, we are given to understand that two main passions which were to govern the son's life – butterflies and literature – came
directly through or from his father (even if their literary tastes sometimes
diverged a bit).

We also learn that while in the eyes of his son, V. D. Nabokov had always
been akin to a deity, he actually became one when young Vladimir began
to fear for his father's life because of an impending duel. The duel was,
fortunately, averted due to a last-minute apology of the other party, but the
note of relief and happiness at seeing his father alive is not allowed to stand
by itself. It is followed in quick succession by the anticipation of the worst
fears of the son being realized in a not-so-distant future, and, from there, by
a move back onto the elevated platform where his father stood that day to
be forever immortalized in his son's memory and through his son's art:

> ten years were to pass before a certain night in 1922, at a public lecture in
> Berlin, when my father shielded the lecturer (his old friend Milyukov) from
> the bullets of two Russian Fascists and, while vigorously knocking down one
> of the assassins, was fatally shot by the other. But no shadow was cast by that
> future event upon the bright stairs of our St. Petersburg house; the large, cool
> hand resting on my head did not quaver, and several lines of play in a difficult
> chess composition were not blended on the board yet.   (*SM*, 193 [ch. 9])

This quick succession of the elevation to future tragedy and back to elevation and thus immortality is a reinforcement of a similar progression
which occurred in chapter 1 with the scene of grateful peasants tossing V. D.
Nabokov up in the air, in a traditional Russian show of enthusiastic approval:

> I would suddenly see through one of the west windows a marvelous case of
> levitation. There, for an instant, the figure of my father in his wind-ripped white
> summer suit would be displayed, gloriously sprawling in midair, his limbs in a
> curiously casual attitude, his handsome, imperturbable features turned to the
> sky . . . Thrice, to the mighty heave-ho of his invisible tossers, he would fly up
> in this fashion, and the second time he would go higher than the first and then
> there he would be, on his last and loftiest flight, reclining, as if for good, against
> the cobalt blue of the summer noon, like one of those paradisiac personages
> who comfortably soar, with such a wealth of folds in their garments, on the
> vaulted ceiling of a church while below, one by one, the wax tapers in mortal
> hands light up to make a swarm of minute flames in the mist of incense, and the
> priest chants of eternal repose, and funeral lilies conceal the face of whoever lies
> there, among the swimming lights, in the open coffin.   (*SM*, 31–32 [ch. 1])

This succession becomes an obvious narrative device, a persistent "motif" that Nabokov "tames" and makes "obedient to . . . my pen" in order to craft his personal agony at the loss of his father into the detached beauty of "an impersonal art form," and, in the process, to make the biography, as written by "a real artist," into a rare and very powerful blend of *both* sympathy and sympathetic imagination.

Writing lives of fictional others . . . and his own

In terms of its positioning within the axes formed by sympathy and sympathetic imagination, the biography of the fictional Yasha Chernyshevski lies somewhere between the life of his more real and more famous namesake and the biographies of Fyodor's and Nabokov's fathers. It is a story of a painful love triangle which provokes a decision to commit a collective suicide because the conflicts are impossible to resolve. Yasha Chernyshevski is, however, the only one who ends up killing himself, while Olya, who is in love with him, and Rudolf, Yasha's beloved who, in turn, is in love with Olya, think better of it once they see their friend dead.

Fyodor, who feels bad for Yasha's parents, nevertheless finds very little about Yasha himself that he can admire: "The more [Mme. Chernyshevski] continued to tell about Yasha, the less attractive he grew: oh, no, he and I have little resemblance to each other . . . And I doubt we would have become friends if he and I had ever met" (*Gift*, 38 [ch. 1]). He finds Yasha humorless, sentimental, and a bad poet to boot, the same qualities which would make him quite unsympathetic in the eyes of Fyodor's creator as well, and yet, in this particular instance, Fyodor's creator has the kind of additional knowledge the young man still lacks.

Listening to the stories about Yasha as told by his grieving parents, Fyodor is witnessing a situation which is the reverse of his own – instead of a young son losing his father, here it is the parents losing their son. Fyodor cannot yet fully comprehend the impact of such a loss but Nabokov, who by the time of writing *The Gift* is already himself a father of a son, can. This knowledge definitely colors the biography of Yasha Chernyshevski who, while not a very "attractive" character, still attains a high degree of poignancy through his unnecessary and untimely death and, more importantly, through the agony it causes his parents. The theme of parents losing – or on the verge of losing – their son becomes a common one for Nabokov after the birth of his own son, as *Bend Sinister* or "Signs and Symbols" readily testify. It should be noted, however, that even prior to the birth of Dmitri Nabokov in 1934, Nabokov was interested in this reversal of his own personal tragedy.

In "Christmas," a story written in 1925, Nabokov (who was at the time roughly the age of Fyodor in *The Gift*, which takes place in the 1920s) contemplated a situation where a father, bearing a strong resemblance to his own, has to face the death of his teenage son, who is an unmistakable portrait of the young Nabokov. The fictional son shares with the real one Nabokov's butterfly collection, his bicycle trips in search of Tamara-Mary-Liusia along the paths of a place which looks remarkably like Vyra, and even his conviction that Goncharov was "a deadly bore" (*Stories*, 135). As the father reads the entries in his late son's journal, he is devastated: "'I-can't-bear-it-any-longer,' he drawled between groans, repeating even more slowly, 'I–can't–bear–it–any–longer . . .'" (*Stories*, 135). The pain is so overwhelming that Sleptsov is about to end his own life when an Attacus moth, a symbol of his son's otherworldly presence, emerges from a chrysalid and makes the father's life more bearable again. Written soon after V. D. Nabokov's death, "Christmas" thus appears to be an almost therapeutic exercise of imagining an even worse scenario: his father having to deal with losing him.

The agony of having lost a son proves to be unbearable for Alexander Yakovlevich, Yasha's father. Doomed to no comfort since even seeing a ghost of his son is, in the end, nothing but a sign of his rapidly progressing mental instability, he rejects the possibility of an afterlife and literally dies of grief: "The following day he died, but before that he had a moment of lucidity . . . saying . . . 'What nonsense. Of course there is nothing afterwards.' He sighed, listened to the trickling and drumming outside the window and repeated with extreme distinctness: 'There is nothing. It is as clear as the fact that it is raining'" (*Gift*, 312 [ch. 5]). There is, in fact, no rain outside, just a tenant above watering his plants, but it is not given to Alexander Yakovlevich to realize the confusion and see the sun shining brightly.

This is an intricate balancing act Nabokov is playing here. He does employ all the powers of his sympathetic imagination as an artist to describe Yasha's last dismal hours before the suicide, and he does extend a significant degree of sympathy and compassion to Yasha's parents because of their unbearable loss which, as a new father, he can now comprehend more fully. And yet, unlike Sleptsov, Yasha's father is deprived of true comfort because, in Nabokov's system of posthumous "awards" (not unlike Bulgakov bestowing "peace" or "light" on his characters at the end of *The Master and Margarita*), Yasha, with all his shortcomings, does not fully deserve the kind of an elevated status which is given to Fyodor's father or Sleptsov's nameless son, both of whom are, of course, largely autobiographical characters. Thus the story which, on its surface, is just about a fictional family, the Chernyshevskis, also becomes, for Nabokov, a substory about his own family, his own loss, and a potential loss that his own father had been spared by a cruel but not utterly sadistic fate.

Many of Nabokov's other fictional biographies of definite "others" seem to end up also being, at least partially, about himself and his family. To give just two examples from his earlier and later works, let us look very briefly at *The Defense* (*Zashchita Luzhina*, 1930) and *Pnin* (1957). In both novels, while the chess prodigy Luzhin and Professor Pnin are very different from Nabokov and, like Yasha but unlike Fyodor, cannot possibly serve as his ostensible alter-egos, the vivid authorial "sympathetic imagination" often goes hand in hand with actual and substantial sympathy toward the protagonists. "Of all my Russian books," Nabokov writes in the introduction to the English translation, "*The Defense* contains and diffuses the greatest 'warmth' . . . In point of fact, Luzhin has been found lovable even by those who . . . detest all my other books" (*Def*, 10). The same can be – and, of course, has been – said about Timofey Pnin. As was the case with Yasha, however, it is often in the distinction that Nabokov seems to invoke between these characters and himself that some of the most striking personal underpinnings of these novels shine through and often translate in yet another loving tribute to his parents.

In *The Defense*, where the focus falls on the nature of the true genius as well as on parental challenges in dealing with an unusually gifted child (which Luzhin's parents do not meet), the subtle autobiographical subtext appears to be Nabokov's own gifts and the way they were carefully nurtured by his parents. The enormously talented Luzhin, mishandled in his childhood by his parents, is doomed to fail where his creator succeeds – in being a true and lasting artist: "Luzhin's . . . plight was that of a writer or composer who, having assimilated the latest things in art at the beginning of his active career and caused a temporary sensation with the originality of his devices, all at once notices . . . that others . . . have left him behind in the very devices where he recently led the way" (*Def*, 96 [ch. 6]). Likewise, in *Pnin*, as much as we may love and admire Timofey, we cannot help being constantly reminded that, despite many things he and his creator may have in common,[15] his "sheer sympathy with failure" (*Pnin*, 35 [ch. 2]) stands in sharp contrast to Nabokov's self-confidence, which was thoughtfully instilled in him by his parents.

The art and lore of "autoplagiarism"

"The future specialist in such dull literary lore as autoplagiarism," Nabokov writes in *Speak, Memory*, "will like to collate a protagonist's experience in my novel *The Gift* with the original event" (*SM*, 37 [ch. 2]). The original event he was talking about was the childhood instance when, without knowing the nature of the daily present his mother had gone out to get him while he was lying sick in bed, he actually "visualized" that it was going to be a pencil but misjudged its size. It turned out to be a showpiece from the shop's window he so often admired, "a giant polygonal Faber pencil, four feet long and correspondingly thick" (*SM*, 38 [ch. 2]). Whether "dull" or not, the question of *The Gift* as an autobiographical *Bildungsroman*, in the tradition – and spirit – of Joyce's *Portrait of the Artist as a Young Man* is, of course, a legitimate one. Fyodor is, after all, the closest alter ego of Nabokov's in all of his fiction, having largely "appropriated" not only his creator's pencil but his childhood, parents, talents, poems, literary views, and, in Zina, even his future wife. Much has been written on the subject of Nabokov's *Gift* as the portrait of Nabokov as a young artist in Berlin, and there is, therefore, no need to dwell on it at much length here.[16] Instead, I would like to conclude this article by pondering Nabokov's epithet "dull," as applied here to "autoplagiarism."

It is, of course, not the art of autoplagiarism which Nabokov obviously loves and in which he excels that gets this unflattering attribute – it is its "literary lore," or critical explorations of what one may consider to be of autobiographical nature in writers' works that Nabokov, in his typical manner, preemptively disdains and discourages. He does so not only out of the general distrust of his critics, mentioned earlier, but also out of fear for his cherished privacy, directed mostly, but not solely, to the Freudians among us. Most importantly, however, he is afraid that the intricate magic of turning "a very personal life story" into "an impersonal art form" which he takes so many pains to conjure and maintain through his memory and imagination will disintegrate when touched by critics' simplistic formulas and unfeeling language. We can argue and disagree, of course, but the roots of his apprehension are legitimate, and it behooves us as critics and readers to tread the personal dimensions of his art sensitively, carefully, and very respectfully.

NOTES

1. Nabokov did, however, warn his first biographer, Andrew Field, that the Chernyshevski biography in *The Gift* was written by someone who was "sort of like me, but I myself wouldn't have written that way" (Andrew Field, *Nabokov: His Life in Part* [London: Hamish Hamilton, 1977], 30).
2. See Galya Diment, "Vladimir Nabokov and the Art of Autobiography," in *Nabokov and His Fiction: New Perspectives*, ed. Julian W. Connolly (Cambridge: Cambridge University Press, 1999), 36–53.
3. Irina Paperno, "How Nabokov's *Gift* Is Made," in *Literature, Culture, and Society in the Modern Age: In Honor of Joseph Frank*, part 2, ed. Edward J. Brown, Lazar Fleishman, Gregory Freidin, and Richard D. Schupbach, Stanford Slavic

Studies 4.2 (Stanford: Dept. of Slavic Languages and Literatures, Stanford University, 1992), 303, 305–7.

4. John Keats, *Selected Letters*, ed. Lionel Trilling (New York: Doubleday, 1956), 166.

5. L. L. Lee, *Vladimir Nabokov* (Boston: Twayne, 1976), 93.

6. Maurice Couturier, *Nabokov* (Lausanne: L'Age d'homme, 1979), 26. I discussed the "myth" of Chernyshevski and what Nabokov does to deflate it in "Nabokov and Strachey," in *Comparative Literature Studies* 4 (1990): 285–97.

7. Edmund Wilson, "Nikolai Gogol–Greek Paidaea," in *The New Yorker*, September 9, 1944): 65.

8. In Brian Boyd, *Vladimir Nabokov: The American Years* (Princeton: Princeton University Press, 1991), 149.

9. Georges Nivat, "*Speak, Memory*," in *The Garland Companion to Vladimir Nabokov*, ed. Vladimir Alexandrov (New York: Garland Publishing, 1995), 677.

10. When discussing *The Gift*, Brian Boyd also points out the importance of the father–son relationship in Nabokov's own identity: "Nabokov felt very strongly that much of what was best in himself came from his father" (Brian Boyd, *Vladimir Nabokov: The Russian Years* [Princeton: Princeton University Press, 1990], 398).

11. It should be noted that V. D. Nabokov, while not a professional lepidopterist like his son or Fyodor's father, was interested in butterflies and was instrumental in provoking Vladimir Nabokov's passion for them – see, for example, in *Speak, Memory*: "I remembered that summer afternoon . . . when he had burst into my room, grabbed my net, shot down the veranda steps – and presently was strolling back holding between finger and thumb the rare and magnificent female of the Russian Poplar Admirable that he had seen basking on an aspen leaf from the balcony of his study" (*SM*, 192 [ch. 9]).

12. This apparent difference is lessened, however, if one recalls that in the nineteenth century there was a twelve-day discrepancy between the Julian calendar used in Russia and the Gregorian calendar used in the West. Thus, July 8 in Russia would have been July 20 in the West. Nabokov comments on the date issue in *Speak, Memory* (*SM*, 13), and it figures in his fiction (see, for example, *Pnin*, 67 [ch. 3]).

13. Boyd, *Russian Years*, 398.

14. Ibid., 43.

15. For a much fuller discussion of autobiographical elements in *Pnin*, see my *Pniniad: Vladimir Nabokov and Marc Szeftel* (Seattle: University of Washington Press, 1997).

16. See, among others, Stephen H. Blackwell, *Zina's Paradox: The Figured Reader in Nabokov's "The Gift"* (Bern: Peter Lang, 2000).

11

ELLEN PIFER

The *Lolita* phenomenon from Paris to Tehran

The history of *Lolita*, Nabokov's third novel in English, is nearly as bizarre as the story related in its pages. The narrator, Humbert Humbert, is a middle-aged European whose benighted passion for a twelve-year-old American girl drives him to make her his mistress. Years before the manuscript was rejected by a series of American publishers, *Lolita*'s author nearly destroyed it himself. On a summer's day in 1950, riddled with doubts about the novel, Nabokov was on his way to the garden incinerator to burn its initial chapters when his wife, Véra, persuaded him to reconsider. As the novelist explained six years later, in his afterword to *Lolita*'s belated American edition, "I was stopped by the thought that the ghost of the destroyed book would haunt my files for the rest of my life" (*Lo*, 312 ["On a Book Entitled *Lolita*"]). Nabokov gradually resumed work on the novel, which he completed in the spring of 1954. After five different American publishers found the subject too hot to handle, *Lolita* was brought out in Paris by the Olympia Press, best known for the frank sexual content of its publications. Rescued from oblivion by the prominent British novelist, Graham Greene, who praised *Lolita*'s artistic merits in the pages of the London *Sunday Times*, the novel quickly became the focus of a legal and literary controversy. Despite its championship by American writers and critics, *Lolita* was not published in the USA until 1958; it quickly became an international bestseller.

"*Lolita* is a special favorite of mine," Nabokov told an interviewer in 1962. "It was my most difficult book – the book that treated of a theme which was so distant, so remote, from my own emotional life that it gave me a special pleasure to use my combinational talent to make it real" (*SO*, 15). In the decade following its *succès de scandale*, the novel achieved widespread critical acclaim, laying to rest the charges of obscenity with which, in certain quarters of the reading (and non-reading) public, it had initially been greeted. With remarkable alacrity, scholars and critics dismissed the shocking nature of Humbert's sexual conduct and turned their attention to mapping the contours of the novel's linguistic design. Thus, in 1970, a mere dozen years after the novel's American debut, Alfred Appel, Jr. could say, "Many readers are more troubled by Humbert Humbert's use of language and lore than by his abuse of Lolita and the law" (*AnL*, xi [Preface]). Appel's landmark edition of the novel, in which he appended to *Lolita*'s three-hundred-page narrative nearly as many pages of scholarly notes and commentary, testifies to the rapidity with which the novel's checkered history has become part of American literary history. As one scholar notes, *The Annotated Lolita* is the "first annotated edition of a modern novel to be published in the lifetime of its author."[1] Revised and reissued in paperback in 1991, Appel's annotated edition also attests to the ongoing fascination of both general and specialized readers with the intricacies of the novel's design. The best studies of *Lolita*, which include Appel's own, demonstrate that close examination of the novel's linguistic patterns and narrative structure does not obviate but rather invites consideration of its moral and psychological dimensions.

Despite the critical acclaim that *Lolita* has garnered since its publication, the controversy sparked by its startling subject has never fully abated. During the past two decades, with increased public attention focused on issues of child abuse, questions have repeatedly been raised concerning Nabokov's choice of subject and his depiction of the sexually exploited child. Also unabated is the suspicion, first voiced by early critics of Nabokov's Russian œuvre, that the author's dazzling language, self-reflexive patterns, and playful word-games reflect his artistic, and narcissistic, arrogance. Early critics of *Lolita* pointed to Nabokov's self-declared dedication to "aesthetic bliss" to support their contention that the novel's design encourages readers to sympathize with the protagonist and artist-figure, Humbert Humbert, to the detriment of the child (*Lo*, 314–15 ["On a Book Entitled *Lolita*"]). Recent commentators – informed by reader-response theories and gender-criticism – are more troubled by the suspicion that Nabokov's art encourages the reader's participation in Humbert's sexual exploitation of a little girl in order to disguise the author's own complicity.[2] In both cases, such critics fail to grasp the ways in which Nabokov deploys the devices of artifice to break the reader's identification with *Lolita*'s narrator.

Embedded in *Lolita*'s text are myriad linguistic devices and literary allusions that, like the implausible coincidences signaling the operation of fate (or "McFate," as Humbert calls it) in the characters' lives, call attention to the novel's status as a work of art. Challenging the conventions of literary realism, Nabokov declares the novel a work of artifice, not the representation of unmediated reality. According to his artistic vision, reality is problematic, elusive, and ultimately unknowable: "You can get nearer and nearer . . . to reality," he says, "but you can never get near enough because reality is an infinite succession of steps, levels of perception, false bottoms" (*SO*, 11).

The act of reading a Nabokov novel, of sifting through its layers of images, associations, and allusions is tantamount to the way each of us attempts to *read* the perceived world. Registered by individual consciousness, the reality we perceive is not an objective entity but a subjective construct; the word "reality" should, therefore, be enclosed within quotation marks (*SO*, 154; *Lo*, 312 ["On a Book Entitled *Lolita*"]). Since human consciousness is itself creative, each individual is engaged in the essentially *artistic* process of creating or recreating, out of the raw materials of existence, the particular shape and significance of the world he or she inhabits. Exploring the analogies between word and world, Nabokov's fiction serves as a model of the universe. In his lexicon, fiction, or *invention*, is not opposed to "reality" but is the very medium through which we know or discover it. "Whatever the mind grasps," he affirms, "it does so with the assistance of creative fancy" (*SO*, 154). That is why, in describing the challenges he faced as a middle-aged Russian novelist seeking to transform himself into an American writer, he says, "It had taken me some forty years to invent Russia and Western Europe, and now [with *Lolita*] I was faced by the task of inventing America" (*Lo*, 312 ["On a Book Entitled *Lolita*"]).

Just as reality, in Nabokov's words, comprises infinite "levels of perception," the "reality" that *Lolita* evokes is fluid, not fixed. What we as readers glean in its structure and design is subject to our own efforts, insights, and levels of perception. As Gabriel Josipovici points out, *Lolita* "does not reveal its secret once and for all; the imaginative effort must be renewed each time it is reread. Ultimately the theme is the imaginative effort itself."[3] That the novelist's arsenal of literary devices and rhetorical ploys is placed at the service of his scurrilous narrator, Humbert Humbert, presents a special challenge to *Lolita*'s readers, particularly those inclined to identify with the character charged with narrating the story. Careful attention to the text reveals the ways in which it is designed to *reveal* what the narrator attempts to *conceal*, or blindly ignores. Readers inattentive to the dual, and duplicitous, nature of the narrator's language in Nabokov's fiction – not only Humbert's language in *Lolita* but Hermann's in *Despair*, Charles Kinbote's in *Pale Fire*, and Van Veen's in *Ada* – are bound to become mis-readers. Humbert gives them fair warning from the outset. Drawing attention to the deceptive as well as evocative power of his language, he announces on his opening page, "You can always count on a murderer for a fancy prose style." Guilty of murder but eager to defend himself, Humbert implicitly acknowledges that high style may well distract readers from the narrator's low designs. All the puns, patterns, and wordplay spawned by his narration both engage our attention and warn us to keep our critical distance from this most *unreliable* of narrators.

Humbert's narration is particularly duplicitous because he is the first among those he would deceive. Only gradually, and with great difficulty, does he face up to the burden of guilt that he bears. When at last he does, he levels the verdict against himself in harsh and spare language bearing little resemblance to the "fancy prose style" in which most of his narrative is cast. Focusing, for once, on the "North American girl-child" rather than the fantasized nymphet, he baldly admits, "Dolores Haze had been deprived of her childhood by a maniac" (*Lo*, 283 [pt. 2, ch. 31]). Humbert's self-condemnation is, however, only one of the perspectives he adopts in his protean narrative. Oscillating between lyric highs and low farce, the narrator's voice modulates from rapturous evocation to mocking self-denigration as his changing moods spin comedy out of despair and tragedy out of farce. Viewed from one vantage, *Lolita* offers a hilarious picture of a cosmopolitan European set adrift in the New World's provincial backwaters. When handsome Humbert arrives as a boarder at the Haze household in suburban Ramsdale, Lolita's widowed mother, Charlotte, can hardly believe her luck. The attraction that his European demeanor exerts on this lonely single mother is equaled only by his abysmal indifference to her full-blown charms. Little does Charlotte realize that Humbert follows her to the altar only because he desires her twelve-year-old daughter. After Charlotte's accidental death, nicely arranged for Humbert by the operations of "McFate," he and his stepdaughter embark on a series of cross-country trips whose sole purpose, for Humbert, is to elude the watchful eyes of nosy neighbors and legal authorities. As they travel aimlessly across the country, he and Lolita spend countless hours confined to the same car or motel room; despite their intense proximity, they never cross the cultural and generational divide gaping between them.

In the course of his narration, Humbert targets numerous aspects of mid-twentieth-century American pop culture – from the celluloid versions of romance and gooey sundaes that Lolita devours to the blandishments of advertising and the cant of "progressive" schools. Darkening these comic effects is the reader's growing awareness that Humbert's hostility to the lure of consumer culture derives not from any authentic concern for the child's welfare but from his obsessive need to keep her to himself. Amusing and devastating in turn, *Lolita* invites laughter at the banalities of the American highway while it poignantly renders the isolation of its characters. Testifying to the difficulty of achieving such artistic equipoise are the two movies adapted from the novel. Each manages to evoke one of the novel's dominant chords: Stanley Kubrick's 1962 film delivers high-flown comedy, while Adrian Lyne's 1997 melodrama is devoid of humor to a remarkable degree.[4]

Lolita also offers a sustained demonstration of Nabokov's multifaceted use of parody as an artistic device. As the author suggests in his earlier novel, *The Real Life of Sebastian Knight*, parody serves not only as a comic device – by burlesquing, or "sending up," other literary styles and works of art – but as "a kind of springboard for leaping into the highest region of serious emotion" (*RLSK*, 89). As we shall see, *Lolita*'s parody of romantic works and themes operates in precisely this way; it both critiques and renews the possibilities for romantic vision. The novel's parodic structure also serves to remind readers of the patently "invented" status of the world they are witnessing. Even before Humbert's narration begins, Nabokov alerts us to the game that the novel initiates between author and reader, prefacing Humbert's narration with a "Foreword" allegedly signed by a psychotherapist named "John Ray, Jr., Ph.D." The mirrored initials of Ray's name (JR, Jr.) already hint at the fictitious nature of this important-sounding personage, who informs us that the author of the memoir we are about to read "died in legal captivity, of coronary thrombosis, on November 16, 1952, a few days before his trial was scheduled to start." Because of his clinical interest in "certain morbid states and perversions," Ray adds, he has been entrusted with the dead man's diary. A host of details relayed by Ray undermine, however, his ostensible bid for authenticity, drawing attention to the fiction in which he, like the other characters, exists. Those familiar with Nabokov's love of anagrams, for example, will detect in Ray's mention of a female biographer, one "Vivian Darkbloom," an anagram of Vladimir Nabokov, whose authorial (and orthographical) presence hovers behind the clinical expert's authoritative-sounding account. In addition to spoofing readers who, like Ray, expect to find in Humbert's narrative a "general lesson," Nabokov parodies the bogus documents that generations of novelists have provided – in the form of fabricated letters, diaries, wills, eyewitness accounts – to gain their readers' credibility (*Lo*, 3–6 ["Foreword"]).

When, however, Ray abandons his didactic tone to extol the narrator's "singing violin [which] can conjure up a tendresse, a compassion for Lolita that makes us entranced with the book while abhorring its author," parody again proves Nabokov's "springboard" to higher regions of thought and emotion (*Lo*, 5 ["Foreword"]). Challenging the premises as well as the devices of literary realism, *Lolita*'s parodic structure invites readers to maintain a kind of double vision: to limn the contours of its cunningly wrought design and, at the same time, to gauge its emotional depths. Viewed from one perspective, the landscape that Humbert and Lolita inhabit takes on the two-dimensional surface of a chessboard – the reader stationed at one end, the author at the other. Moving his characters through the narrative, Nabokov plants both clues and false leads to keep readers on their mental toes. The game intensifies with the introduction of Humbert's secret rival, whose identity is not revealed until Humbert learns it from Lolita at the end.

Three years after she succeeds in escaping from him, Lolita, "hopelessly worn at seventeen," encounters Humbert for the last time. Only the "dead leaf echo" of his enchanting nymphet, she is now pregnant and married to a young man, Dick Schiller, who knows nothing of her past. When Humbert insists that she reveal the identity of the "fiend" who stole her from him, she does so in a whisper. Withholding that information from his readers, Humbert coyly says that "she emitted . . . the name that the astute reader has guessed long ago" (*Lo*, 252 [pt. 2, ch. 23]; 271–72, 277 [pt. 2, ch. 29]). Nabokov was aware, of course, that many readers would fail, on first reading, to detect the clues to Clare Quilty's identity embedded in the text. For those duly caught out, the pieces of the puzzle do not fall into place until later. Humbert's final encounter with Lolita also evinces the way in which parody drives the game that each of Nabokov's novels sets in motion. Peppered with allusions to Prosper Mérimée's *Carmen* – the melodramatic tale of jealous love that inspired Bizet's famous opera – Humbert's account provokes the reader's conventional expectations only to overturn them. As he toys with the gun which he will use to kill Quilty, he mentally addresses Lolita as his "Carmen" or "Carmencita," begging her to come away with him. Playing upon the reader's fear that, when she refuses, Humbert – like the jealous lover, José, in Mérimée's novella – will kill her, he adds, "Then I pulled out my automatic – I mean, this is the kind of fool thing a reader might suppose I did. It never even occurred to me to do it" (*Lo*, 278–80 [pt. 2, ch. 29]).

Far from seeking to destroy her, Humbert here recognizes that, "more than anything I had ever seen or imagined on earth, or hoped for anywhere else," he loves "*this* Lolita, pale and polluted, and big with another's child." As he gazes at the young woman whose life he "polluted," Humbert is, for once, frank. For her, he notes, their "poor romance" was no romance at all, simply "a bit of dry mud caking her childhood." More harsh still is his recognition that Quilty is, by Lolita's own confession, the only man she ever loved. She is fond of her young husband, she explains; but for Quilty – the "famous" playwright, celebrity, "genius" – she reserves her awe. To her he is still "a great guy," despite the fact that, after helping to arrange her escape from Humbert, Quilty turned out to be "a complete freak in sex matters" and wanted her to participate in all kinds of "filthy things," including group sex and pornographic movies. When "she refused to take part because she loved him," he "threw her out" (*Lo*, 272–78 [pt. 2, ch. 29]). Bested by a rival whose cunning and perversity exceed his own, Humbert spends years trying to uncover the identity of his shadowy alter ego. When he finally does, he projects onto Quilty his own self-loathing and rage for revenge. If, by killing Quilty, Humbert seeks to absolve himself from guilt, the project backfires. True to Nabokov's parody of novelistic conventions, Humbert's destruction of his "double" affords him no relief. After pulling the trigger in an attempt to discharge his "load of revenge," Humbert finds that he has failed: "Far from feeling any relief, a burden even weightier than the one I had hoped to get rid of was with me" (*Lo*, 304 [pt. 2, ch. 35]).

Like Quilty, Humbert is a pervert. What makes him so fascinating a character, however, is not his predatory sexual conduct. "Anybody can imagine those elements of animality," he tells the reader (*Lo*, 134 [pt. 1, ch. 29]). More intriguing, and less predictable, is the source of Humbert's obsession, the fuel that fires his ardent imagination. Humbert's "nympholepsy," as Thomas Frosch observes, "is aesthetic as well as sexual; the nymphet in the child is perceived by the mind."[5] The statement would read even more accurately if the terms were reversed: "sexual as well as aesthetic." For as Humbert states in a passage echoing Nabokov's well-known disdain for Freud's theories of sexuality, "It is not the artistic aptitudes that are secondary sexual characters as some shams and shamans have said; it is the other way around: sex is but the ancilla of art" (*Lo*, 259 [pt. 2, ch. 26]). Employing the Latin word for "maidservant," Humbert's statement upends the notion that art is a sublimation, or "secondary" characteristic, of sexuality. Instead, Humbert suggests that his sexual desire for the child's body depends on (or attends) his aesthetic drive: it is the way his imagination conjures the nymphet's image that holds him in thrall.

The nature of Humbert's obsession is revealed, early on, by the "time terms" he substitutes for "spatial ones" when attempting to pinpoint "the perilous magic of nymphets." The romantic landscape he evokes belongs to a private world of enchantment where time is suspended: "I would have the reader see 'nine' and 'fourteen' as the boundaries – the mirrory beaches and rosy rocks – of an enchanted island haunted by those nymphets of mine and surrounded by a vast, misty sea." Among young girls between the ages of nine and fourteen, the bewitched nympholept discovers those few whose true nature, he says, "is not human but nymphic," or "demoniac" (*Lo*, 16 [pt. 1, ch. 5]; 134 [pt. 1, ch. 29]). But as his narrative makes clear, it is Humbert's obsessed imagination that is demonic, transforming the helpless child into a figment of his fantasy. Conjured by his imagination, the nymphet Lolita is summarily dispossessed of the surname and genealogy that belong to Dolores Haze, the daughter of Charlotte Haze and her deceased husband, Harold. The etymology of the word *nymphet* further suggests the unfortunate consequences that Humbert's perverse imagination has for the child. Beyond its many associations with Greek myth and religion, the *nymph* designates, in entomological terms, "an immature stage of a hemimetabolic insect"; in contrast to a butterfly, it "does not undergo complete metamorphosis."[6] Inflicting his private fantasy of the nymphet – a mythical creature who must "never grow up" – on an immature "girl-child" whose natural right is to do just that, Humbert would stunt both her growth and her freedom (*Lo*, 19, 21 [pt. 1, ch. 5]). In order to satiate his desire for the nymphet, he resorts to "terrorizing" the child with threats of abandonment or incarceration in a "juvenile detention home" (*Lo*, 149, 151 [pt. 1, ch. 1]).

The perversity of his desire notwithstanding, Humbert's narrative is a labor of love, love for the elusive beauty of the nymphet as perceived by him. The desire to "fix once for all the perilous magic of nymphets" is, he says, what inspires the writing of his memoir (*Lo*, 134 [pt. 1, ch. 29]). In this aim Nabokov's narrator is supremely successful, rendering in resonant detail his vision of the nymphet's unique beauty – from the "glistening tracery of down on her forearm" to the "gooseberry fuzz of her shin" and "the quicksilver in the baby folds of her stomach" (*Lo*, 41, 45 [pt. 1, ch. 11]; 162 [pt. 2, ch. 2]). So enchanted is Humbert with the nymphet that the child's tears only serve to increase his ardor. He relishes the delicate "tinge of Botticellian pink" that the sting of unhappiness brings to her "tender" complexion. As the text here makes clear, it is Dolores Haze's misery that produces the singular aesthetic effects – the "raw rose about the lips, those wet, matted eyelashes" – that intensify Humbert's rapture for the nymphet, obliterating any concern for the child (*Lo*, 64 [pt. 1, ch. 15]).

The way in which Humbert's imagination works, eclipsing the child's identity in order to evoke the tantalizing nymphet, is described early on in the novel as solipsistic. In a crucial scene that takes place one Sunday morning in the livingroom of the Haze household, Humbert recounts the occasion on which he first achieved, onanistically, sexual ecstasy with his nymphet. As the child sprawls next to him on the couch, carelessly flinging her legs across his lap, Humbert, with tingling nerves, marvels at the nature of his great good luck. Slowly, painstakingly, he begins to fit "her shameless innocent shanks and round bottom" to the contours of his lap until, after a series of excruciating maneuvers, he manages to achieve climax. Reveling in his "self-made seraglio," Humbert, characteristically oblivious to the child's responses, assumes that she knows "nothing" of what has transpired. The reader, on the other hand, notes the way that the twelve-year-old has, during the course of Humbert's convulsions, "wiggled, and squirmed," and thrown "her head back." It is Humbert who proves unknowing, confident that "Lolita had been safely solipsized." He adds, "What I had madly possessed was not she, but my own creation, another, fanciful Lolita – perhaps, more real than Lolita . . . and having no will, no consciousness – indeed, no life of her own" (*Lo*, 60–62 [pt. 1, ch. 13]). Here, in his dual role as protagonist and narrator, Humbert reveals both the blinding force of his solipsistic obsession and, perhaps unwittingly, the intricate life of the child whose identity, at the time, he failed to acknowledge.

Impelled by the disparity between what he calls "my fancy and nature's reality," Humbert delights in a "vision" forever "out of reach, with no possibility of attainment." His quest for "the great rosegray never-to-be-had" aligns him with other romantic dreamers inspired by ineffable longing (*Lo*, 264 [pt. 2, ch. 27]). His true precursors are not the pedophiles of psychiatric case history but those literary personae – Don Quixote, Emma Bovary, Jay Gatsby – whose ideal visions are wedded to impossibility. Like them, Humbert suffers the fatal affliction of infinite longing, an unquenchable passion for the "inaccessible object" of desire.[7] Humbert's narrative is rife with allusions to romantic works of fiction and poetry, including those of Edgar Allan Poe. It was Poe's love for his cousin and child-bride, Virginia Clemm (whom he married when she was thirteen and he twenty-seven), that inspired his poem "Annabel Lee," whose language serves as a subtext throughout the novel (see *AnL*, 328–32, 357–58 [Notes]). Addressed to the speaker's dead bride, "Annabel Lee" celebrates the romantic lover's transcendent desire, his faith in "a love that [is] more than love" (stanza 2, l. 3). Parodying the language and imagery of Poe's poem throughout his narration, Humbert identifies his own childhood sweetheart, who died of typhus at the age of twelve, as "Annabel Leigh," even calling her his "dead bride" (*Lo*, 39 [pt. 1, ch. 10]). From the poem's title to its remote setting in a "kingdom by the sea," Poe's lyric inspires Humbert's visions of a romantic kingdom where love transcends mortal as well as moral law.

In ardent pursuit of his private kingdom, or "intangible island of entranced time," Humbert feeds on the beauty of a child whom he has imaginatively transformed into the "mythopoeic nymphet" (*Lo*, 17 [pt. 1, ch. 5]; 186 [pt. 2, ch. 8]). In describing the rapture that overtakes him when he first gazes on the nymphet Lolita, Humbert even likens himself to a vampire: "the vacuum of my soul managed to suck in every detail of her bright beauty" (*Lo*, 39 [pt. 1, ch. 10]). Significantly, he fails to distinguish between his vampirish appetite and the vulnerability of his prey. Thus, after his first, fateful night with Lolita in The Enchanted Hunters hotel, Humbert is "anointed and ringed with the feel of her body" on which, like some "fairytale vampire," he has left "a purplish spot." Far from belonging to a twelve-year-old, it is for him "the body of some immortal daemon disguised as a female child" (*Lo*, 39 [pt. 1, ch. 10]; 139 [pt. 1, ch. 32]). In thrall to his fantasizing imagination, Humbert is at once vampire and victim, predator and prey.

As his narrative progresses, however, certain "smothered memories" begin to surface in Humbert's memory, and his efforts to attribute his actions to the "demonic" power of the nymphet grow increasingly lame (*Lo*, 284 [pt. 2, ch. 32]). Never do his attempts at self-justification prove more unconvincing than when he adopts the role of a watchful father bemoaning the "definite drop in Lolita's morals." When, after months of slavish subjection to his sexual demands, Lolita begins to counter with her own mercenary ones, Humbert laments to the reader: "Knowing the magic and might of her own soft mouth, she managed to raise the bonus price of a fancy embrace to three, and even four bucks" (*Lo*, 185–86 [pt. 2, ch. 7]). He even admits to burgling her room in order to confiscate her hard-won allowance, which, he fears, she may use to make her escape. The flagrant contradiction between Humbert's adopted role as Lolita's guardian and his demands as vampirish lover undermines the appeals he makes to the reader's sympathy. With unwitting explicitness, he exposes the gruesome reality operating beneath his pose as concerned parent when he describes having to take the sick child to a local hospital: "She was shaking from head to toe. She complained of a painful stiffness in the upper vertebrae – and I thought of poliomyelitis as any American parent would. Giving up all hope of intercourse, I wrapped her up in a laprobe and carried her into the car" (*Lo*, 240 [pt. 2, ch. 22]). Humbert's casual reference to his "hope" for intercourse explodes his pretensions to fatherly "concern" and brings home to the reader, yet again, the dreadful incongruity between the child's fragile innocence and the adult's fierce appetite.

The theme of abortive childhood, which sounds like a threnody throughout the novel, culminates in the reader's discovery that seventeen-year-old Dolores Haze – now "Mrs. Richard F. Schiller" – dies in childbirth, "giving birth to a stillborn girl" (*Lo*, 4 ["Foreword"]). More precisely, it is Nabokov's re-reader who makes that discovery, since the information relayed in the Foreword, ostensibly written by John Ray, Jr., has little significance for those who have not yet embarked on the novel. This sad end to Lolita's brief life remains unknown to Humbert, who concludes his memoir with the expectation that "Dolly Schiller will probably survive me by many years" (*Lo*, 308 [pt. 2, ch. 36]). Although Humbert's remorse for having destroyed Lolita's childhood is articulated relatively late in his narrative, this crucial recognition underlies his efforts to render not only the nymphet's perilous magic but the poignant reality of the hapless orphan. Within the text, in other words, Lolita's vital presence as a child rather than a nymphet depends on Humbert's capacity to penetrate the bars of his obsession.

The complexity of Humbert's psychology and narrative voice is not found in Nabokov's earlier treatment of nymphet-obsession, a 1939 novella composed in Russian under the title *Volshebnik* and posthumously translated into English as *The Enchanter*. Recounted in the third-person, the narrative tracks the main character's single-minded desire for a little girl until, his secret exposed by the screams of a waking child, he dashes into the street to meet his death. Here, in contrast to *Lolita*, it is the protagonist, rather than the child's mother, who is run over by a hurtling car (*En*, 92, 95). Dead before he can consummate his criminal lust, "the enchanter" is spared Humbert's remorse but also lacks his emotional range and depth. Nabokov, by his own account, "was not pleased" with this early effort, because, as he said in his afterword to *Lolita*, "the little girl wasn't alive. She hardly spoke" (*Lo*, 312 ["On a Book Entitled *Lolita*"]). It was only later, while writing a different work in a different country and language, that he "managed to give [the child] some semblance of reality" (*AnL*, lvi [Introduction]). In *Lolita*'s first-person narrator Nabokov created a character whose voice and vision prove sufficiently complex to reflect, within the frame of the fiction, the identity of the child eclipsed by his desire.

If Humbert's fixation with the nymphet constitutes, as earlier suggested, a form of romantic longing, the means by which he penetrates the confines of his solipsistic obsession also engages the power of romantic vision. This time, however, the romantic's store of images and metaphors is placed at the service of the child herself. As his narrative winds to its close, Humbert finds himself recalling a scene that took place when he and Lolita were still living in Beardsley. On the way to a concert he overhears Lolita say to her friend, "You know, what's so dreadful about dying is that you are completely on your own." And "then it struck me," Humbert says, "that I simply did not know a thing about my darling's mind and that quite possibly, behind the awful juvenile clichés, there was in her a garden and a twilight, and a palace gate – dim and adorable regions which happened to be lucidly and absolutely forbidden to me, in my polluted rags and miserable convulsions" (*Lo*, 284 [pt. 2, ch. 32]). Once again Humbert marshals the romantic formulae of a remote and melancholy kingdom, with its faint echoes of Poe's "Annabel Lee" and its "kingdom by the sea" – but with a crucial difference. Now this remote "kingdom," with its secret "garden," has nothing to do with the "pubescent park" where, in his reveries, Humbert disports with his nymphets (*Lo*, 21 [pt. 1, ch. 5]). It signifies, rather, the child's inner kingdom, her own pristine world of dreams, thoughts, desires – still intact and "forbidden" to him, despite all his invasive actions. Employing his prodigious imagination to conjure, for once, the life and longing of someone other than he, Humbert succeeds, however briefly, in penetrating the bars of his solipsistic perception, paying homage to the child's independent identity. Surfacing in his consciousness like "limbless monsters of pain," these "smothered memories" bear witness to the knowledge he can no longer repress: the knowledge that he, with his insatiable demands and "miserable convulsions," wrested from Dolores Haze – this "North American girl-child" – her inalienable right to life, liberty, and the pursuit of happiness (*Lo*, 283–84 [pt. 2, chs. 31–32]).

The "poison" that fatally infected Humbert with nympholepsy, he tells us, was his "premature" and unconsummated love for Annabel Leigh. If so, we might add, the disease that afflicts his fierce but blinkered imagination is his blindness to the child (*Lo*, 18 [pt. 1, ch. 5]). In his transgressions against the source and symbol of creative imagination, Humbert proves a false avatar of romantic faith and freedom – betraying the legacy bequeathed him by Rousseau, Wordsworth, and Blake. For the Romantics, the child – whose innocence has not yet been ravaged by experience, whose wonder at the world is still fresh – embodies the human being's creative potential. Similarly Nabokov, in his autobiography *Speak, Memory*, envisions the birth of each nascent consciousness as a glorious flowering, a "stab of wonder" that recapitulates the dawn of human consciousness in the history of evolution (*SM*, 298). For a writer who once described consciousness as "the only real thing in the world and the greatest mystery of all," the child occupies a revered position in the ultimate scheme of things (*BS*, 188). Given Nabokov's vision of reality, the admission that Humbert makes at the end of his story is both personally and philosophically damning: "it was always my habit and method to ignore Lolita's states of mind while comforting my own base self" (*Lo*, 287 [pt. 2, ch. 32]). By traducing, rather than honoring, Lolita's childhood, Humbert betrays both Dolores Haze and the creative "mystery" of human consciousness. By the same token, his capacity to break through his solipsistic vision, as he does in acknowledging the child's autonomous being and "states of mind," entails a significant renewal of romantic vision.

While Humbert's confession of guilt at the end of the novel does not manage "to save" his "soul," as he apparently hopes, it does afford him a modicum of saving grace (*Lo*, 308 [pt. 2, ch. 36]). Drawing on the powers of imagination to evoke the nymphet's elusive beauty, he also proves capable, albeit from hindsight, of acknowledging the child and the deprivation she suffered at his hands. After their first night together in The Enchanted Hunters hotel, shortly before Humbert informs Lolita that she is an orphan, he describes the "oppressive, hideous constraint" that suddenly comes over him. As the "lone child, an absolute waif" sits next to him in the car, Humbert has the distinct feeling that he is "sitting with the small ghost of somebody I had just killed." It is this ghost – the ghost of Lolita's dead childhood – that will eventually return to haunt him, even though at this moment, as he frankly tells us, "somewhere at the bottom of that dark turmoil I felt the writhing of desire again, so monstrous was my appetite for that miserable nymphet" (*Lo*, 140 [pt. 1, ch. 32]). Only in art can Humbert restore to the child he tyrannized – the child whose "life," as he says, he "broke" – some semblance of the autonomy he denied her (*Lo*, 279 [pt. 2, ch. 29]). The nature of his (highly qualified) redemption is aesthetic as well as moral, for it depends less on his expressed remorse than on the vital image of the child he recreates in his narrative. Alongside the elusive nymphet rapturously celebrated in his memoir Humbert resurrects the image of Dolores Haze, who haunts the pages of his narrative as she haunts his memory. This link between the ethics and aesthetics of Nabokov's fiction has generated increasing interest among critics and readers, laying to rest his early reputation as an aesthete indifferent to the ethical concerns of human beings.

A recent tribute to this often overlooked dimension of *Lolita* occurs in a memoir bearing the singular title, *Reading* Lolita *in Tehran*.[8] Authored by an Iranian professor currently living in the USA, the book's opening chapter describes a privately held class that met every week for two years, beginning in the fall of 1995, in the Tehran apartment of the author, who had recently resigned her academic post at a local university. For this small, hand-picked group of students, all women, the centerpiece of the assigned reading list – which included novels by Austen, James, and Flaubert – was *Lolita*. Summarizing their discussion of the novel, Azar Nafisi says, "'Moppet,' 'little monster,' 'corrupt,' 'shallow,' 'brat' – these are some of the terms assigned to Lolita by her [early] critics. Then there are others," Nafisi adds, "who condemn *Lolita* because they feel Nabokov turned the rape of a twelve-year-old into an aesthetic experience. We in our class disagreed with all of these interpretations. We unanimously . . . agreed with Véra Nabokov," who privately commented in her diary: "I wish . . . somebody would notice the tender description of the child's helplessness, her pathetic dependence on monstrous HH, and her heartrending courage all along[,] culminating in that squalid but essentially pure and healthy marriage, and her letter, and her dog."[9]

The source of Nafisi's unidentified citations is *Véra*, Stacy Schiff's 1999 biography of Nabokov's wife; in a later passage of the biography, Schiff quotes a similar "plea for the heroine's humanity" made by Mrs. Nabokov in 1959: "She [Lolita] cries every night, and the critics are deaf to her sobs."[10] That Véra Nabokov was an astute reader of her husband's work comes as no surprise, particularly to those aware of the couple's half-century of intellectual partnership, which began two years before their wedding in 1925 and ended only with Nabokov's death in 1977. That young Iranian students living under the rule of the ayatollahs could respond with similar insight is, on the other hand, both surprising and revealing. As Nafisi relates in her memoir, these sheltered young women – forced to hide their faces, in public, behind a veil and condemned, even imprisoned if found to be wearing lipstick or nail polish – proved astute readers of *Lolita*. After entering the privacy of Dr. Nafisi's house and throwing off their black veils, they responded with nuanced understanding and appreciation of a work banned by the censors as a symbol of Western decadence. Humbert's efforts to pose as Lolita's guardian in order to control her every action struck a chord with these young women, all of whom were being subjected to the watchful "protection" of an invasive regime. Perhaps that is why they so readily grasped the distinction that Humbert himself comes to make between the "North American girl-child," Dolores Haze, and the figment of his dreaming mind. For, as Nafisi comments in a passage that alludes to the romantic trappings of Humbert's fantasy while exposing its underlying tyranny, "Whoever we were – and it was not really important what religion we belonged to, whether we wished to wear the veil or not, whether we observed certain religious norms or not – we had become the figment of someone else's dreams. A stern ayatollah, a self-proclaimed philosopher-king, had come to rule our land. He had come in the name of a past, a past that, he claimed, had been stolen from him. And he now wanted to re-create us in the image of that illusory past."[11]

Nabokov, who cultivated the condition of exile in which he lived for most of his life, would have relished, I think, Nafisi's dramatic testament to the way that *Lolita*'s wide readership has transcended not only national borders but the stranglehold of a repressive regime and its attempt to crush the individual and the freedoms of imagination. By the time that he and his family, having fled France as Hitler's troops were overrunning Europe, arrived in America, Nabokov had every reason to be personally and artistically exhausted. Instead, however, through a monumental act of imagination this Russian-born author and exile managed, as John Updike says, "to bring an entirely new audacity and panache to American literature" (*LL*, xxvii [Introduction]). In the process of reinventing America so brilliantly in *Lolita*, Nabokov did even more than turn himself into an American writer: he infused the American language with new vitality and vision. Many contemporary writers, along with Updike, have paid tribute to Nabokov's contribution to English and American letters – among them Martin Amis, Don DeLillo, John Barth, Herbert Gold, and Edmund White. White, for one, credits Nabokov, along with his fellow Russian-émigrés Igor Stravinsky and George Balanchine, with helping to fashion a new definition of American art and culture. Alluding to Nabokov's other career as a distinguished lepidopterist, White says, "More glorious and surprising in his metamorphosis than any butterfly he ever stalked, Nabokov, the Russian master, turned himself into a writer in English, the best of the century."[12]

NOTES

1. Christine Clegg, ed., *Vladimir Nabokov,* Lolita: *A Reader's Guide to Essential Criticism* (Cambridge, UK: Icon, 2000), 66.

2. See, for example, the discussion of critics Naomi Wolf, Virginia L. Blum, Andrew Brink, Trevor Neely, Jeffrey Berman, and Brandon S. Centerwall in Ellen Pifer, "Her Monster, His Nymphet: Nabokov and Mary Shelley," in *Nabokov and His Fiction: New Perspectives*, ed. Julian W. Connolly (Cambridge, UK: Cambridge University Press, 1999), 158–60 and attending notes. For a brief overview of earlier critical commentary, see Ellen Pifer, *Nabokov and the Novel* (Cambridge, MA: Harvard University Press, 1980), 11–13 and attending notes.

3. Gabriel Josipovici, "*Lolita*: Parody and the Pursuit of Beauty," in Josipovici, *The World and the Book: A Study of Modern Fiction* (London: Macmillan, 1971), 220.

4. See Ellen Pifer, "Reinventing Nabokov: Lyne and Kubrick Parse *Lolita*," in *Nabokov at Cornell*, ed. Gavriel Shapiro (Ithaca, NY: Cornell University Press, 2003), 68–77.

5. Thomas R. Frosch, "Parody and Authenticity in *Lolita*," in *Nabokov's Fifth Arc: Nabokov and Others on His Life's Work*, ed. J. E. Rivers and Charles Nicol (Austin: University of Texas Press, 1982), 177.

6. Kurt Johnson and Steve Coates, *Nabokov's Blues: The Scientific Odyssey of a Literary Genius* (Cambridge, MA: Zoland Books, 1999), 36.

7. Denis de Rougemont, *Love Declared: Essays on the Myths of Love*, trans. Richard Howard (New York: Random House, 1963), 51. For French and Russian literary precursors of Nabokov's nymphet, see D. Barton Johnson, "'L'Inconnue de la Seine' and Nabokov's Naiads," *Comparative Literature* 44.1 (1992): 225–48.

8. Azar Nafisi, *Reading* Lolita *in Tehran: A Memoir in Books* (New York: Random House, 2003).

9. Nafisi, *Reading* Lolita, 40.

10. Stacy Schiff, *Véra (Mrs. Vladimir Nabokov)* (New York: Random House, 1999) 235–36, 255.

11. Nafisi, *Reading* Lolita, 28.

12. Edmund White, "Nabokov: Beyond Parody," in *The Achievements of Vladimir Nabokov*, ed. George Gibian and Stephen Jan Parker (Ithaca, NY: Cornell University, 1984), 26.

12

MICHAEL WOOD

Nabokov's late fiction

I should like to steal up on Nabokov's late fiction with a quiet query about the term. It is in one sense synonymous with "last fictions," as we now speak of Richard Strauss's *Four Last Songs*, although he didn't call them that. Lateness of this kind is a matter of chronological time, and may imply an achieved maturity, a sense of autumn. The *Oxford English Dictionary* gives "flowering or ripening at an advanced season of the year" among its meanings. But with Nabokov no matter of time is only a matter of time, and lateness in the work of distinguished artists often has another, qualitative meaning, far from negative but indicating, nonetheless, a certain quirkiness, hinting not merely at maturity but also at something beyond maturity.[1] Since all of Nabokov's work is quirky, we shall have to show, if we wish to pursue this thought, that the quirkiness itself changes its color or its tone or its intensity in the late novels, and that is what I shall try to do in this essay.

Transparent shadows

The late fiction, in most of the overviews of the career, and in both of my senses of lateness, consists of three books: *Ada* (1969), *Transparent Things* (1972), *Look at the Harlequins!* (1974). But I want to suggest we can glimpse Nabokov's incipient lateness (in the second sense) just a little earlier: in the last page or so of Charles Kinbote's commentary in *Pale Fire* (1962). Here is a fictional character who already has a plausible claim to (at least) two identities beside his own. The Zemblan professor is, if we take him at his fulsome word, the exiled king of his country; and if we trust a certain hysterical fluster in the book's index and elsewhere, he is an exiled Russian who has invented not only the kingship but Zembla itself. As he ends his story, however, he starts to speculate on who else he may become. "I shall continue to exist. I may assume other disguises, other forms, but I shall try to exist. I may turn up yet, on another campus, as an old, happy, healthy, heterosexual Russian, a writer in exile . . . Oh, I may do many things!" (*PF*, 300–301). The ebbing confidence of these announcements ("I shall continue to exist," "I shall try to exist") hints at the suicide Nabokov assigns to Kinbote in a conversation recorded in *Strong Opinions* (*SO*, 74), and the full paragraph contains several options of existence related to the plot, the internal world so to speak, of *Pale Fire*. But Kinbote at least glimpses the possibility of a life resembling that of his creator, that is, seems to see, within the fiction, a person and a career we know to be located outside the fiction, rather as Joyce's Molly Bloom suddenly and surprisingly turns out to know her author's name,[2] and as the narrator of Proust's *A la Recherche du temps perdu* allows us to wonder on a couple of occasions whether he is or isn't called Marcel.[3] We can't of course be sure that the old happy healthy heterosexual Russian writer evoked in *Pale Fire* is Nabokov himself, because the description is far from exclusive, and in any case this figure is not a person but an imagined possibility. But then the quirky point is even firmer. If Nabokov is just one of several actual writers who meet the specifications, then the possibility is not only imagined (by Kinbote) but lived (by others). The real Nabokov becomes, for Kinbote, something like a denizen of the hallucinated Terra the characters of *Ada* see from their own Demonia; and Kinbote himself begins to resemble Vadim Vadimovich in *Look at the Harlequins!* a man haunted by a writerly twin, the shadow of the creator he will never know. Even the rather stolid Hugh Person, in *Transparent Things*, who mainly fails to hear the calls coming from another world ("Here's the person I want. Hullo, person! Doesn't hear me" [*TT*, 1 (ch. 1)]), is said to have "experienced the sensation . . . of there existing behind him – at his shoulder, as it were – a larger, incredibly wiser, calmer and stronger stranger . . ." The narrator continues, with a mysterious comment we shall need to return to, "and had he been without that transparent shadow, we would not have bothered to speak about our dear Person" (*TT*, 98 [ch. 25]).

Nabokov has conjured up these extrafictional visions before: in *Invitation to a Beheading* (1935–1936) in *The Real Life of Sebastian Knight* (1941), in *Bend Sinister* (1947). There is a moment in each book when the ontological walls give way (or could give way) and allow a fictional character to cross over into another zone of existence – also fictional, but so eerily akin to our own world that for a moment we believe it is that world, the world of history and time we share with the author. In the first example, Cincinnatus divides himself into two persons, one of them counting loudly towards the fall of M'sieur Pierre's ax, and the other stepping away not only from the execution but from the whole scene of the fiction, which collapses like a stage set: "and amid the dust, and the falling things, and the flapping scenery, Cincinnatus made his way in that direction where, to judge by the voices, stood beings akin to him" (*IB*, 223 [ch. 20]). Beings like us, we imagine, whose privacy and individuality may be thought of as opacity, and who are not, we hope, going to be sentenced to death for failing to be completely transparent to others. The second example shows the narrator speculating, in the last sentence of his text, that he and his half-brother Sebastian may be the same person, and then adding "or perhaps we both are someone whom neither of us knows" (*RLSK*, 203 [ch. 20]). That "someone" could be anyone, of course. But it's tempting to think that the narrator, brooding on questions of identity and existence, has faintly glimpsed his own (and Sebastian's) fictional condition.

The third example is the most complicated in Nabokov's earlier work. In *Bend Sinister*, the author tells us in his Introduction, "an anthropomorphic deity impersonated by me . . . experiences a pang of pity for his creature and hastens to take over" (*BS*, xviii). The deity ends the pain of his suffering character, the philosopher Adam Krug, by allowing him "a sudden moonburst of madness" in which he perceives "the simple reality of things," namely that neither he nor his dead wife nor his tortured son can have suffered because they are in a novel, only figments of someone else's imagination, "merely my whims and megrims," as Nabokov puts it (*BS*, xviii, xiv). We should always pause when Nabokov uses the words "simple" or "reality" – or "merely" for that matter. There is a simple reality here – Nabokov is writing a book – but there are other realities too. When Nabokov says, in the same Introduction, that "nothing on earth really matters, there is nothing to fear, and death is but a question of style" (*BS*, xviii), he is not evading a difficult issue but framing it in a delicately oblique way which actually leaves all the pain intact. We might think of all the things Pnin, in another novel, has taught himself to forget: unvisited memories are forgotten only in a very special sense. Krug has to go mad to attain his insight into his existential condition – scarcely an attractive solution. What's more, the supposed solution will not help him in his fictional world, the only one where he actually lives, any more than it would help Nabokov or any other living writer if a god were to drive him crazy and reveal his puppet status. Death is a question of style as long as the death is a written one, that is, doubly someone else's: not yours, and belonging to a character made of words. Krug's world disappears the way Cincinnatus's does ("the wall vanished, like a rapidly withdrawn slide" [*BS*, 240 (ch. 18)]), and of course the idea that totalitarian regimes are hodgepodges of fantasy, massive evasions of real humanity, is not without its truth. The trouble, as Nabokov knew all too well, is that such fantasies have, in recent history, been able to muster all the instruments of material power.

Dying by the book

None of these characters, however, comes quite as close to seeing, or more precisely to inventing, his actual author as Kinbote does. It's true that Pnin meets up with a character, "a prominent Anglo-Russian writer," who resembles his author in certain respects, but Pnin didn't create this character, and although Pnin escapes from Waindell College, neither he nor anyone in his fictional world even dreams of an escape from the book into a historical America. The project of Nabokov's late work, I want to suggest, is the second part of what Vadim Vadimovich, in *Look at the Harlequins!* calls an "interview with posterity" (*LATH*, 227 [pt. 6, ch. 1]). The first part is conducted in the meticulously orchestrated sentences of *Strong Opinions* and concerns Nabokov's picture of himself as a writer. He imagines posterity, which happily hasn't arrived yet, as continuous with the present, and not requiring a separate address. The second part of the interview is found in the last novels, and involves a fictional exploration of what it means to write fiction. It means, in Nabokov's practice, to redraw but never deny the world of brutal fact, the contingent realm of death and history and madness. The pain and the beauty of this work lie in its intricate blend of success and failure in the redrawing – sometimes it is better to fail than to succeed – and in its close portrait of the redrawing process itself.

In the strictest sense posterity began for Nabokov in July 1977, but the characters in his last novels run into it all the time, that is, they contemplate not death but whatever awaits them on death's other side. The axiom that Vadim Vadimovich decides to "twist . . . into a jingle," as he says, is in its most obvious meaning a literary rule: no dead narrators.

> The I of the book
> Cannot die in the book [*LATH*, 239 (pt. 7, ch. 1)].

The rule condemns the post-suicide narrative of Quentin Compson in Faulkner's *The Sound and the Fury,* and questions the joke which underlies Machado de Assis's *Memorias Postumas de Bras Cubas,* where the narrator is, as he says, less an author who has died than a dead man who has taken up authorship, not an *autor difunto* but a *difunto autor.* But the jingle has a pathos which goes well beyond a literary prescription. Vadim is saying he can't die if he is writing, and by implication, won't die as long as his writing continues. But then is he writing as his sentences die away at the end of the book? If the crumbling syntax represents a man falling asleep, the writer is still in control (miming loss of control). His represented self will return to consciousness, and no doubt to a good life as an old, happy, healthy, heterosexual Russian writer in America, endlessly loved by the young woman he calls "you." But one day he will die, in this way or another, and what if the syntax represents the moment of death rather than a sinking into sleep? All that's necessary for this is the breaking of a literary rule. The rule, like all rules perhaps, states what should happen rather than what does and acquires in this reading the flavor of an eager wish. It also expresses, with a slight trucu- lence, the one chance any writer can cling to come what may: that he or she will die, as Van and Ada Veen hope to, into a book. "One can even surmise," we read in *Ada*, "that if our time-racked, flat-lying couple ever intended to die they would die, as it were, *into* the finished book . . ." (587 [pt. 5, ch. 6]).

Do they die in this way? Yes, but do they die only in this way? Neither they nor their book can tell us, because they have placed themselves so firmly under the (not entirely secure) protection of Vadim's rule. The conditional moods ("if our . . . couple ever intended to die they would die") suggest a choice where there is ultimately none, and at an earlier moment Van has been even more emphatic: "Throw him out. Who said *I* shall die?" (535 [pt. 4]). The I of this book has no plans for dying in or out of the book, or indeed for recognizing death at all, except in one extraordinary moment, when Van allows himself to write "I am because I die" (153 [pt. 1, ch. 24]). Van and Ada themselves presumably devised and checked the Family Tree which follows the title page of *Ada* (and in the Library of America edition precedes Nabokov's own dedication to Véra). Among the dates there we find those of Aqua Durmanov 1844–1883, Daniel Veen 1838–1893, Marina Durmanov 1844–1900, Lucette Veen 1876–1901, Demon Veen 1838–1905, Andrew Vinelander 1865–1822, Van Veen 1870–, Ada Veen 1872–. An editor's note on the next page but one tells us "With the exception of Mr. and Mrs. Ronald Oranger, a few incidental figures, and some non-American citizens, all the persons mentioned by name in this book are dead." Mr. Oranger, the editor, is still alive and therefore confirms Vadim's rule. It's scrupulous of him not to tamper with the text, even when there are missing dates. But we do know by inference that Van and Ada, like Humbert Humbert, are dead by the time we read them, since their scheme was to have the memoirs published only posthumously. Posterity gets its interview then, because it is posterity, but the text itself is very reluctant to let anyone die, or to die itself. Van is ninety-seven years old, in terrible pain, and terminally ill: "The Veens had believed for a whole summer of misery (or made each other believe) that it was a touch of neuralgia" (587 [pt. 5, ch. 6]). Their doctor says it isn't "a person or persons" who need to be cured before it is too late, but a book. "It was," Van/Nabokov writes laconically. It was too late, or it was cured? Both, it seems. The book was cured, and then driven back into critical condition, a perfect metaphor for a death that must come but can never be seen arriving.

A clean copy, it seems, is too close to a prepared corpse, and even "a regular inferno" is a form of life. Violet, soon to be Mrs. Oranger, is Van's typist.

> What everybody thought would be Violet's supreme achievement, ideally clean, produced on special Atticus paper in a special cursive type (a glorified version of Van's hand), with the master copy bound in purple calf for Van's ninety-seventh birthday, had been immediately blotted out by a regular inferno of alterations in red ink and blue pencil. One can even surmise that if our time-racked, flat-lying couple ever intended to die . . .   (587 [pt. 5, ch. 6])

In *Transparent Things* the management of posterity has been handed over to a series of eccentric angels or ghosts. For certain privileged observers, any place in the world, and in this case the main street of a town in Switzerland, "teems with transparent people and processes, into which and through which we might sink with an angel's or author's delight . . ." (*TT*, 44 [ch. 13]). "Or author's" is a clue to the particular speaker or writer of this text. He says "I" in the first line of the book, but also says "we" in italics a few lines down, as if to emphasize the class of persons or non-persons he belongs to. "We depend on italics to an even greater degree than do, in their arch quaintness, writers of children's books" (92 [ch. 24]). And who is he, who are they? His fluent but occasionally curious English suggests he is R., a German-American writer, alive and then dead in the narrative and therefore undoubtedly dead at the time of writing – apparently a blatant infringement of Vadim's rule. But then "dead" in this text may be just an uninformed manner of speaking, and material death, the death Van Veen refuses and that comes for us all, is elided once again, this time because it may be only a change of state:

> This is, I believe, *it*: not the crude anguish of physical death but the incomparable pangs of the mysterious mental maneuver needed to pass from one state of being to another.
>
> Easy, you know, does it, son.
>
> (104 [ch. 26])

"They" then are the dead who care about the living, who call to them and shadow them, and R. needs his italics both to identify this elusive group and to insist on the slenderness of the power. They know more than mere mortals – how many times a loved person has been unfaithful, for example – but they cannot put their knowledge to very active use.

> Direct interference in a person's life does not enter our scope of activity . . . The most we can do when steering a favorite in the best direction . . . is to act as a breath of wind and to apply the lightest, the most indirect pressure such as *trying* to induce a dream that we *hope* our favorite will recall as prophetic if a likely event does actually happen. On the printed page the words "likely" and "actually" should be italicized too, at least *slightly* . . .   (92 [ch. 24])

All this diffidence is more than justified, since the spirit of R. cannot at all help the protagonist of the novel, Hugh Person, who dies, or "dies," in a terrible hotel fire. "We thought that he had in him a few years of animal pleasure . . . but after all it was for him to decide, for him to die, if he wished" (99 [ch. 25]). One of Hugh's "last wrong ideas," we learn, was that the human cries he heard "were the shouts of people anxious to help him, and not the howls of fellow men" (104 [ch. 26]). It is perhaps not far-fetched to see this sentence as a revision of the ending of *Bend Sinister*. In each case a well-disposed creature on another plane of being knows a truth that is unavailing for the suffering person. The second time the unavailing nature of the knowledge is clearer, and the reader is reminded of the howls.

Partir c'est mourir un peu . . .

In *Strong Opinions*, Nabokov is rather scathing about critics who missed the simple riddle of the narrator's identity in *Transparent Things*. That wasn't the worst of it, though. The very notion of transparency seems to have, in Nabokov's words, "baffled the wise and misled the silly." Wise and silly alike thought the novelist's business was "seeing through things," whereas "that kind of generalization is not only a dismal commonplace but is specifically untrue. Unlike the mysterious observers in *Transparent Things*, a novelist is, like all mortals, more fully at home on the surface of the present than in the ooze of the past" (*SO*, 194, 195). The tone and texture of this remark are so different from those of *Transparent Things* itself that we go straight back to the book with renewed questions. If the mortal novelist inhabits the surface of the present, what do we make of the novelist's presentation of an ex-novelist who makes the same recommendation but has trouble following it himself?

> When *we* concentrate on a material object, whatever its situation, the very act of attention may lead to our involuntarily sinking into the history of that object. Novices must learn to skim over matter if they want matter to stay at the exact level of the moment. Transparent things, through which the past shines! (*TT*, 1 [ch. 1])

It's hard not the feel the ambivalence here, and hard to attribute it all exclusively to R. There is a real charm in those transparent things and that shining (far from oozing) past, and R. has told us why: the past is seductive because the future is unreal. Certainly there is virtue in staying at the exact level of the moment, and it is lucky for novels and novelists that "sexual love is less transparent than many other much more complicated things" (17 [ch. 6]). But Nabokov's own practice suggests that novices who wish to become experts may do best of all not just to skim but to know when to skim and when to sink a little. This is why R., in a sentence I have already quoted, writes of sinking as "an angel's or author's delight."

Transparency means many things in Nabokov. In *Invitation to a Beheading* it evokes the standardized, administered notion of identity which obtains in a totalitarian world – and perhaps also in certain democratic worlds too, if they have bureaucratized themselves sufficiently. In *Look at the Harlequins* it represents a form of insanity, a uncontrolled spatial equivalent to the sinking though time of *Transparent Things*. At one point when he is trying to explain his mental difficulties with the organization of space, Vadim sees the walls of an American dining room open up on to a phantasmatic audience: "through the translucid unpleasant walls I could make out – without looking! – rows and tiers of dim spectators, with the sense of a sign in my brain meaning 'standing room only' in the language of madness" (176 [pt. 4, ch. 4]). *Transparent Things* doesn't disavow these meanings, indeed the fact that even a knowledgeable writerly ghost can't resist transparency points up its dangers. The title of the novel signals a certain pathos of things, too transparent, too vulnerable to the past, to enjoy their own moment in the sun. But it also points to the durability of the past, to the long history which lingers even in the smallest object, and which therefore has not died.

This durability is the great theme of *Ada*, of course, an apologia for life, as Jean Blot nicely says.[4] But just as the death that is not pictured drives much of the passion in this book, so preoccupations which appear to be denied recur again and again at crucial moments. These preoccupations take many forms – anxieties about reality, resurgences of morality, intermittences of energy and power – and their final effect is to insert a stripe of darkness into memory itself, as if a triumphant love was not only a victory over time but itself a kind of danger or damage.

"But *this* . . . is certain, this is reality," Ada exclaims, insisting as firmly as her author could wish on the surface of the present, "this is pure fact – this forest, this moss, your hand, the ladybird on my leg, this cannot be taken away, can it?" Four words in parenthesis – from Van, from Ada herself at a later time? – tell us and her "it will, it was" (*Ada*, 153 [pt. 1, ch. 24). But was it? The writing remembers, so who or what has lost this "reality"? I don't think the parenthesis is talking about the deaths of Van and Ada, or is written from beyond the end of the book. The loss occurs within their lives, and their finding the moss and the forest in their memory dilutes the sorrow but doesn't abolish it. There is a peculiar Proustian pain in this perception. Just as the narrator of *A la Recherche du temps perdu* must first resurrect his grandmother in his mind in order fully to grieve for her death, so Van and Ada can't recall their early love without also recalling the missing, wasted years of their adult lives.

The whole text of *Ada* is a doubly haunted flashback: it knows it will reach happiness, but it knows how much absence and trouble lie along the way. Read with these concerns in view, Van and Ada's "family chronicle" seems littered with loaded words, with expressions and intimations they would surely strike out if they had one more round with their red ink and blue pencil. Van rather grandly implies that he doesn't know what "incestuous" means (19 [pt. 1, ch. 3]), and he tells his father he has "no regrets" about his consumed passion for his sister. Well, he would have told his father if he had sent the letter containing this claim (309 [pt. 1, ch. 42]). And he does tell his father, in conversation, that "we just did not care" (442 [pt. 2, ch. 11]). But if this is so, why does the notion of incest keep recurring, as if Nabokov were organizing an improbable tribute to Freud? Children play anagrams and come up with the words "insect" and "nicest," along with the non-word "scient." It takes only one more instant for the word "incest" to appear (85 [pt. 1, ch. 13]. "He was omniscient," Van writes of himself. "Better say, omni-incest" (394 [pt. 2, ch. 5]). He sends Lucette away because he refuses "to complicate matters by entering into yet another incestuous relationship" (467 [pt. 3, ch. 3]). Does this language reflect long-suppressed guilt? No, only an awareness that Van and Ada do not live in a world of their own making. Van's father says, "I have bribed many officials in my wild life but neither you nor I can bribe a whole culture, a whole country" (443 [pt. 2, ch. 11]). And Ada herself had earlier said to Van, "One can't bribe one's parents, and waiting forty, fifty years for them to die is too horrible to imagine – I mean the mere thought of *anybody* waiting for such a thing is not in our nature, is mean and monstrous" (264 [pt.1, ch. 38]). It is possible, Nabokov is saying, to be innocent in one's own eyes and guilty in the world's, and for neither condition to cancel the other out. The world may be wrong but it is the world, not only "sufficient" as Van says (21 [pt. 1, ch. 3]), but all there is, in spite of the dreams of Terra and the forking paths of fiction.

It is in this sense, I think, that we should read all the conventional, moralizing terms that Van applies to his and Ada's love. He is not a conventional moralist – not a moralist at all – but he does not inhabit a separate universe, and the purest private diction is always marked by what Roland Barthes calls the language of others.[5] This love is "early, too early" (73 [pt. 1, ch. 12]), it first occurs in a "fatal summer" (140 [pt. 1, ch. 22]) it is a "much too premature and in many ways fatal romance" (148 [pt. 1, ch. 24]). Van sees himself as "a nasty young satyr" (110 [pt. 1, ch. 18]). The siblings indulge in sex "freely, and dirtily, and delightfully" (126 [pt. 1, ch. 20]); one of their meetings is "beastly, but beautiful" (180 [pt. 1, ch. 29]). "Heights of happiness" for Van are preceded by "shame" and "agony" (431 [pt. 2, ch. 9]). A joke about *amour-propre* and *sale amour* (168 [pt. 1, ch. 27]) comes from

Tolstoy, but we can ask why it has to appear at all. "Their immoderate exploitation of physical joy amounted to madness and would have curtailed their young lives had not summer . . . begun to hint lazily at possible failings and fadings" (139 [pt. 1, ch. 22]). This proposition may be a bit of belated boasting rather than any sort of self-critique, but even so a normative judgment, the view of "the average physiologist" (139 [pt. 1, ch. 22]), has got itself represented. It's not that Van and Ada have any doubts about their love or their right to love each other. It's that the social impossibility of their love, richly present in the real and imagined world outside it, also has a persistent presence within it – and it is an impossibility which turns out to include not only incest but any freely indulged sexual appetite. Indeed, we may read incest in the novel as an extreme figure for a lurking taboo on outright sexual joy.

Of course Van and Ada overcome this, and live happily almost ever after – once they have reached the ages of fifty-two and fifty. We cannot and should not deny their splendid success. But they live surrounded by transparent things, and no late years will ever catch up with their first summer of 1884.

Et mourir c'est partir un peu trop

Other worlds abound in Nabokov, as Vladimir Alexandrov has persuasively shown.[6] There are past worlds, alternative worlds, posterities, travestied histories, novels within novels, ghostly acrostics, shades of shades, versions of the hereafter. They are all different from each other, and the differences matter. But there is a dimension in which these worlds come together, and are no longer really separable. When a character in Nabokov first stumbles on a hint of another world, he doesn't know which of several other worlds he may have met. He knows only the aura of otherness, the sensation of doubling, and I want to return now to R.'s claim, in *Transparent Things*, that he and his astral companions will bother to speak only about people who have such sensations.

The implication is that for R., and perhaps ideally for the late Nabokov and for us, the most interesting persons, in fiction and in fact, are those who suspect that their own world is not all there is, who persistently perceive, like Vadim Vadimovich for example, "a certain insidious and relentless connection with other states of being which were not exactly 'previous' or 'future,' but definitely out of bounds, mortally speaking" (*LATH* 7 [pt. 1, ch. 2]). Or who, like Van Veen, are sure their own world is the only one but display a passionate, indeed professional interest in those who believe otherwise. Believing otherwise is itself, we might say, a reasonable definition of what fiction does and is. And yet Nabokov never fails to suggest in his last novels that such belief is a form of madness: a clinical condition in *Ada*, a set of "morbid terrors" in *Look at the Harlequins!* (*LATH* 7 [pt. 1, ch. 2]), and in its most benign form, in *Transparent Things*, a "curious sensation" – curious and rare since we are told that the sensation is known only to our hero and to "three famous theologians and two minor poets" (98 [ch. 25]).

The sensation Hugh Person has in *Transparent Things* is "of there existing behind him – at his shoulder, as it were – a larger, incredibly wiser, calmer and stronger stranger, morally better than he. This was . . . his main 'umbral companion' . . ." (98 [ch. 25]). Allowing for the different temperament of the perceiver, which converts a companion into a demon, this is precisely the experience of Vadim Vadimovich in the later novel:

> I now confess that I was bothered . . . by a dream feeling that my life was the non-identical twin, a parody, an inferior variant of another man's life, somewhere on this or another earth. A demon, I felt, was forcing me to impersonate that other man, that other writer who was and would always be incomparably greater, healthier, and crueler than your obedient servant.
>
> (*LATH* 89 [pt. 2, ch. 3])

Charles Kinbote's fleeting fantasy of becoming a version of Nabokov is a strange intuition. He has stumbled on his author, so to speak. But it's hard to imagine him wanting to be that author, let alone managing to achieve this new identity, and he would not be cheered by the idea of being a fiction. One of his frightened dreams about Queen Disa, we remember, is "that she had become a character in a novel." His next dream-thought is "that she was dead," and the quick sequence suggests an equivalence (*PF*, 212).

In *Transparent Things* and *Look at the Harlequins!* this fear, which was a faint speculation in *The Real Life of Sebastian Knight* and an ambiguous promise of release in *Invitation to a Beheading* and *Bend Sinister*, becomes a recurring suspicion of two undeniable truths: that one is living in a novel, and that the novel is written by someone like Nabokov. This is not how the suspicion presents itself, of course. We scarcely know how Hugh Person feels about his "umbral companion," even if we do know a little more about how the companion views his job. And Vadim Vadimovich's recurring intuition is a nightmare, which Nabokov discreetly but lovingly elaborates throughout the book. Vadim, the author of *Tamara*, *Camera Lucida* and *The Dare*, is repeatedly mistaken for the person who wrote *Mary*, *Camera Obscura*, and *The Gift*. His pen name is V. Irisin. At one point he jokingly thinks he may become a lepidopterist (although he has earlier said "I know nothing about butterflies" [*LATH* 97 (pt. 2, ch. 5), 34 (pt. 1, ch. 7)]), and at another moment finds himself on a mountainside in the Rockies with a "dream sensation of having come empty-handed – without what? A gun? A wand?" (156 [pt. 4, ch. 1]). How will he ever know that what he is lacking is his author's but-terfly net? Receiving a pompous lecture from his daughter's headmistress, he can't "shake off the feeling of its all being a nightmare that I had had or would have in some other existence, some other bound sequence of numbered dreams" (174 [pt. 4, ch. 4]). What he is half-remembering here is not a piece of Nabokov's life but a conversation Humbert Humbert has in *Lolita*, and Vadim is in the same fictional country, at least phonetically, when he invents for himself the name Dumbert Dumbert (143 [pt. 3, ch. 3]). His worst fear is "that even *Ardis*, my most private book, soaked in reality, saturated with sun flecks, might be an unconscious imitation of another's unearthly art" (234 [pt. 6, ch. 2]), although in a moment of real happiness he is able to put that suspicion from his mind. We note the variability of the nightmare – Vadim is some author's character in this or another book, Vadim is a par-ody or impersonation of that author – along with its consistency. In each case Vadim has the sense of "a sudden connection with another world" (96 [pt. 2, ch. 5]), as he would have if his intimations were of immortality, a realm of spirits, a hereafter, a Proustian past, or John Shade's "involute abode" (*PF*, 63 [ll. 817–18]) where the artist-creators of our universe play their silent game.

Hugh Person's shadow and the figure of whom Vadim, inversely, thinks he may be only a shadow are not quite the same. The first is R., a novelist within a novel, the second is Nabokov, a historical person. But they attract the same language. One is "wiser, calmer . . . stronger . . . morally better" than the fictional character; the other is "greater, healthier, and crueler." We may pause over the compliments Nabokov seems to be handing himself and his surrogate (and we may wonder whether "crueler" is a compliment), and we may remember that he is casually picking up a very ancient and traditional metaphor. If the artist is a god in relation to his work, then this relation may picture, in miniature, God's interest in design and his aloofness from the world, his availability only to certain intuitions and acts of faith. We find this metaphor, and especially the attention to design in this sense, throughout Nabokov's writing, critical and creative. But here, in this late fiction, we are looking at a particular turn of the trope, a quirky critique of the very ideas Nabokov himself holds dear. He concentrates not on the perception of pattern but on the sense of the flawed copy, the feeling of secondariness that haunts our first and perhaps our only lives.

Vadim's interview with posterity is predicated on the notion that he feels his life may be (and we know it is) "a parody . . . of another man's life, somewhere on this or another earth." He is not going to be released into his own fictionality, like Adam Krug, because that fictionality is itself his nightmare; and he is not going to invent Nabokov, as Kinbote fleetingly does, because an uninvented Nabokov is already dogging him. Like Van Veen, who can't die and must die, and like Hugh Person, who loses his wrong ideas and his life at the same time, Vadim Vadimovich inhabits a fiction which is after all a form of reality, our reality, the reality of our hopes and fears. The suggestion is not that this world or the other is a fantasy or in any way unreal, but that the life we live may be seen as a real novel which one day will end. Wondering what happens to fictional characters when their story is over – perhaps they live for ever but don't know it themselves, perhaps they and their books are forgotten before the reader drops off to sleep – is a way of wondering whether our lives are ever entirely our own. We don't need to live in a novel in order to ask this question, and we don't need to believe or disbelieve in a god in order to answer it. We need only worry a little about whether we could be better than we are, whether another calmer, healthier self awaits us somewhere; and whether we could be worse than we are, assume another self which is merely stronger and crueler. We may never know the fate of these possible selves, but we shall be the richer for having known their shadows, and one day it will be too late to wonder.

NOTES

1. See T. W. Adorno, "Spätstil Beethovens," in *Musikalische Schriften* IV (Frankfurt: Suhrkamp, 1982), 13. "The ripeness of the late works of significant artists does not resemble that of fruit . . . they lack all the harmony that classical aesthetics is accustomed to demand from the work of art" (my translation). Adorno goes on to suggest that late works characteristically engage more rather than less with the conventions of the given art form.
2. She says in the middle of a long monologue "O Jamesy let me up out of this." James Joyce, *Ulysses* (London: The Bodley Head, 1960), 914.
3. See Marcel Proust, *A la Recherche du temps perdu* (Paris: Gallimard, 1988), III:583, 663. The interesting point, in this context, is not the still putative name of the narrator but the fact that the fictional character unmistakably knows the name of his author.
4. Jean Blot, *Nabokov* (Paris: Editions du Seuil, 1995), 196.
5. Roland Barthes, *S/Z* (Paris: Editions du Seuil, 1970), 190.
6. Vladimir Alexandrov, *Nabokov's Otherworld* (Princeton: Princeton University Press, 1991), passim.

3
RELATED WORLDS

13

BARBARA WYLLIE

Nabokov and cinema

"Funny thing," said Darwin one night, as he and Martin came out of a small Cambridge cinema, "it's unquestionably poor, vulgar, and rather implausible, and yet there is something exciting about all that flying foam, the femme fatale on the yacht, the ruined and ragged he-man swallowing his tears."
Vladimir Nabokov, *Glory*, 83 (ch. 20)

Darwin's passing comment in the 1932 novel, *Glory*, encapsulates the fundamental antagonism that characterizes Nabokov's own attitude towards moving picture art. On the one hand, cinema epitomizes the worst of commercially driven, populist culture and yet, on the other, it generates a compelling dynamic of excitement and wonder that is inarguably, and perpetually, fascinating. Nabokov, an avid filmgoer throughout most of his life, delighted in the movies as a source of pure entertainment. The films he cited as his favorites were mostly comedies – the slapstick features of the 1920s and 1930s, starring Charlie Chaplin, Buster Keaton, Harold Lloyd, Laurel and Hardy, and the Marx Brothers – from which he could recall specific scenes in meticulous detail (*SO*, 163). From the same era he mentioned films by Fritz Lang, as well as Murnau's *The Last Laugh* (1924), Wiene's *The Hands of Orlac* (1925), and Sternberg's *Shanghai Express* (1932),[1] although he was later to claim that the names of these directors "never meant anything" to him (*SO*, 163) as if, incongruously, he had never bothered to connect the films he had seen with the people who made them. Nabokov also demonstrated a similar indifference to some of the greatest figures in cinema history. At a Hollywood dinner party in 1960 he is reported to have asked John Wayne what he did for a living. "I'm in pictures," he replied.[2] Nabokov did not fail, however, to recognize Marilyn Monroe, and also met and befriended Billy Wilder,[3] along with James Mason, who played the part of Humbert Humbert in Stanley Kubrick's 1962 film adaptation of *Lolita*. Such incidents have created the impression that Nabokov was merely an "average movie-goer" who had "seen more films than he [was] able or care[d] to remember."[4] During their years in Europe and America the Nabokovs were indeed regular filmgoers.[5] Véra Nabokov recalled seeing Greta Garbo in Clarence Brown's scandalous story of love and betrayal, *Flesh and the Devil* (1926), but of all her films, Nabokov singled out the Hollywood classic *Ninotchka* (1939), directed by Ernst Lubitsch, in which Garbo plays a steely Soviet emissary gradually broken down by the combined charms of cosmopolitan, capitalist Paris and leading-man Melvyn Douglas.[6] Once in Switzerland, however, Nabokov's movie-going came to an end. In 1974, Nabokov commented that in the fifteen years since leaving America he had been to the cinema only two or three times.[7] Nevertheless the Nabokovs did have a television set on which he saw Orson Welles's seminal *Citizen Kane* (1941) for the first time in 1972.[8] Interestingly, Nabokov's favorite part of the film was "the clutter of the final sequence," reminiscent of the chaotic interior of Pavor Manor in *Lolita*. The extent to which he lost touch with contemporary developments in film during this period is perhaps best exemplified by his ignorance of one of the biggest screen phenomena of the late twentieth century, James Bond (*SL*, 537–38).

Nabokov responded positively to the first major study of cinema in his work (published in 1974), conceding that the "basic idea, [of] my constantly introducing cinema themes, and cinema lore, and cinematophors (VN) into my literary compositions cannot be contested of course" (*SL*, 537). This was a rare concession, since Nabokov never elucidated the processes of his deployment of film in his fiction, nor explained its ramifications in terms of his central creative preoccupations. From his everyday life there are very few recorded incidents that reveal the true extent of his immersion in film lore, although it is possible to get a sense of Nabokov's spontaneity, and his inability to resist the temptation of turning a real-life scenario into a remembered movie sequence. In a letter to Edmund Wilson, for example, Nabokov describes his attempts to contact him during a recent visit to New York in fanciful emulation of a scene from a 1940s *film noir* – "I rang up the Princeton Club – and slowly put down the receiver as they do in the movies"[9] – whilst Alfred Appel, Jr. recalls Nabokov enacting, with mischievous relish, the opening sequence of Robert Siodmak's *The Killers* (1946), a film adapted from a short story by Ernest Hemingway:

> Nabokov and I entered the dimly lit bar of the Montreux Palace Hotel. Standing at the bar he ordered a scotch, and I asked for a well-known aperitif which was not in stock. "Good!" said Nabokov, "that's no drink for a man." Our rather tight-fitting overcoats still on, we began a three-way badinage with the barman . . . "We're like Hemingway's killers," observed Nabokov, speaking out of the corner of his mouth in mock-gangster fashion. Pointing to his wide-brimmed grey fedora, placed in gentlemanly fashion on a bar stool, Nabokov said, "I should return it to my head, no?, and heighten the realism."[10]

Nabokov's opinion of the movies was, nevertheless, ambivalent. It is apparent that he had little patience for "the grotesqueness of cinematic cliché."[11] Friends described how he would "single out intentionally an inept American film" and "literally shake with laughter, to the point where . . . he would have to leave the hall."[12] It was precisely this element of *poshlust*[13] that inspired his first overtly cinematic novel, *Laughter in the Dark* ("I wanted to write the entire book as if it were a film," he commented[14]), and informed the characterizations of many of his compromised protagonists, from Smurov to Albinus, Hermann Karlovich, Humbert Humbert, and Van Veen.

Throughout his career, Nabokov looked to the movies not simply as a form of delightful escapism, but also as a potential source of revenue. Like many other émigrés in interwar Berlin, he took advantage of the opportunities to work as an extra in the city's growing film industry, befriended "screen starlets,"and even auditioned for acting roles. Apparently, Nabokov was "exceptionally ready to believe in his own success."[15] He also wrote original scenarios for the screen and negotiated the sale of film rights to his fiction with European and American producers. It would be easy to conclude that Nabokov's interest in the movie business was purely financial, but in the few accounts that exist describing these negotiations it is quite apparent that Nabokov's enthusiasm was not generated simply by the promise of fame and fortune. In 1932, for example, Nabokov met, through former Moscow Art Theatre director Sergei Bertenson, Hollywood producer/director Lewis Milestone to discuss an adaptation of his story, "The Potato Elf." Apparently Nabokov "grew very excited" at Milestone's proposals, telling Bertenson that "he literally adore[d] the cinema and watch[ed] motion pictures with great keenness." Following this meeting he continued to send Bertenson synopses and story ideas, as well as copies of his recent novels, *Camera Obscura* and *Despair*, in the hope that they might be taken up.[16] At the same time, it is evident that Nabokov considered his work as an extra as something more than just a useful source of income. A fellow émigré writer, Ivan Lukash, recalled a particular episode with Nabokov in a Berlin cinema when, by chance, they found themselves watching one of the films in which Nabokov appeared. Although he was subsequently unable to remember the title of the film (*SO*, 161), the experience evidently had a considerable impact: "As his face gleamed and faded, he pointed himself out on the screen, but the sequence was over so quickly that Lukash simply scoffed, thinking Nabokov had invented this moment of stardom."[17]

Nabokov's excitement at this fleeting vision parallels the fervor with which many of his protagonists pursue their cinematic dreams. This "keenness" also extends to his manipulation of the processes, styles, and techniques of film-making in his fiction, which both generates a thematic context for the preoccupations of his movie-obsessed characters and introduces a new narrative and perceptual dimension that impacts upon fundamental notions of time, memory, mortality, and the imagination.

Nevertheless, Nabokov's stance remained contradictory and evasive. In September 1958, during negotiations over the film rights for *Lolita*, he stated that "my supreme, and in fact only, interest in these motion pictures is money" (*SL*, 261). Nabokov's deal with James Harris and Stanley Kubrick for the rights to *Lolita* was certainly lucrative, consisting of $150,000 plus 15 percent of the producers' profits. In addition, Nabokov was paid $100,000 for writing the screenplay for the 1962 Harris/Kubrick production, and the film returned $3,700,000 in the US box office alone.[18] As a consequence of *Lolita*'s success, the figures involved in subsequent rights negotiations became higher and higher. In April 1968, prior to the publication of *King, Queen, Knave* (Nabokov's new translation of *Korol', dama, valet*), a $100,000 contract for the movie rights had already been negotiated, whilst bidding for the rights to *Ada* began at $1,000,000.[19] In 1964 and again in 1970, Nabokov was approached by Alfred Hitchcock to collaborate on film projects, but on both occasions the plans came to nothing. Nabokov commented that he and Hitchcock shared a certain "humour noir." It is perhaps no coincidence, therefore, that the only film of his that he could recall seeing was the 1955 black comedy, *The Trouble with Harry*.[20] Apart from their "humour noir" Nabokov and Hitchcock shared other key characteristics – a penchant for puzzles and game-playing, a fascination with ways of seeing and voyeurism, with complex patternings of themes and imagery, doubles and doubling, and a sophisticated manipulation of narrative conventions.[21]

Lolita was the first of Nabokov's novels to be filmed. This was followed, in 1969, by British director Tony Richardson's version of *Laughter in the Dark*, scripted by playwright Edward Bond. Richard Burton had been originally cast to star, but was replaced by Nicol Williamson. Nevertheless, "despite all this talent, the film [proved] flat and unprofitable."[22] At the Cannes Film Festival in 1972, Polish film-maker Jerzy Skolimowski's adaptation of *King, Queen, Knave*, starring Gina Lollobrigida and David Niven, was nominated for the Palme D'Or, as was German director Rainer Werner Fassbinder's *Despair* in 1978, starring Dirk Bogarde with a screenplay by Tom Stoppard.[23] Several of Nabokov's stories and novels have also been adapted for television – *Bend Sinister* (Germany, 1970), *Invitation to a Beheading* (Germany, 1973), *Maschenka* (*Mary*) (joint European production, with a screenplay by John Mortimer, 1986), *Mademoiselle O* (France, 1994), and *An Affair of Honour* (Estonia, 1999). Short film adaptations include *Skazka* (*A Nursery Tale*, Germany, 1997), and *Christmas* (USA, 2000).[24] In 2000, Marleen Gorris's adaptation of *The Luzhin Defense* (*The Defense*) was released in the United States, starring John Turturro and Emily

Watson,[25] whilst in 1997, another American production, this time a new version of *Lolita*, opened to a storm of controversy. The film had initially been rejected by US distributors, who were reluctant to back a film about pedophilia at a time when new anti-child-pornography legislation was about to be passed. The film claimed to be more faithful to Nabokov's novel than Kubrick's version, but audiences were made immediately wary by its choice of director. Since the early 1980s, British film-maker Adrian Lyne had been producing fast-paced, highly-charged and sexually provocative, yet commercially successful, mainstream Hollywood features (*Flashdance, 9½ Weeks, Fatal Attraction, Indecent Proposal*). Unsurprisingly, his *Lolita* presented the child heroine as a sexual predator, with a worldly maturity far beyond her twelve years, and more akin to a twenty-first-century teenager than an adolescent from the late 1940s. Jeremy Irons played a wistful, emotionally vulnerable Humbert Humbert, a victim of tragedy and grief, haunted by the memory of his lost love, Annabel Leigh, ruthlessly manipulated and inevitably betrayed by Lolita. This version had none of the humor or wit of Kubrick's original and was also, disappointingly, considering the supposedly more liberal age in which it was made, deeply chauvinistic.

It is not difficult to argue the validity of a sympathetic interpretation of Humbert Humbert's tale, considering that the novel is narrated solely from his point of view and is cast as a "love story," yet it is interesting to see how Nabokov's and Schiff's screenplays diverge in terms of intent.[26] Nabokov's Humbert Humbert is "horrible," "abject," and a "shining example of moral leprosy" (*Lo Screen*, 3). He tortures Lolita mentally, emotionally, and also physically. It is made quite plain that she is forced to negotiate every favor, that Humbert Humbert is a depraved and grotesque captor, consumed by irrational jealousy and prepared to use physical violence to keep her with him, and it is this that drives her to Quilty.

Kubrick's version emphasized the detective-story aspect of the novel, but shifted its primary focus away from the question of "who did Humbert kill?" to "why did Humbert kill Quilty?"[27] The film also displays a skillful use of comedy and irony, reminiscent of Nabokov's very distinctive "humour noir," which successfully renders the complexity of the relationships among Humbert Humbert, Charlotte, and Lolita. Meanwhile, the situation's true perversity and decadence is exposed through Peter Sellers's eccentric portrayal of Quilty, who represents the flip side of Humbert Humbert's impeccably maintained demeanor of propriety. Quilty's strangeness is compounded by the enigmatic presence of his silent companion, Vivian Darkbloom (the incarnation of Nabokov's fictional alias), with whom he practices judo, amongst other things: "She throws me all over the place," he reports with a wry smile. Although Nabokov did not care for the slapstick sequence featuring "the collapsing cot" at The Enchanted Hunters, and "the frills of Miss Lyon's elaborate nightgown" (*Lo Screen*, xiii), the film included some ingenious set pieces – the opening confrontation at Pavor Manor played across a ping-pong table, Humbert Humbert drunk in the bathtub following Charlotte's accident (which Nabokov singled out as "delightful"), the scene at a drive-in movie with both Charlotte and Lolita clasping Humbert Humbert's knee, his breakdown at the hospital in Elphinstone, and Quilty's visit to the house in Beardsley, masquerading as Dr. Zempf, a German psychologist (a Sellers character that prefigures Dr. Strangelove in Kubrick's film of 1964).

Nabokov spent six months from April to September 1960 in a house off Sunset Boulevard working on his script. In July, he presented Kubrick with a 400-page draft. Kubrick commented that it was "too unwieldy, contained too many unnecessary episodes, and would take about seven hours to run."[28] Nabokov's screenplay was also full of cumbersome cinematic devices – animated sequences, voice-overs and obtuse camera set-ups – more reminiscent of the chiaroscuro style of 1920s German Expressionist film than the sophisticated visual economy of the contemporary American product. On delivery of the final draft in September, Kubrick set about reworking it into a tightly structured film that retained the book's thematic texture and its moral integrity. Although Harris and Kubrick told Nabokov that his was "the best screenplay ever written in Hollywood," in an interview in 1993, Harris admitted that Nabokov's "huge" script was "unfilmable": "'You couldn't make it. You couldn't even *lift* it.'"[29] In the end, Nabokov was disappointed that "only ragged odds and ends of [his] script" had been used (although he retained sole credit for the screenplay and received an Oscar nomination in 1963). Nevertheless, he acknowledged that "Kubrick was a great director" and that "his *Lolita* was a first-rate film with magnificent actors" (*Lo Screen*, xii). Kubrick did, however, pay attention to the parts of Nabokov's screenplay that worked cinematically – particularly the Ramsdale High School summer dance sequence, the scenes with Humbert Humbert and Lolita on the road, and the final sequence at the Schillers' house. He also demonstrated a sensitivity to the pathos of the story and Nabokov's distinctive use of imagery,[30] whilst the film's cyclic structure dramatized its pivotal themes of entrapment and self-destruction.

Kubrick's working method was well suited to adapting Nabokov's novel. "The perfect novel from which to make a movie" he stated, "is not the novel of action but, on the contrary, the novel which is mainly concerned with the inner life of its characters."[31] One of the main criticisms of Kubrick's film was that, rather than closely follow the course of Nabokov's story, it inserted scenes that were not in the novel in order to fulfill its own dramatic purpose and allowed the Quilty/Humbert Humbert conflict to dominate.

This was, however, a deliberate device deployed by Kubrick to ensure that the adaptation made cinematic sense. His focus on character, he argued, provided him with a starting point from which he could "invent action" that was "an objective correlative of the book's psychological content, [that would] accurately dramatize this in an implicit, off-the-nose way without resorting to having the actors deliver literal statements of meaning."[32] At the same time, severe censorship constraints forced him to underplay the story's sexual dynamic. Instead, he amplified its comic aspect. Film critic Pauline Kael described the film as "the first *new* American comedy since those great days in the forties when Preston Sturges recreated comedy with verbal slapstick [i.e. Screwball comedy]. *Lolita* is black slapstick."[33]

That Nabokov was, in fact, more than merely an "average movie-goer" is most evident in his fiction, however. Apart from incorporating the styles and themes of film into the very fabric of his writing, covert allusion to particular actors and movies indicate the scope of Nabokov's exposure to a vast array of films and film stars during his time in Europe and America. This would encompass the movies of the silent era – German Expressionist as well as Soviet and European avant-garde film, the epics of Cecil B. DeMille and D. W. Griffiths, Mack Sennett's slapstick comedies – and later the Hollywood gangster movie, the Western, American *film noir* and Screwball comedy. In *Mary*, his first novel, Nabokov transposed an entire scene from *The Hands of Orlac*,[34] whilst in *Lolita* there are references to contemporary films as disparate as the romantic epic *Gone with the Wind* (*Lo*, 117 [pt. 1, ch. 2], 156 [pt. 2, ch. 2]), and *noir* thrillers *Brute Force* and *Possessed* (*Lo*, 262 [pt. 2, ch. 26]). In Nabokov's penultimate novel, *Transparent Things*, there is even an oblique reference to Edward G. Robinson as he appeared in John Huston's *Key Largo* (*TT*, 30 [ch. 10]). In *The Gift*, Fyodor takes his mother to see what is patently a Soviet film, reminiscent of Pudovkin's *Mother* or Eisenstein's *Strike* (*Gift*, 90 [ch. 2]), and as a student in Cambridge, Sebastian Knight goes to see Westerns and Charlie Chaplin comedies (*RLSK*, 47 [ch. 5]). At the same time, Martha Dreyer idolizes a fictional movie star, an actor called Hess, whilst the intensely beautiful, glamorous, but dangerous femmes fatales played by Greta Garbo and Marlene Dietrich inspire Margot's cinematic aspirations in *Laughter in the Dark*. There are covert allusions to Garbo contained in descriptions of Ada and Cordula de Prey (*Ada*, 165, 167 [pt. 1, ch. 27]),[35] and the films that are made and screened in the novel – Marina's *A Torrid Affair*, Vronsky's *Les Enfants Maudits*, Ada's *The Young and the Doomed* and *Don Juan's Last Fling*, and Vitry's *Letters from Terra* – serve as distorted reflections of the various stages of Van and Ada's affair. *Don Juan's Last Fling*, however, also functions as a key plot device. It is a critical catalyst in Lucette's suicide, at the same time provoking an overwhelming fit of jealousy in Van that drives him to pursue Ada's fleeting image "from flick-house to flick-house" (*Ada*, 481 [pt. 3, ch. 5]): a "singular" yet double-edged "quest" that feeds his sense of desolation and desire (*Ada*, 500 [pt. 3, ch. 5]). It could be argued, however, that Van's almost pathological obsession with the film is revealing of the extent to which he identifies with its hero. It seems more than a coincidence that several versions of the story have been produced by Hollywood, the most famous of which, made in 1926 and starring matinée idol John Barrymore, showed Don Juan planting "191 kisses on various females during the course of the film, an average of one every 53 seconds."[36] In the same way that such films cataloged the philanderings of an infamous rake, so Van's chronicle can be read as a catalog not only of his infidelities, but also of his sexual conquests, thus reinforcing the antagonistic moral dynamic embedded in his commentary.

Nabokov's characters also take their cinema-going seriously. Humbert Humbert and Lolita, for example, "[take] in, voluptuously and indiscriminately . . . one hundred and fifty or two hundred programs" (*Lo*, 170 [pt. 2, ch. 3]) in their first year on the road (on average three to four films a week). What would normally be an innocent pastime is transformed here into a cynical manipulation, however. Humbert Humbert is eager to get Lolita into a darkened room where he can fondle her discreetly, while she is both placated and distracted by her favorite movies – "musicals, underworlders, and westerners" (*Lo*, 170). The dynamic of *poshlust* is also often present in these episodes, generated particularly by gratuitous sentimentalism. Martin's Uncle Henry is known to cry at the movies (*Glory*, 35 [ch. 9]); Pnin, although "bored by Chaplin," bursts into tears in a fit of nostalgia brought on by a Soviet propaganda film (*Pnin*, 81–82 [ch. 3]); and Luzhin is moved to a rare demonstration of emotion by an overly romantic movie, which happens to be the first he has ever seen (*Def*, 191–92 [ch. 12]). There are also those who either try or succeed in making their careers in films. Ganin, the hero of *Mary*, works as an extra, Lik is known for his "excellent job in the bit part of a stutterer" (*Stories*, 462), and whilst Margot's screen debut is a dismal failure (*Laugh*, ch. 22), Ada and her mother, Marina, enjoy long, intermittently successful acting careers.

In terms of his fiction, the cinematic elements of his first novel, *Mary*, demonstrate Nabokov's intention to put his own experiences to immediate artistic use. The "raw bit of 'real life'" presented by Ganin, the "tuxedoed extra" (*SO*, 161) generates a sense of actuality and contemporaneity but also epitomizes Nabokov's approach to the exploration of cinema throughout his work: "Nothing was beneath his dignity; more than once he had even sold his shadow . . . to work as a movie extra on a set . . . where light seethes with a mystical hiss from the huge facets of lamps that were aimed, like cannon, at a crowd of extras, lit to a deathly brightness" (*Mary*, 9 [ch. 2]).

Ganin's experience both expresses the impact of the medium on Nabokov's imagination and demonstrates the complexity of his response to it. Whilst there is an explicit suggestion that there is something ominous and dangerous in the film-making process – "an undefinable but quite definite sense of mystery and dread"[37] – there is also something intensely compelling in the idea of offering oneself up to annihilation by the overwhelming power of the studio lights, or being rendered utterly anonymous, engulfed in a vast crowd of strangers. The notion that "nothing was beneath his dignity" is, therefore, critical in the context of this sense of wonder, and there is an implication of pride in this statement that counteracts its negative aspect. It is also significant that Ganin claims not to have sold *himself* but his "shadow," appropriately, to this phantom world. Conventional associations of life with light and death with darkness are subverted, but the sense of conflict they generate remains unresolved. Ganin's stance, therefore, exemplifies the inherent ambivalence of Nabokov's treatment of film in his fiction.

Nabokov claimed to "think in images" (*SO*, 154). His son, Dmitri, commented that "his writing . . . was all there, inside his mind, like film waiting to be developed."[38] Cinematic perspective is also integral to Nabokov's exposition of themes of memory and mortality. Processes of film and photography not only grant his protagonists a superhuman visual capability, but the calculated manipulation of the camera eye also offers them supremely privileged points of vantage which are crucial in their struggle to overcome the degenerative forces of time. The artificial quality of this mode of narrative presentation in turn magnifies preoccupying questions of objective and subjective cognition but also serves, paradoxically, as the only reliable means of apprehending "reality" in time and space. As Nabokov argued, the problem of perceiving any given situation as "real" can only be solved by means of "the apparatus to reproduce those events optically within the frame of one screen," namely, a "video" camera (*SO*, 154). At the same time, the photographic image is perceived as an independent dimension and an alternative realm of existence, one which is both aspirational and terrifying. For Ganin, the submission of his shadow to this ghostly realm is profoundly disturbing and reductive, rendering him vulnerable, amorphous, transitory, and yet for others, particularly Humbert Humbert or Van Veen, film offers a form of refuge, the potential for transformation, the means by which to realize their creative ideals, and an alternative realm of existence that defies the ravages of time and the oblivion of death that awaits them.

Cinema's power to transform and transcend mundane reality is a key dynamic in Nabokov's fiction. Romantovski's comment on the movies in the 1933 story "The Leonardo" – "in real life it is all considerably duller" (*Stories*, 364) – echoes the universal response to the medium that Darwin expresses in *Glory*. More fundamentally, however, cinema provides Nabokov's protagonists with a ready source of diverse scenarios from which to draw and a vast array of personae to emulate in their, often unsuccessful, attempts to control their worlds and the people in them. In *The Eye*, Smurov submits himself utterly to the camera perspective to wield an unchallenged authority over his narrative: "Whenever I wish, I can accelerate or retard to ridiculous slowness the motions of all these people, or distribute them in different groups, or arrange them in various patterns, lighting them now from below, now from the side . . . For me their entire existence has been merely a shimmer on a screen" (*Eye*, 90). In *Despair*, Hermann Karlovich not only believes himself to be a literary genius *manqué*, but also a great undiscovered film director, whereas in *Laughter in the Dark*, Margot's schemes are inspired by silent screen melodramas, and in *Lolita*, Humbert Humbert adopts the role of a "great big handsome hunk of movieland manhood" (*Lo*, 39 [pt. 1, ch. 10]) to attract his "starlet" (*Lo*, 65 [pt. 1, ch. 15]), who in turn appears in various film guises, from the femme fatale to Screwball heroine.

Van Veen, however, has a real screen actress at his disposal, bringing the fantastic, tantalizing world of film into the very center of his existence. At the same time, Van emulates the cinematic mode in order both to retain his proximity to Ada and to assert absolute control over the presentation of their history, but he is not alone in his desire to create an idealized version of the past, not simply for posterity, but for his own personal gratification. Marina is determined that "someday [her] past must be put in order" (*Ada*, 253 [pt. 1, ch. 38]), and that she should imagine the process in terms of film is not only appropriate as a reflection of her own immersion in the medium as a movie actress, but also significant in that she inadvertently describes the exact process of Van's "chronicle":

> Someday, she mused, one's past must be put in order. Retouched, retaken. Certain "wipes" and "inserts" will have to be made in the picture; certain telltale abrasions in the emulsion will have to be corrected; "dissolves" in the sequence discreetly combined with the trimming out of the unwanted, embarrassing "footage" and definite guarantees obtained; yes, someday – before death with its clapstick closes the scene.   (*Ada*, 253–54 [pt. 1, ch. 38])

Film is directly associated with the processes of memory in the novel, such that Van keeps a precious remembered vision of Ada, an "enduring mosaic" of "random images and expressions" that remains unchanged and undimmed by the passage of time. Although the vision is imaginary, it has the vivid and potent quality of film, "a definite picture that he knew he had never seen in reality" which "[remains] within him more real than any actual memory" (*Ada*, 296–98 [pt. 1, ch. 41]). The importance of film and photography to Van's system of memory also takes on a tangible form in the Lucinda Museum which he opens in Manhattan: "A miniature museum just two stories high, with a still growing collection of microphotographed paintings from all public and private galleries in the world" (*Ada*, 336 [pt. 2, ch. 1]). Significantly, the collection also contains an archive of Ada's films, viewable "by arrangement" only (*Ada*, 568 [pt. 5, ch. 1]).

Lolita, too, becomes immortalized in the photographic chamber of Humbert Humbert's memory. The cinematic trope underpins Humbert Humbert's pursuit of Quilty and is played out in the allusions to slapstick comedy and the Western in the murder scene at Pavor Manor.[39] It is also fundamental to both Humbert Humbert's depiction of his relationship with Lolita, and the dramatization of his own predicament throughout the narrative. Most distinctive is Humbert Humbert's assumption of the role of *noir* hero, the figure faced with a dilemma "generated by his own weakened moral awareness" and who "gradually loses the battle against a strong urge to succumb to something he knows is likely to destroy him."[40] Humbert Humbert plays out this role most explicitly in his revenge scenario, which is introduced by the allusions to gangsters and molls in his "Carmen" song (*Lo*, 61–62), and concluded at the end of the novel when he runs his Melmoth into a ditch (*Lo*, 306–307).[41]

The misguidedness of replacing reality with a cinematic fantasy is perhaps most ruthlessly demonstrated by Albinus's relationship with Margot in *Laughter in the Dark*. His infatuation with her is inspired directly by the place in which he first lays eyes on her – a movie theater. When he first sees Margot she is described as a "creature gliding about in the dark" (*Laugh*, 23 [ch. 2]), but initially it is more the sensation of her in the "velvety darkness" of the cinema which attracts him (20). Ironically, his first good look at her is colored by his initial sense of physical attraction compounded by the context in which she appears – "He stared at her face almost in dread. It was a pale, sulky, painfully beautiful face" (21). Albinus so wants to see beauty in Margot's face because of the realm from which she seems to emerge that he ignores its pallor and the predominant aspect of her personality – sulkiness – which it expresses, although at the same time it presents the archetypal image of the screen diva.

In Margot, Albinus finds a tangible embodiment of perfection only attainable in films. He is often presented in a captivated state of reverie induced by a vision of Margot, and yet these visions are contrived simply to fulfill and subscribe to his cinematically informed desires. Margot's skill in emulating screen goddesses proves to be limited, whereas Albinus's deluded vision escalates to a point where it overrides every other faculty of perception, long before the event of his physical blinding: "Margot sat up and smiled plaintively. Tears only added to her beauty. Her face was aflame, the iris of her eyes was dazzling, and a large tear trembled on the side of her nose: he had never before seen tears of that size and brilliance" (*Laugh*, 119 [ch. 14]). With this image their aspirations merge. Margot, who so desires to be a screen icon becomes one in Albinus's eyes. This vision directly echoes the on-screen close-up of an anonymous actress in the story of 1924, "A Letter That Never Reached Russia," which epitomizes the tantalizing power and beauty of the cinematic image: "the huge face of a girl with gray, shimmering eyes and black lips . . . approaches from the screen, keeps growing as it gazes into the dark hall, and a wonderful, long, shining tear runs down one cheek" (*Stories*, 138).

Once they are together, Margot's playacting is extremely effective on this man so preoccupied with film imagery. No matter how vulgar and contrived her behavior, to Albinus, Margot's passionate role-playing is genuine and overwhelming: "There were stormy scenes at home, sobs, moans, hysteria. She flung herself on the sofa, the bed, the floor. Her eyes sparkled brilliantly and wrathfully; one of her stockings had slipped down. The world was swamped in tears" (*Laugh*, 192 [ch. 24]).

Albinus is cruelly and brutally victimized as a result of his slavish devotion to this visual incarnation of a romantic ideal and, it could be argued, that in destroying him so utterly, Nabokov is condemning the potency of the cinematic image and the filmic perspective as an alternative mode of perception. At the same time, however, Margot, who calculatedly generates and manipulates a cinematic persona, apparently thrives, indicating that the fundamental issue is not the validity or otherwise of film as an additional fictive dimension, but the deployment and incorporation of cinematic elements as a means of establishing and maintaining autonomy and asserting control, both in terms of characterization and narrative.

Nabokov's depiction of film in his work is not entirely negative, however. While Van's purpose in his narrative manipulations is to "retouch" and "retake" the past, essentially to fabricate a lie, the same process offers a means of obliterating pain. In *Bend Sinister*, Krug deploys the cinematic mode to alter the past: "The script of daytime memory," he comments, "is far more subtle in regard to factual details, since a good deal of cutting and trimming and conventional recombination has to be done by the dream producers" (*BS*, 63 [ch. 5]). The role of the "dream producers" recalls F. Scott Fitzgerald's archetypal Hollywood mogul Monroe Stahr as he watches the day's rushes: "Another hour passed. Dreams hung in fragments at the far end of the room, suffered analysis, passed – to be dreamed in crowds, or else discarded."[42] This allusion extends to Nabokov also, who is, after all, a "dream producer" of sorts, a creator of fictional illusions. The notion of the dream quality of reality is also emphasized here – "the recurrent dream we all know . . . was in Krug's case a fair rendering of the atmosphere of the original version" (*BS*, 63 [ch. 5]). It is significant that the evocation of an "atmosphere" is sufficient to reconstitute the past, suggesting that the present also is nothing more than a sensation, intangible, illusory. In *Bend Sinister*, Nabokov deploys a synthetic medium to explore and express Krug's reality, but also, ultimately, to negate it. Yet this is not an act of denial, but simply a transformation. The film/narrative enables a shift in perspective, and it is this that grants Krug a form of release from the tyranny of memory and the agony of loss.

Film and photography are also inextricably linked with the processes of imagination and creativity in Nabokov's work, and in this respect are distinctly positive. The "game of intricate enchantment and deception" (*SM*, 125 [ch. 6]) that characterizes Nabokov's art is key to the cinematic experience, and whilst the process of film-making and projection may be cumbersome, the resulting product is inspirational. The slide shows in *Speak, Memory* mirror the screening of the film in Nabokov's story of 1943, "The Assistant Producer." "Tonight we shall go to the movies" (*Stories*, 546) announces the story's narrator, while Nabokov declares at the opening of chapter 8 of his autobiography, "I am going to show a few slides" (*SM*, 153 [ch. 8]). Central to this section are Lenski's magic lantern shows, but Nabokov extends this into a motif that runs throughout the chapter: "The next picture looks as if it had come on the screen upside down. It shows our third tutor standing on his head" (157). Lenski's shows are, however, tedious and monotonous, and their manner of presentation frustratingly amateurish. His assistant, a "dejected-looking university student" is overwhelmed by the "elaborate apparatus" (162) he has been charged to operate and the sequence grinds to a halt as he struggles to find the "fourth slide, having got it mixed up with the used ones" (165). The whole episode is reminiscent of the assistant producer's efforts to keep control of his projector – "but my reel is going too fast" (*Stories*, 549), he cries. Nevertheless, the awkwardness of the machinery is counteracted by the marvelous effect of simply throwing light through the slides. "How tawdry and tumid they looked, those jellylike pictures" Nabokov comments, "but, on the other hand, what loveliness the glass slides . . . revealed when simply held between finger and thumb and raised to the light" (*SM*, 166 [ch. 8]). At the same time, the slides function as a system of memory: "In looking back I find the pattern curiously clear, and the images appear within memory's luminous disc as so many magic-lantern projections" (153–54).

In the opening of *Speak, Memory*, Nabokov describes the family life of "a young chronophobiac" just before he was born, witnessed, significantly, in a series of home movies in which he discovers, with horror, that he "did not exist at all" and, worse still, that "nobody mourned his absence." Nabokov concludes that "our existence is but a brief crack of light between two eternities of darkness" (*SM*, 19 [ch. 1]). Paradoxically, whilst the film exposes Nabokov's absence and circumscribes his existence, it also provides incontrovertible evidence of his presence in the world. The cinematic motif is compounded by the image of the "crack of light," reminiscent of the beam of a movie projector cutting through the darkness of a cinema auditorium, the beam serving as a metaphor for life. In *Bend Sinister*, the beam of light represents the imagination and its ability to transcend time and connect the past with the present, and the real and fictional worlds. At a critical moment in the novel, Nabokov "[slides] along an inclined beam of pale light" (*BS*, 233 [ch. 18]) to reach his fictional protagonist, Krug, who is incarcerated in a prison-house of tortuous dreams and fears. The channel of light acts as a link between the real and the imaginary, serving as an amorphous bridge between two worlds which are both equally baffling and alien. Not only does this provide a significant insight into Nabokov's understanding of his creativity, but it is also revealing of the centrality of the apparatus of film to his art.

Perhaps the most positive prospect afforded by a manipulation of the cinematic mode is to be found in *Transparent Things*, and the perspective of the spirit of the dead writer, R., who watches over Hugh Person's world. Nabokov commented in a 1962 interview that "we live surrounded by more or less ghostly objects" (*SO*, 11). *Transparent Things* dramatizes its ghostly world in a process of inversion, whereby the tangible proves to be illusory, and the intangible emphatically real. R.'s "ghostly" perspective enacts Nabokov's conception of reality as "an infinite succession of steps, levels of perception, false bottoms," a reality that is ultimately and inevitably "unquenchable, unattainable" (*SO*, 11). In death, R. has been granted a privileged perspective that transcends time and space, such that past and present exist together on an equal plane, and it is only through a process of "pulling focus" that distinctions between them can be realized. R.'s vaunted, limitless visual capability emulates the mechanics of photography, and the narrative is dominated by his "camera eye" which perpetually switches from long to medium and short focus in his depiction of Hugh's tortured existence. The tension and anxiety generated by the prospect of their own mortality which motivates so many of Nabokov's protagonists to find ways of overcoming the regressive forces of time is of no consequence in this scenario. Far from being "heartless"[43] and "dehumanized,"[44] R.'s perspective proves to be eternal, positive, and infinitely expansive, and the novel presents, perhaps most explicitly in the entirety of Nabokov's work, the potential for release from the constraints of mortality and a means of escape from the "prison of time," that is otherwise "spherical and without exits" (*SM*, 20 [ch. 1]).

The antagonism and ambivalence that characterizes Nabokov's treatment of film in his fiction remains an unresolved yet highly potent dynamic. The notion that as a creative medium it offers the potential to access alternative realms of existence is, however, at once palpable and compelling, provocative and elusive, existing equally and undiminished as both a positive and negative force in Nabokov's art.

NOTES

1. Alfred Appel, Jr., *Nabokov's Dark Cinema* (New York and Oxford: Oxford University Press, 1974), 137, 58.
2. Ibid., 58.
3. Ibid., 236.
4. Ibid., 58.
5. Brian Boyd, *Vladimir Nabokov: The Russian Years* (Princeton: Princeton University Press), 363.
6. Appel, *Nabokov's Dark Cinema*, 41, 187.
7. Ibid., 57.
8. Ibid.
9. Letter dated October 22, 1956 in *Dear Bunny, Dear Volodya: The Nabokov–Wilson Letters, 1940–1971*, ed. Simon Karlinsky (Berkeley, CA: University of California Press, 2001), 337.
10. Appel, *Nabokov's Dark Cinema*, 208.
11. Boyd, *Russian Years*, 363.
12. Ibid.
13. Nabokov's version of the Russian term for the "obviously trashy," false or vulgar (see *LRL*, 309–14; and *SO*, 100–101).
14. Appel, *Nabokov's Dark Cinema*, 258–59.
15. Boyd, *Russian Years*, 229, 232–33.
16. Ibid., 376. See also Appel, *Nabokov's Dark Cinema*, 137.
17. Boyd, *Russian Years*, 205.
18. See Richard Corliss, *Lolita* (London: BFI Publishing, 1994), 18, 64, 80.
19. Brian Boyd, *Vladimir Nabokov: The American Years* (Princeton: Princeton University Press, 1991), 532.
20. See *SL*, 361–66; and Appel, *Nabokov's Dark Cinema*, 129.
21. For more, see, James A. Davidson, "Hitchcock/Nabokov: Some Thoughts on Alfred Hitchcock and Vladimir Nabokov," in *Images: A Journal of Film and Popular Culture*, 3 (http://www.imagesjournal.com/issue03/features/hitchnab1.htm [accessed July 2003]).
22. Boyd, *American Years*, 532. For Nabokov's opinion on the film, see Appel, *Nabokov's Dark Cinema*, 134–35.

23. For commentaries on *Despair*, see David Robinson, "Fassbinder After Despair," *Sight and Sound* 46.4 (1977): 216–17; Edward M. V. Plater, "The Externalization of the Protagonist's Mind in Fassbinder's *Despair*," *Film Criticism* 9.3 (1987): 29–43; Peter Ruppert, "Fassbinder, Spectatorship, and Utopian Desire," *Cinema Journal* 28.2 (1989): 28–47; and Wallace Watson, "The Bitter Tears of RWF," *Sight and Sound* 2.3 (1992): 24–29.

24. See Dieter E. Zimmer, "A Nabokov Filmography," on "Zembla, the Nabokov Website" (http://www.libraries.psu.edu/nabokov/forians.htm), and listings on the "Internet Movie Database" (http://www.imdb.com). Details of *An Affair of Honour* can be found at http://www.luebeck.de/filmtage/99/program/essays/estland.html, and François Rossier's adaptation of "A Nursery Tale" at http://www.berlinale-talentcampus.de/talents/652.php (accessed July 2003). Thanks to Alice Lotvin Birney at the Library of Congress, Washington, DC, for details on Serge Gregory's film, *Christmas*.

25. See Steven Poole's article, "The Nabokov Gambit," in *The Guardian*, August 25, 2000, in which he also discusses the film versions of *Laughter in the Dark*, *King, Queen, Knave*, *Despair*, and *Lolita*, as well as Alfred Hitchcock's invitation to Nabokov to write the screenplay for *Frenzy* (1972) (also at http://books.guardian.co.uk/departments/classics/story/0,6000,358450,00.html [accessed July 2003]).

26. See Suellen Stringer-Hye, "An Interview with Stephen Schiff," on "Zembla" (http://www.libraries.psu.edu/nabokov/schiff1.htm), and Alan A. Stone, "Selling (Out) Nabokov: A Humorless New *Lolita* Makes Satire for Tragedy," *Boston Review*, October–November 1998 (http://bostonreview.mit.edu/BR23.5/stone.html [accessed July 2003]).

27. Dan E. Burns, "Pistols and Cherry Pies: *Lolita* from Page to Screen," *Literature/Film Quarterly* 12.4 (1984): 246.

28. Boyd, *American Years*, 408; see also Appel, *Nabokov's Dark Cinema*, 232–34.

29. Corliss, *Lolita*, 19.

30. For commentary, see Thomas Allen Nelson, "Lolita: Kubrick in Nabokovland," in *Kubrick: Inside a Film Artist's Maze* (Bloomington, IN: University of Indiana Press, 1982), 54–78.

31. Stanley Kubrick, "Words and Movies," *Sight and Sound* 30 (1960–1961): 14.

32. Ibid.

33. Pauline Kael, "Lolita," in *I Lost It at the Movies. Film Writings 1954–1965* (New York: Marion Boyars, 1994), 205.

34. See Appel, *Nabokov's Dark Cinema*, 137.

35. See Don Barton Johnson's posting "ADA & Garbo," on NABOKV-L, 30 August 2003 (http://listserv.ucsb.edu/archives/nabokv-l.html).

36. See the Internet Movie Database http://www.imdb.com/title/tt0016804/trivia (accessed August 2003).

37. Gavriel Moses, *The Nickel Was for the Movies: Film in the Novel from Pirandello to Puig* (Berkeley and Los Angeles, CA: University of California Press, 1995), 113.

38. Dmitri Nabokov, "On Revisiting Father's Room," in *Vladimir Nabokov: A Tribute*, ed. Peter Quennell (London: Weidenfeld and Nicolson, 1979), 129.

39. See Michael Wood, *The Magician's Doubts: Nabokov and the Risks of Fiction* (London: Chatto and Windus, 1994), 130–33.

40. See A. Silver and E. Ward, eds., *Film Noir. An Encyclopedic Reference to the American Style*, 3rd edn (New York: Overlook Press, 1992), 6.
41. Appel, *Nabokov's Dark Cinema*, 222.
42. F. Scott Fitzgerald, *The Last Tycoon* (London: Penguin, 1965), 70.
43. Boyd, *American Years*, 601.
44. David Rampton, *Vladimir Nabokov: A Critical Study of the Novels* (Cambridge: Cambridge University Press, 1984), 166.

14

LEONA TOKER

Nabokov's worldview

Vladimir Nabokov repeatedly went on record rejecting sociopolitical engagement as a writer's duty. His non-*engagé* stance earned him the suspicion of the readers who expect novelists to critique the social order, negotiate its change, or teach the audience how to live. It also earned him the hostility of those who believe that emphasis on aesthetics rather than an emphatic promotion of values conducive to "bringing up a better generation in a safer world" (*Lo*, 8) may be a sufficient reason for, as it were, turning pedophilia into a thing of beauty.

Yet even if Nabokov's concern with aesthetics dominates his ideology ("what makes a work of fiction safe from larvae and rust is not its social importance but its art, only its art" [*SO*, 33]), it is not exclusive. Its link with his ethical concepts and metaphysical preferences emerges from, for instance, the connotations of definition of "aesthetic bliss," in the Afterword to *Lolita*, as "a sense of being somehow, somewhere, connected with other states of being where art (curiosity, tenderness, kindness, ecstasy) is the norm" (*Lo*, 314–15): the expression "other states of being" refers not only to states of heightened aesthetic perception but also to states of quickened ethical awareness and to states of metaphysically refined consciousness. Here I shall discuss Nabokov's worldview in terms of this interconnectedness of his poetics, ethics, and metaphysical outreach, also taking into consideration some of the political aspects of his stance.

Aesthetics

In contrast to *engagé* writers, Nabokov did not seek to influence the reader's ideology via direct sociopolitical or ethical theses in the plots or the idea-content of his works. He saw ethical value in aesthetic experience itself and created conditions for such experience on the part of their readers. These conditions can be discussed under three rubrics that redescribe some of the on-record principles of Nabokov's poetics: vitality, refinement, and saturation.

The *vitality* of Nabokov's prose style is a matter of the force of unforgettable single images (the dying swan trying to get into a boat in *Speak, Memory*, Dolly Haze at tennis in *Lolita*, the oversize slippers of Cincinnatus and the well-worn ones of Sonia Zilanov), of the dynamism with which would-be static descriptions are transformed into accounts of the flow of the perceiving consciousness, and of the transformations of states of consciousness in the course of the same sentence or paragraph. Nabokov's own term for such a cluster of effects was "enchantment": a writer may be seen as "a storyteller, as a teacher, and as an enchanter. A major writer combines all these three . . . but it is the enchanter in him that predominates" (*LL*, 5). Unlike "charm" or "spell," enchantment does not amount to arrested motion: separate images are imprinted in the reader's memory in retrospect, but in the process of reading they are part of the flux of consciousness, the lived time of imaginative cooperation with the text.

The principle of *refinement* is phrased negatively in Nabokov's on-record remarks: it consists in the exclusion of common, heavy-duty, ready-made tired forms of language and thought – except for parodic purposes. Nabokov was engaged in a lifelong struggle against the type of pompous vulgarity that is referred to by the lapidary Russian term *poshlost* (see *NG*, 63–74), a term that in Russian carries weaker class-contempt connotations than are felt in its English translations. The common is kept away from Nabokov's authorial prose not because of his aristocratic claims but because it is a deadwood encumbrance on the flow of consciousness modeled by his style. For the same reason it is often represented in the speech and behavior of the characters who are the butt of Nabokov's satire. Nabokov's ridiculing of the lifeless forms of language and thought is in tune with the main idea of Henri Bergson's seminal essay "Laughter": what makes us laugh is a combination of the mechanical with the living.[1]

Nabokov, who continued writing Russian poetry long after he had switched to English as the language of his prose, seems to have explored to the full the aesthetic potentialities of the contact of languages and the kinds of cultural consciousness that the languages embody.[2] Refining away the ready and gelled, the common and the vulgar – except for parodic purposes – is also one of the conditions of the vitality of Nabokov's prose.

The *saturation* of the prose text consists in the richness of the semiotic and symbolic loads of meaning economically signaled by lexical choices, collocations, and recurrences. What remains unsaid frequently impinges on the shape of what is said in the text ("the little I can express would not have been expressed, had I not known more" [*SO*, 45]),[3] so that a slight lexical change can alter the whole ethical or aesthetic construct of a passage – this, no doubt was one of the reasons for Nabokov's and his family's insistence on controlling, as much as polyglotically possible, the work of his translators. The effect of this feature of Nabokov's texts on the reader consists in creating a feeling of minor revelations waiting to happen, of the unexpected joy of epiphanies, of gratitude to other readers who facilitate the discoveries, and, not seldom, moments of shame at having overlooked clues, connections, allusions, challenges. The sophistication of the patterns of meaning is dependent on intertextual links as well as on internal patterns of significance created by the paradigmatic recurrence of images and motifs and by the syntagmatic reciprocal influence of words in collocation. The latter effect is indirectly commented on in *Invitation to a Beheading*, where Cincinnatus laments his inability to write in such a way as to make "a commonplace word" come alive and "share its neighbor's sheen, heat, shadow, while reflecting itself in its neighbor and renewing the neighboring word in the process, so that the whole line is live iridescence" (*IB*, 93 [ch. 8]). Through the reference to "live iridescence," the idea of semantic enrichment through collocation is connected to the vitality of the style and the synaesthetic potential of the imagery. Ironically, in the above complaint about the elusiveness of the writer's art, Cincinnatus appeals not only to the reader's visual sense but also to fluctuating tactile sensations ("sheen, heat, shadow") and to the auditory sense (mainly through the alliterations, such as *sh*are, *sh*een, *sh*adow).

The aesthetic effect of Nabokov's works is based not only on matters of style and imagery but also on intricate and often witty structural patterns that characterize both his plots and their episodic constituents.[4] The ending of a novel, whether *Invitation to a Beheading*, or *Pnin*, or *Transparent Things*, tends to create a different perspective on the foregoing material, turning a repeated reading into an entirely new and qualitatively different experience. An analogous effect is also created by the camouflaged complexities of separate details. His demand that literary study be conducted with "the passion of science and the patience of poetry" involved a set of preferences ("the specific detail to the generalization, images to ideas, obscure facts to clear symbols, and the discovered wild fruit to the synthetic jam" [*SO*, 7]) which must be read as a counterpart of the ethics of literary form evolved in his own works.

Ethics

"By all means place the 'how' above the 'what,' but do not let it be confused with the 'so what'" (*SO*, 66). "So what" may here be understood to pertain to the total aesthetic impact of the work as opposed to localized effects; it may also refer to the ethics of addressivity: since each segment of a literary text is an event in the experience of the reader, the shape of the segment (the "how") is ethically significant – more so, perhaps, than its content (the "what"). The ethics of literary form is rooted in the formative influence of individual aesthetic experience, "the telltale tingle between the shoulder-blades" (*LL*, 64), *in its own right* rather than via the idea content of the works.[5]

The philosopher Richard Rorty reads Nabokov's dictum "that little shiver behind is quite certainly the highest form of emotion that humanity has attained when evolving pure art and pure science" (*LL*, 64) as a comment on the sense of the term "pure" in "pure art and pure science" (art or science unadulterated by pragmatic bias) – and finds it "compatible with saying that 'the ability to shudder with shame and indignation at the unnecessary death of a child . . . is the highest form of emotion that humanity has attained while evolving modern social and political institutions.'"[6] Yet Nabokov's ensuing ethical statement – that the capacity "to wonder at trifles – no matter the imminent peril – these asides of the spirit, these footnotes in the volume of life are the highest form of consciousness, and it is in this childishly speculative state of mind, so different from common sense and its logic, that we know the world to be good" (LL, 374) – gives provocation even to Rorty: "If you want your books to be read rather than respectfully shrouded in tooled leather, you should try to produce tingles rather than truth."[7] Yet Rorty has also been the first to point to the connection between Nabokov's denial of the rational basis of aesthetic experience with A. E. Housman's view of poetry – not as verse in general but as the rare indefinably genuine quality of some verse – expressed in *The Name and Nature of Poetry* ("the best-known manifesto in English of what Nelson Goodman calls "the Tingle-Immersion" theory of aesthetic experience"[8]). Regarding the appeal of poetry as "more physical than intellectual," Housman has enumerated several kinds of somatic responses to it, such as "a shiver down the spine," "a constriction of the throat and a precipitation of water to the eyes," and a piercing sensation in "the pit of the stomach."[9] Oriental mysticism (to which Nabokov was supremely indifferent) grants the spine the ability to promote transcendent states. So does vivisection: Galvani's *incantesimo* (enchantment) referred to the momentary cessation of the heartbeat upon insertion of a needle into a frog's spinal cord. No wonder that Nabokov associates aesthethic fastidiousness (in *Mary*, *Despair*, *Laughter in the Dark*, *Lolita*, and *Ada*) with callousness or cruelty.

References to the base of the spine as the seat of aesthetic experience suggest the need to develop – through exercise – the necessary intellectual poise. According to Bergson, whereas in primitive organisms perception is equivalent to action (an amoeba immediately recoils from an irritant that it perceives), in complex organisms, perception is *delayed* action; this still means, however, that the organism perceives that which is relevant to its survival and determines its conduct. The education of human senses consists in learning to perceive what is, on the contrary, *not relevant* for any practical endeavor, to perceive details for their own sake.[10] By educating our senses we thus learn to admire the world around us with the kind of disinterestedness that Immanuel Kant held to be the *sine qua non* of aesthetic experience.

Yet the education of the senses means learning to perceive not only the "useless" beauty but also the "irrelevant" pain of another human being, that which appeals to pity. The readers' belated insights into the complexities of Nabokov's characters and their motives reenact the characters' own contrite post-factum responsiveness to the pain of others. By partial camouflage of the suffering of the people who surround the protagonists (symptoms of this suffering are allowed into the text, even if in an understated manner), Nabokov creates the conditions for us to recognize the callous reluctance of imagination not only in the characters but also in ourselves: perhaps the camouflage should not have been effective? This aspect of his art can be read as a protest against the near-universality of unconscious or deliberate callousness, one of the most widespread transnational cultural phenomena of the century in which he lived.

Yet if, as ample historical evidence can show, aesthetic sensitivity cannot automatically produce moral responsiveness, neither does a conscious commitment to the good of individual others suffice for compassionate attention: one often has to be *trained* to perceive implicit appeals to sympathy. In his lecture on Kafka, Nabokov defined art as "beauty plus pity" (*LL*, 251). His works are, indeed, punctuated with signals of the characters' suffering, often camouflaged but not beyond recognition if one's attentiveness has been appropriately trained. The heightening of one's disinterested sensitivity to and curiosity about the environment available to the senses may also sharpen one's sensitivity to signs of another's pain – but only given a prior general commitment of the will to the good of others – the kind of commitment which Sebastian Knight manifests when (*RLSK*, 109 [ch. 12]) he returns to pick up an advertisement in order not to slight the stranger who hands out throwaways (Sebastian's tragic flaw is his inability to maintain the same ideologically motivated commitment to people with whom he has genuine emotional ties). One can form this commitment through tears at the dismissal of the beloved governess or through an occasional "disgust" at recollecting one's past conduct (*SM*, 33 [ch. 2]). By itself, this commitment is not a sufficient condition of ethical discipline: it must be supplemented by a proficiency of disinterested attention. "Curiosity" should go together with "pity" and, when not spontaneous, attention to the suffering of others can be enhanced through aesthetic training.

The ethical ideology evolved in Nabokov's fiction can be described as an idealistic variety of rational individualism: moral values are derived not from a vision of a collective good but from respect and concern for the rights of the individual – so long as that individual's aims do not encroach on the rights of other individuals. Some of Nabokov's characters (Martin Edelweiss, Fyodor Godunov-Cherdyntsev, Timofey Pnin, John Shade) respect the rights of others to an independent identity; others solipsistically ignore that right (Ganin, Dreyer, Van Veen); still others actively violate it (Hermann, Humbert, Kinbote).

The characters of the first group, however, sometimes embark on pursuits that conflict with their self-interest or with the well-being of their families, pursuits that are either entirely selfless or motivated by transcendent aims. Most of them can be described as ethical idealists: they believe in doing what is intrinsically right, even though they often fail to live up to this belief and are sometimes trapped in conflicts between different criteria for telling the right from the wrong. Their armor of rational individualism is, in the best tradition of classical Russian and American fiction, occasionally breached by a hankering after a capacity for supererogation, for acts that transcend or clash with one's rationally calculable duty.

By contrast, in the characters of the second group rational individualism has degenerated into egoism. Their experience challenges the reader to analyze their fundamental ethical misprisions or self-delusions and to admit having temporarily endorsed such misprisions in the process of reading.[11] Nabokov once half-earnestly predicted that "one day a reappraiser will come and declare that, far from having been a frivolous firebird, I was a rigid moralist kicking sin, cuffing stupidity, ridiculing the vulgar and the cruel – and assigning sovereign power to tenderness, talent, and pride" (SO, 193). His fiction creates the conditions not only for aesthetic experience but also for a study of the character's attitudes and acts in terms of culturally symptomatic ethical tendencies.

Metaphysics

Whereas the terms "tenderness," "curiosity," and "kindness" in Nabokov's definition of "aesthetic bliss" establish links between aesthetics and ethics, the terms "states of being" and "ecstasy" point in the direction of metaphysicals: "states of being" are an ontological issue, whereas "ecstasy" can be understood both as a transcendent mystical state or a state of heightened aesthetic attention. As is now widely recognized,[12] one of the concerns traceable throughout Nabokov's work is with the mystery of the relationship of matter and spirit and of life (before birth and) after death: "The cradle rocks above an abyss, and common sense tells us that our existence is but a brief crack of light between two eternities of darkness. Although the two are identical twins, man, as a rule, views the prenatal abyss with more calm than the one he is heading for" (*SM*, 19 [ch. 1]).

Nabokov's views on the darkness on both sides of the cradle underwent modifications. In his younger days he was ready to confront the possibility of the extinction of individual consciousness after death: the 1928 poem "Rasstrel" ("Execution") envisages "merciless darkness" ("neumolimaia t'ma" [*Stikhi*, 209]) following a young man's execution. This poem, however, was not included in Nabokov's later bilingual collection *Poems and Problems* (1981) – as if, with the eventuality of death growing more real, and with the growing need to extend comfort to the future bereaved, skepticism about the survival of consciousness after death became less bearable. Nabokov's fragment "Ultima Thule" describes a bereavement-motivated series of attempts to draw the solution of the mystery of death out of the person who seems to have had it revealed to him and to have gone insane as a result:[13] the protagonist's double bind is that the solution of the mystery is, by definition, a knowledge of life after death, and death, the irreversible, is a condition of its attainment. The most one is able to achieve when alive is "leakings and drafts" from another dimension (*SM*, 35 [ch. 2]) – impressions that one is at liberty to regard as promises that the other dimension exists and awaits one at the end of the road. Earthly beauty and the leaps of the spirit at its sight are "pocket money" icons of "the real wealth, from which life should know how to get dividends in the shape of dreams, tears of happiness, distant mountains" (*Gift*, 164 [ch. 3]).

Under the influence of *Invitation to a Beheading*, where the protagonist is victimized for the crime called "gnostical turpitude" (*IB*, 72 [ch. 6]), the relationship between earthly life and the transcendent realm in Nabokov's worlds is most often imagined on the basis of gnostical dualism: the material world is a product of a sinister swerve in the spiritual realm, upon which human spirit has been entrapped in a spurious universe "hastily assembled" (*IB*, 51 [ch. 4]) by a demiurge. Each human being is believed to possess a spark, a splinter of the real world; the recognition of this spark in oneself, fidelity to it, its cultivation, brings one closer to the "state of being" in which the genuine life of the soul "is the norm."

Yet gnosticism cannot provide an unhedged description of Nabokov's metaphysics, if only because he claimed to be "an indivisible monist" (*SO*, 85). Gnostical imagination, Christian symbolism, Romantic search for wholeness, Schopenhauer's poesy, and Bergson's vision were *alternative* takes on experience – visions with which Nabokov's own intuitions had various affinities. For example, the gnostical attitude to the individual is in tune with Nabokov's somewhat romantic sense that while non-pragmatic sensitivity to one's environment needs to be fostered, its cultivation is not a formation of a new quality so much as a reawakening of the property that one has already possessed. Children are endowed with that capacity for self-forgetful concentrated receptiveness to external stimuli: it is with "a child's care" that Truth holds a secret in its hands (*Gift*, 224 [ch. 4]).[14] Adaptation to everyday practical and social life obliterates the child's capacity for an aesthetically heightened visionary state of consciousness. Cincinnatus C., the "gnostic" dissident in *Invitation*, is often described in terms of childish purity, childish sullenness, and childish frailty tormented by an adult sense of being.

In *Speak, Memory*, however, Nabokov describes the birth of his own sense of time and of being as "tremendously invigorating." It was a comparison of the ages of his parents, thirty-three and twenty-seven, with his own age of four, that brought about his sense of himself as separate from the world around him, along with the realization, as he continued merrily "strutt[ing] and trott[ing]" (*SM*, 22 [ch. 1]) along a path,[15] that the world had been there before his entrance. Nabokov describes this revelation as his second baptism, "on more divine lines" than the literal first one: "I felt myself plunged abruptly into a radiant and mobile medium that was no other than the pure element of time. One shared it – just as excited bathers share shining seawater – with creatures that were not oneself but that were joined to one by time's common flow, an environment quite different from the spatial world" (21). This early intuition is akin to a Bergsonian view of reality as pure time and of time not as a static medium but as a mobile one, as flow, change, heterogeneity into which one inserts the mobility of one's own inner life. The image of the path in this episode is a symbol of the spatial vision that results from the intellectualization of time.[16] By contrast, the flow of time is, in *Speak, Memory*, consistently associated with images of moving water, as when "the endless tumultuous flow of a water mill [gives] the spectator (his elbow on the handrail) the sensation of receding endlessly, as if this were the stern of time itself (*SM*, 72–73 [ch. 3]).[17]

Nabokov comments on his first epiphany in the following terms: "the beginning of reflexive consciousness in the brain of our remotest ancestor must surely have coincided with the dawning of the sense of time." The key word in this extrapolation of philogenesis from ontogenesis ("the theory of recapitulation" [*SM*, 21 (ch. 10)]) is the epithet "reflexive." Comparison with the Russian version of the autobiography shows that the word "reflexive" is here used not in the sense of "deliberative, thoughtful" but in the sense of "directed back upon the agent or subject,"[18] – "osoznanie sebia."[19] Elsewhere Nabokov would describe this kind of reflexive consciousness as "[b]eing aware of being aware of being" (SO, 142).

In the infant years preceding the "second baptism," the child's consciousness is not aware of itself: the infant may have been aware of the world but not of his own being in the world, and still less of "being aware of being." The elderly Nabokov's retrospective knowledge of having been there without knowing it merges with the four-year-old boy's positive emotion at realizing that his mother had come into the world before he did and his father even earlier, that each of them was, hence, a separate individual being rather than a "tender incognito" (SM, 22 [ch. 2]). The joy of the moment is also the joy of the discovery of love, because the *sine qua non* of love – as of life itself ("The cranium is a space-traveller's helmet. Stay inside or you perish" [P, 20 (ch. 1)]) – is separateness. The second baptism does not bring the fear of nonexistence, of not having existed, because it entails the intuition of one's having existed without knowing it, in the mobile medium where consciousness becomes reflexive only after it separates out and only when it has realized its own discreteness. The darkness before the rocking cradle may be an epistemological rather than an ontological blank.

If the blank before the first conscious memory is that of an unreflexive finite consciousness, and if conscious personal history is the history of the finite consciousness that is aware of itself, the protagonist of the novel in *Bend Sinister* (1947) entertains the possibility that the darkness after death may be not nothingness but just a different state of being.[20] The "intelligence" of the protagonist, the philosopher Adam Krug, cannot accept death as "the transformation of physical discontinuity into the permanent continuity of a nonphysical element, nor can it accept the inanity of accumulating incalculable treasures of thought and sensation . . . to lose them all at once and forever in a fit of black nausea followed by infinite nothingness" (BS, 99 [ch. 6]). When he is moved to reformulate this dichotomy in terms of death being "either the instantaneous gaining of perfect knowledge" or "absolute nothingness," his intellect still reproaches him: "Who could have believed that his powerful brain would become so disorganized?" (BS, 175 [ch. 14]). But later the intellect begins to give way to intuition, and Krug writes about the blending of the finite individual consciousness into the "infinite consciousness" (BS, 192 [ch. 16]), a consciousness without a personal subject, synonymous with "perfect knowledge" and "permanent continuity of a nonphysical element." An extrapolation of the finite/infinite and reflexive/unreflexive parameters might suggest a homogeneity of the infinite unreflective consciousness after death and before birth; Nabokov does not comment on this in his own name but gives his thoughtful but confused Adam Krug the hypothesis that if we do not feel "abject panic" at the thought of the infinite past "on the minus side of the day of our birth" this is because we "have already gone through eternity, have already non-existed once and have discovered that this *néant* holds no terrors whatever." The abyss in front, Krug believes, "is borrowed . . . from the infinite past" (*BS*, 192–93 [ch. 16]).

In the fifties a further change takes place in Nabokov's fiction: the idea of the unreflexiveness of consciousness after death seems to lose its attractiveness. Perhaps because the issue of one's own death is dwarfed by the pain caused by the death of others, ideas such as the "permanent continuity of a nonphysical element," and of attempts "of a point in space and time to identify itself with every other point," are replaced by the motif of ghosts. The consciousness of a ghost is usually imagined as personal, reflexive: the theme of ghosts may be of greater consolatory power (especially in the short story "The Vane Sisters")[21] even though treated with many grains of salt since "human despair seldom leads to great truths" (*P*, 58 [ch. 2]). The protagonist of Nabokov's *Pnin* dimly believes in "a democracy of ghosts. The souls of the dead, perhaps, formed committees, and these, in continuous session, attended to the destinies of the quick" (*P*, 136 [ch. 5]). Such fantasies return to the images of the lost friends part of the discreteness which they are denied by the idea of "infinite consciousness." For a bereaved Nabokovian character a ghost is an emotion-fraught memory of the dead, often in the shape of images that used to constitute their "properties" when alive.

In a literary work a character is a verbal construct, a combination of motifs; "a ghost" can be interpreted as the reprise of a character's specific leitmotif after that character's death in the story-time (earnest discussions of ghosts as literally haunting the worlds of Nabokov's novels[22] needlessly personify leitmotifs). If in his early fiction recurrent imagery tended to suggest the interpenetration of states of consciousness, in his later fiction it is more closely associated with the theme of the memory of the dead.

Such a use of recurrent imagery points to the possibility (also raised by Joyce in *Ulysses* and by Borges in "Tlön, Uqbar, Orbis Tertius") that the interpenetrating states of consciousness might be intersubjective. Different people may step into the same state of perception-oriented consciousness: in *Pnin*, for example, many of the perceptions and thoughts of the protagonist can, on a repeated reading, seem to be shared with those of the Anglo-Russian narrator who eventually takes over his job; this may well be the case with parts of the narrator's and his brother's experience in *The Real Life of Sebastian Knight*, with Fyodor's and his father's experience in *The Gift*, or Darwin's and Martin's at the end of *Glory*. Such moments seem to be instances of a fleeting recuperation of the irrecoverable; they connect also to the meaning of Nabokov's cryptic remark that he does not "believe in time" (*SM*, 139). In the Russian version of the autobiography this passage reads "I do not believe in the fleetingness of time" ("mimoletnost' vremeni"[23]): by contrast to Heraklitus and Bergson, Nabokov felt that one could, with some effort, step into the same stream twice: "I like to fold my magic carpet, after use, in such a way as to superimpose one part of the pattern upon another." The sense of timelessness achieved this way is enhanced in moments of immersion in one's favorite landscape ("among rare butterflies and their food plants"), when "ecstasy" is underpinned by a sense of "oneness with sun and stone" and a "thrill of gratitude to whom it may concern – to the contrapuntal genius of human fate or to tender ghosts humoring a lucky mortal" (*SM*, 139 [ch. 6]). The verb "humoring" at the end of this metaphysical passage brings back the self-irony which repeatedly curtails Nabokov's autobiographical outreach to "great truths." The "tender ghost" of the passage may well refer to the thoughts about the writer's father, V. D. Nabokov, also a lepidopterist, who, during Nabokov's "second baptism," had emerged from having been previously perceived as a "tender incognito." And if the moments comparable to those Wordsworthian joys can – one wishes to think – be shared with the lost loved ones, they may perhaps be also shared, unknowingly and without pooling the affect, with other living people: such a possibility is staged in the short story "Recruiting" where the narrator attributes his own wave of happiness to a shabby old stranger who may, for all one knows, be experiencing the same elation at the sight of a sunny scene. Nabokov knew that even in the countries governed by totalitarian dictatorships, there live, in various forms of hiding (symbolically exemplified by the self-camouflage strategies of Cincinnatus and of his father in *Invitation to a Beheading*), "fellow dreamers" who keep the same "irrational and divine standards during the darkest and most dazzling hours of physical danger, pain, dust, death" (*LL*, 373).

Politics

Though Nabokov rejected the obligations of an *engagé* writer, he did not ignore the political situation around him:[24] from "the much abused ivory tower" which he recommended as a "fixed address," one was supposed "to dash down to buy the evening paper" (*LL*, 371). His detached view from above may have helped safeguard him from the errors caused by the political involvement of such writers as Koestler or Sartre. His family fled from the Bolshevik takeover at practically the last possible moment; and it was likewise almost at the last moment before the German onslaught that he escaped, with his wife and child, from France in 1940: in both cases he must have seen that further lingering would be lethal. References scattered throughout his work show that he had a good understanding of what was happening in the Soviet Union; and, in *Pnin*, the details of the protagonist's thoughts about the death of Mira Belochkin show that he had read materials concerning Nazi concentration camps of the kind in which his younger brother Sergei lost his life. His political views were not identifiable with those of any party; they were liberal – in the classical sense of believing in individual freedom short of encroaching on the freedom and property of others, as well as in the more modern sense of being opposed to all forms of cruelty and terror.

Yet Nabokov's ideas about human conduct in the face of totalitarianism seem to have changed in the course of his life. His belief in intellectual life as separateness, as resistance to the pressures of cultural environment, in combination with the yearning for intersubjective sharing of experience, provided a context for valorizing the fragmentariness of vision. Whereas most of Nabokov's modernist contemporaries deplored what they saw as the fragmentation of the modern world, in his pre-World War II fiction Nabokov presented the deliberate fragmentation of experience in positive terms, as a measure against totalitarian assault on individual difference. The error of Cincinnatus in *Invitation to a Beheading* is a paranoid granting of solidity to the world in which he is trapped, allowing it to be a whole rather than a threadbare patchwork of fragments: "Involuntarily yielding to the temptation of logical development, involuntarily (be careful, Cincinnatus!) forging into a chain all the things that were quite harmless as long as they remained unlinked, he inspired the meaningless with meaning, and the lifeless with life" (*IB*, 155 [ch. 14]). In "Signs and Symbols" a holistic vision, supplemented with the tendency of seeing the whole as hostile and as peculiarly hostile to oneself, is presented as a psychotic condition, the "referential mania." According to the lucidly deranged Falter in Nabokov's "Ultima Thule," "logical development inexorably becomes an envelopment"(*Stories*, 514). If the world is in fragments, this is where it ought to be: the stage set of *Invitation* eventually collapses and disintegrates in a way that, in 1934, prophetically foreshadows the long-awaited collapses of the totalitarian regimes which the novel evokes. The very notion of the "world" is totalizing; Nabokov responded to it by asking "whose world?" (*SO*, 135). In the short story "Tyrants Destroyed," the narrator, who feels guilty for not having stopped, killed, subverted a future dictator when he could still do it, eventually concludes that he can oppose the tyrant by destroying his image in his own mind. This internal imaginative solution supplements Cincinnatus's decision not to play by the rules of his jailors but to treat them, Alice-in-Wonderland fashion, as not much more than a pack of cards.

World War II seems to have deprived Nabokov of this type of imaginative consolation by philosophy. In retrospect, writing about Russian émigré life in Europe in the thirties, he remembered having viewed the "spectral Germans and Frenchmen in whose more or less illusory cities" he had "happened to dwell" as transparent figures "cut out of cellophane." Yet this illusory self-defense from the alien environment would collapse each time one needed a "visa" or other official dispensation: an "awful convulsion" would then show "who was the discarnate captive and who the true lord" (SM, 276 [ch. 14]). *Bend Sinister*, the first novel that Nabokov completed after the war, constitutes an admission of the powerlessness of self-dissociation from political events. Not only does the protagonist, Adam Krug, fall victim to an unscrupulous regime which can take hold of him through his love for his child; he himself is partly responsible, through his inconsiderate thought-lessness as a schoolmate of the future dictator and later through his near-exclusive absorption in his professional and private emotional life, for the rise of this regime. By contrast to *Invitation*, moreover, in *Bend Sinister*, Nabokov does not deny the possibility of authentic spiritual life in conforming citizens: each "Etermon" (Everyman) may be harboring something quaintly genuine behind his colorless façade:

> All of a sudden transfigured, his eyes narrowly glowing, Mr. Etermon (whom we have just seen mildly pottering about his house) locks himself up in the bathroom with his prize – a prize we prefer not to name; another Etermon, straight from his shabby office, slips into the silence of a great library to gloat over certain old maps of which he will not speak at home; a third Etermon with a fourth Etermon's wife anxiously discuss the future of a child she has managed to bear him in secret during the time her husband . . . was fighting in a remote jungle land where, in his turn, he has seen moths the size of a spread fan, and trees at night pulsating rhythmically with countless fireflies. No, the average vessels are not as simple as they appear. (BS, 79 [ch. 5])

Yet this authentic life of the everyman is, in *Bend Sinister*, fatally disconnected from public life, which is thereby allowed to go to seed. In a 1968 interview Nabokov noted that "[a]verage reality begins to rot and stink as soon as the act of individual creation ceases to animate a subjectively perceived texture" (SO, 118). The word "ceases" signifies that Nabokov does not deny the existence and the powers of creative perception and perhaps does not limit it to the artistic and intellectual elite, but he disapproves of channeling this perception away from the segments of reality left behind by the main thrust of creative activity: the debris has to be reabsorbed into the life of the spirit and perhaps the toil of reabsorption may be not less creative than the initial pathfinding drive.

However that may be, it remains unclear to what extent the principle of a constant maintenance of "average reality" transcends individual agenda. Or to what extent "subjectively perceived texture" can be extended to public life. "Animat[ing] subjectively perceived" texture apparently involves consciousness of uncertainties not only in matters of metaphysics but also those of politics and ethics. Nabokov's aesthetic achievement, moreover, lies not so much in raising such questions in individual readers as in activating the alertness to stimuli, in spurring and training creative perception. It is up to the readers themselves to commit themselves to directions in which, after such schooling, their "curiosity, tenderness, kindness" may be channeled – just as it is up to the readers to determine the relative position of the pursuit of "ecstasy," the fourth constituent in Nabokov's definition of "aesthetic bliss," in the texture of their own lives.

NOTES

1. The effect of the comic, according to Bergson, is corrective: if we wish to avoid being ridiculed, we shall disembarrass our lives from the lifeless gelled accretions of stencil and habit; see Bergson, "Laughter," in *Comedy* (Garden City: Doubleday Anchor, 1956), 61–190, especially 73–79.
2. Another naturalized American, Hannah Arendt, noted that an emigrant is capable of using the language of his adopted country in a more vivid and flexible way if he keeps his own mother tongue as well; if the native language is lost, the acquired one tends to be cliché-ridden even when correct and idiomatic; see Arendt, *Essays in Understanding 1930–1954*, ed. Jerome Kohn (New York: Harcourt Brace, 1994), 13.
3. See also L. Toker, "Nabokov's *Nikolai Gogol*: Doing Things in Style," in *Nabokov at Cornell*, ed. Gavriel Shapiro (Ithaca: Cornell University Press, 2003), 136–47.
4. For the relationship of such patterns and the concern with human commitments see my *Nabokov: The Mystery of Literary Structures* (Ithaca: Cornell University Press, 1989).
5. Cf. Arthur Schopenhauer's belief that aesthetic contemplation has the power of silencing, for its duration, the (intrinsically evil) immanent Will objectified in the individual subject; *The World as Will and Representation*, vol. I, trans. E. F. J. Payne (New York: Dover, 1969), 363.
6. Rorty, *Contingency, Irony, and Solidarity* (Cambridge: Cambridge University Press, 1989), 147.
7. Rorty, *Contingency*, 152. Rorty's infelicitous choice of lexis, e.g., "tingling trifles" (151), "to arouse the senses – to cause tingles" (152), "special sorts of people like Nabokov, who have specially wired brains" (153n) as opposed to people "whose brains are not wired to produce tingles" (151), comes close to describing aesthetic experience as a near-onanistic little pleasure. For a sustained engagement with Rorty's essay see my article "Liberal Ironists and the 'Gaudily Painted Savage': On Richard Rorty's Reading of Vladimir Nabokov," *Nabokov Studies* 1 (1994): 195–206.
8. Rorty, *Contingency*, 149n.

9. All of these are a matter of setting up "in the reader's sense a vibration corresponding to what was felt by the writer." See Housman, *The Name and Nature of Poetry* (Cambridge: Cambridge University Press, 1940), 47, 12.

10. See Henri Bergson, *Matter and Memory*, trans. Nancy Margaret Paul and W. Scott Palmer (London: Allen and Unwin, 1929), 46–48.

11. Rorty discusses striking examples of this phenomenon in *Contingency*, 163–64.

12. This subject is discussed at length in Julian Moynahan, "A Russian Preface for Nabokov's *Beheading*," *Novel* 1 (1967): 12–18; Sergej Davydov, *"Teksty-Matreshki" Vladimira Nabokova* (Munich: Otto Sagner, 1982); D. B. Johnson, *Worlds in Regressions: Some Novels of Vladimir Nabokov* (Ann Arbor: Ardis, 1985), 185–223; Vladimir E. Alexandrov, *Nabokov's Otherworld* (Princeton: Princeton University Press, 1991); and Gennady Barabtarlo, *Aerial View: Essays on Nabokov's Art and Metaphysics* (New York: Peter Lang, 1993).

13. The quasi-prophet's name, Falter, the German for butterfly, plays on the faltering quest for the soul, Psyche, "the myth behind the moth" (*Ada*, 437 [pt. 2, ch. 10]).

14. Cf. Nabokov's valorization of the "childishly speculative state of mind" (*LL*, 374). In the title of one of Sebastian Knight's novels, "Lost Property" may be understood not as *lost possessions* but as a *lost feature* or *capacity*.

15. On the image of the path see also Brian Boyd, *Vladimir Nabokov: The Russian Years* (Princeton: Princeton University Press, 1990), 44–45.

16. For Bergson, intellectualized time turns into, or is contaminated by, space; see *The Creative Mind*, trans. Mabelle L. Andison (New York: Philosophical Library, 1946), 34. In Nabokov's *Ada* Van Veen refers to Space as "the comedy villain, returning by the back door with the pendulum he peddles, while I grope for the meaning of Time" (*Ada*, 538 [pt. 4]).

17. See also L. Toker, "Nabokov and Bergson on Duration and Reflexivity," in *Nabokov's World*, vol. I: *The Shape of Nabokov's World*, ed. Jane Grayson, Arnold McMillin, and Priscilla Meyer (Basingstone: Palgrave, 2002), 132–40.

18. *Webster's New Collegiate Dictionary*, based on *Webster's New International Dictionary*, 2nd edn (London: G. Bell, 1951), 711.

19. Vladimir Nabokov, "Drugie berega," in *Terra Incognita* (Moscow: DEM, 1990), 7.

20. Cf. Schopenhauer, *The World as Will and Representation*, vol. I: 411–12.

21. See also Michael Wood, *The Magician's Doubts: Nabokov and the Risks of Fiction* (London: Pimlico, 1995), 79.

22. In W. W. Rowe's *Nabokov's Spectral Dimension* (Ann Arbor: Ardis, 1981) ghosts are presented, rather mechanically, as ubiquitous. Less flawed, but likewise unnecessarily literalizing of the metaphor of "ghost" ("what is boded must be embodied" [*BS*, 108 (ch. 7)]) are Brian Boyd's "The Problem of Pattern: Nabokov's *Defense*," *Modern Fiction Studies* 33 (1987): 575–604; and his *Vladimir Nabokov's* Pale Fire: *The Magic of Artistic Discovery* (Princeton: Princeton University Press, 1999); as well as Gennady Barabtarlo's "Grandmother's Charm (*The Enchanter*)," in *Aerial View: Essays on Nabokov's Art and Metaphysics* (New York: Peter Lang, 1993), 39–75; these materials, however, usefully connect their observations with the ethical aspects of the structure: Barabtarlo's article, for instance, shows that the implied author's view of the little girl's mother (in some ways the precursor of Charlotte Haze) in *The Enchanter*

is much more positive than the view of the story's first-person proto-Humbertian narrator.

23. Nabokov, "Drugie berega," 86.
24. For important comments on Nabokov's politics see, for instance, Mikhail Geller, "Nabokov i politika," in *Vladimir Nabokov et l'émigration. Cahiers de l'émigration russe* (Paris, 1993), vol. II: 11–17; and Charles Nicol, "Politics," in *The Garland Companion to Nabokov*, ed. Vladimir Alexandrov (New York: Garland, 1995), 625–28.

Alexandrov, Vladimir E. *Nabokov's Otherworld*. Princeton: Princeton University Press, 1991.

Alexandrov, Vladimir E., ed. *The Garland Companion to Vladimir Nabokov*. Garland Reference Library of the Humanities 1474. New York: Garland, 1995.

Alter, Robert. "Nabokov's Game of Worlds." In *Partial Magic: The Novel as a Self-Conscious Genre*. Berkeley: University of California Press, 1975. 180–217.

"Nabokov and Memory." *Partisan Review* 58 (1991): 620–29.

Amis, Martin. *The Sublime and the Ridiculous. Nabokov's Black Farces*. London: Weidenfeld and Nicolson, 1979.

"*Lolita* Reconsidered." *The Atlantic Monthly* 270.3 (September 1992): 109–20.

Appel, Alfred, Jr. *Nabokov's Dark Cinema*. New York: Oxford University Press, 1974.

"Introduction." In Vladimir Nabokov, *The Annotated Lolita*. Ed. with preface, intro., and notes Alfred Appel, Jr. New York: Vintage International, 1991.

Appel, Alfred, Jr., and Charles Newman, eds. *Nabokov: Criticism, Reminiscences, Translations and Tributes*. Evanston: Northwestern University Press, 1971.

Averin, B., N. Malikova, and A. Dolinin, eds. *V. V. Nabokov: Pro et contra*, 2 vols. St. Petersburg: Izd. Russkogo Khristianskogo gumanitarnogo instituta, 1997–2001.

Bader, Julia. *Crystal Land: Artifice in Nabokov's English Novels*. Berkeley: University of California Press, 1972.

Barabtarlo, Gennady. *Phantom of Fact: A Guide to Nabokov's* Pnin. Ann Arbor: Ardis, 1989.

"Those Who Favor Fire (On *The Enchanter*)." *Russian Literature Triquarterly* 24 (1991): 89–112.

Aerial View: Essays on Nabokov's Art and Metaphysics. New York: Peter Lang, 1993.

Beaujour, Elizabeth Klosty. *Alien Tongues: Bilingual Russian Writers of the "First" Emigration*. Ithaca: Cornell University Press, 1989.

Belobrovtseva, Irina, et al., eds. *Kul'tura russkoi diaspory: Vladimir Nabokov – 100*. Tallinn: Trü Kirjastus, 2000.

Berberova, Nina. *The Italics are Mine*. Trans. Philippe Radley. New York: Harcourt, Brace and World, 1969.

Berdjis, Nassim Winnie. *Imagery in Nabokov's Last Russian Novel* (Dar), *Its English Translation* (The Gift) *and Other Prose Works of the 1930s*. Frankfurt: Peter Lang, 1995.

Blackwell, Stephen H. *Zina's Paradox: The Figured Reader in Nabokov's* Gift. Middlebury Studies in Russian Language and Literature 23. New York: Peter Lang, 2000.

Bloom, Harold, ed. *Vladimir Nabokov*. Modern Critical Views. New York: Chelsea House, 1987.

ed. *Lolita*. Modern Literary Characters. New York: Chelsea House, 1993.

Boyd, Brian. "Nabokov's Russian Poems: A Chronology." *The Nabokovian* 21 (Fall 1988): 13–28.

Vladimir Nabokov: The Russian Years. Princeton: Princeton University Press, 1990.

Vladimir Nabokov: The American Years. Princeton: Princeton University Press, 1991.

"'Even Homais Nods': Nabokov's Fallibility or How to Revise *Lolita*." *Nabokov Studies* 2 (1995): 62–86.

Nabokov's Pale Fire: *The Magic of Artistic Discovery*. Princeton: Princeton University Press, 1999.

Nabokov's Ada: *The Place of Consciousness*. Ann Arbor: Ardis, 1985. Rev. edn. Christchurch, NZ: Cybereditions, 2001.

Boyd, Brian, and Robert Michael Pyle, eds. *Nabokov's Butterflies: Unpublished and Uncollected Writings*. Boston: Beacon Press, 2000.

Brown, Edward J. "Nabokov, Chernyshevsky, Olesha, and the Gift of Sight." In *Literature, Culture, and Society in the Modern Age: In Honor of Joseph Frank*. Part 2. Ed. Edward J. Brown, Lazar Fleishman, Grogory Freidin, and Richard D. Schopbach. Stanford Slavic Studies 4.2. Stanford: Dept. of Slavic Languages and Literatures, Stanford University, 1992. 280–94.

Buks [Buhks], Nora. *Eshafot v khrustal'nom dvortse*. Moscow: Novoe literaturnoe obozrenie, 1998.

Clancy, Laurie. *The Novels of Vladimir Nabokov*. New York: St. Martin's, 1984.

Clegg, Christine, ed. *Vladimir Nabokov*, Lolita: *A Reader's Guide to Essential Criticism*. Cambridge, England: Icon Books, 2000.

Connolly, Julian W. "The Function of Literary Allusion in Nabokov's *Despair*." *Slavic and East European Journal* 26 (1982): 302–13.

"The Otherworldly in Nabokov's Poetry." *Russian Literature Triquarterly* 24 (1991): 329–39.

Nabokov's Early Fiction: Patterns of Self and Other. Cambridge: Cambridge University Press, 1992.

Connolly, Julian W., ed. *Nabokov's* Invitation to a Beheading: *A Critical Companion*. Evanston: Northwestern University Press, 1997.

ed. *Nabokov and His Fiction: New Perspectives*. Cambridge: Cambridge University Press, 1999.

Corliss, Richard. *Lolita*. London: British Film Institute, 1994.

Cornwell, Neil. *Vladimir Nabokov*. Plymouth: Northcote House, 1999.

Couturier, Maurice. *Nabokov*. Lausanne: L'Âge d'Homme, 1979.

Nabokov ou la tyrannie de l'auteur. Paris: Seuil, 1993.

Couturier, Maurice, ed. *Lolita*. Figures mythiques. Paris: Editions Autrement, 1998.

Davydov, Sergej. *"Teksty-Matreshki" Vladimira Nabokova*. Munich: Otto Sagner, 1982.

Dembo, L. S., ed. *Nabokov: The Man and His Work*. Madison: University of Wisconsin Press, 1967.

Diment, Galya. *Pniniad: Vladimir Nabokov and Marc Szeftel*. Seattle: University of Washington Press, 1997.

Dolinin, Alexander. "Caning of Modernist Profaners: Parody in *Despair*." *Cycnos* 12.2 (1995): 43–54.

"Nabokov's Time Doubling: From *The Gift* to *Lolita*." *Nabokov Studies* 2 (1995): 3–40.

"Istinnaia zhizn' pisatelia Sirina," in Vladimir Nabokov, *Sobranie sochinenii russkogo perioda*, 5 vols. St. Petersburg: Symposium, 1999–2000. Vol. I: 8–25. Vol II: 9–41. Vol. III: 9–41. Vol. IV: 9–43. Vol. V: 9–39.

Field, Andrew. *Nabokov: His Life in Art*. Boston: Little, Brown and Co., 1967.

Nabokov: His Life in Part. New York: Viking, 1977.

Foster, John Burt, Jr. *Nabokov's Art of Memory and European Modernism*. Princeton: Princeton University Press, 1993.

Foster, Ludmila A. "Nabokov in Russian Emigré Criticism." In Proffer, *A Book of Things About Vladimir Nabokov*, 42–53.

Fowler, Douglas. *Reading Nabokov*. Ithaca: Cornell University Press, 1974.

Gibian, George, and Stephen Jan Parker, eds. *The Achievements of Vladimir Nabokov*. Ithaca: Center for International Studies, Cornell University, 1984.

Grabes, Herbert. *Vladimir Nabokov's Fictitious Biographies*. The Hague: Mouton, 1977.

Grayson, Jane. *Nabokov Translated: A Comparison of Nabokov's Russian and English Prose*. Oxford: Oxford University Press, 1977.

"*Rusalka* and the Person from Porlock." In *Symbolism and After: Essays on Russian Poetry in Honour of Georgette Donchin*. Ed. Arnold McMillin. Worcester, England: Bristol Classical Press, 1992. 162–85.

Vladimir Nabokov. Penguin Illustrated Lives. London: Penguin, 2001.

Grayson, Jane, Arnold McMillin, and Priscilla Meyer, eds. *Nabokov's World*, 2 vols. Basingstoke: Palgrave, 2002. Vol. I: *The Shape of Nabokov's World*. Vol. II: *Reading Nabokov*.

Green, Geoffrey. *Freud and Nabokov*. Lincoln: University of Nebraska Press, 1988.

Greenleaf, Monika. "Fathers, Sons and Imposters: Pushkin's Trace in *The Gift*." *Slavic Review* 53 (1994): 140–58.

Haber, Edythe C. "Nabokov's *Glory* and the Fairy Tale." *Slavic and East European Journal* 21 (1977): 214–24.

Hyde, G. M. *Vladimir Nabokov: America's Russian Novelist*. Critical Appraisals Series. London: Marion Boyars, 1977.

Johnson, D. Barton. *Worlds in Regression: Some Novels of Vladimir Nabokov*. Ann Arbor: Ardis, 1985.

"Preliminary Notes on Nabokov's Russian Poetry: A Chronological and Thematic Sketch." *Russian Literature Triquarterly* 24 (1991): 307–27.

"'L'Inconnue de la Seine' and Nabokov's Naiads." *Comparative Literature* 44.3 (1992): 225–48.

Johnson, D. Barton, with Wayne C. Wilson. "Alphabetic and Chronological Lists of Nabokov's Poetry." *Russian Literature Triquarterly* 24 (1991): 355–415.

Johnson, Kurt, and Steve Coates. *Nabokov's Blues: The Scientific Odyssey of a Literary Genius*. Cambridge, MA: Zoland Books, 1999.

Juliar, Michael. *Vladimir Nabokov: A Descriptive Bibliography*. Garland Reference Library of the Humanities 656. New York: Garland, 1986.

Karlinsky, Simon. "Nabokov and Chekhov: The Lesser Russian Tradition." In Appel, Jr. and Newman, 7–16.

Karlinsky, Simon, ed. *Dear Bunny, Dear Volodya: The Nabokov–Wilson Letters, 1940–1971*. Revised and expanded edition. Ed., annotated, and with an introductory essay by Simon Karlinsky. Berkeley: University of California Press, 2001.

Kellman, Steven G., and Irving Malin, eds. *Torpid Smoke: The Stories of Vladimir Nabokov*. Amsterdam: Rodopi, 2000.

Lee, L. L. *Vladimir Nabokov*. Boston: Twayne, 1976.

Lodge, David. "What Kind of Fiction did Nabokov Write? A Practitioner's View." *Cycnos* 12.2 (1995): 135–47. Reprinted in *The Practice of Writing*. London: Secker and Warburg, 1996.

Lokrantz, Jessie T. *The Underside of the Weave: Some Stylistic Devices Used by Vladimir Nabokov*. Studia Anglistica 11. Uppsala: Acta Universitatis Upsaliensis, 1973.

Long, Michael. *Marvell, Nabokov: Childhood and Arcadia*. Oxford: Oxford University Press, 1984.

Maddox, Lucy. *Nabokov's Novels in English*. Athens, GA: University of Georgia Press, 1983.

Martynov, G. G. *V. V. Nabokov: Bibliograficheskii ukazatel'*. St. Petersburg: Folio-Press, 2001.

Mason, Bobbie Ann. *Nabokov's Garden: A Guide to* Ada. Ann Arbor: Ardis, 1969.

McCarthy, Mary. "A Bolt from the Blue." *New Republic* (June 4, 1962): 21–27. Reprinted in Page, *Nabokov*, 124–36.

Mel'nikov, N. G., ed. *Klassik bez retushi: Literaturnyi mir o tvorchestve Vladimira Nabokova*. Moscow: Novoe literaturnoe obozrenie, 2000

Meyer, Priscilla. *Find What the Sailor Has Hidden: Vladimir Nabokov's* Pale Fire. Middletown: Wesleyan University Press, 1988.

Morris, Paul D. "Vladimir Nabokov's Poetry in Russian Emigré Criticism: A Partial Survey." *Canadian Slavonic Papers* 40.3–4 (1998): 287–310.

Morton, Donald E. *Vladimir Nabokov*. New York: Frederick Ungar, 1974.

Moynahan, Julian. "A Russian Preface for Nabokov's *Beheading*." *Novel* 1 (1967): 12–18.

Vladimir Nabokov. Minneapolis: University of Minnesota Press, 1971.

Nabokov, Dmitri. "The *Lolita* Legacy: Life with Nabokov's Art." *The Nabokovian* 37 (Fall 1996): 8–29.

Naumann, Marina Turkevich. "Nabokov as Viewed by Fellow Emigrés." *Russian Language Journal* 28. 99 (1974): 18–26.

Blue Evenings in Berlin: Nabokov's Short Stories of the 1920s. New York: New York University Press, 1978.

Nicol, Charles, and Gennady Barabtarlo, eds. *A Small Alpine Form: Studies in Nabokov's Short Fiction*. New York: Garland, 1993.

O'Connor, Katherine Tiernan. "Rereading *Lolita*, Reconsidering Nabokov's Relationship with Dostoevskij." *Slavic and East European Journal* 33 (1989): 64–77.

Olson, Lance. *Lolita: A Janus Text*. New York: Twayne, 1995.

Packman, David. *Vladimir Nabokov: The Structure of Literary Desire*. Columbia, MO: University of Missouri Press, 1982.

Page, Norman, ed. *Nabokov: The Critical Heritage*. The Critical Heritage Series. London: Routledge and Kegan Paul, 1982.

Paperno, Irina. "How Nabokov's *Gift* Is Made." In *Literature, Culture, and Society in the Modern Age: In Honor of Joseph Frank*. Part 2. Ed. Edward J. Brown, Lazar Fleishman, Gregory Freidin, and Richard D. Schupbach. Stanford Slavic Studies 4.2. Stanford: Dept. of Slavic Languages and Literatures, Stanford University, 1992. 295–322.

Parker, Stephen Jan. *Understanding Vladimir Nabokov*. Columbia, SC.: University of South Carolina Press, 1987.

Pifer, Ellen. *Nabokov and the Novel*. Cambridge, MA: Harvard University Press, 1980.

Pifer, Ellen, ed. *Vladimir Nabokov's* Lolita: *A Casebook*. Oxford: Oxford University Press, 2003.

Polsky, Svetlana. "Vladimir Nabokov's Short Story 'Easter Rain.'" *Nabokov Studies* 4 (1997): 151–62.

Proffer, Carl R. *Keys to Lolita*. Bloomington: Indiana University Press, 1968.

Proffer, Carl R., ed. *A Book of Things About Vladimir Nabokov*. Ann Arbor: Ardis, 1974.

Quennell, Peter. *Vladimir Nabokov: A Tribute*. New York: William Morrow, 1980.

Raguet-Bouvart, Christine. *Lolita: un royaume au-delà des mers*. Bordeaux: Presses Universitaires de Bordeaux, 1996.

Rampton, David. *Vladimir Nabokov: A Critical Study of the Novels*. Cambridge: Cambridge University Press, 1984.

Vladimir Nabokov. New York: St. Martin's Press, 1993.

Rivers, J. E., and Charles Nicol, eds. *Nabokov's Fifth Arc: Nabokov and Others on His Life's Work*. Austin: University of Texas Press, 1982.

Ronen, Irena, and Omry Ronen. "'Diabolically Evocative': An Inquiry into the Meaning of Metaphor." *Slavica Hierosolymitana* 5–6 (1981): 371–86.

Rorty, Richard. "The Barber of Kasbeam: Nabokov on Cruelty." In *Contingency, Irony, and Solidarity*. Cambridge: Cambridge University Press, 1989. 141–68.

Roth, Phyllis A. "Toward the Man behind the Mystification." In Rivers and Nicol, 43–59.

Roth, Phyllis A., ed. *Critical Essays on Vladimir Nabokov*. Critical Essays on American Literature. Boston: G. K. Hall, 1984.

Rowe, William Woodin. *Nabokov's Deceptive World*. New York: New York University Press, 1971.

Nabokov's Spectral Dimension. Ardis: Ann Arbor, 1981.

Shapiro, Gavriel. *Delicate Markers: Subtexts in Vladimir Nabokov's* Invitation to a Beheading. Middlebury Studies in Russian Language and Literature 19. New York: Peter Lang, 1998.

Shapiro, Gavriel, ed. *Nabokov at Cornell*. Ithaca: Cornell University Press, 2003.

Schiff, Stacy. *Véra (Mrs. Vladimir Nabokov)*. New York: Random House, 1999.

Schiff, Stephen. *Lolita: The Book of the Film*. New York: Applause, 1998.

Schuman, Samuel. *Vladimir Nabokov: A Reference Guide*. Boston: G. K. Hall, 1979.

Shakhovskaia [Shakhovskoy], Zinaida. *V poiskakh Nabokova*. Paris: La presse libre, 1979.

Sharpe, Tony. *Vladimir Nabokov*. London: Edward Arnold, 1991.

Shrayer, Maxim. *The World of Nabokov's Stories*. Austin: University of Texas Press, 1999.

Sisson, Jonathan Borden. "Cosmic Synchronization and Other Worlds in the Work of Vladimir Nabokov." Ph.D. diss., University of Minnesota, 1979.

Smith, Gerald S. "Nabokov and Russian Verse Form." *Russian Literature Triquarterly* 24 (1991): 271–305.

Stegner, Page. *Escape into Aesthetics: The Art of Vladimir Nabokov*. New York: The Dial Press, 1966.

Stuart, Dabney. *Nabokov: The Dimensions of Parody*. Baton Rouge: Louisiana State University Press, 1978.

Tammi, Pekka. *Problems of Nabokov's Poetics: A Narratological Analysis*. Suomalaisen Tiedeakatemian Toimituksia Annales Academiae Scientiarum Fennicae B 231. Helsinki: Suomalainen Tiedeakatemia, 1985.

   Russian Subtexts in Nabokov's Fiction: Four Essays. Tampere: Tampere University Press, 1999.

Toker, Leona. *Nabokov: The Mystery of Literary Structures*. Ithaca: Cornell University Press, 1989.

Updike, John. Introduction to *Lectures on Literature*, by Vladimir Nabokov. Ed. Fredson Bowers. New York: Harcourt Brace Jovanovich / Bruccoli Clark, 1980.

Wood, Michael. *The Magician's Doubts: Nabokov and the Risks of Fiction*. Princeton: Princeton University Press, 1995.

Wyllie, Barbara. *Nabokov at the Movies: Film Perspectives in Fiction*. Jefferson, NC: McFarland, 2003.

Zimmer, Dieter E. *Nabokovs Berlin*. Berlin: Nicolai, 2001.

Zunshine, Lisa, ed. *Nabokov at the Limits: Redrawing Critical Boundaries*. New York: Garland, 1999.

CAMBRIDGE COMPANIONS TO LITERATURE

CAMBRIDGE COMPANIONS TO CULTURE